Kath

A GERMAN WORD FAMILY DICTIONARY

Подруге —

"Светильник для тела есть око. Итак, если око твое будет чисто, то всё тело твое будет светло; если же око твое будет худо, то все тело твое будет темно. Итак, если свет, который в тебе, тьма, то какова же тьма?"

———

„ Nicht will wohllauten
„ Der deutsche Mund
„ Aber lieblich
„ Am stechenden Bart rauschen
„ Die Küsse."
„

парень-камень

A GERMAN
WORD FAMILY
DICTIONARY

TOGETHER WITH ENGLISH EQUIVALENTS

HOWARD H. KELLER

UNIVERSITY OF CALIFORNIA PRESS

Berkeley   Los Angeles   London

University of California Press
Berkeley and Los Angeles, California

University of California Press, Ltd.
London, England

ISBN: 0-520-03291-8

Library of Congress Catalog Card Number: 76-19988

Printed in the United States of America

1 2 3 4 5 6 7 8 9 0

FOR MY WIFE HELGA
AND MY DAUGHTER CHRISTIANE VERA

σοὶ δὲ θεοὶ τόσα δοῖεν, ὅσα φρεσὶ σῇσι μενοινᾷς,
ἄνδρα τε καὶ οἶκον, καὶ ὁμοφροσύνην ὀπάσειαν
ἐσθλήν· οὐ μὲν γὰρ τοῦ γε κρεῖσσον καὶ ἄρειον,
ἢ ὅθ᾽ ὁμοφρονέοντε νοήμασιν οἶκον ἔχωσιν
ἀνὴρ ἠδὲ γυνή· πόλλ᾽ ἄλγεα δυσμενέεσσι,
χάρματα δ᾽ εὐμενέτῃσι, μάλιστα δέ τ᾽ ἔκλυον αὐτοί."

The Odyssey, VI, 180-185

CONTENTS

ACKNOWLEDGMENTS

The computer age has brought with it ghostwriters of a new kind—people who write and debug data processing algorithms. It is thus fitting that my first expression of thanks goes to Tommy Wilkins of the Murray State University Computer Center. Wilkins worked out countless numbers of computer routines over a two year period and remained as helpful and optimistic at the finish as he was at the start of the project. William Freeman Smith, Jr., must also share my gratitude for his programming and processing help because of the many nights he spent preparing the German data for the *German Root Lexicon* which in turn became source tapes for this present work.

The funds for this project were provided by several grants from the Murray State University Committee on Institutional Studies and Research. I wish to thank these committee members and the two chairpersons, Lynn Bridwell and Kenneth Harrell, for the faith that they have shown in this and other projects over the past seven years.

An acknowledgment of gratitude must also be made to Constantine W. Curris, president of Murray State University, again to Kenneth Harrell, this time as dean of the College of Humanistic Studies, and finally to John W. Ferguson, chairman of the Department of Foreign Languages, for the support that these gentlemen have shown to language studies. Their encouragement was a significant factor in keeping this research project going through some difficult stages.

Very special thanks are also due to Bill Sams, Director of the Murray State University Computer Center, for the more than routine support that our computer specialists have given my various computer projects. Bill Coker was always available for special programming, and Pattie Crider and Nancy Lovett volunteered their skills for keypunching 16,000 data cards—and saved me the need to train a bevy of students for the job.

The German students at Murray State have also been most helpful during the planning and development of this book, and I would like to give special mention to my three student workers, Kathy Caufield, Tim Wibking, and Bill Gardner, for the high quality of their work.

I would like to use these pages to thank Professor J. Alan Pfeffer for his comments on the early stages of the manuscript, and Professor Herbert Lederer for his thoughts on the feasibility of the study and for permission to quote from his *Reference Grammar of the German Language*. I also delight in having this opportunity to thank Udo Strutynski at the University of California Press for his insights and suggestions during every phase of the production of this work.

My final and deepest gratitude goes to my wife, Helga, to whom this book is dedicated. Helga worked closely with me on every aspect of this book since its inception in October 1970 and helped me through countless phases of typing, checking translations, and rewriting the work numerous times. Most important, however, was the good humor and encouragement that Helga gave me during a project that would be finished "next year for sure."

High standards have been set for books in the last hundred years. At the beginning of *Alice's Adventures in Wonderland*, Alice thought to herself: "What's the use of a book without pictures or conversations?" Thomas Love Peacock complained further that "a book that furnishes no quotations is, *me judice*, no book—it is a plaything." This book would be a further disappointment in that it lacks narration, plot, and even paragraphs! It is hoped, however, that this work will be a valuable tool that will give an unusual insight into German word formation. Although the many people mentioned above have contributed greatly to this project, I claim full responsibility for any lacunae and errors in the German corpus as well as for faulty translations that may have survived numerous data runs and editing checks.

Howard H. Keller

Murray, Kentucky
June 1977

A German Word Family Dictionary, by Howard H. Keller

ERRATA

pages xviii and xxviii are transposed

p. 130	vor lieg en	*reads* a chain on the door, etc.
		should read lie before s.o.; be in hand, be submitted; be under consideration
p. 155	Pfleg erin	*reads* fosterer, male nurse; etc.
		should read fosterer, female nurse; . . .
p. 177	ver sand en	*reads* silt up; peter out, come to nothing REMOVE FROM "SAND siehe SEND" WORD GROUP
p. 177	Ver sand ung	*reads* siltation REMOVE FROM "SAND siehe SEND" WORD GROUP
p. 289	zu av	ADD THE FOLLOWING LISTING: zu p to, towards, up to; at, in, on; in addition to

INTRODUCTION

The *German Word Family Dictionary* is a reference work that presents a very important and useful phenomenon of the German language: the prefix-root system. Each German word in this dictionary is listed in alphabetical order, but starting with the first letter of its root. This root ordering differs from a normal dictionary in that a word is listed under its root rather than under its prefix. The difference from a "tergo" or reverse dictionary is that all members of a root family are listed together, rather than in different sections, such as verbs (under -en), nouns (under -ung), adjectives (under -lich), etc. For example, *Auftrag* would normally be found under *auf-* in a conventional dictionary, but is found under 'TRAG' in the GWFD, and is listed together with the approximately eighty other words that also have 'TRAG' as their root and that therefore constitute the 'TRAG' word family.

A conventional dictionary listing gives a definition of an individual word, but it throws no light on the extension of the word family in question, nor does it give the full range of translations that the individual word shares with as many as 50 or 100 paronyms. The arrangement of the GWFD provides a different perspective to the normal method of vocabulary listing, and helps solve some of the problems that one meets in increasing one's German vocabulary:

1. Each German word family is listed in column format so that the user can obtain an overview of the full extent of each word family.

2. Each word family is accompanied by an English translation of all German words, and these translations are also given in column format to the right of the German words. These English glosses give the user an insight into the semantic range and development of each German word family. The student is thus able to see both the literal and the figurative extensions of each root development.

3. The GWFD brings order to the problem of confusing look-alikes (e.g., *Aufsatz* and *Aussatz; Betrag* and *Beitrag; Vertrag* and *Vortrag*) by listing these similar sets in close proximity to one another, and by presenting an English translation for each word to highlight the difference.

4. As the student becomes familiar with the common semantic denominator of a given family, he finds it easier to "guess" or "predict" the meaning of new prefixed words that he encounters for the first time in his reading.

5. A word family arrangement also encourages the student to learn the less frequent members of a family for which he might already know ten or twenty of the more frequent words. For example, a student who is already acquainted with the more frequent derivatives of TRAG such as *Auftrag, Betrag, Vertrag, Vortrag* will be interested in learning the meaning of *Antrag, Beitrag, nachträglich, Übertragung,* and so forth.

Depending on the approach to this productive word family system, these prefix-root combinations can be regarded either as a complicated system of confusing look-alikes or as an inherently economical system of ordering words grouped around familiar roots. It is intended that the GWFD will give the student an unusual vantage point from which to view this productive system of word families.

ROOTS, BASES, RADICALS, AND STEMS

The reader will see frequent use of the term "root" in this dictionary, and a short clarification of the terms "root" and "stem" would be in

order. The designation "root" is used for a word element from which
other words are formed (etymological sense) or for a word element to
which prefixes and suffixes may be added (morphological sense). Many
standard dictionaries and works in descriptive linguistics also use the
terms "base" and "radical" as a synonym for root, and most works are
careful to define their terms to avoid misunderstandings.

An example of a root in the etymological sense is the Indo-European
root dekm̥ which ultimately accounts for the German word 'zehn' and
the English word 'ten.' Derivational processes often span many centuries and can be traced through successive stages of a given language.
For this reason derivations such as 'zehn' and 'ten' from dekm̥ are
called *diachronic* derivations:

Proto-Indo-European *dekm̥ > Proto-Germanic *tehan (also: Gothic taíhun;
Latin decem) > Old High German zehan > Middle High German zehen > Modern
High German zehn.
In like manner, Proto-Germanic *tehan > Old English tīen, tēne, tȳn > Middle
English ten > Modern English ten.

An example of a root in morphology is the German root TRAG
which forms the basis of numerous German words by a process of adding various adjective-forming, adverb-forming, noun-forming, and
verb-forming suffixes (derivational suffixes) in combination with one
or several prefixes. All the following sample word derivations exist at
the same time in a given stage of the language and thus are called *syn-
chronic* derivations:

Noun	*Verb*	*Adjective*
Träg er	trag en	trag bar
Träg erin		
Träg heit		
Ab trag	ab trag en	ab träg lich
Ein trag		
Ein träg lich keit		ein träg lich
Ein trag ung	ein trag en	

The GWFD uses the term "root" in this latter, morphological, sense. This dictionary does not present etymologies of words, and presents only German words that exist in the contemporary period of High German.

The word "stem" is used in a somewhat more limited and technical sense than the word "root" and designates that part of a word to which inflectional endings are added. Some typical inflectional endings are plural and case markers for nouns; person, number, and tense markers for verbs; comparative and superlative degree markers for adjectives, and so forth.

One stem may contain one root and several prefixes (e.g., be auf *trag* en, sich her auf be *müh* en) or several roots with one or several prefixes (e.g., un *wahr schein* lich, *herz* er *freu* end). Stems with several roots are termed complex or multi-root words in this dictionary in contrast to simplex or single-root words. There is a relatively small number of complex (multi-root) words in the GWFD, and a listing of them is found after the lists of prefixes and suffixes.

SOURCES FOR GERMAN WORDS AND ENGLISH TRANSLATIONS

This dictionary draws its German word inventory from Gerhard Wahrig's *Deutsches Wörterbuch*[1] and its English translations from *Langenscheidt's New College German Dictionary*.[2] A logical selection procedure was used to produce a word family dictionary of workable proportions:

1. At least one member of each word family had to be in the first three thousand most frequent German words. (The word frequency list used for this determination is J. Alan Pfeffer's *Grunddeutsch: Basic (Spoken) German Dictionary*.)[3]

---

[1]Gerhard Wahrig, *Deutsches Wörterbuch* (Gütersloh: Bertelsmann, 1968).

[2]Heinz Messinger, *Langenscheidt's New College German Dictionary,* new ed. (Berlin: Langenscheidt, 1973).

[3]J. Alan Pfeffer, *Grunddeutsch: Basic (Spoken) German Dictionary* (Englewood Cliffs, N.J.: Prentice-Hall, 1970).

2. Each word family must have at least three prefixed members in Wahrig's *Deutsches Wörterbuch*.

Langenscheidt's *New College German Dictionary* provided a final screening device for infrequent or "mechanical" derivations—new words that merely represent a different part of speech for a form already listed and add no new semantic meaning to the form already given. A decision was made that if the German word from Wahrig did not also appear in Langenscheidt's College it would not be included in the GWFD. This decision had the beneficial effect of excluding many mechanical applications of noun-forming, verb-forming, and adjective-forming suffixes. Thus, Wahrig lists the following examples in the TRAG family whereas the Langenscheidt's College omits several of these examples:

Wahrig	*Langenscheidt's College*
ab trag en	ab trag en
Ab trag ung	
aus trag en	aus trag en
Aus trag ung	
Bei trag	Bei trag
bei trag en	bei trag en
Bei träg er	
ge trag en	ge trag en
Ge trag en heit	
nach träg lich	nach träg lich
Nach träg lich keit	

Many words contained in Wahrig and omitted in Langenscheidt's College are often used in conversation and writing, but they add little insight to the development of the various word families. Their absence in the GWFD gives an aspect of streamlining and directness to each root portrayal.

The GWFD emphasizes single-root words, e.g., *Hinterrad, Vorderrad, ausrädeln,* and only includes the small number of very frequent multi-root words that appear in the Pfeffer three thousand word frequency list. It is well known that German has a propensity for almost

		- later than, following upon	nachklassisch, nachlaufen, nachträglich
35.	NEBEN	- directly touching on, neighboring, beside, "side-", branching off	Nebenzimmer, Nebenstrasse
		- parallel with, synchronous	Nebengleis
		- joining, being added to	Nebenfluss
		- in addition, supplemental, extra	Nebenverdienst
		- incidental, existing in addition	Nebenprodukt
		- of secondary or lesser importance	Nebenrolle, Nebenstrasse
		- rounding off, completing	Nebenbücher
36.	NIEDER	- lower	Niederdeutsch, Niederlande
		- down, downward	niederbeugen, niederbrechen
37.	OB (shortened form of OBEN or OBER)	- onto s.o. or s.t.; toward, opposed to, accommodating	obliegen, obsiegen, obwalten, Obdach, Obhut
38.	OBER	- located above, situated higher	Oberarm, Oberteil
		- "Upper" in geographical names	Oberbayern, Oberitalien
		- higher in rank, the highest in rank	Oberbürgermeister, Oberleutnant
		- the highest, sole responsibility; generic, embracing everything	Oberbefehlshaber, Oberbegriff, Oberleitung
39.	RÜCK	- back, rear	Rückschritt
		- "re-"	Rückberufung, rückversichern
		- return, giving back, going back	Rückgabe, Rückgang, rückständig
40.	ÜBER	- more, in excess	überbieten, übertreiben, überlasten
		- to the other side of, across	überbrücken, überschreiben, übersetzen, Übersee
		- above, higher than	überirdisch, Überschrift
		- further than	überleben, überlaufen

ETYMOLOGICAL INFORMATION

A distinction must be made here between a word family dictionary and an etymological dictionary. The only essential goal of the former is simply to list together all words that share the same root, declare that this grouping of words is a word family, skip a line, and then present the next group of words sharing a common root. Dictionaries of etymology, on the other hand, present a great wealth of information concerning word forms in earlier stages of the language as far back as the "proto" or "Ur" period, and very often the reconstructed Indo-European root is also given. Degrees of relationships with other words and the cognate words themselves are often listed. Many diverse phonomena such as borrowing, loan translation, semantic shift, Indo-European root developments (basic, suffixed, prefixed, nasalized, o-grade, zero-grade, lengthened-grade, shortened, etc.) are all essential considerations of an etymological dictionary.[4] A complete etymological dictionary will often contain a brief listing of scholarly opinion in *every* word article. A word family dictionary cannot present this sophisticated information, and it would be a mistake to look for it there.[5]

An etymological dictionary often presents only a very few prefixed extensions of an individual root when it gives an analysis of that root. For this reason, a word family dictionary and an etymological dictionary complement one another quite well.

There are really only two major areas where form and etymology are at variance, and consequently where a word family dictionary might make use of etymological information: separating homographs into their individual groupings, and referencing cognate families to one another.

All homographs among the roots have been split into their two (or three or four) subgroups and have been listed separately. Thus,

---

[4]See the following two reviews of Worth's *Russian Derivational Dictionary* for divergent views of the role of etymology in a word family dictionary: Howard H. Keller in *Language,* 48 (Spring 1972), 197-200, and Howard I. Aronson in *Slavic and East European Journal,* 18 (Winter 1974), 454-456.

[5]An interesting survey and discussion of all manner of etymological dictionaries has recently been completed: Yakov Malkiel, *Etymological Dictionaries: A Tentative Typology* (Chicago: University of Chicago Press, 1975).

KEHR₁ 'turn, go' and KEHR₂ 'sweep' or WEIN₁ 'cry' and WEIN₂ 'wine' are presented as different families. Often a family will have members with very different meanings within its listing (e.g., KRIEG 'get' and 'wage war'; SCHON, obSCHON, SCHONen, and SCHÖN; KOMMen and beKOMMen; beREIT and REITen; etc.), but these families have not been split if all the members are descendants of the same stem.

Cognates and ablaut variants of major families are listed separately in this dictionary according to their own subfamilies. They do contain a "SIEHE" reference to their main root form, however. Thus, the BRUCH family has 14 members, and this family is in turn related to BRECH; SCHRIFT has 23 members which are in turn cognates of SCHREIB. These assignments are based on Kluge's *Etymologisches Wörterbuch der deutschen Sprache.*[6]

WORD FAMILY DICTIONARIES, ROOT DICTIONARIES, AND DERIVATIONAL DICTIONARIES

Since the earliest centuries of language analysis, there has been a multiplicity of conventionally ordered dictionaries and word lists, and even a surprisingly large number of back-ordered ("backward" or "tergo") word lists. The number of root dictionaries — working from the middle out to the front and then to the back — is quite small. It is even more surprising that Russian has had two excellent word family dictionaries for several years, Catherine A. Wolkonsky's *Handbook of Russian Roots*[7] and Dean S. Worth's *Russian Derivational Dictionary,*[8] while the first wide-ranging study of German word families was my own *German Root Lexicon,*[9] published in 1973. Partial studies of both Russian and German root developments have appeared at various times

[6]Friedrich Kluge, *Etymologisches Wörterbuch der deutschen Sprache*, 20. Auflage (Berlin: Walter de Gruyter, 1967).

[7]Catherine A. Wolkonsky and Marianna A. Poltoratzky, *Handbook of Russian Roots* (New York: Columbia University Press, 1961).

[8]Dean S. Worth, Andrew S. Kozak, and Donald B. Johnson, *Russian Derivational Dictionary* (New York: American Elsevier, 1970).

[9]Howard H. Keller, *German Root Lexicon*, Miami Linguistics Series No. 11 (Coral Gables: University of Miami Press, 1973).

(George Z. Patrick's *Roots of the Russian Language* [1938][10] and Florence Hastings's *Studies in German Words and their Uses* [1911].)[11] These last two works are very frustrating to use in that they seem to omit more prefix-root combinations than they include for a given word family.

The present GWFD is an outgrowth of the *German Root Lexicon,* but with a number of significant differences. The GRL is a German-only word list of all prefixed simplex (single-root) words found in Wahrig's *Deutsches Wörterbuch.* There are no English translations in the GRL. In addition there are no non-prefixed stems. Thus, *Abzug, Anzug,* and *Aufzug* are included, but *Zug,* and *zügig* are not included. The GRL is a computerized reordering of every prefix/single-root combination in Wahrig, and thus contains many "families" of one word each. The GRL presents all word families in a column format, and this is a significant advantage for giving a graphic overview of the structure and extent of each word family. The GWFD is the only bilingual root dictionary that also maintains a column presentation for all word families *and* their English translations.

A complete description of the derivational morphology of English, French, Spanish, German, or Russian is still far in the future. A number of interesting works have appeared in recent years for various Indo-European languages, and it is hoped that the GWFD will have made a significant contribution as the beginning of a complete analysis of German derivational morphology.

---

[10]George Z. Patrick, *Roots of the Russian Language* (New York: Pitman, 1938).
[11]Florence Hastings, *Studies in German Words and Their Uses* (Boston: D. C. Heath, 1911).

PREFIXES

This list of prefixes used in the dictionary is followed by a list of examples as an attempt to suggest the various meanings or functions of each prefix. Several of these prefixes are very productive and are used in forming a great number of German words (e.g., BE, ER, GE, VER) and several other prefixes form a relatively small number of words (e.g., INNE, AFTER, FÜR).

1. AB	16. ENT/EMP	31. LOS	46. VER
2. ABER	17. ER	32. MISS	47. VOLL
3. AFTER	18. ERZ	33. MIT	48. VON
4. AN	19. FERN	34. NACH	49. VOR
5. ANT	20. FORT	35. NEBEN	50. VORDER
6. AUF	21. FÜR	36. NIEDER	51. WEG
7. AUS	22. GE	37. OB	52. WEIT
8. AUSSEN	23. GEGEN	38. OBER	53. WEITER
9. AUSSER	24. HER	39. RÜCK	54. WIDER
10. BE	25. HIN	40. ÜBER	55. WIEDER
11. BEI	26. HINTER	41. ÜBRIG	56. ZER
12. DA	27. IN	42. UM	57. ZU
13. DAR	28. INNE	43. UN	58. ZURÜCK
14. DURCH	29. INNEN	44. UNTER	59. ZUSAMMEN
15. EIN	30. INNER	45. UR	60. ZWISCHEN

DESCRIPTION OF PREFIXES

The description of the origin, development, and use of prefixes is an interesting and wide-ranging study, and there are many good surveys of prefixes in the various published grammars and structural analyses of German. The only phenomenon concerning prefixes that would merit mention here is that, when used with verbs, some prefixes are always inseparable (the prefix does not become a verb complement in certain conditions) and some prefixes are either separable or inseparable. The prefix is always *un*stressed when it is *in*separable, and in the case of verbal prefixes that may be separable *or* inseparable, the inseparable verbs often have an abstract or figurative meaning. It remains for a more specialized grammar or beginning language textbook to give some further finer points on usage.

Inseparable Prefixes (always unstressed when before a verb):
    BE, ENT/EMP, ER, GE, HINTER, MISS, OB, VER, ZER.

Separable or Inseparable Prefixes (this dictionary places an apostrophe before a verbal prefix to indicate that it is stressed [and therefore separable] and after the verbal prefix to indicate that it is unstressed [and therefore inseparable]):
    DURCH, ÜBER, UM, UNTER, VOLL, WIDER, WIEDER.

    Example: *über'setz en* 'translate'
             (Ich übersetze den Brief ins Deutsche.)
             'über setz en 'pass over, cross, ferry over'
             (Ich setze die Leute mit meinem Boot über.)

1.	AB	- separation, removal	abschaffen, abschaben
		- lessening, reducing	abtragen, abziehen
		- beginning, starting	abreisen, abfahren
		- downward motion or direction	abspringen, abfallen
		- refusal, denial, cancelation, annulment	absagen, ablehnen
		- strengthening, intensification	abbetteln, abängstigen
		- copying, imitation	abschreiben, abmalen

2. ABER (originally a comparative of AB)
    - falseness, worthlessness, nega-   Aberglaube, Aberwitz
     tion
    - again; repetition   abermals

3. AFTER   - after, behind   Afterpacht
            - inferior, false, imperfect,   Aftergelehrter, Afterrede
             undeveloped

4. AN   - attachment, fastening,   anbinden, angrenzen,
           touching, approaching   anhängen
           - motion toward or to s.o. or s.t. jemanden anschreiben, einen
                          Punkt anpeilen
           - beginning of an action or a   anstimmen, anfaulen
             process
           - strengthening, growth,   anschwellen, anbauen,
             increase   anhäufen
           - forcefulness, exactness,   sich etwas anhören, ansehen
             accuracy

5. ANT (originally the full form that corresponds to the unaccented ENT)
    - toward, against   Antlitz, Antwort

6. AUF   - up, upward   aufblicken, aufliegen
           - opening   aufbrechen, aufschliessen
           - end s.t., bring to completion   aufbrauchen, aufessen,
                          auflesen
           - sudden or brief action   aufflammen, aufschreien

7. AUS   - movement away from, move- ausgehen, aussenden, aus-
           ment outward   rufen, ausstellen
           - movement forward, movement ausbrechen, ausgraben
             from inside a place
           - completion, termination, com- ausstrecken, auskochen, aus-
             plete finish   weinen
           - choice from several possibilities auslesen, auswählen

8. AUSSEN - outside, exterior, external, Aussenhafen, Aussenseite
            outer
           - external, foreign   Aussenamt, Aussenpolitik

9. AUSSER - besides, in addition   ausserdem, ausserordentlich
           - outside, exterior, external   ausserehelich, ausserhalb

10.	BE	- direction	befallen, sich begeben
		- effect on s.o. or s.t. which is of limited duration	begiessen, bekämpfen
		- completion, doing s.t. well or thoroughly	besiegen, bedecken
		- around, on all sides	belagern, beschneiden
		- bring the action of an intransitive verb to bear upon an object	belecken, bespritzen, bestrahlen, bewässern
		- supply, furnish, or endow with s.t.	bedachen, beflügeln, begrenzen, bemasten, beseelen
		- derivatives from nouns	beerdigen, berücksichtigen, begnadigen, benachrichtigen
11.	BEI	- beside, in addition, extra, additional	Beifilm, Beiwagen, Beigericht, Beiladung
		- nearness, proximity	beiliegen, beistehen
		- motion or tendency toward	beitreten, beikommen
		- add s.t. in addition	beimischen, beigeben, beitragen, beiordnen
12.	DA	- there, here	dabei
		- then, at that time	damals
13.	DAR	- to: movement away from the speaker	darreichen
		- gift, loan, offering	darbieten, darbringen, Darlehen
14.	DURCH	- through	durch'reisen, den Kuchen mit Rosinen durch'backen, durchsichtig
		- across	'durchreisen, Durchmesser
		- thorough	'durcharbeiten, 'durchbacken
15.	EIN	- motion into, penetration into s.t.	einfahren, einnehmen, einstecken
16.	ENT/EMP	- movement away from s.t., out of s.t.	entfliehen, entgleisen, entschuldigen
		- a reversal: the opposite of the simple verb	spannen + entspannen, verloben + entloben
		- beginning of an activity	entbrennen, entfachen, ent-

			zünden, empfinden
		- separation, removal, with- drawal (often in paired forms)	fliehen + entfliehen; sagen + entsagen; wenden + ent- wenden
17.	ER	- reference to the inner person: cause s.t., effect s.t.	sich erkälten, erfreuen, ermuntern
		- produce, generate, or beget s.t.	erbauen, erzeugen
		- getting or obtaining s.t. by effort or hard work	erbitten, erhalten, ersingen
		- bring about a result	erkunden, erwarten
		- emphasis on the beginning or the brevity of an action	erschauern, erzittern, erblü- hen, erröten
		- die, kill	ertrinken, ersticken, erlöschen, ermorden
18.	ERZ	- an intensification of meaning, usually with pejorative conno- tation	erzdumm, Erzgauner
		- "Arch-", with positive meaning	Erzbischof, Erzengel, Erzher- zog
19.	FERN	- far away, distant, remote, "tele-"	Ferngespräch, Fernseher, Fernblick, fernbleiben
20.	FORT	- away, away from, off, to an- other place, further, continu- ing	fortgehen, fortsetzen
21.	FÜR	- for, in favor of	Fürbitte, Fürsorge, Für- sprache
22.	GE	- entrance into a state or condi- tion: the completion of an action	gewähren, genehmigen
		- a collection or union of per- sons, things, or related parts	Geäst, Gebirge, Gestirn
		- the result of an action	Gefüge
		- the characteristic of the con- cept expressed in the source word	gewitzt

23.	GEGEN	- opposition, weakening, hostile, harmful	gegeneinander, Gegengift
		- response, consequence	Gegenleistung
		- counter, confirming; opposite member of a pair	Gegenzeichen
24.	HER	- motion toward the speaker	herkommen, herfahren
25.	HIN	- motion away from the speaker	hinfahren, hinkommen
26.	HINTER	- behind (in place or time), after	Hintergrund, Hinterhof
		- rear part of s.t.	Hinterbein, Hinterschiff, Hinterleib, Hinterrad
27.	IN	- into, in; within, inside	inländisch, Inlaut, Inschrift
28.	INNE	- within, a part of	innehaben, innehalten
29.	INNEN	- inside, interior, indoors, inner	Innenansicht, Innenseite
		- interior, domestic	Innenminister, Innenpolitik
30.	INNER	- internal, inner	innerparteilich
31.	LOS	- away from s.t., off or gone from s.t.	losschrauben, loslösen
		- a sudden beginning (especially after overcoming obstacles)	loslaufen, losschreiben
32.	MISS	- failure, error; s.t. false; the opposite of a simple verb	misslingen, missfallen
33.	MIT	- "co-", "syn-"; with, together with	mitgehen, mithalten, mitspielen, Mitarbeit
		- companion, member	Mitglied, Mitmensch
34.	NACH	- behind, after	nachlaufen, nachtrauern, nachsegeln; Nachkriegszeit
		- in addition	nachexerzieren, nachfordern
		- imitating, copying; testing, examining	nachbilden, nacherzählen, nachmessen, nachrechnen, nachschreiben
		- again, one more time	nachschneiden, nachpolieren

unlimited stem compositions, and if all the multi-root words from Wahrig were included in the GWFD, the sense of the word families would be lost. Thus, among the multi-root compounds with -RAD the more common *Fahrrad* and *Motorrad* are included and the far less common *Uhrrad, Wasserrad, Wagenrad, Auszugwellenrad,* and *Beiwagenmotorrad* are excluded. It must be noted that there are some 136 multi-root words that have -RAD as a second or last element. It is also generally true that the meaning of these composita are easily deduced from adding together the meanings of the two component parts: e.g., *Wagenrad* 'car wheel, wagon wheel' = *Wagen* 'car, wagon' + *Rad* 'wheel'.

The English translations of German words from the Langenscheidt dictionary were at times rather extensive, and so I made a decision to shorten each English translation to a maximum of seven words. It was decided at the outset that the GWFD would not compete with a conventional German-English dictionary where certain German words require as many as two or three page-length columns of English translations for each word. The resultant English columns omit many technical terms and leave out many synonyms and fine shades of meaning. They do form manageable columns, however, which permit the user to view the entire expanse of a German word family with a maximum of one skipped line between German words.

There will no doubt be lacunae in the English glosses, and there are most certainly bound to be personal preferences in individual German words where the user would prefer a different set of English equivalents from those contained in this dictionary. Certainly a desired effect for the GWFD would be for the user to exclaim every so often: "My God, he's hit the nail on the head with his translation of *liebenswürdigerweise*" or "He has captured the very essence of *gegeneinanderhalten.*" It would obviously be very difficult to sustain this wished-for exactitude for 12,500 German words however, since no two languages can be translated on a one-to-one basis. Thus I found solace in the doctrine of "traduttore — traditore" (one man's meat is another man's *poisson*) and resolved to paint a broad picture of each German word in the hopes of giving an effective and concentrated feeling for the extent of each German word family.

41.	ÜBRIG	- remaining, residual, left over	übrigbehalten, übrigbleiben, übriglassen

42.	UM	- embracing, enclosing, surrounding in a spatial sense	umarmen, umzingeln
		- change of direction, attitude, or position	umkehren, umstürzen, umziehen
		- change or alteration of a shape or form	umbauen, umformen
		- in a circle around a central point	umbinden, umgehen, umhängen

43.	UN	- designates negation or the opposite: "non-", "un-", "in-"	unerwünscht, unhöflich, unübersehbar, undiskutabel
		- (for nouns) designates a large mass or amount	Unmenge, Unzahl
		- s.t. defective, bad, unnatural, worthless, unpleasant	Unsitte, Unbehagen, Unmensch, Unkraut
		- a strong intensification of the meaning of the stem	Untat, Untier, Untiefe

44. UNTER (with the accent on the prefix)

		- put or place s.t. down, below, lower	unterlegen, unterschieben

(with the accent on the stem)

		- motion downward or motion below s.t.	unterdrücken, untergraben, untermalen
		- not take place, cease, remain undone	unterbleiben, unterbrechen, unterlassen
		- located below, located underneath	unterentwickelt, unterirdisch
		- "Lower" in geographical names, lower in rank	Unteritalien, Unteroffizier

45.	UR	- the beginning, the first	urgermanisch, Urmensch, Urtext, Urzustand
		- intensification of the meaning of the stem, designation of a high degree, very	uralt, urkomisch
		- authenticity, often signifying unused	Urkraft, Urzustand
		- a preceding or following generation	Urgrossvater, Urenkel

46.	VER	- wrong or improper doing, a mistake or error in an action	verbauen (Gebäude), ver-schneiden (Stoff), verbilden (Charakter), sich verrechnen, sich verhören, verbieten, sich etwas verbieten
		- complete an action, sustain an action to the end; consume, use up	verbrauchen, verdursten, verklingen, verwelken
		- increase, intensify, enhance or augment a state or condition	verdichten, veredeln, ver-grössern, verschliessen
		- change or transformation	verfinstern, verflüssigen, verkohlen
		- bring together	verflechten, verknüpfen, vermischen
		- go away, go forth; disappear	verjagen, verlieren, verschüt-ten, verlassen
		- waste, spoilage, disappearance	verrosten, verfaulen, verge-hen
		- protecting, fastening; hinder-ing, obstructing, refusing	verkleben, vernageln, verrie-geln, verweigern
		- waste or consume time in an action	versäumen, verschlafen, vertanzen
		- derivations from adjectives	verbittern, verfremden, ver-schönern
		- derivations from nouns	verfilmen, vergolden, ver-kitschen
47.	VOLL	- full, filled up	(sich) vollsaugen, vollgiessen
		- full, complete, whole	Vollmilch, vollständig, voll-kommen
		- full, ample	Vollgas
48.	VON	- from	voneinander
49.	VOR	- forward	sich vorbeugen, vordringen, vorlaufen, vorschicken
		- earlier than, before s.t.	vorchristlich, vordatieren
		- toward the outer side or the front side; put forward	vorhängen, vorlegen
		- as an example, model, or pattern	vorleben, vormachen, vor-schreiben

50.	VORDER	- before (in place or time) - front part of s.t. - present time	Vordergrund, Vorderhof Vorderbein, Vorderrad Vorderhand
51.	WEG	- away, gone, removed	weggehen, weglassen, weg- schicken
52.	WEIT	- far-reaching, large, sweeping - broad, large	weitgehend, weitläufig, weit- tragend weitherzig, weitspurig, weit- maschig
53.	WEITER	- continue to, not stop doing s.t. - to another person, to a third person - to other people - (for nouns) further, continu- ing, without interruption	weiterarbeiten, weiterklingeln weitergeben, weiterverkaufen weitersagen, weitererzählen Weiterbildung, Weiterfahrt
54.	WIDER	- against, contrary, opposite, back, "re-"	Widerrede, Widerruf
55.	WIEDER	- again, "re-"	wiederaufnehmen, wieder- erzählen
56.	ZER	- separation, breaking to pieces, scattering	zerfliessen, zerreissen, zer- trennen, zerteilen, zer- brechen, zerfallen
57.	ZU	- close, cover - motion toward a goal - add to, attach to, give in addi- tion to	zuschliessen, zumachen, zuschütten auf jemanden zugehen, zukommen zugeben, zusetzen, zuzählen
58.	ZURÜCK	- back: return to the departure point - backward, behind, remaining at the starting point	zurückgehen, zurückstellen, zurückwinken zurückbleiben, zurücklassen

59.	ZUSAMMEN	- be together, be near one another	zusammenbleiben, zusammensitzen
		- come to one another, come together	zusammenfegen, zusammenkommen
		- bring to one another, bring together	zusammenbinden
		- unite, join	zusammenschweissen
		- harmonize, agree, correspond, conform	zusammenklingen, zusammenpassen
		- (slang) in two, in pieces, smashed, broken	zusammenschlagen
		- (slang) for emphasis	sich etwas zusammenlügen
60.	ZWISCHEN	- between, intermediate, "inter-"	Zwischenraum, Zwischensatz, Zwischenhandel

INDEX OF SUFFIXES

45. IG	adj 6. *	72. SAM	adj 9. *
46. IN	noun 13. *	73. SCHAFT	noun 20. *
47. ISCH	adj 7. *	74. SCH EN	verb 6.
48. IS IER EN	verb 11.	75. SEIT IG	adj 33.
49. KEIT	noun 11. *	76. SEIT S	adv 17.
50. LAST IG	adj 31.	77. SEL	noun 19. *
51. LEER	adj 16.	78. S EN	verb 4.
52. LEI	adj 17.	79. ST	noun 21. *
53. LEIN	noun 2. *	80. SÜCHT IG	adj 34.
54. LICH	adj 8. *	81. T	noun 22. *
55. LICH	adv 4.	82. TÜCHT IG	adj 35.
56. LICH EN	verb 13.	83. TUM	noun 23. *
57. LING	noun 14. *	84. UN FÄH IG	adj 36.
58. LING S	adv 15.	85. UNG	noun 24. *
59. LOS	adj 18.	86. VOLL	adj 21.
60. MAL	adv 9.	87. WÄRT S	adv 18.
61. MAL S	adv 16.	88. WEG	adv 11.
62. MASS EN	adv 10.	89. WEG S	adv 19.
63. MÄSS IG	adj 32.	90. WEIL IG	adj 37.
64. NIS	noun 15. *	91. WEISE	adv 12. *
65. PF EN	verb 9.	92. WEND IG	adj 38.
66. RECHT	adj 19.	93. WERT	adj 22.
67. REICH	adj 20.	94. WERT IG	adj 39.
68. RICH	noun 16.	95. WID R IG	adj 40.
69. S	adv 2. *	96. WILL IG	adj 41.
70. S	noun 17. *	97. WÜRD IG	adj 42.
71. SAL	noun 18. *	98. Z EN	verb 5.

*Descriptions for the suffixes marked with an asterisk were taken from Herbert Lederer, *Reference Grammar of the German Language* (New York: Scribner's, 1969).

DESCRIPTION OF SUFFIXES

ADJECTIVE-FORMING SUFFIXES

SUFFIX	part of speech from which adjective is formed	examples	how used/remarks
1. BAR	N (mainly) V (sometimes)	sichtbar, fruchtbar erfüllbar, unbezahlbar	Expresses the possibility of s.t. being done. Exhibits the character of a process.
2. EN	N	golden, wollen	Designates a material.
3. ERN	N	hölzern, gläsern, eisern	Designates a material.
4. HAFT	N, ADJ	krankhaft, mädchenhaft	Designates the type of quality.
5. HAFT IG	N, ADJ	wahrhaftig, leibhaftig	The additional suffix -IG can be added to -HAFT.
6. IG	—	freudig, gefällig, hiesig, dortig	Shows a condition or a similarity (sometimes with Umlaut.)
7. ISCH	N, PN (mainly) V (sometimes)	arabisch, chemisch, kindisch malerisch, zeichnerisch	Denotes origin, property, or characteristic (often negative: weibisch and kindisch vs. weiblich and kindlich.)
8. LICH	—	freundlich, zerbrech-lich, ärgerlich	Denotes characteristic qualities (-LICH was originally a noun meaning "body.")

9. SAM　　abstract N, V,　arbeitsam, lenksam,
　　　　　ADJ　　　　　langsam

The following adjectival suffixes could also be viewed as the second half of a complex (multi-root) stem. The majority of these "suffixes" can also exist as independent words with a generally similar meaning: e.g., ARM, BEREIT, FREI, LEER, VOLL.

10. ARM	N	geistarm, blutarm, nikotinarm	Expresses the scarcity or minimal presence. Often the source noun expresses elements or ideas. Is often used in pairs with -REICH.
11. BE REIT	N	startbereit, kampf-bereit, abwehrbereit	Expresses preparedness or readiness. Often used with nouns of motion (starting and stopping) and with nouns of combat and defense.
12. BREIT	N	haarbreit, fingerbreit	Expresses width or broadness.
13. FREI	N	bleifrei, sturmfrei, portofrei	Expresses freedom from or lack of something. Often used with nouns designating chemical elements, physical obstacles, or financial costs.
14. GE MÄSS	N	standesgemäss, ver-tragsgemäss, ord-nungsgemäss	Expresses conformity or agreement.
15. GE RECHT	N	stilgerecht, mundge-recht, formgerecht	Expresses conformity or agreement.
16. LEER	N	geistleer, blutleer, inhaltleer	Expresses absence or void.

17. LEI	Numerals	einerlei, zweierlei, allerlei	Forms a series of variative numerals that express a number of kinds or types. A linking -ER- is used.
18. LOS	N (mainly)	gedankenlos, wertlos, sinnlos	Expresses the absence of a quality. It is often a negative member in pairs with -VOLL.
19. RECHT	N (mainly)	senkrecht, regelrecht, winkelrecht	Expresses either a geometric relationship of right angles or a relationship of conformity.
20. REICH	N	geistreich, blutreich, erfolgreich	Expresses fullness, richness or abundance. Corresponds to English -FULL. Is often used in pairs with -ARM.
21. VOLL	N (mainly)	gedankenvoll, wertvoll, sinnvoll	Expresses fullness. Is often used in pairs with -LOS or sometimes -FREI.
22. WERT	N	sehenswert, bemerkenswert, empfehlenswert	This suffix is usually attached to a noun which has been formed by the suffix -EN or -UNG, and which itself is derived from a verb. The suffix indicates that the source action is worthy or valuable.

The following series of suffixes ending in -IG are really compounds in which the real suffix is -IG, which is added to a complex (multi-root) stem: thus, *affenartig* is really *Affenart + ig,* not *Affen + artig.*

23. ART IG	N, ADJ	aalartig, fremdartig, grossartig	Indicates a kind, a manner, or a resemblance.
24. BE DÜRF T IG	N	liebesbedürftig, erholungsbedürftig	Expresses a need or a requirement.
25. BÜRT IG	ADJ	ebenbürtig, vollbürtig, edelbürtig	Expresses a relationship of birth, parentage, or rank.
26. FÄH IG	N	arbeitsfähig, kampffähig, zahlungsfähig	Expresses the capability or ability to do something.
27. FÄLL IG	N, V	baufällig, schwerfällig, straffällig	The original idea is "to fall." Expresses the related ideas of heaviness, or susceptibility or liability.
28. FALT IG	Numerals	dreifaltig, hundertfaltig	Corresponds to English "-FOLD". Used with individual numbers to designate a specific number of times.
29. FERT IG	N	kampffertig, schlüsselfertig; schlagfertig	Expresses a readiness or preparedness.
30. FÖRM IG	N	kreisförmig, bohnenförmig	Expresses similarity of form or shape.
31. LAST IG	N	kopflastig, schwanzlastig, steuerlastig	Expresses burden or weight.
32. MÄSS IG	N	vernunftsmässig, beispielmässig, regelmässig	Expresses the idea of moderateness or fitness. Can also be used to show the close relationship or "use" of the stem-noun.

33. SEIT IG	ADJ, Numerals	vielseitig, zweiseitig, gleichseitig	Expresses the number or type of sides or directions.
34. SÜCHT IG	V; some ADJ and N	eifersüchtig, habsüchtig, selbstsüchtig	Expresses a craving or addiction or preoccupation.
35. TÜCHT IG	N	geschäftstüchtig	Expresses capability, suitability, or skill.
36. UN FÄH IG	N	arbeitsunfähig, kampfunfähig, zahlungsunfähig	Used in a small number of words that express the opposite of FÄHIG: the inability or incapability of doing something.
37. WEIL IG	ADJ, N	zeitweilig, langweilig	Expresses duration of time.
38. WEND IG	ADJ, N	notwendig	Expresses a reciprocal or intensive relationship.
39. WERT IG	ADJ, Numerals	vollwertig, minderwertig	Expresses worth or value.
40. WID R IG	N	folgewidrig, verkehrswidrig	Expresses an adverse or contrary relationship. Often associated with the English prefix "COUNTER-".
41. WILL IG	N, ADJ	freiwillig, hilfswillig	Expresses willingness, readiness, or docility.
42. WÜRD IG	N, V (sometimes)	glaubwürdig, erbarmungswürdig, vertrauenswürdig	Expresses worth or deservedness. Often occurs with prefixed nouns ending in -UNG.

ADVERB-FORMING SUFFIXES

SUFFIX	part of speech from which adverb is formed	examples	how used/remarks
1. E	ADJ	lange, stille, balde	Many of these words are either obsolescent or have become colloquial. They still frequently occur in poetic usage.
2. S	N, ADJ	tags, rechts;	The -S is originally the genitive ending of masc.
3. ENS	N, ADJ	meistens, erstens	or neuter nouns. By analogy it can occur with feminine nouns (nachts.)
4. LICH	ADJ	freilich, kürzlich, sicherlich	In English the cognate adverbial ending -LY is vastly more productive. In German there are only a few words that are exclusively adverbs which are formed with -LICH.

The following adverbial suffixes could also be viewed as the second half of a complex (multi-root) stem. The majority of these "suffixes" can also exist as independent words with a generally similar meaning: e.g., ART, MAL, WEG, WEISE.

5. ART	ADJ, Article	derart, welcherart, allerart	Expresses extent or means. Used only with der, welcher, solcher, aller.

6. HALB	Article, Demonstrative PN	deshalb, dieserhalb	Expresses "for the sake of."
7. HALB EN	Pronoun-Adjective; Article	meinethalben, deinethalben	Expresses "for the sake of."
8. HALB ER	N	gesundheitshalber, anstandshalber	Expresses "for the sake of": a reason or an intended benefit.
9. MAL	Numbers	einmal, zehnmal, hundertmal	Expresses the number of times something has happened.
10. MASS EN	ADJ	einigermassen, gewissermassen, versprochenermassen	Expresses extent or manner. A linking -ER- is used.
11. WEG	ADJ	frischweg, glattweg, kurzweg	Denotes manner.
12. WEISE	N, ADJ	paarweise, stufenweise, ausnahmsweise	Denotes manner.

The following series of suffixes ending in -S could also be intepreted as compounds in which the real suffix is *only* -S, which is added to a complex (multi-root) stem: thus, *jedenfalls* could be considered to be *jeden + fall + s* as well as *jeden + falls*.

13. DING S	ADJ	allerdings, neuerdings	Used with ALL, NEU, SCHLECHT, GLATT, PLATT. An intensification force is often present. A linking -ER- is used.
14. FALL S	ADJ	gleichfalls, jedenfalls	Forms ADV as well as CONJUNCTION. Ex-

			presses the idea of way, event, case, or eventuality.
15. LING S	N, ADJ, V, ADV, Prepositions	bäuchlings, rücklings, blindlings	Denotes manner. Indicates position or direction toward something. (Usually with umlaut)
16. MAL S	ADJ	damals, vielmals, mehrmals	Denotes time or number of times.
17. SEIT S	N	1. väterlicherseits, linkerseits	1. Expresses side.
	Pronoun-Adjective	2. meinerseits, seinerseits	2. Expresses a personal reference or viewpoint.
18. WÄRT S	N (mainly)	vorwärts, ostwärts, heimwärts	Denotes direction toward. Corresponds to the English -WARD.
19. WEG S	ADJ	geradewegs, keineswegs	Denotes manner.

NOUN-FORMING SUFFIXES

SUFFIX	gender	part of speech from which noun is formed	examples	how used/remarks
1. CHEN	Neut	N	Städtchen, Mädchen	Forms diminutives (usually with umlaut).
2. LEIN	Neut	N	Schneiderlein, Brüderlein	Forms diminutives (usually with umlaut).

3. DE	Fem + Neut	V	Freude, Gebäude	
4. E	Fem	V or Adj	Hilfe, Bitte	Often with umlaut or vowel change.
			Säge, Winde	Often designates tools or instruments.
5. EI	Fem	V or N	Zauberei, Schreiberei	An intensive activity, sometimes with a derogatory connotation.
			Bücherei, Molkerei	A place of business, occupation, or activity.
6. EL	Masc (mainly) Fem (occasionally)	V	Hebel, Flügel	Often indicates tools or instruments.
7. EN	Masc (mainly) Fem (occasionally)	—	See below for examples.	

This suffix has no appreciable meaning. It is used with words that denote: an instrument (Spaten, Bogen, Haken); a place for storing or securing s.t. (Laden, Schuppen, Hafen); a part of the body (Magen, Rücken, Daumen); in some cases an abstract idea (Glaube(n), Friede(n), Schreck/Schrecken). As an infinitive ending it can be used as a nominalization of most verbs (das Treiben, das Tun, das Sprechen). This is a mechanical application of a grammatical process, and all cases of infinitive used as noun are neuter.

8. ER	Masc	V (mainly)	Verkäufer, Schneider Bettler, Holländer	Designates occupations (umlaut). Characterizes persons by a particular attribute or place of origin.

9. FALT	Numerals	N	Einfalt, Zwiefalt, Vielfalt Sorgfalt	Corresponds to English "-FOLD."
10. HEIT	Fem	N, Adj, or Participles	Schönheit, Gottheit	A condition or a characteristic.
11. KEIT	Fem	N, Adj, or Participles	Dankbarkeit, Freundlichkeit	A condition or a characteristic. Used after the suffixes BAR, IG, LICH, SAM, and often after EL and ER.
12. ICHT	Neut	N, Adj, V	Kehricht; Dickicht, Röhricht, Tannicht	A collective idea (Kehricht) or a collection or gathering of plants.
13. IN	Fem	Masc N	Freundin, Königin	Indicates a female counterpart.
14. LING	Masc	V, Adj, other N	Lehrling, Sträfling	Describes a person by means of the condition or activity in which he finds himself. (Usually with umlaut.)
			Schwächling, Bitterling Frühling, Silberling	Often diminutive or strongly pejorative. Some older formations are impersonal.
15. NIS	Neut or Fem	V, Adj, other N	Gefängnis, Finsternis	Designates actions, conditions, or things.
16. RICH	Masc	N	Enterich, Ganserich	Original meaning was "ruler." Present use is greatly weakened in force from "ruler." Is used to designate the

				male of several species of birds. It can also be used for certain plants.
			Weiderich, Hederich	
17. S	Masc	V	Knicks, Klaps, Schnaps, Schwips	
18. SAL	Neut (mainly)	V (mainly)	Schicksal, Trübsal	
19. SEL	Neut (mainly)	V (mainly)	Mitbringsel, Überbleibsel	
20. SCHAFT	Fem	N (mainly), Adj and Participles (sometimes)	Grafschaft, Lehrerschaft, Freundschaft, Verwandtschaft	Collective nouns that designate territory, a group, a condition, or a property.
21. ST	all genders	V	der Gewinst, das Gespinst, die Kunst (können)	Forms abstract nouns.
22. T	Fem	V	Fahrt, Wacht, Tracht	
23. TUM	Neut (mainly)		Fürstentum, Bürgertum Reichtum, Irrtum	Designates territory or group. May also show abstract qualities.
24. UNG	Fem	V (often verbs) with prefixes)	Haltung, Voraussetzung, Mitteilung	A very widely used suffix.

VERB-FORMING SUFFIXES

SUFFIX	part of speech from which verb is formed	examples	how used/remarks
1. EN	—	haben, sehen, gehen	This is by far the most frequent infinitive suffix for German verbs. Indeed, with very few exceptions, all German infinitives are formed with either -EN, -ELN, or -ERN.

The infinitive suffix (-EN, -ELN, -ERN, etc.) is the same suffix that is used for the first and third plural endings (wir haben, sie haben) as well as for the polite/formal singular and plural endings (Sie haben) of verbs.

2. ELN	—	betteln, streicheln	1. Iteration: the frequent occurrence and repetition of an activity.
		prasseln, zappeln	2. Rapidity.
		lächeln, tröpfeln	3. Diminutive force.
		schmeicheln, heucheln, klügeln	4. Depreciatory force.
		Es füchselt, anheimeln	5. Likeness, similarity, close association.
3. ERN	—	schnattern, stottern, flackern	1. Frequent repetition or continuation of an action, often in jerks or in an unsteady motion.

		mich schläfert, trinkert, durstert	2. The irresistible desire of doing that which is implied in the stem. Especially frequent in impersonal construc- tions. (Obsolete)
4. SEN	—	japsen, knipsen, klecksen, mucksen	Iterative force and weak diminutive force.
5. ZEN	—	lechzen, jauchzen, grunzen	Iterative force and weak diminutive force.
6. SCHEN	—	quietschen, löschen	Iterative force and weak diminutive force.
7. CHEN	V	horchen ← hören	This is actually the strengthening of the final consonant of the stem, and expresses an intensification of the meaning of the stem.
8. CKEN	V	bücken ← biegen	This is actually the strengthening of the final consonant of the stem, and expresses an intensification of the meaning of the stem.
9. PFEN	V	rupfen ← raufen	This is actually the strengthening of the final consonant of the stem, and expresses an intensification of the meaning of the stem.
10. IEREN	N (frequently)	marschieren, buch- stabieren, halbieren	This suffix has no dis- tinct meaning. It was originally a French ending, but is now

affixed to German as
well as to foreign
stems.

11. ISIEREN	—	egalisieren, nasalisieren, organisieren	This suffix corresponds to a great extent to the English suffix -IZE.
12. EIEN	N (frequently)	prophezeien, benedeien, maledeien	This suffix has no distinct meaning. It often corresponds to the foreign ending -EI in nouns.
13. LICHEN	ADJ	verehelichen, versinnlichen, ermöglichen	This often corresponds to an adjective ending in -LICH. The verb is usually prefixed, and is transitive.

COMPLEX WORDS

The following is a list of all complex (multi-root) words found in the dictionary. These complex word forms are all found in the first three thousand words of German and are all members of a productive word family. They are listed in the dictionary according to their second root, and are presented after the full series of simplex words in a given family is completed.

Mitt el alter	NN
Zeit alter	NN
Hand arbeit	NF
Mund art	NF
Sport art	NF
Zahn arzt	NM
Eisen bahn	NF
Strasse n bahn	NF
wo bei	
steh en bleib en	
Augen blick	NM
Fuss boden	NM
Zahn bürst e	
irgend ein	

Woche n end e	NN
Abend ess en	NN
Mit tag ess en	NN
viel fach	A
zwei fach	A
so fern	
recht fert ig en	
statt find en	
Spazier gang	NM
so gar	
acht geb en	
spazier en geh en	
zu grund e geh en	
so gleich	
Flug hafen	NM
fest halt en	
sich fest halt en	
Haus halt	NM
aller hand	AV
Gast haus	NN
Kauf haus	NN
Krank en haus	NN
Rat haus	NN
wo her	
barm herz ig	
wo hin	
Bahn hof	NM
Streich holz	NN
Früh jahr	NN
Leb en s jahr	NN
Schul jahr	NN
Welt krieg	NM
Grund lag e	
Deutsch land	NN
stund en lang	AV
Zeit lang	NF
grund leg end	
Wasser leit ung	
kenn en lern en	
irre mach en	
Denk mal	NN
Merk mal	NN

jeder mann	PN	
Kauf mann	NM	
Schutz mann	NM	
Weih nacht en	NN	
Mass nahm e		
so ge nann t	A	
teil nehm en		
wahr nehm en		
ausser orden t lich		
Sport platz	NM	
Auf nahm e prüf ung		
Ge sicht s punkt	NM	
Mitt el punkt	NM	
Stand punkt	NM	
Zeit punkt	NM	
Fahr rad	NN	
Motor rad	NN	
Haupt sach e		
Tat sach e		
Grund satz	NM	
grund sätz lich		
haupt säch lich		
tat säch lich	AV	
Staub saug er		
Welt an schau ung		
wahr schein lich		
Regen schirm	NM	
wunder schön	A	
Kühl schrank	NM	
Zeit schrift	NF	
Hand schuh	NM	
Mitt el schul e		
Volk s schul e		
Volk s hoch schul e		
Fern seh en	NN	
Schau spiel	NN	
Schau spiel er		
dem ent sprech end		
Gross stadt	NF	
selbst ständ ig		
selbst ver ständ lich		
fest steh en		

fest stell en	
Fest stell ung	
Halt e stell e	
Schrift stell er	
Tank stell e	
Früh stück	NN
eifer sücht ig	
All tag	NM
Ge burt s tag	NM
heut zu tag e	AV
Brief träg er	
Gross vater	NM
so weit	
not wend ig	
Not wend ig keit	
Land wirt	NM
Land wirt schaft	
land wirt schaft lich	
Natur wiss en schaft	
kenn zeich n en	
Frei zeit	NF
gleich zeit ig	
Jahr es zeit	NF
Lehr zeit	NF
Mahl zeit	NF
Schul zeit	NF
Flug zeug	NN
Werk zeug	NN
Wohn zimmer	NN
all zu	AV
nah e zu	AV
wo zu	

ABBREVIATIONS

The following abbreviations are used with the German words in this dictionary and are taken from Wahrig's *Deutsches Wörterbuch*. The grammatical information is placed five spaces after each German word and the stylistic and regional information is placed approximately eight spaces after each word. Words limited to a particular technical usage are relatively infrequent in this dictionary, and words restricted to regional usage are very rare.

The grammatical information is limited to part of speech and gender notation and is given in cases of ambiguity or in instances where the gender is not immediately clear from the suffix. Thus, for example, nouns ending in -UNG or -KEIT such as *Achtung, Ähnlichkeit* are not labeled NF, verbs ending in -EN such as *arbeiten, tragen* are not labeled V, and adjectives ending in -LICH such as *ärgerlich, freundlich* are not labeled A. It is suggested that the reader use this grammatical information together with the information contained in the list of suffixes.

Grammatical Information

NM	masculine noun	(der)
NF	feminine noun	(die)

NN	neuter noun	(das)
NP	plural noun	(die-PL)

A	adjective
AV	adverb
P	preposition
C	conjunction

Stylistic Information

A	archaic or obsolete
B	business or trade
C	chancery
G	grammatical term
H	hunting term
I	rare
L	legal
M	military
N	nautical
O	sport
P	poetic
S	slang
T	technical or scientific

Regional Usage

AU	Austrian
CH	Swiss
LG	lower German
NG	north German
RH	Rhine
UG	upper German

WORD FAMILY DICTIONARY

her ab	av	down, downward
hin ab	av	down, downwards; down there
vor ab	av	in advance; first of all; beforehand; tentatively

Acht nf	outlawry, ban, proscription; attention
acht bar	respectable, honorable
Acht bar keit	respectability, honorableness; reputability, creditableness
acht en	respect, esteem; abide by laws; respect rights
ächt en	outlaw, proscribe
acht en s wert	estimable, respectable
acht los	inattentive, unheeding, careless; inconsiderate
Acht los ig keit	inattention, heedlessness, carelessness; disrespect, discourtesy
acht sam	attentive to; careful of
Acht sam keit	attentiveness; carefulness
Acht ung	attention; respect, esteem, regard
acht ung s voll	respectful
be acht en	pay attention to, heed; note, notice, observe; bear in mind
be acht lich	noticeable, marked, considerable; remarkable
Be acht ung	attention, notice; consideration, regard; observance
er acht en	consider, judge, deem, think
miss acht en	disregard, ignore, neglect; slight, despise
Miss acht ung	disregard, neglect; disdain
Ob acht nf	attention
un acht sam	inattentive; absent-minded; careless, negligent
Un acht sam keit	carelessness, negligence, inadvertance
ver acht en	despise, hold in disdain; scorn
Ver ächt er	despiser
ver ächt lich	contemptuous, disdainful, scornful; contemptible, vile

Ver acht ung	contempt, disdain
un be acht et	unnoticed
un ge acht et p	regardless of, irrespective of, notwithstanding; despite
be ob acht en	observe, watch; scan, survey; shadow s.o.
Be ob acht er	observer
Be· ob acht ung	observation
un be ob acht et	unobserved

ahn d en	avenge; punish
Ahn d ung	revenge; punishment
ahn en	anticipate, foresee; have a foreboding of; devine, sense; suspect
Ahn ung	presentiment, hunch; foreboding; misgiving; suspicion; idea
ahn ung s los	unsuspecting, without misgivings; innocent
ahn ung s voll	full of prensentiment; ominous, portentous
Vor ahn ung	presentiment, foreboding
un ge ahn t	undreamt-of, unthought-of; unexpected, unhoped-for

Ahn nm	ancestor, forbear; grandfather
ähn el n	look like, resemble, bear a remote resemblance to
ähn lich	resembling; similar to, like, alike; analogous to
Ähn lich keit	resemblance to, likeness to
un ähn lich	unlike, dissimilar
Ur ahn nm	great grandfather
Ur ahn e nf	great grandmother

alt a	old
Alt e nm	old man
Ält es te	elder, senior
ält lich	elderly, oldish
ur alt a	very old, very ancient
ver alt en	become obsolete, go out of date, go out of fashion

alter: siehe alt	
Alter nn	age; old age
älter a	older
alter n	grow old, age, advance in years
Alter tum	antiquity
alter tüm lich	ancient, antique; archaic; antiquated
Alter ung	seasoning
über alter t	superannuated, obsolete
Ueber alter ung	obsolescence, superannuation
Mitt el alter nn	Middle Ages
Zeit alter nn	age, era

Amt nn	office; post; task; official duty, function; agency, bureau
amt ier en	hold office, be in charge

amt lich	official
ausser amt lich	unofficial, non-official; private
Be amt e	official, functionary, officer, executive; public servant
Be amt en schaft	bureaucracy
Be amt en tum	civil servants
Be amt in	official, functionary, officer, executive; public servant
Fern amt nn	long-distance telephone exchange
Neben amt nn	subsidiary office
Unter be amt er	subordinate official

an av	on, onward; up
dar an av	on that, at that, in that; thereby; thereon
fort an av	henceforth, from now on
her an av	up this way, near, to the spot
hin an p av	up, upwards; up to
neben an av	next door, in the next room; close by
vor an av	before, at the head, in front of

ander	other; different; second; next; opposite
ander er seit s	on the other side, on the other hand
änder n	change, alter; modify; vary
ander s av	otherwise; differently
ander s	else
Änder ung	change, alteration; modification; variation
ab änder lich	alterable, modifiable, variable; commutable
ab änder n	alter, change; vary; modify; correct, revise, recast; amend
Ab änder ung	alteration, modification; rectification, revision
'um änder n	change, alter, modify; rearrange
ver änder bar lich	changeable, variable
ver änder n	alter, change; vary
sich ver änder n	change one's place, take another situation
Ver änder ung	change, alteration; variation, fluctuation
un ab änder lich	unalterable, irrevocable, definite
un ver änder lich	unchangeable, invariable; constant, stable
Un ver änder lich keit	unchangeability
un ver änder t	unchanged, just as it was, the same as before

Angst nf	fear, anxiety; fright, dread, terror; anguish
ängst ig en	alarm, frighten, strike with fear; worry
sich ängst ig en	be afraid of, be alarmed about, be worried about
ängst lich	anxious, fearful; uneasy, nervous; timid
Ängst lich keit	anxiety, nervousness; timidity; scrupulousness
angst voll	fearful, frightened, terrified
be ängst ig en	make anxious, make uneasy, worry, alarm, frighten
Be ängst ig ung	anxiety, uneasiness, worry

Antwort nf	answer, reply, retort
antwort en	answer, reply, retort; react, respond

be antwort en	answer, reply to
Be antwort ung	answer, reply
Rück antwort nf	reply
über 'antwort en	deliver up, give over, surrender
ver antwort en	answer for, account for
sich ver antwort en	justify o.s.
ver antwort lich	responsible, answerable
Ver antwort lich keit	responsibility; accountability
Ver antwort ung	responsibility; justification
ver antwort ung s los	irresponsible
ver antwort ung s voll	responsible
un be antwort et	unanswered
Mit ver antwort ung	joint responsibility
un ver antwort lich	irresponsible; inexcusable, unwarrantable
Un ver antwort lich keit	irresponsibility, inexcusability

Arbeit nf	work, labor, toil, effort, trouble; employment; composition
arbeit en	work, work hard, labor, toil, drudge; be employed
Arbeit er	workman, worker, laborer; artisan, craftsman, handy-man
Arbeit erin	working-woman, factory girl, factorywoman
Arbeit er schaft	working classes, workmen; personnel, crew
arbeit sam	industrious, diligent; busy, active
Arbeit sam keit	industry, diligence; activity
arbeit s los	out of work, unemployed
Arbeit s los e	unemployed person, jobless person
Arbeit s los ig keit	unemployment
ab arbeit en	work off; overtask; repay by working
sich ab arbeit en	sweat; overwork o.s.; wear off
auf arbeit en	work up; renovate; finish; catch up on s.t.; work off
aus arbeit en	work out, elaborate, prepare; write, compose
Aus arbeit ung	elaboration, perfection, finishing touch; composition
be arbeit en	machine; influence s.o.; revise; work, cultivate; handle
Be arbeit er	reviser, compiler, author, editor; adaptor
Be arbeit ung	working, revision; arrangement; machining
'durch arbeit en	work through; train; knead
sich 'durch arbeit en	get through, make one's way through
ein arbeit en	train on the job
er arbeit en	gain by working, earn
hin arbeit en	aim at
los arbeit en	work away at
Mit arbeit nf	cooperation, collaboration; assistance
mit arbeit en	cooperate, collaborate; contribute to, be on the staff of
Mit arbeit er	collaborator, coworker, correspondent, contributor
nach arbeit en	touch up, refinish, recondition; work from a model

Neben arbeit	nf	extra work, spare-time work
über 'arbeit en		do over again, revise
sich über 'arbeit en		overwork o.s.
Ueber arbeit ung		revision, touching up, modified text; overwork
'um arbeit en		remodel, revise; correct, improve, work over
Um arbeit ung		working over, revision; correction, improvement
ver arbeit en		manufacture; use up; handle; fabricate, process
Ver arbeit ung		working up, using up, manufacturing, machining, fashioning
Vor arbeit	nf	preparatory work, ground work
vor arbeit en		prepare s.t., prepare the ground for
Vor arbeit er		foreman, leading hand, chief operator
Zusammen arbeit	nf	cooperation, mutual support, team-work
zusammen arbeit en		work together, cooperate, collaborate
sich hin auf arbeit en		work one's way up
her aus arbeit en		work out, form, modulate; elaborate
sich hin durch arbeit en		make one's way through; study from beginning to end
sich hin ein arbeit en		make o.s. thoroughly acquainted with, familiarize o.s. with
ent gegen arbeit en		counteract, thwart, oppose, work against, buck
un ver arbeit et		unwrought
Hand arbeit	nf	work done by hand, handmade object

arg	a	bad; morally bad, wicked, evil; malicious
Arg	nn	malice, harm
Ärg er		annoyance, vexation, irritation, chagrin, anger
ärg er lich		angry, annoyed, vexed, irritated
ärg er n		annoy, anger, vex, irritate, exasperate, madden; provoke, tease
sich ärg er n		feel angry, be annoyed, be vexed by, fret at
Ärg er nis	nn	scandal, offense
arg los		guileless; innocent, harmless; unsuspecting; unsuspicious
Arg los ig keit		guilelessness; innocence, harmlessness
ver arg en		hold s.t. against s.o., blame s.o. for s.t.
ver ärg er n		annoy, vex, anger
Ver ärg er ung		annoyance, irritation

Arm	nm	arm
Ärm el		sleeve
ärm el los		sleeveless
arm ier en		arm, equip; shield; sheath; reinforce; armor
Arm ier ung		armament, equipment
arm voll		armful
Ober arm	nm	upper arm
um 'arm en		embrace, hug
Um arm ung		embrace, hug
Unter arm	nm	forearm

arm	a	poor

ärm lich	poor; shabby
Ärm lich keit	poorness; shabbiness, misery
Arm ut nf	poverty; destitution, indigence, penury; lack, deficiency
ver arm en	become poor, become impoverished
Ver arm ung	impoverishment, pauperization

Art nf	kind, sort
art ig	well-behaved, polite, courteous; nice, pretty
Art ig keit	good behavior; politeness, niceness; prettiness
Art ung	character, nature
Ab art nf	variety, species; modification; version
ab art en	deviate from type, vary; degenerate
ab art ig	abnormal
aus art en	degenerate; turn rowdy, get out of hand
Aus art ung	degeneration
ent art en	degenerate; deteriorate
Ent art ung	degeneration, deterioration; abnormality
nach art en	take after s.o.
Un art nf	bad habit, bad trick; incivility; ill-breeding
un art ig	rude, uncivil, ill-bred; naughty
Unter art nf t	subspecies, subvariety
Mund art nf	dialect; patois, vernacular
Sport art nf	type of sport

Arzt nm	physician; medical practitioner, doctor
Ärzt in	lady doctor, lady physician
ärzt lich	medical
Ober arzt nm	assistant medical director
Unter arzt nm	junior surgeon, physician assistant
ver arzt en s	take care of s.o., doctor s.o.
Zahn arzt nm	dentist

Atem nm	breath; breathing, respiration
atem los	breathless
at m en	breathe, respire
At m ung	breathing, respiration
auf at m en	give a sigh of relief
aus at m en	breathe out, exhale; breathe one's last breath
Aus at m ung	exhalation
ein at m en	inhale, breathe in
Ein at m ung	inhalation

auf av	up, upwards; open; awake; astir
dar auf av	on it, on that; on top of it; thereupon
her auf av	up, upwards; up here
hin auf av	up, upwards, up there
vor auf av	ahead, at the head, out in front, to the fore, before, foremost
da hin auf av	up there

aus av	out; over; finished; done with

dar aus	av		from this, from that; of it; thence; therefrom
durch aus	av		throughout, thoroughly; absolutely, definitely, by all means
her aus	av		out
hin aus	av		out, out there; outside
über aus	av		exceedingly, extremely
vor aus	av		in front, ahead
da hin aus	av		out there, out that way

---

ausser	c		except that, but that; if not
Äusser e	nn		outside, exterior, outward appearance
ausser halb	p		out of, outside; beyond
äusser lich			external, exterior, outward
Äusser lich keit			exterior, external appearance
äusser n			utter, express; advance; show, manifest
äusser st	av		extremely, exceedingly, utterly, highly
Äusser ung			utterance, statement, declaration; remark, observation, comment
sich ent äusser n			get rid of; divest o.s. of, discard, dispose of
Rück äusser ung			reply
ver äusser lich			alienable; negotiable
ver äusser n			alienate; transfer; dispose of, sell
Ver äusser ung			alienation; disposal, sale
un ver äusser lich			inalienable
Un ver äusser lich keit			inalienability

---

back en		bake; fry; dry fruit; burn; fire brick
Bäck er		baker
Bäck erei		bakehouse, bakery
an back en		bake gently
'durch back en		bake thoroughly
durch 'back en		bake s.t. with s.t.; bake a cake with raisins
Ge bäck	nn	baker's ware; pastry, fancy cake, cookie
zusammen back en	s	bake together

Bahn	nf	course, path; track; road, way
bahn en		beat a path, clear, open up a path
bahn frei		free station
Neben bahn	nf	local railroad line
Eisen bahn	nf	railroad; train
Strasse n bahn	nf	streetcar, trolleycar

---

band:	siehe bind	
Band	nm	volume; tome
Band	nn	string, cord
Band age	nf	bandage
Bänd chen		small ribbon; small volume
Band e		company, troop, team
bänd er n		form into ribbons; stripe, streak
bänd ig en		tame; break in a horse
Bänd ig er		tamer; conqueror
Bänd ig ung		taming; breaking in

Ein band nm	book binding; cover
un bänd ig	unruly, intractable; tremendous
Ver band nm	binding; bracing
an band el n	make advances to s.o., flirt with s.o.; pick a quarrel

Er barm en nn	pity, compassion, commiseration; mercy
er barm en	move s.o. to pity
er bärm lich	pitiful, pitiable; miserable, wretched; paltry, mean
Er bärm lich keit	pitiableness, misery
er barm ung s los	pitiless, merciless; relentless
er barm ung s voll	full of pity, compassionate

barm-herz ig	merciful, lenient; compassionate; charitable
Barm-herz ig keit	mercy; compassion, charity
un barm-herz ig	unmerciful, merciless, pitiless, relentless
Un barm-herz ig keit	unmercifullness

Bau nm	building, construction, structure; build
bau en	build, construct; make s.t.; grow, cultivate; rely on s.t.
Bau er	farmer, peasant; pawn in chess, jack in cards
Bäu erin	farmer's wife, peasant woman
bäu er lich	rural, rustic
Bau er schaft	peasantry, farmers
Bau er n tum nn	peasantry, farmers
bau lich	architectural, constructional, structural
Bau lich keit en np	buildings; architecture
Bau ten np	buildings, structures
Ab bau nm	reduction, cut; separation; dismantling; dismissal
ab bau en	work, take down, remove; demolish; reduce; dismantle
An bau nm	annex, wing; cultivation, tillage
an bau en	till, cultivate, grow corn; add a new wing
Auf bau nm	erection, assembly; reconstruction; body, superstructure
auf bau en	build up, erect, rebuild, construct; display
Auf bau ten np	superstructure; set
Aus bau nm	outbuilding; jetty; enlargement; perfection, completion
aus bau en	improve; finish, complete; extend, develop; support
be bau en	build on; till, cultivate, farm
Be bau ung	cultivation; covering with buildings
Ein bau nm	interior, installation, mounting, assembly
ein bau en	build in, install; fix, mount; insert
er bau en	build up, construct, erect; found; edify
sich er bau en	be edified by, be pleased with
Er bau er	builder, constructor, designer, erector, architect
er bau lich	edifying, devotional; encouraging, gratifying, pleasing
Er bau ung	building, erection, construction; edification, uplift

Ge bäu de	nn		building, edifice, structure, house, office building
Ober bau	nm		work above ground, superstructure; roadbed
Ueber bau	nm		superstructure
über 'bau en			build over
Um bau	nm		rebuilding, reconstruction, alterations; reorganization
'um bau en			rebuild, reconstruct; reorganize, reform, remodel
um 'bau en			build around
Unter bau	nm		substructure, infrastructure; foundation, support, base, groundwork
unter 'bau en			underpin, lay the basis of
ver bau en			build up; build badly; spend in building
Vor bau	nm		front structure, porch
vor bau en			build out, build in front of; guard against, prevent
zu bau en			wall up, wall in
Zusammen bau	nm		assembly, assemblage, erection
zusammen bau en			mount, assemble, set up, erect
Wieder auf bau	nm		reconstruction, rebuilding; rehabilitation
wieder 'auf bau en			rebuild, reconstruct
un be bau t			uncultivated, untilled; undeveloped; vacant
Hinter ge bäu de	nn		back building, rear building
Neben ge bäu de	nn		adjacent building, annex
Vorder ge bäu de	nn		front building

Bauch	nm	belly
bauch ig		bellied, bulged; convex
Bauch ung		convexity; bulge; swelling, inflation
aus bauch en		bulge out, belly out
Aus bauch ung		bulge
Ober bauch	nm	epigastrium
Unter bauch	nm	hypogastrium

bei	av	by, near
an bei	av	herewith, find enclosed; attached
da bei	av	near at hand, close by
her bei	av	here, hither
neben bei	av	by the way, incidentally; besides, moreover
vor bei	av	along, by, past; over, gone
wo bei		in which, where, which

Bein	nn	leg; bone
Bein ling		leg of a stocking
Ge bein	nn	bones; skeleton
Hinter bein	nn	hind leg
Ueber bein	nn	node, exotosis
Vorder bein	nn	foreleg

beiss en	gnaw at, gnaw on
ab beiss en	bite off
an beiss en	bite at, take a bite of
aus beiss en	bite out
durch 'beiss en	bite through, bite off, bite in two

'durch beiss en		bite through, bite in two
sich 'durch beiss en		fight s.t. out, struggle through s.t.; weather the storm
ver beiss en		suppress
zer beiss en		bite through, bite to pieces, crunch
zu beiss en		bite; snap
zusammen beiss en		clench one's teeth

bell en		bark
an bell en		bark at
Ge bell	nn	barking

bes: siehe bess		
Bes te	nn	the best thing
bes t ens	av	best

besser	a	better; improved; superior; respectable
Besser es	nn	something better, something superior
sich besser n		make better; improve; ameliorate
Besser ung		amelioration, improvement; change for the better
besser ung s fäh ig		improvable
auf besser n		raise, increase salary; improve prices
Auf besser ung		rise, raise, increase of pay, improvement of prices
aus besser n		mend, repair, fix; overhaul; patch up; darn; restore art
Aus besser ung		repair, mending, patching
Ver besser er	i	improver; reformer, corrector
ver besser n		improve, ameliorate; correct, rectify; modify; revise
Ver besser ung		improvement; correction, rectification
un ver besser lich		incorrigible, inveterate

bet en		pray to God; say one's prayers
an bet en		adore, worship, idolize
An bet er		worshiper, adorer; admirer
An bet ung		adoration
Ge bet	nn	prayer
her bet en	s	pray mechanically, rattle off prayers
nach bet en	s	repeat mechanically, echo, parrot
Nach bet er	s	thoughtless repeater, parrot
vor bet en		recite a prayer to s.o.
un ge bet en	a	uninvited, unasked

Bett	nn	bed, bedstead; cot
bett en		put s.o. to bed
Bett ung		bedding; bed-plate; bed
ein bett en		embed
Ober bett	nn	coverlet
'um bett en		put into another bed
Unter bett	nn	underbedding, underblankets

Beug e		bend; curve; flexure

beug en	bend, bow, flex
sich beug en	bow down, bend down, stoop
Beug ung	bending; flexion; flexure, bend
nieder beug en	bend down, bow; depress, weigh down
un beug sam	inflexible, unshakable, uncompromising, adamant, hard-shell
Un beug sam keit	inflexibility; unshakability
ver beug en	bow to
Ver beug ung	bow
vor beug en	prevent, obviate; guard against
sich vor beug en	bend forward
Vor beug ung	prevention
sich hin aus beug en	lean out
un ge beug t	unbent, uncurbed

Beut e	booty, captured material
Beut el	bag; purse
beut el n	shake; bolt, sift flour; bag; bulge
Aus beut e	gain, profit; yield, output
aus beut en	exploit; work, make the most of, take advantage of
Aus beut er	exploiter, slavedriver
Aus beut ung	exploitation
er beut en	capture, take as booty, carry off

bieg en	bend, bow; flex limbs; curve; camber wood; turn a corner
bieg sam	pliable, flexible
Bieg sam keit	pliability; flexibility; suppleness
Bieg ung	bend
ab bieg en	bend off; turn aside, deflect; take care of s.t., handle a matter
aus bieg en	bend outwards, deflect
ein bieg en	bend inwards, turn inwards
'um bieg en	bend over; turn down, turn up
ver bieg en	bend, twist, distort

biet en	offer; treat; present difficulties; afford pleasure
sich biet en	present itself
an biet en	offer, tender
sich an biet en	offer one's services, volunteer
auf biet en	proclaim; publish banns; call up, summon; mobilize; muster
Auf biet ung	summoning; proclamation; immobilization
aus biet en	offer, exhibit
dar biet en	offer, present; perform, play
Dar biet ung	performance, presentation
sich er biet en	offer to do s.t., volunteer to do s.t.
Ge biet nn	territory; ground; district, region; area
ge biet en	order s.o. to do s.t.; enjoin; direct, require, command
Ge biet er	master, lord, governor, ruler, commander

Ge biet erin	mistress
ge biet er isch	commanding; imperious, authoritative, dictatorial; peremptory
über 'biet en	outbid; surpass, outdo
unter 'biet en	underbid; undercut in price; undersell competitors
ver biet en	forbid, prohibit; ban, rule out, outlaw
An er biet en nn	offer, proposal

Bild nn	picture, painting, drawing, photograph, image; sight, spectacle
bild en	form; make, produce, compose; shape, mold; educate, train
sich bild en	form, be formed; educate o.s.
bild end	formative; educational, instructive
bild lich	pictorial, graphic; figurative, metaphorical
Bild ner	sculptor; educator
Bild nerei	sculpture
bild ner isch	sculptural
Bild nis nn	portrait, likeness
bild sam	formable, ductile, plastic
Bild sam keit	plasticity, ductility
Bild ung	education; culture, development
Ab bild nn	copy, likeness, image
ab bild en	copy, portray; model
Ab bild ung	illustration, copying; sketch, image, picture
aus bild en	form, develop; educate; cultivate, improve
sich aus bild en	study for, perfect o.s.
Aus bild er	instructor, trainer, coach
Aus bild ung	education, training; accomplishment, development
'durch bild en	develop fully, perfect; design, construct
Durch bild ung	thorough education
sich ein bild en	imagine, believe, think; pride o.s. on; fancy s.t.
Ein bild ung	imagination, idea, illusion, fancy; conceit
fort bild en	keep on studying
Fort bild ung	advanced training
Ge bild e nn	creation, product; work, formation; form, vision, image
ge bild et	educated, cultured, civilized, well-bred
miss bild en	misshape
Miss bild ung	deformity, malformation
Nach bild nn	copy, counterfeit, imitation, replica, facsimile
nach bild en	copy, imitate, reproduce, simulate, counterfeit
Nach bild ung	replica, copy
Rück bild ung	regeneration, regression, involution
'um bild en	transform; remodel, reconstruct, reorganize; reform
Um bild ung	transformation; remodelling, reconstruction, reorganization; reform
Un bild en np	inclemency of weather
Un bild ung	lack of education, illiteracy
Ur bild nn	prototype, ideal
ver bild en	form wrongly; educate badly, spoil

Vor bild nn		pattern, model, standard, example
vor bild en		train, prepare
vor bild lich		exemplary, model, typical, representative
Vor bild ung		preparatory training
weiter bild en		develop
Weiter bild ung		advanced training, further development
sich zurück bild en		reform, form again
Zurück bild ung		involution
her an bild en		train; educate, bring up
ein ge bild et		imaginary; conceited; fantastical
un ge bild et		uneducated, uncivilized; rude, ill-bred, unpolished
un aus ge bild et		uncultivated, undeveloped, untrained
be bild er n		illustrate a book
Be bild er ung		illustration
ver bild lich en		symbolize; illustrate

bill ig		equitable, fair, just; reasonable, cheap, inexpensive
bill ig en		approve of, consent to, agree to; sanction
bill ig er weise	av	fairly, in all fariness; justly
Bill ig keit		fairness, equity, justness; reasonableness
Bill ig ung		approval, approbation, sanction, consent
Un bill nf		injury, wrong
un bill ig		unfair, unreasonable; inequitable
Un bill ig keit		unfairness, inequity
miss bill ig en		disapprove of, frown upon
Miss bill ig ung		disapproval, disapprobation, rejection
ver bill ig en		reduce the price of, lower in price, cheapen
Ver bill ig ung		reduction in price, cheapening
zu bill ig en		grant, concede, allow; award

Bind e		band
bind en		bind, tie, fasten, attach; pack; bundle
sich bind en		bind o.s.. engage, o.s., oblige o.s., commit o.s.
Bind er		tie
Bind ung		bond, bonding; cross-weaving
ab bind en		untie, unbind, loosen, remove, tie off; wean
an bind en		bind, tie up, fasten
auf bind en		untie, undo, loosen; tie up; truss up, turn up
ein bind en		bind a book
ent bind en		dispense, release, excuse; disengage, liberate, set free
Ent bind ung		dispensation, release, exemption
Ge bind e nn		bundle
los bind en		untie, unfasten, loosen
um 'bind en		tie around; put on an item of clothing
'um bind en		tie around; put on apron
unter 'bind en		tie up, ligate; stop, call a halt to; forestall, obviate
ver bind en		tie together, bind; link, join, unite, connect
ver bind lich		binding, obligatory, compulsory; obliging
Ver bind lich keit		obligation, liability, commitment; obligingness
Ver bind ung		union; bond, alliance; combination; connection

vor bind en s	tie s.t. on, put s.t. on
zu bind en	tie up, bind up; bandage; blindfold the eyes
zusammen bind en	bind together, tie together
An ge bind e nn	gift, present
un ver bind lich	not binding, not obilgatory; informal; noncommital
Un ver bind lich keit	non-obligation, noncommittal attitude; disobliging manner

birg: siehe berg	
Ge birg e nn	mountain range, mountains
ge birg ig	mountainous
Vor ge birg e nn	promontory, cape; foothills

biss: siehe beiss	
Biss nm	bite
Biss chen	a little; a little bit; a trifle; somewhat; slightly
Biss en nm	bit, morsel, mouthful, bite; savory tidbit
biss en weise av	by bits
biss ig	biting
Biss ig keit	snappishness; bitingness; sarcasm
Ge biss nn	teeth; denture, set of artificial teeth
Im biss nm	light meal, snack
ver biss en a	crabbed, morose; grim
Ver biss en heit	sourness of temper, moroseness; doggedness

Bitt e	request; entreaty; supplication, petition; invitation
bitt e av	please
bitt en	request; beg, entreat; implore, beseech; trouble o.s. for
Ab bitt e	apology
ab bitt en	apologize to s.o. for s.t., beg one's forgiveness
aus bitt en	request s.t., ask for s.t., demand s.t.
er bitt en	beg for, ask for, request
Für bitt e	intercession
her bitt en	ask to come, ask to one's house
ver bitt en	refuse to tolerate s.t., not stand for s.t.
her auf bitt en	ask s.o. to come up
her ein bitt en	invite s.o. to come in, ask s.o. in
un er bitt lich	inexorable, pitiless
Un er bitt lich keit	inexorability; pitilessness
zurück er bitt en	ask back

bitter a	bitter
Bitter keit	bitterness
bitter lich	bitterish
Bitter ling	yellow-wort
er bitter n	embitter, exasperate; incense
Er bitter ung	exasperation, bitterness; embitterment, animosity
ver bitter n	embitter, fill with bitterness
Ver bitter ung	bitterness of heart

Bläs chen	small bubble
Blas e	bubble
blas en	blow
Bläs er	player of a wind instrument; the wind section of an orchestra
blas ig	bubbly; like blisters
ab blas en	blow off, blow away; sandblast; release gas; call off, cancel
auf blas en	blow up; inflate
aus blas en	blow out; blow down a furnace; exhaust steam
Aus bläs er	exhaust; blowout
ein blas en	blow into; inject into; insufflate with s.t.; whisper s.t. to s.o.
Ein bläs er	prompter
Ge bläs e nn	blower, engine blast
'um blas en	blown down, blown over
weg blas en	blow off, blow away
auf ge blas en a	puffed up, inflated; arrogant, conceited
Auf ge blas en heit	arrogance, conceit

Blatt nn	leaf
Blätt chen	small leaf, leaflet
blätt er ig	leafy, foliated
blätt er n	turn over the leaves
blatt los	leafless
Bei blatt nn	supplement
ab blätt er n	strip the leaves off, defoliate
'durch blätt er n	glance through a book, leaf through
ent blätt er n	strip of leaves, defoliate
sich ent blätt er n	shed leaves
'um blätt er n	turn over the page

Bleib e s	shelter, place to stay
bleib en	remain; stay; continue, keep; be left
auf bleib en	remain open; stay up
aus bleib en	stay away, stay out, fail to appear
da bleib en	stay, remain
fern bleib en	keep away, absent o.s., not come, not attend
fort bleib en	stay away; fail to return
nach bleib en	remain behind, lag behind; be kept in
Ueber bleib sel	remainder, remnant, holdover
übrig bleib en	be left, remain to
unter 'bleib en	be left undone; not take place, be discontinued, cease
Ver bleib nm	whereabouts
ver bleib en	be left, remain
weg bleib en	stay away; be omitted
zu bleib en s	remain closed, remain shut
zurück bleib en	remain behind; be left behind; survive; be left over, fall behind
un aus bleib lich	inevitable, unfailing
da bei bleib en	persist in it, abide by it, stick to it

steh en	bleib en	stop, come to a halt; stay, remain, be left behind

---

	Blick	nm	look at
	blick en		look, glance at
An	blick	nm	look, sight, view, aspect; spectacle
an	blick en		look at, glance at; view, eye
auf	blick en		look up, glance up, raise one's eyes
Aus	blick	nm	outlook, prospect, view
Durch	blick	nm	view, vista, perspective; peep
'durch	blick en		look through; become apparent, peep out, show
Ein	blick	nm	view
er	blick en		see, perceive; discover, catch sight of, spot
Fern	blick	nm	distant view, vista
Hin	blick	nm	with regard to
hin	blick en		look, glance
nach	blick en		look after, follow with one's eyes
Rück	blick	nm	counterdemand; reclamation
Ueber	blick	nm	survey; summary, review, synopsis
über	'blick en		glance over; overlook, survey; view, assess
weg	blick en		look away
her ab	blick en		look down at s.o., despise s.o.; look s.o. up and down
hin aus	blick en		look out, gaze out
um 'her	blick en		look around o.s.
hin über	blick en		look over, look across
her vor	blick en		look out, peep out from behind; look out the door
Augen	blick	nm	moment, instant

---

	blieb: siehe bleib	
Hinter	blieb ene	surviving dependant, survivor

---

	blüh en	bloom, blossom, flower; be in bloom
	Blüt e	blossom, bloom
ab	blüh en	droop, wither; fade
auf	blüh en	burst into blossom, bloom out, open; flourish, prosper
er	blüh en	blossom out, come into flower; grow into a beauty, flourish
ver	blüh en	fade, wither

	Blum e	flower
	Blüm chen	little flower, floweret
	blum en reich	abounding in flowers; flowery
	blum ig	flowery
ge	blüm t	flowered, flowery; sprigged, with floral design
ver	blüm t	veiled, allusive; figurative
un ver	blüm t	plain, direct, blunt

	Blut nn	blood
	blut arm	bloodless, anemic
	blut en	bleed

	Blut er	bleeder, hemophiliac
	blut ig	bloody, blood-stained; bleeding; sanguinary
	blut leer	bloodless, anemic
	blut los	bloodless, anemic
	Blut ung	hemorrhage
aus	blut en	cease bleeding; bleed to death
durch	'blut en	supply with blood
Ge	blüt nn	blood; lineage, race
Nach	blut ung	secondary hemorrhage; after-bleeding
un	blut ig	bloodless
ver	blut en	bleed to death
voll	blüt ig	full-blooded; plethoric

	Boden nm	ground
	boden los	bottomless
Fuss	boden nm	floor

	Boot nn	boat
aus	boot en	put into boats, disembark; oust; put out of the running
Bei	boot nn n	dinghy
ein	boot en	embark

	bot: siehe biet	
	Bot e nm	messenger; errand-boy; commissionaire; carrier
	bot mäss ig	subject; obedient
	Bot mäss ig keit	dominion, jurisdiction; sway, rule
	Bot schaft	message, communication; news; embassy
	Bot schaft er	ambassador
	Bot schaft erin	ambassadress
er	böt ig	be ready to do s.t., offer one's help
Ge	bot nn	order, command; rule
Ver	bot nn	prohibition, ban
ver	bot en a	forbidden, prohibited; illicit; foul
Vor	bot e	forerunner
An ge	bot nn	offer
Auf ge	bot nn	public notice, citation
Gegen an ge	bot nn	counteroffer
Ueber an ge	bot nn	excessive supply

	brach: siehe brech	
	brach av	fallow, uncultivated; idle, unused
	Brach e	fallow land
	Brach en nn	allowing land to lie fallow
Ge	bräch nn t	fallow land

	brach: siehe bring	
an ge	brach t	seasonable, suited
auf ge	brach t	angry, furious
her ge	brach t a	customary, established, usual, traditional
un an ge	brach t a	out of place, unsuitable, inopportune

	brand:	siehe brenn
	Brand	nm	fire, blaze, flames; gangrene; blight, mildew
	brand en	surge, break, roar of waves
	brand ig	having a burnt smell, burnt; gangrenous; blighted
	Brand ung	surf, breakers, surging of waves
Ab	brand nm t	consumption, wear; oxidation, melting loss; combustion

	brann:	siehe brenn
ab ge	brann t	broke, out of money; burnt down
un ge	brann t	unroasted, green; raw; unfired, unburned

	brat en	roast, frizzle
	Brat en	nm	roasting; roast meat
an	brat en	roast gently
'durch	brat en	roast thoroughly

	Brauch	nm	custom; use, habit; practice
	brauch bar	useful
	Brauch bar keit	usefulness, fitness, serviceability
	brauch en	be in need of, want, need; use, make use of
	Brauch tum	nm	customs; folklore
auf	brauch en	use up, consume, exhaust
Ge	brauch	nm	use, employment
ge	brauch en	use, make use of, avail o.s. of; employ, apply to; handle
ge	bräuch lich	in use; current, ordinary, common; customary, usual
Miss	brauch	nm	abuse, misuse, improper use
miss	brauch en	abuse, take advantage of; misuse, misapply
miss	bräuch lich	c	improper
un	brauch bar	useless, unserviceable; waste; impracticable
Un	brauch bar keit	uselessness
Ver	brauch	nm	consumption
ver	brauch en	consume, use up; spend; wear out, exhaust; waste
Ver	brauch er	consumer, user
un ge	bräuch lich	unusual; obsolete
un ge	brauch t	unused, quite new

	brech bar	breakable
	Brech bar keit	breakability
	Brech e	break, gap
	brech en	break; violate, infringe; vomit, throw up
	Brech er	breaker, crusher
	Brech ung	breaking; light refraction
ab	brech en	pick, pluck; break off, pull down; stop, cut short
sich ab	brech en	burn one's boats
an	brech en	begin; break, open; dawn
auf	brech en	break open, burst; set off, depart
aus	brech en	break out; vomit; originate, arise, spring
durch	'brech en	pierce, perforate; cut one's way; run through
'durch	brech en	break through, break forth, force one's way, cut through

ein brech en	break open, force open, break in; give way; burglarize
Ein brech er	burglar, housebreaker
er brech en	break open, open; vomit
Ge brech en nn	deficiency, defect; infirmity, affliction
ge brech lich	weak, fragile, brittle, rickety, decrepit, frail
Ge brech lich keit	infirmity, frailty, decrepitude, weakness, feebleness
los brech en	break off, break out, burst out
nieder brech en	break down
um 'brech en	make up into pages
'um brech en	break down; plough up, break up
unter 'brech en	interrupt, shut off, disconnect, interdict, switch off
Unter brech er	interrupter, break; cutout, circuit breaker
Unter brech ung	interruption, break, disconnection, intermission, stop
ver brech en	commit a crime, perpetrate
Ver brech en nn	crime, felony
Ver brech er	criminal, offender, delinquent, felon, culprit
ver brech er isch	criminal
zer brech en	break into pieces, shatter, smash; rupture; fracture
zer brech lich	fragile, brittle, breakable, flimsy, friable
Zer brech lich keit	fragility, brittleness
zusammen brech en	break down, collapse, crumble
her ein brech en	fall, break in, set in; come upon
her vor brech en	break forth, issue out, break through, rush out
un zer brech lich	unbreakable, non-breakable

breit a	broad, wide; square chin; large, vast, spacious
Breit e	breadth, width; spaciousness
aus breit en	spread out; extend, expand; unfold; display; propagate; diffuse
sich aus breit en	spread; extend, expand; gain ground, make headway; travel; scatter
Aus breit ung	spread; extension, expansion; propagation, circulation, diffusion
'unter breit en	lay under, spread under
unter 'breit en	lay before s.o., submit to s.o., refer to a higher court
ver breit en	spread; diffuse; propagate, disseminate
ver breit er n	widen, broaden
sich ver breit er n	broaden, widen
Ver breit er ung	widening

brenn bar	combustible, burnable; inflammable
Brenn bar keit	combustibility; inflammability
brenn en	burn; singe; distil, curl, wave
sich brenn en	burn; be ablaze
Brenn er	distiller
Brenn erei	distillery
ab brenn en	burn down, destroy by fire; burn off; refine, temper, spark
an brenn en	catch fire, begin to burn

aus brenn en	burn out; bake bricks; cauterize; cut out, weld
'durch brenn en	burn through, burn a hole in
ein brenn en	burn into; anneal colors; bake lacquer
ent brenn en	be inflamed; blaze up; break out; start
nieder brenn en	burn down, burn to the ground
ver brenn en	burn
Ver brenn ung	burning, combustion; deflagration; cremation
un ver brenn bar	incombustible

bring en	bring, get; yield, produce
Bring er	bringer, conveyor
ab bring en	take off, remove; dissuade
an bring en	attach to, apply to, place, bring; put forward
auf bring en	bring up, produce, get open; raise
aus bring en	bring out, take off; hatch
bei bring en	bring forward, bring by; put across, teach
dar bring en	bring, offer, present; make a sacrifice
'durch bring en	bring through, put through; waste
ein bring en	bring in a bill; invest; gather in; show profit
er bring en	bring forth
fort bring en	move away, carry away; get on
her bring en	bring here, bring up
hin bring en	bring, carry to a place; lead to, accompany; spend
hinter bring en	give notice of s.t.; denounce, bring charges against
mit bring en	bring along with
Mit bring sel nn	present, souvenir
nach bring en	bring after
über 'bring en	bear, deliver; convey, carry
Ueber bring er	bearer
'um bring en	kill, slay, murder; destroy, liquidate
'unter bring en	place; lodge, house, accommodate; invest
Unter bring ung	lodgings, accommodation, housing; placing; investment
ver bring en	spend, pass
voll 'bring en	accomplish, achieve, perform; carry out, fulfill
vor bring en	say, put forward; utter; propose, express; argue
weg bring en	take away, remove, take out
weiter bring en	help on; get on, make progress
'wieder bring en	bring back, restore, return to
zu bring en	bring to, take to; spend the time
Zu bring er	feeder, conveyer
zurück bring en	bring back, return
zusammen bring en	collect, assemble; bring together, reconcile
her an bring en	bring near
her auf bring en	bring up, take up
her aus bring en	bring out, get out, take out; publish, edit; solve
her bei bring en	bring forward, produce
her ein bring en	bring in, harvest, gather in
hin ein bring en	take in, bring in, get in
wieder 'ein bring en	make up for; retrieve
ent gegen bring en	carry towards; offer, confer

hin über	bring	en		bring over, bring across
her um	bring	en	s	get over; talk over
her unter	bring	en		bring down, get down; reduce
hin unter	bring	en		get down
her vor	bring	en		bring forth, produce, generate; cause; utter
Her vor	bring	ung		bringing forth, production, creation
un wieder	bring	lich		irrecoverable, irretrievable
aus ein				
ander	bring	en		part, separate

---

	broch:	siehe brech	
un ge	broch	en	a	unbroken, not refracted
un unter	broch	en	a	uninterrupted, unbroken; continuous, continually

---

	bruch:	siehe brech	
	Bruch	nm		break, breaking; fracture, rupture; breach, violation
	Bruch	nm	i	marsh, bog, swampland
	bruch	ig		marshy, boggy
	brüch	ig		fragile, full of cracks; brittle, friable
	Brüch	ig	keit	fragility, crackedness; flawy, friability
Ab	bruch	nm		breaking off, pulling down; rupture; damage, injury
An	bruch	nm		beginning, opening, break; dawn
Auf	bruch	nm		break-up, start; departure, setting-out
Aus	bruch	nm		outbreak, eruption; escape, flight; explosion, burst
Durch	bruch	nm		breach, rupture, piercing, eruption; breakthrough
Ein	bruch	nm		burglary; invasion, raid; breakthrough, penetration
Um	bruch	nm		revolutionary change, change-over; landslide; page-proof
Zusammen	bruch	nm		breakdown, collapse, failure, ruin; smash
un ver	brüch	lich		inviolable

	Bruder	nm	brother
	Brüder	chen	little brother
	brüder	lich	brotherly, fraternal
	Brüder	lich keit	brotherliness, fraternity
	Brüder	schaft	brotherhood, fellowship
Ge	brüder	np	brothers
Mit	bruder	nm	brother, fellow, comrade, confrere
sich ver	brüder	n	fraternize
Ver	brüder	ung	fraternization
	Buch	nn	book, volume
	buch	en t	enter into the books, make an entry of; post; reserve s.t.
	Büch	erei	library
Gegen	buch	ung	cross-entry
'um	buch	en	transfer to another account
Um	buch	ung	transfer
ver	buch	en	book

---

	bund:	siehe bind

Bund	nn	bond of people; agreement; conspiracy, alliance; band; bundle, bunch
Bünd chen		small band; small bundle; cuff of a sleeve
Bünd el		bundle, bunch; packet, parcel, package
Bünd el ei		conspiracy, plot; bundling together, bunching together
bünd el n		bundle up, make a bundle of s.t., tie into bundles, bunch together
bünd ig		concise, precise, terse, curt; convincing argument
Bünd ig keit		conciseness, precision, succinctness, terseness; conclusiveness
bünd isch		belonging to an association, belonging to a league
Bünd nis	nn	alliance, league, confederacy, pact
bünd weise	av	in bundles
Aus bund	nm	personification, incarnation; paragon, model
aus bünd ig	i	unusual, extraordinary
Ge bund	nn	bundle, bunch
ge bund en	a	bound, fixed; latent, slurred; bonded, maintained, tied; in verse
Ge bund en heit		restraint, constraint, restriction; dependence
Ver bund	nm	compound, combine; interlocking system
sich ver bünd en		ally o.s. with s.o., ally o.s. against s.o.
Ver bund en heit		connection with, ties with; attachment to, affection for
Ver bünd eter	nm	ally, confederate
an ge bund en		short, curt, abrupt, brusque, brief
un ge bund en	a	unbound, in sheets; loose, untied, free, uncombined; unattached
Un ge bund en heit		independence, unrestraint

Burg	nf	castle
Bürg e	nm	bail, bailsman, surety; security, guarantor
bürg en		post bail for, stand surety for
Bürg schaft		security, surety, guarantee

burger:	siehe burg 2	
Bürger	nm	citizen; townsman
Bürger in		townswoman
bürger lich		civil, civic; middle-class
Bürger lich e		commoner
Bürger schaft		citizens
Bürger tum	nn	citizenship
aus bürger n		deprive of citizenship; expatriate
Aus bürger ung		expatriation
ein bürger n		naturalize
Ein bürger ung		naturalization

Bürst e	brush; crew cut
bürst en	brush
ab bürst en	brush clothes; brush off dust
aus bürst en	brush out
Zahn	

bürst e	toothbrush

Buss e	penitence, penance; repentance; satisfaction; penalty, fine
büss en	atone for, make amends
Büss er	penitent
buss fert ig	penitent, repentant; contrite
Buss fert ig keit	repentance; contrition
ab büss en	expiate, atone for, serve a sentence
Ein buss e	loss, damage
ein büss en	forfeit, lose
ver büss en	serve, complete a sentence
Zu buss e	allowance; contribution, additional payment

Christ	nm	Christian
Christ en heit		Christendom, the Christian world
Christ en tum	nn	Christianity
christ lich		Christian
un christ lich		unchristian
vor christ lich		pre-Christian

Dach	nn	roof
dach förm ig		roofshaped, rooflike
ab dach en		slope, slant
ab dach ig		variety, species, modification; variety, version
Ab dach ung		slope, declivity; glacis; ramp
be dach en		roof
Be dach ung		roofing
Ob dach	nn	shelter, lodging
ob dach los		unsheltered, homeless
Ob dach los er		homeless person
Ob dach los ig keit		homelessness
über 'dach en		roof over, shelter

dacht: siehe denk		
Dacht el nf s		slap in the face
An dacht	nf	devotion, prayers
an dächt ig		devout, devotional; absorbed, attentive
Be dacht	nm	consideration, care, deliberation, forethought
be dächt ig		considerate, discreet, slow, deliberate
Be dächt ig keit		circumspection, caution
be dacht sam		considerate, cautious, prudent, circumspect
Be dacht sam keit		considerateness, caution, thoughtfulness
Ge dächt nis		memory, remembrance, recollection, reminiscence
Ver dacht	nm	suspicion, distrust
ver dächt ig		suspected of, suspicious; spurious, phony
un be dacht	a	inconsiderate, thoughtless, rash, indiscreet
Vor be dacht	nf	forethought, premeditation
un ver dächt ig		unsuspected
ver dächt ig en		cast suspicion on s.t.
Ver dächt ig ung		calumny, insinuation

	Dampf nm	steam; vapor; smoke; exhalation, odor
	dampf en	steam, emit steam; give off vapor; smoke, fume
	dämpf en	steam a food
	Dampf er	steamer, steamship
	Dämpf er	damper; mute; baffle, muffler; pressure cooker
	dampf förm ig	vaporous
	dampf ig	steamy, vaporous
	dämpf ig	sultry, sweltering
	Dämpf ung	damping
Ab	dampf nm	exhaust steam
ab	dampf en s	evaporate; steam off, pull out; beat it
ein	dampf en	evaporate
ver	dampf en	evaporate, vaporize
Ver	dampf er	evaporator
Ver	dampf ung	evaporation
Voll	dampf nm	full steam

	Dank nm	thanks, gratitude; reward; acknowledgement
	dank p	owing to, thanks to
	dank bar	thankful; grateful; obliged; worthwhile; profitable; paying
	Dank bar keit	gratitude, gratefulness, thankfulness
	dank en	thank, return thanks, decline with thanks
	dank en s wert	deserving of thanks, commendable, meritorious
ab	dank en	resign, retire from office; abdicate, renounce the throne
Ab	dank ung	discharge, dismissal; resignation, retirement; abdication
sich be	dank en	thank, express one's thanks, thank s.o. for s.t.
Un	dank nm	ingratitude, ungratefulness
un	dank bar	ungrateful, thankless, unthankful; unrewarding
Un	dank bar keit	ingratitude; thanklessness
ver	dank en	owe s.t. to s.o., have s.o. to thank for s.t.

	dank: siehe denk	
Ge	dank e nm	thought; idea; notion; reflection; speculation
ge	dank en los	thoughtless
Ge	dank en los ig keit	thoughtlessness
ge	dank lich	intellectual, mental
Hinter ge	dank e nm	reservation; ulterior motive
Neben ge	dank e nm	secondary thought

	darf: siehe durf	
Be	darf nm	need, want, requirement; needs, demand for
un be	darf t s	inexperienced; naive, gullible

	Dauer nf	duration; continuance; permanence; period, length of time
	dauer haft	durable, lasting
	Dauer haft ig keit	durability, lastingness; solidity; stability
	dauer n	continue, last; take time, require time
	dauer nd av	lasting, permanent; durable, enduring; continuous, constant

an	dauer	n	last, continue, keep on; persist
an	dauer	nd a	lasting, continuous; persistent, incessant
Aus	dauer	nf	perseverance; endurance
aus	dauer	n	hold out, last
aus	dauer	nd	persevering, enduring, patient; plodding; persistent, tenacious
Fort	dauer	nf	continuance
fort	dauer	n	continue, last, persist
über	'dauer	n	outlast, outlive

---

be	dauer lich	regrettable, deplorable, sad
be	dauer n	sympathize; feel sorry for

	Deck	nn	deck
	Deck	e	cover, covering; surface; coverlet; counterpane, quilt
	Deck	el	lid, cover; top, cap; watch-cap
	deck	en	cover; slate a roof, thatch a roof
sich	deck	en	cover
	Deck	ung	covering
ab	deck	en	uncover; untile; unroof; clear the table; mask s.t., cover s.t.
Ab	deck	er	renderer, flayer
Ab	deck	erei	rendering establishment
auf	deck	en	uncover, lay bare, unveil, reveal, expose; detect
be	deck	en	cover, screen; coat; shelter, protect; escort a convoy
Be	deck	ung	cover; protection, safeguard
ein	deck	en	cover; straddle; buy back, cover up roses
ent	deck	en	discover; strike; detect, find out, reveal, disclose
Ent	deck	er	discoverer
Ent	deck	ung	discovery, detection; disclosure, exposure
Ge	deck	nn	cover; menu
Hinter	deck	nn	quarterdeck, poopdeck
Ober	deck	nm	upper deck of ship
über	'deck	en	cover s.t. over; overlap; conceal; veil, shroud
Unter	deck	nn	lower deck of ship
Ver	deck	nn	covering; awning
ver	deck	en	cover up; hide, conceal; mask, screen, veil, cloak
Vorder	deck	nn	fore-part of the deck
zu	deck	en s	cover up; conceal
Zwischen	deck	nn	between decks, steerage
un be	deck	t	uncovered; bare
un ge	deck	t	uncovered; unsheltered, unprotected, exposed

---

	denk bar	thinkable, conceivable, imaginable, possible
	denk en	think; believe, suppose, imagine; remember, recall
	Denk er	thinker, philosopher
	denk er isch	thinking, intellectual
	Denk mal nm	monument, memorial
an	denk en	remembrance, memory, keepsake, souvenir, token
aus	denk en	find out; invent

sich aus denk en	think out; imagine, think up
Be denk en nn	deliberation, reflection; scruple, hesitation
be denk en	consider, deliberate on, reflect on, think over
sich be denk en	deliberate
be denk en los	unscrupulous
be denk lich	dubious, scrupulous; doubtful, risky, serious
Be denk lich keit	doubtfulness, scruple; seriousness, gravity
durch 'denk en	think over
er denk en	imagine, conceive, invent, fabricate, think out
er denk lich	imaginable, possible; conceivable
ge denk en	mention, honor; intend
hin denk en s	what are you thinking of
nach denk en	meditate, think over, reflect on
nach denk lich	reflecting, meditative, thoughtful, pensive
über 'denk en	ponder on, reflect upon, think over; consider, brood
un denk bar	unthinkable, inconceivable
un denk lich	immemorial
ver denk en	find fault with, blame s.o. for
weiter denk en	mindful of; provident, far-sighted
zurück denk en	think back on, recall to memory
un be denk lich	unhesitating, unobjectionable, harmless, without scruples
sich hin ein denk en	put o.s. in s.o.'s place
An ge denk en nn	remembrance, recollection
ein ge denk av	mindful of
un vor denk lich	immemorial
hin zu denk en	add in thought

Deut elei	sophistry, quibble, hair-splitting
deut el n	quibble
deut en	point at; interpret, construe
deut lich	clear, distinct, plain; articulate; legible; obvious; outspoken
Deut lich keit	clearness, distinctness, plainness; bluntness, plain speaking
Deut ung	interpretation, explanation, construction
an deut en	indicate; hint, intimate, imply; suggest; foreshadow
An deut ung	indication; hint
aus deut en	interpret, explain
be deut en	signify, mean; imply; represent; be important, matter; portend
be deut end	important, major; considerable; distinguished, eminent, great
be deut sam	significant, suggestive
Be deut ung	meaning, significance
be deut ung s los	insignificant, of no account; meaningless
Be deut ung s los ig keit	insignificance; harmlessness
be deut ung s voll	significant; weighty, of great consequence, momentous
hin deut en	point to s.t., indicate s.t., suggest s.t.

miss deut en		misinterpret, misconstrue
Miss deut ung		misinterpretation, false construction
'um deut en		give a new interpretation to
un deut lich		indistinct; vague; blurred; illegible
Un deut lich keit		indistinctness, vagueness; obscurity
Neben be deut ung		secondary meaning, connotation
un be deut end		insignificant; slight, negligible, trifling; minor
Ur be deut ung		original meaning
Vor be deut ung		foreboding, omen, portent
ver deut lich en		make clear, elucidate; illustrate

deutsch	a		German
Deutsch	nn		German, the German language
Deutsch e	nm		German
Deutsch e	nn		German, the German language
Deutsch tum	nn		German character, Germanity
ein deutsch en			Germanize
nieder deutsch	a		low German
un deutsch	a		un-German
ur deutsch	a		thoroughly German, German to the core
Ver deutsch ung			Germanization

dicht en		compose, write
Dicht er		poet; author, writer
Dicht erin		poetess; authoress, writer
dicht er isch		poetic
Dicht er ling		would-be poet, poetaster
Dicht ung		poetry; fiction; poem, poetical work; work of fiction
an dicht en		ascribe s.t. to s.o.; address verses to s.o.
er dicht en		invent, fabricate, trump up
Er dicht ung		fiction; figment, invention, fabrication
Ge dicht nn		poem, piece of poetry
Nach dicht ung		adaptation, free version

dicht a		tight, impervious; leakproof; compact, closely packed
Dicht e		density
dicht en		make tight
un dicht a		not tight; leaky, not waterproof, porous
ver dicht en		condense; solidify; compress, concentrate
Ver dicht er		steam condenser
Ver dicht ung		condensation; compression; concentration

dien en		serve
Dien er		manservant; footman, valet
Dien erin		maidservant, maid
dien er n		bow and scrape
Dien er schaft		servants, domestics
dien lich		useful, serviceable; expedient, suitable, handy; wholesome
Dien st nm		service; duty, function; situation, post, employment

dien st bar	subservient
Dien st bar keit	subjection, servitude, bondage
dien st be reit	ready for service; obliging
dien st fäh ig	fit for active service, able-bodied
dien st fert ig	zealous, assiduous; obliging; officious
dien st frei	be off duty
dien st lich	official
dien st un fäh ig	unfit for service; disabled
dien st will ig	ready for service; obliging
ab dien en	serve one's time, do one's military service
An dien ung b	tender, offer; delivery
aus dien en	serve one's time
be dien en	serve, wait on; attend upon; work, operate, control, manipulate
sich be dien en	help o.s.
Be dien te	servant, valet; lackey, footman
Be dien ung	service
ver dien en	deserve; earn, gain, make money
ab ver dien en	work off debt

---

dienst: siehe dien	
Aussen dienst nm	field work; outside work, outside duty
ausser dienst lich	unofficial, private, extraofficial; off-duty; unofficially
be dienst et	be employed by s.o., be in one's service
Be dienst ete	employee, civil servant
Gegen dienst nm	reciprocal service, service in return
Innen dienst nm	indoor work, office work
inner dienst lich	internal
Ver dienst nn	merit, service; worth, worthiness; credit, honor
Ver dienst nm	earnings, wages; salary; income; gain, profit
ver dienst lich	creditable, meritorious, deserving
ver dienst los	meritless
ver dienst voll	creditable, meritorious, deserving
Neben ver dienst nm	secondary income, additional income, extra earnings, extra profit

---

Ding nn	thing; object; matter, affair
ding fest	arrest, take s.o. into custody
ding lich	real
Ding s nn	thing, what's-its-name; gadget
be ding en	condition, stipulate, require, necessitate, presuppose, cause
be ding t	conditional; dependent upon, contingent on; limited; qualified
Be ding t heit	limitation; relativity
Be ding ung	condition; provision, clause, stipulation
be ding ung s los	unconditional
Ge ding e nn t	bargain; agreement; piecework, contract work
Neben ding e np	secondary matters
Un ding nn	absurdity; impossibility; monstrosity
ver ding en	rent o.s. out; put s.o. to service with s.o., apprentice s.o.

sich ver ding en		go into service, hire o.s. out, apprentice o.s.
Zwischen ding	nn	intermediate, cross, halfway object
un ab ding bar		unalterable; inalienable
Un ab ding bar keit		inalienability
aus be ding en		stipulate
Gegen be ding ung		counterstipulation
un be ding t		unconditional; absolute; positive
Vor be ding ung	s	precondition, prerequisite, basic requirement
aller ding s	av	to be sure

Donner	nm	thunder
donner n		thunder
nieder donner n		come down with a crash
ver donner n	s	sentence s.o. to prison, condemn s.o., force s.o. to do s.t.
ver donner t	s	bewildered, thunderstruck
auf ge donner t	s	dressed up to the nines, in full feathers, dolled up

drang:	siehe dring	
Drang	nm	pressure, stress, hurry; urge; eagerness; impulse; oppression
Dräng elei	s	pushing, shoving, jostling
dräng el n	s	push, shove, jostle s.o.
sich dräng el n	s	push one's way to the front, squeeze one's way to the front
dräng en		push, shove, force; be urgent; aspire to s.t.
Dräng er		pusher, slave driver
Dräng erei		pushing, shoving
Dräng sal	nf	affliction, distress; anguish, agony; tribulation, hardship
drang voll		crowded, thronged, oppressive
ab dräng en		push s.o. aside, shove s.o. away, force s.t. aside; deflect s.t.
An drang	nm	crush, press, rush; run on s.t.; congestion of the blood
an dräng en		crowd, press, push
auf dräng en		thrust s.t. upon s.o.; intrude into one's mind
sich auf dräng en		force o.s. upon s.o., thrust o.s. on s.o.; intrude upon s.o.
be dräng en		press s.o. hard, oppress; harry, pester, plague
Be dräng er		oppressor
Be dräng nis		distress, need, anguish, affliction, tribulation
Be dräng te		oppressed person, harassed person
Be dräng ung		oppression, harassment; distress, need, anguish
sich 'durch dräng en		push one's way through, elbow one's way through
ein dräng en		crowd in upon s.o.
fort dräng en		push away, push s.t. aside; desire to go away
Ge dräng e	nn	thronging, crowding, pushing, shoving; crowd; difficulties, dilemma
Ge dräng t heit		shortness, brevity, conciseness, compactness, succinctness
hin dräng en		thrust o.s. there, push o.s. there

nach dräng en	press after, crowd after; push from behind; pursue closely
um 'dräng en	throng around, crowd around
ver dräng en	displace; oust s.o., drive s.o. out; replace; repress, suppress
Ver dräng ung	displacement; replacement; repression, suppression, ejection
vor dräng en	press forward, push forward
zurück dräng en	push s.o. back, press s.o. back; repress, repel, restrain
zusammen dräng en	crowd together, crush together; condense
her an dräng en	press forward
hin aus dräng en	push s.o. out, shove s.o. out, force s.o. out
sich her bei dräng en	crowd around; press near, press forward
her ein dräng en	push one's way in
hin ein dräng en	force s.o. into s.t., push s.o. into s.t.; push one's way in

---

drau:	siehe droh	
be dräu en	p	threaten, menace

Dreh nm	twist
dreh bar	revolving, rotating, rotary; swivelling
dreh en	turn
sich dreh en	revolve around; be centered around
Dreh er	turner, lathe-handle
Dreh ung	turn
ab dreh en	twist off; turn off; switch off; strip; turn down
an dreh en	turn on; switch on; start up, start; screw on
auf dreh en	untwist, unravel; turn on; loosen a screw, unscrew
aus dreh en	turn off; switch off; hollow
'durch dreh en	crank the engine through, swing; mince meat
ein dreh en	turn in
los dreh en	twist off
über 'dreh en	overwind a watch; overspeed an engine; strip a thread
'um dreh en	turn around, whirl around, spin around
Um dreh ung	turning around; turn
ver dreh en	distort, wrench, twist; sprain; roll one's eyes
Ver dreh t heit	craziness
Ver dreh ung	twisting, distortion
zu dreh en	turn off
zurück dreh en	turn back, put back
her um dreh en	turn around

---

dring en	force one's way through, break through; penetrate, pierce
dring end	urgent, pressing; imminent
dring lich	pressing, urgent
Dring lich keit	urgency; priority
an dring en	push forward, press on; draw near, advance
auf dring lich	obtrusive, importune, pushing; gaudy, showy

Auf dring lich keit	obtrusiveness, importunity
durch 'dring en	penetrate, pierce; pass through; fill; inspire
'durch dring en	get through, penetrate; leak out; succeed, prevail
Durch dring ung	penetration, pervasion
ein dring en	enter forcibly, break in, burst in; intrude, penetrate
ein dring lich	insistent, urgent, emphatic; striking, impressive, forcible
Ein dring lich keit	insistence, urgency; force
Ein dring ling	intruder, invader
vor dring en	advance, press forward, make headway, forge ahead
vor dring lich	urgent, most important, claiming priority
Vor dring lich keit	urgent nature, priority
zu dring lich	importunate, obtrusive; intruding, forward
Zu dring lich keit	importunity, obtrusiveness, forwardness; improper advance
her auf dring en	arise from below, float up
un durch dring lich	impenetrable; impervious; inscrutable
her ein dring en	enter forcibly
her vor dring en	proceed, come from, issue from

droh en	threaten, menace
Droh ung	threat, menace; intimidation
an droh en	threaten s.o., menace s.o. with s.t.
An droh ung	threat, menace; warning
be droh en	threaten, menace
be droh lich	threatening, ominous
Be droh ung	threat, menace

Druck nm	pressure, squeeze; stress; print, printing; issue
druck en	print
Druck er	printer, printing device
Drück er	latch, latchkey; trigger; thumb release; press button
Druck erei	printing office, printery, printing shop
druck s en s	hesitate, beat around the bush
Ab druck nm	copy, print, proof; mark, impression
ab druck en	print off, strike off; publish; imprint, impress
ab drück en	squeeze off, pull the trigger, shoot
an drück en	press, squeeze close to; put on speed
Auf druck nm	print, imprint, impress, stamp; printing
auf druck en	stamp on, print on, imprint
auf drück en	impress; press open, break open
Aus druck nm	expression, phrase, term, word
aus druck en	work off; print at full length, finish printing
aus drück en	squeeze out, wring clothes; express, utter
sich aus drück en	express o.s.
aus drück lich	express, explicit, formal, strict; expressly, intentionally
aus druck s los	expressionless, blank, vacant
aus druck s voll	expressive, significant, suggestive

be druck en	print on
be drück en	oppress, harass, wrong, persecute, torment
be drück end	oppressive; depressing
Be drück er	oppressor
Be drück ung	oppression; pressure
'durch drück en	press through; enforce
Ein druck nm	impression, sensation; effect
ein druck en	imprint, impress
ein drück en	press in; crush, squash, flatten
ein druck s los	unimpressive
ein druck s voll	impressive
er drück en	squeeze to death, oppress; crush, stifle
Fern druck er	teleprinter, teletype apparatus, ticker
ge drück t	depressed, low; difficult
Ge drück t heit	depression
Gegen druck nm	reaction, resistance; back pressure, counterpressure
los drück en	fire, fire off
Nach druck nm	energy, vigor, stress; weight; reprint, reproduction
nach druck en	reprint
nach drück lich	energetic, strong, emphatic, forcible
Nieder druck nm t	low pressure
nieder drück en	weigh down; depress, oppress
Ueber druck nm	overprint; excess pressure; surcharge
über 'druck en	overprint
Um druck nm	transfer, reprint
Unter druck nm	underpressure, reduced pressure
unter 'drück en	suppress, oppress, crush, repress
Unter drück er	oppressor, suppressor
Unter drück ung	oppression, suppression, repression
ver drück en	eat up
sich ver drück en s	slink away
Vor druck nm	first impression; form, blank, schedule
Wider druck nm	reaction, counterpressure; backing up
zer drück en	crush, mash, grind; wrinkle, crease
zu drück en	close, shut
zusammen drück en	compress
Zusammen drück ung	compression
Wieder ab druck nm	reprint
wieder 'ab druck en	reprint
her aus drück en	press out, squeeze out
be ein druck en	impress
sich her um drück en s	hang around, shirk one's work

---

drucks: siehe druck	
her um drucks en s	hem and haw

---

drung: siehe dring	
ge drung en a	stocky, thickset, squat, stumpy, compact
Ge drung en heit	stockiness, squatness, stumpiness, compactness

---

duld en	bear patiently, endure, suffer, tolerate, permit, put up with

	Duld er	sufferer
	duld sam	tolerant, indulgent, patient, forebearing
	Duld sam keit	tolerance, forbearance
	Duld ung	toleration, sufferance
	er duld en	endure; suffer
	Er duld ung	endurance; submission, toleration
	Ge duld nf	patience, indulgence, forbearance; perseverance
sich ge duld en	have patience; wait patiently
	ge duld ig	patient; indulgent, forbearing
	un duld sam	intolerant
	Un duld sam keit	intolerance
Un ge duld nf	impatience

	durch av	through; by, by means of; throughout, during
da durch av	through there, that way
hin durch av	through; throughout; across
zwischen durch av	at intervals, occasionally; through

	dürf en	be permitted, be allowed, have the right
	dürf tig	needy, indigent
	Dürf tig keit	neediness, indigence; poverty
be dürf en	need, want, require; be in need of
Be dürf nis	need, want; necessity, requirement
be dürf nis los	having few wants; frugal
Be dürf nis los ig keit	absence of wants; frugality
be dürf t ig	needy, poor, indigent; in need of, requiring
Be dürf t ig keit	neediness, indigence, destitution
hin dürf en s	be allowed to go there
zurück dürf en s	be allowed to go back, be allowed to return

	eben a	even; level, flat, plane
	eben av	evenly; exactly, precisely
	Eben e	plain; flat land, level ground
	eben fall s av	likewise, also; too, as well
	Eben heit nf	evenness; smoothness
	eben mäss ig	symmetrical, well proportioned; harmonious; shapely, beautiful
un eben a	uneven; rough, rugged, bumpy
ein eb n en	level, plane, grade

	edel a	noble, aristocratic
un edel a	ignoble, base
ver edel n	ennoble, refine, purify; process; finish; improve; enrich s.t.
Ver edel ung	refinement; improvement; processing, finishing

	Ehe nf	marriage
	ehe lich	conjugal, matrimonial; wedded, married life; born in wedlock
	ehe lich en	marry
	Ehe lich keit	legitimacy of a child
	Ehe los ig keit	single life, celibacy

ausser ehe lich	illegitimate, born out of wedlock; extramarital
un ehe lich	illegitimate, born out of wedlock
Un ehe lich keit	illegitimacy
vor ehe lich	prenuptial, premarital
sich ver ehe lich en	marry

ehr bar	honorable, upright, respectable; honest
Ehr bar keit	honesty, respectability, integrity
Ehr e nf	honor; distinction; dignity, pride; reputation
ehr en	honor; pay tribute to; respect, esteem; revere
ehr en haft	honorable, high-principled, honest
Ehr en haft ig keit	honesty, uprightness, integrity
ehr en halb er av	for honor's sake
Ehr en mal nn	monument; war memorial; cenotaph
ehr en voll	honorable; glorious, creditable
ehr en wert	honorable, respectable
ehr lich	honest
ehr lich	frankly, to tell the truth
Ehr lich keit	honesty; uprightness; reliability, loyalty; fairness
ehr los	dishonorable, infamous
Ehr los ig keit	dishonorableness, infamy; perfidy
ehr sam	honorable, upright, respectable; honest
Ehr ung	honor, tribute
ehr würd ig	venerable, reverend; patriarchal
Ehr würd ig keit	venerableness
be ehr en	honor; favor
ent ehr en	dishonor a woman, disgrace, degrade
Ent ehr ung	dishonoring, disgrace; degradation
Un ehr e	dishonor
un ehr en haft	dishonorable
un ehr lich	dishonest, insincere
Un ehr lich keit	dishonest; insincerity; duplicity
ver ehr en	revere, venerate, look up to; worship, admire, adore
Ver ehr er	worshipper; admirer
Ver ehr ung	reverence; veneration, worship

Eifer nm	eagerness
Eifer er	zealot, fanatic
eifer n	be zealous, be eager, strive, strain for; declaim, inveigh
eif r ig	eager, zealous, passionate, ardent; enthusiastic; officious
an eifer n	stimulate, incite
sich er eifer n	get excited, fly into a rage
Er eifer ung	excitement; passion, exasperation, vehemence
nach eifer n	emulate; compete with
Nach eifer ung	emulation
Ueber eifer nm	over-zeal
über eif r ig	over-zealous

eigen a	particular, special; proper, inherent; one's own; odd

eigen art ig	peculiar; odd, characteristic; individual, special, original
eigen s av	expressly, on purpose; particularly
Eigen schaft	quality; attribute, distinctive feature, characteristic
eigen t lich	real, true, actual; essential; precise, proper; intrinsic
Eigen tum nn	property
Eigen tüm er	owner, proprietor
eigen tüm lich	peculiar, special; characteristic, inherent; odd, strange
Eigen tüm lich keit	peculiarity; oddity; characteristic, peculiar feature
eig n en	suit s.o., fit s.o.
sich eig n en	be peculiar in s.o., be inherent in s.o.
Eig n ung	qualification, fitness, aptitude
un eigen t lich	not proper, not real
ur eigen a	one's very own; innate, inherent
sich an eig n en	appropriate to o.s., make one's own; master; annex; usurp
An eig n ung	appropriation, acquisition; adoption; conversation; annexation
ent eig n en	expropriate, dispossess
Ent eig n ung	expropriation
sich er eig n en	happen, come to pass, occur, take place
Er eig n is nn	event; occurrence, incident, affair; phenomenon
ge eig n et	fit; qualified for; suited, proper, appropriate to
über 'eig n en	make s.t. over, assign, transfer; convey real estate to
Ueber eig n ung	assignment, transfer, conveyance
zu eig n en	dedicate a book
Zu eig n ung	dedication; appropriation
un ge eig n et	unfit; unqualified; inopportune

Eil e nf	haste
eil en	make haste, hasten, hurry; hustle, rush
eil end s av	in a hurry, hastily; in haste, posthaste
eil fert ig	hasty; rash
Eil fert ig keit	hastiness; rashness
eil ig	hasty, speedy, hurried; urgent, pressing; prompt
eil ig st av	utmost dispatch, in great haste, posthaste
sich be eil en	hasten, hurry, make haste, hustle
'durch eil en	hasten through, pass through in haste; cover
durch 'eil en	hasten through, hurry through, cover a distance
ent eil en	hasten away, be gone; escape; slip away
er eil en	overtake, catch up with
fort eil en	hurry away, run off
hin eil en	hurry there, hasten there, rush to the spot
nach eil en	hasten after, run after; lag
über 'eil en	precipitate, rush
Ueber eil ung	precipitance, rashness, overhaste
vor eil ig	hasty, rash, precipitate
Vor eil ig keit	rashness, overhaste, precipitancy
zurück eil en	hasten back

vor aus	eil en		hurry on ahead, hurry in advance
her bei	eil en		approach in haste, rush to the scene, come running
ent gegen	eil en		hasten to meet; rush into one's ruin
da hin	eil en		hurry along; pass swiftly, fly
da von	eil en		hurry away, hasten off

dar	ein	av	into it, into that; therein
her	ein	av	in, in here, into
hin	ein	av	into, inside
da hin	ein	av	in there

	ein	a		one
	ein ander	pn		each other; one another; mutually
	Ein heit			unit; unity; oneness; standard; unit point; time
	ein heit lich			homogeneous, integrated, uniform, coherent, consistent
	Ein heit lich keit			homogeneity, integrity; uniformity; coherence
	ein ig			united
	ein ig e	a		several, some, a few
	ein ig er mass en			to some extent; somewhat; rather, fairly
	ein s	pn		one, one thing
	ein sam			lonely, lonesome, solitary
	ein sam keit			loneliness, solitude; seclusion; lonely place
	ein st	av		once, at one time, erstwhile; in the days of old
	ein zel n	a		single, solitary; particular, special; individual; isolated; odd
	ein zig	a		only; single, sole; unique, peerless
un	ein ig			disagreeing, disunited, discordant, divided
Un	ein ig keit			disagreement; dissension, discord, disharmony
Ver	ein	nm		union
ver	ein bar			compatible, consistent
un ver	ein bar			incompatible
Un ver	ein bar keit			incompatibility
an	ein ander	av		together
auf	ein ander	av		one on top of the other, one against the other
aus	ein ander	av		asunder, apart; separate
bei	ein ander	av		together
durch	ein ander	av		confusion
Durch	ein ander	nn		disorder, disarray, confusion, mess, muddel
für	ein ander	av		for each other, for one another
gegen	ein ander	av		against one another; reciprocally, mutually
hinter	ein ander	av		one after the other, one by one; in succession
in	ein ander	av		into one another, into each other
mit	ein ander	av		with each other; together, jointly, at the same time
nach	ein ander	av		one after another, successively; by turns
Neben	ein ander	nn		coexistence, simultaneousness
neben	ein ander	av		side by side, abreast; together, simultaneously
über	ein ander	av		one upon the other
um	ein ander	av		around each other
unter	ein ander	av		one beneath the other

von ein ander	av	of each other
vor ein ander	av	one in front of the other, one behind the other, face to face
zu ein ander	av	to each other, to one another
ver ein bar en		agree upon, arrange
Ver ein bar keit		compatability, reconcilability
Ver ein bar ung		agreement, understanding; arrangement, appointment, convention
ver ein heit lich en		unify, standardize
Ver ein heit lich ung		unification, standardization
ver ein ig en		unite, join; combine
Ver ein ig ung		union, consolidation; combination, assembly; confluence
ver un ein ig en		disunite, set at variance
‿sich ver un ein ig en		fall out, break, split up
ʻwieder ver ein ig en		reunite
Wieder ver ein ig ung		reunion
ver ein sam en		become isolated, grow lonely
Ver ein sam ung		isolation
irgend ein		any, anyone, some, someone

einzel:	siehe ein 2	
ver einzel t		single, singular; in isolated cases, sporadically

Eis	nn	ice; ice cream
eis frei		free from ice, ice-free
eis ig		icy, glacial
ent eis en		free from ice; defrost, de-ice
Ent eis ung		defrosting; de-icing, ice elimination
los eis en	s	wangle
ver eis en		freeze; be covered with ice, ice up
Ver eis ung		freezing; icing, glaciation

elter lich		parental
Elter n	np	parents
elter n los		parentless, orphaned
Elter n schaft		parentage
Ur elter n	np	ancestors
Vor elter n	np	forefathers, ancestors, progenitors

End e	nn	end
end en		come to an end, close, terminate; cease, finish, stop
end ig en		come to an end, close, terminate; stop, finish
end lich		final, ultimate; limited
End lich keit		finiteness
end los		endless, interminable; boundless; infinite
End ung		ending, termination
be end en		finish, complete, terminate; bring to an end; close, conclude
Be end ung		ending, termination, conclusion, close; completion
un end lich	a	endless; infinite; boundless

un end lich	av	infinitely
ver end en		perish, die
voll 'end en		finish; terminate, complete; round off; perfect
voll end s	av	entirely, wholly, quite; altogether
Voll end ung		finishing, completion; perfection
un voll end et		unfinished
Be end ig ung		ending, termination, conclusion, close; completion
Woche n end e	nn	weekend

eng	a	narrow; tight; clinging; crowded, closely packed; close
Eng e		narrowness; closeness; tightness; narrow passage
be eng en		cramp, narrow; choke; confine, restrain, hamper
ein eng en		constrict; confine, narrow down, hem in, limit; cramp
ver eng en		narrow; contract
sich ver eng en		narrow; contract
ver eng er n		narrow; contract
Ver eng er ung		narrowing; contraction

Erb e	nm	heir, successor; beneficiary under a will; legatee; devisee
erb en		inherent, fall heir to, succeed to one's property
Erb in		heiress
erb lich		hereditary, inheritable
Erb schaft		inheritance; estate; legacy
An erbre	nm	next heir, heir to entailed property
An erb e nm r		be one's heir, succeed to one's property, inherit s.t. from s.o.
ent erb en		disinherit, cut s.o. out of a will
Ent erb ung		disinheriting
er erb en		inherit
Mit erb e		coheiress
Nach erb e		reversionary heir
ver erb en		leave, bequeath, will to; transmit; hand down
sich ver erb en		be hereditary
Ver erb ung		leaving, bequeathing
Vor erb e	nn	heir in tail, estate in fee tail
Vor erb schaft		estate in fee tail

Ernt e		harvest; crop, produce
ernt en		harvest, gather in, reap
ein ernt en		gather in, harvest; gain, win
Miss ernt e		bad harvest, crop failure
Nach ernt e		aftercrop; aftermath

erst	av	first; at first, originally; previously; only, just
erst e	a	first
erst en s	av	first, in the first place; to begin with, for one thing
Erst er e	nm	the former
Erst ling		first-born child

erst mal ig	a	first
erst mal s	av	for the first time
vor erst	av	first of all; for the present, for the time being
zu erst	av	first of all, in the first place, above all; in the beginning

ess bar		eatable, edible
ess en		eat
Ess en	nn	eating; food; meal, repast; lunch, dinner; supper
Ess er		eater
auf ess en		eat; consume
aus ess en		eat up; clear, empty dish; pay for
mit ess en		dine with s.o.; partake of one's meal
Mit ess er		blockhead, comedo
'über ess en		overeat
sich über 'ess en		overeat
weg ess en		eat up
Abend ess en	nn	supper, dinner
Mit tag ess en	nn	lunch, dinner, noon meal

ew ig		eternal; everlasting, perpetual; endless, unending; external
Ew ig keit		eternity; everlastingness, perpetuity
ew ig lich	p	externally; forever
ver ew ig en		perpetuate; immortalize

Fach	nn	compartment, partition, division; partition
fäch el n		fan, blow gently, waft
Fäch er		fan
fach ge mäss		workmanlike, competent, skillful
fach lich		professional, special, technical
Fach schaft		all the students of a university department
an fach en		blow into a flame, fan, kindle
ent fach en		kindle, set ablaze; arouse, provoke
Neben fach	nn	subsidiary subject; minor field of specialization
zu fäch el n		fan s.o.
viel fach	av	repeatedly, frequently; many times
zwei fach	a	double, twice, twofold

fäh ig	capable, qualified, liable to; competent, efficient, clever
Fäh ig keit	capability; qualification, competence, efficiency; talent
un fäh ig	incapable, unable; unfit, incompetent; inefficient
Un fäh ig keit	incapacity, inability, incompetence; inefficiency
be fäh ig en	enable to do; qualify
be fäh ig t	fit, capable of; talented, gifted
Be fäh ig ung	qualification, fitness; aptitude, talent; skill, competence

fahr bar	movable, mobile, travelling; navigable
Fähr e	ferry, ferryboat

fahr en	go, drive, ride, travel; run
Fahr er	driver, motorist; rider
Fahr erei	tedious travelling, journeying
fahr ig	fidgety, jumpy; fickle, erratic; careless; nervous, hurried
Fahr ig keit	nervousness, jitteriness, jumpiness; fickleness, carelessness
Fahr nis nf	movable goods, chattels, movables
Fahr t nf	journey, trip; drive, ride; voyage; excursion; speed, motion
Fähr te nf	track, trace; trail, spoor, scent
ab fahr en	start, leave, depart for, sail for
Ab fahr t nf	departure, setting out; putting to sea; descent
an fahr en	begin to move; drive up to, arrive
An fahr t nf	driving up, arrival; descent
auf fahr en	rise, ascend; drive up, jump up; collide
Auf fahr t nf	ascension, driving up; driveway
aus fahr en	drive out, take a drive, ascend; wear out
Aus fahr t	drive, ride, excursion; doorway, gateway, exit; departure
be fahr bar	passable; practicable; navigable
be fahr en a	much frequented road, much travelled
be fahr en	pass over; navigate
Bei fahr er	passenger, assistant driver, auxiliary rider
durch 'fahr en	pass through, drive through, sail through, go through
Durch fahr t nf	passing, passage, gateway, channel
ein fahr en	carry in, break in; arrive, drive in
Ein fahr t nf	entrance, gateway
ent fahr en	escape, slip out of
er fahr en a	expert, experienced, seasoned, skilled, conversant with
er fahr en	hear, learn from, experience; find out; suffer
Er fahr ung	experience, practice, skill, knowledge
Fern fahr t nf	long-distance trip
fort fahr en	drive away, remove, start, depart; keep on
Ge fahr nf	danger, peril, menace, risk, hazard
ge fähr lich	dangerous, perilous, risky, hazardous, critical
Ge fähr lich keit	dangerousness
ge fahr los	safe, without danger
Ge fahr los ig keit	safety, security
Ge fähr t nn	vehicle
Ge fähr te	companion, fellow, comrade, associate
ge fahr voll	dangerous, perilous
her fahr en	bring here; move along, come along in a car
Her fahr t nf	journey back, return journey, return trip
hin fahr en	drive there, drive, convey to a place, go to a place
Hin fahr t nf	voyage out, journey there
los fahr en	depart; fly out at; fall upon s.o.
mit fahr en	ride with
Nach fahr nm	descendant
nach fahr en	drive after, go after, follow

nieder fahr en		come down, descend
Rück fahr t	nf	return journey, return trip
über 'fahr en		run over s.o.
'über fahr en		drive over; cross; run past; ferry over
Ueber fahr t		passage, crossing, ferrying over
'um fahr en		run down, take the round-about way
um 'fahr en		drive around, sail around; double; circumnavigate
Ver fahr en	nn	method, manner, dealing
ver fahr en		proceed, act, work; manage, deal
sich ver fahr en		take the wrong road, lose one's way
Vor fahr	nm	forefather, ancestor
vor fahr en		drive up to, stop at
Vor fahr t	nf	right of way, priority in traffic
weg fahr en		carry away, remove, leave; drive away
wider 'fahr en		happen, befall, meet with
zer fahr en	a	rutted; absent-minded, thoughtless, giddy
Zer fahr en heit		giddiness, thoughtlessness, absent-mindedness, carelessness
zu fähr en		drive on, go on, drive towards
Zu fahr t	nf	drive in
zurück fahr en		drive back, go back, start back; recoil; convey back
zusammen fahr en		bring together; shrink; start at, collide
her ab fahr en		come down, descend
her an fahr en		pull in
her auf fahr en		go up, drive up
hin auf fahr en		drive up, ride up
her aus fahr en		drive out, slip out, rush out; slip from one's tongue
un be fahr bar		impracticable, impassable
vor bei fahr en		drive past
un er fahr en	a	inexperienced, inexpert, untrained, unskilled
Un er fahr en heit		inexperience
un ge fähr	av	about, around, roughly, approximately, probable
un ge fähr lich		not dangerous, harmless, inoffensive
her über fahr en		carry over, transport, cross, pass
her um fahr en	s	take a drive, drive around
hin unter fahr en		go down
vor ver fahr en		preliminary procedure
aus ein ander fahr en		separate suddenly, go asunder, go apart

---

fahrd:	siehe fahr	
ge fährd en		endanger, imperil
un ge fährd et		safe, out of danger

Fall	nm	fall, tumble, plunge; downfall, decline, recession
Fall	nm	case, instance, example; matter, situation
Fall e		trap, pitfall; latch of a lock
fall en		fall, fall down, drop; recede, descend
fäll en		fell, cut down a tree; pass judgement, reach a decision
fäll ig		due, payable, collectible, mature

	Fäll ig keit		maturity, expiration
	fall s		in case, if, in the event of, supposing, provided that
	Fäll ung	t	precipitation
Ab	fall	nm	fall; slope; desertion; decrease; waste, garbage
ab	fall en		fall down; slope; go to waste
ab	fäll ig		sloping; disapproving, derogatory
An	fall	nm	attack; shock, fit; reversion
an	fall en		attack, assault, assail
an	fäll ig		susceptible
auf	fall en		fall upon; astonish, surprise, strike
auf	fall end	a	striking, conspicuous, outstanding, remarkable
auf	fäll ig		striking, conspicuous, outstanding, remarkable
Aus	fall	nm	ally; falling-out; deficit, loss, shortage; stoppage
aus	fall en		fall out, come out, sally forth; be omitted
aus	fäll ig		aggressive; insulting
be	fall en		befall; fall on, fall upon; strike, attack
Bei	fall	nm	approbation, applause, cheers, approval, assent
bei	fäll ig		favorable, assenting, approving
Durch	fall	nm t	falling through; failure; diarrhea
'durch	fall en		fall through; fail; be unsuccessful
Ein	fall	nm	downfall, collapse; invasion; flash of inspiration
ein	fall en		fall in, fall down; join in; invade
ent	fall en		fall from, escape; fall to
Fort	fall	nm	cessation, discontinuing
fort	fall en		cease; fall away; be abolished
Ge	fäll e	nn	slope, incline; fall; expenses, rents, income
ge	fall en		please, like, suit; put up with s.t.
Ge	fall en	nn	pleasure, kindness, favor
Ge	fall ener		fallen person; the dead, the killed
ge	fäll ig		complaisant to, pleasing; courteous
Ge	fäll ig keit		complaisance, courteousness; kindness, favor
ge	fäll ig st	av	please
her	fall en		fall upon, come upon; attack
hin	fall en		fall down
hin	fäll ig		weak, decaying, shaky, obsolete, perishable
Hin	fäll ig keit		weakness, infirmity, debility, decrepitude, shakiness
miss	fall en		displease
Miss	fall en	nn	displeasure, dislike
miss	fäll ig		displeasing, unfavorable, disparaging, disagreeable
nieder	fall en		fall down
Rück	fall	nm	recidivism, relapse, reversion
rück	fäll ig		recidivous, relapsing, revertible
Ueber	fall	nm	sudden attack, hold-up, raid
über	'fall en		attack suddenly, holdup, surprise, seize
über	fäll ig		overdue
Um	fall s	nm	fall, tumble; sudden change of opinion
'um	fall en		fall down, fall over, tumble, drop; give in
Un	fall	nm	accident, disaster, misfortune
Ver	fall	nm	decay, ruin, decline; failure; maturity, expiration
ver	fall en		go to ruin, decline; grow weaker; mature, expire

Vor	fall	nm	occurrence, incident, event
vor	fall	en	occur, happen, take place
Weg	fall	nm	omission
weg	fall	en	fall away, cease, be omitted, be abolished
Zer	fall	nm	ruin, decay, decadence, dissociation, decomposition
zer	fall	en	fall to pieces, fall into ruin, decay
Zu	fall	nm	chance, accident, occurrence, event, coincidence
zu	fall	en	close, fall to, fall on
zu	fäll	ig	accidental, incidental, casual; by chance, at random
Zu	fäll	ig keit	chance, casualness, casualty, contingency
zurück	fall	en	fall back, relapse; be reflected
zusammen	fall	en	fall down, collapse; coincide with
Zwischen	fall	nm	incident, episode
her ab	fall	en	fall down
un auf	fäll	ig	inconspicuous, conservative, modest, unassuming
Her ein	falls	nm	bad business, failure; swindle
her ein	fall en	s	be taken in, fall for, be cheated
hin ein	fall en		fall in
aus ge	fall en	a	unusual, odd, strange
un ge	fäll ig		disobliging, unkind
Un ge	fäll ig keit		disobligingness, discourtesy
her unter	fall en		fall down
hin unter	fall en		fall down
aus ein ander	fall en		fall in pieces

---

	falsch	a	false; wrong, incorrect; erroneous
	Falsch	nn	falseness
	fälsch en		falsify; forge, fake; counterfeit
	Fälsch er		falsifier; forger, counterfeiter; faker; adulterator
	Falsch heit		falseness, falsity
	fälsch lich		false; fraudulent; incorrect, wrong; erroneous, by mistake
	Fälsch ung		falsification; faking; forgery; counterfeiting; adulteration
ab	fälsch en	o	divert the ball
ver	fälsch en		falsify, alter fraudulently; adulterate
Ver	fälsch ung		falsification; adulteration
un ver	fälsch t		unadulterated, pure; genuine
Un ver	fälsch t heit		genuineness

---

	falt bar		foldable
	Falt e		fold; wrinkle
	fält el n		gather, pleat, plait, frill
	falt en		fold; pleat, plait; crease; shirr cloth
	falt en los		without folds; unwrinkled, smooth
	Falt er		butterfly, moth
	falt ig		folded; plaited, pleated; wrinkled, puckered
Ein	falt	nf	simplicity
ein	fält ig		simple-minded; innocent, naive; silly, foolish

ent falt en	unfold; expand, spread; unroll, unfurl; deploy, spread out
sich ent falt en	unfold; deploy, spread out; expand, unfold, develop
Ent falt ung	unfolding
zusammen falt en	fold up; furl a sail
aus ein	
ander falt en	unfold
Sorg falt nf	care, attention; conscientiousness, meticulousness; caution

falz: siehe falt	
Falz nm	crease, fold; guard; slip; joint, seam
falz en	crease, fold; sheet, bead, seam; shave
ein falz en	fold in, fold up; rebate; notch, bottom

Fang nm	capture, catch, bag, haul; coup de grace; tusk, claws
fang en	catch, capture, take prisoner; trap, net
Fäng er	catcher
ab fang en	catch, seize; stab; intercept
An fang nm	beginning, commencement, opening; elements
an fang en	begin, set about, start
An fäng er	beginner
an fäng lich	initial, original, at first
an fang s av	at first, in the beginning, originally
auf fang en	snap up, catch, snatch; cushion shocks, parry
be fang en	confused, shy, self-conscious; prejudiced
Be fang en heit	confusion, prejudice, shyness, bias, constraint
ein fang en	catch, seize, arrest, trap
Emp fang nm	reception, welcome; receipt, delivery
emp fang en	receive, get; welcome; become pregnant
Emp fäng er	receiver, addressee; radio set
emp fäng lich	susceptible, responsive, sensitive, impressionable
Emp fäng lich keit	susceptibility, sensibility, receptivity
Emp fäng nis	conception
Ge fang ener	prisoner, captive
Ge fang en schaft	captivity, custody, imprisonment, confinement
Ge fäng nis	prison, jail, cage, imprisonment
Um fang nm	circumference, periphery, perimeter; range, extent, size
um 'fang en	encircle, surround, embrace
um fäng lich	extensive, comprehensive; bulky, spacious
Unter fang en nn	venture, bold attempt, enterprise, undertaking
unter 'fang en	attempt, dare, venture
ver fang en	take effect, tell on
sich ver fang en	become entangled, get ensnared; betray o.s.
ver fäng lich	insidious, embarrassing, awkward; indecent; risky
weg fang en s	catch away, intercept
Ur an fang nm	first beginning
ur an fäng lich	original, primeval
un be fang en a	free, natural, ingenuous, impartial, unembarrassed

Un be fang en heit	impartiality, unaffectedness, ease, candor
un emp fäng lich	unreceptive, unsusceptible, dull, apathetic
un ver fäng lich	harmless

Farb e	color; hue; tint; shade; pigment
färb en	color, tinge; dye; stain
farb en reich	richly colored
Färb er	dyer; stainer
Färb erei	dye-house; dye-works
farb ig	colored; chromatic; stained
Farb ig e	colored person, black person
farb los	colorless
Farb los ig keit	colorlessness
Färb ung	coloring, coloration; pigmentation of skin; hue, tinge
ab färb en	lose color; stain, bleed
auf färb en	lift, touch up; dye again, redye
ent färb en	discolor, decolorize; bleach
sich ent färb en	turn pale, lose its color, discolor
Ent färb ung	decolorization, bleaching
Gegen farb e	complementary color
miss farb ig	discolored
nach färb en	redye, color again, redip
'um färb en	redye, dye again
ver färb en	discolor
sich ver färb en	lose color, change color

Fass nn	cask, barrel; keg; vat, tub
fass bar	tangible; comprehensible
Fäss chen	small barrel, small cask, keg
fass en	seize, grasp, take hold of; catch, apprehend
sich fass en	bite
fass lich	comprehensible, conceivable
Fass lich keit	comprehensibility, conceivability
Fass ung	mounting, frame, support; lamp holder, socket; setting
fass ung s los	disconcerted, perplexed; aghast, speechless
Fass ung s los ig keit	bewilderment, perplexity; shock, dismay
fass weise av	by the barrel
ab fass en	intercept; arrest; compose, write, draft; draw up
an fass en	take hold of, grasp, seize; touch, handle; treat
auf fass en	conceive; understand, comprehend, grasp; interpret, construe
Auf fass ung	conception; interpretation; apprehension, grasp; opinion
be fass en a	touch, handle
ein fass en	enclose; fence in; border, edge; frame a picture
Ein fass ung	enclosure; fence, railing; rim, border, edge
er fass en	seize, grasp, catch; clutch, grip; comprise
Er fass ung	registration, recording, listing; consideration
Ge fäss nn	vessel
ge fass t	calm, composed; resigned

'um fass en	grasp, grip; enclose, surround; embrace; encircle; include
um 'fass en	grasp, grip; enclose, surround; embrace, include
Um fass ung	embracing, encompassing; enclosure
un fass bar	incomprehensible, inconceivable, impalpable
un fass lich	incomprehensible, inconceivable, impalpable
'unter fass en	take one's arm
ver fass en	compose, write, pen some lines
Ver fass er	author, writer
Ver fass ung	state, condition; disposition, state of mind; system
zu fass en	make a grab; catch, seize, clutch, grasp for
zusammen fass en	comprise, comprehend, embrace; combine, concentrate; condense, sum
Zusammen fass ung	collection; concentration; summary, resume; condensation
vor ge fass t	preconceived

faul a	rotten; foul, putrid; brittle metal; decayed teeth
Fäul e	rot
faul en	rot, decay, putrefy
Faul heit	laziness, idleness, sluggishness
faul ig	rotten; putrid; moldy; rotting, putrescent
Fäul nis	rottenness; putrefacation; decay, decomposition; putrescence
ab faul en	rot and fall off
an faul en	begin to rot, go bad
'durch faul en	rot through
ober faul a s	very unusual, fishy
ver faul en	rot, molder, decay, putrefy

feg en	furbish, rub; clean, wipe; scour; sweep
ab feg en	sweep off
aus feg en	sweep out

Fehl nm	blemish, flaw, fault
fehl en	be absent; have failed to come; be missing; lack, be wanting
Fehl er	defect; drawback; mistake, error; flaw, blemish
fehl er frei	faultless, perfect
fehl er haft	faulty; defective, deficient; incorrect
fehl er los	faultless, perfect
un fehl bar	infallible, unerring; unfailing
Un fehl bar keit	infallibility
ver fehl en	miss
Ver fehl ung	offense; mistake; lapse

Be fehl nm	command; order, bidding
be fehl en	command, order, direct; instruct, tell, bid; decree
be fehl end	mandatory; commanding, imperative
be fehl er isch	imperious, dictatorial, peremptory, bossy
emp fehl en	recommend; commend
sich emp fehl en	commend itself, be recommended

Emp	fehl	ung	recommendation
an be	fehl	en a	order s.o. to do s.t., commit s.t. to one's charge
Gegen be	fehl	nm	counterorder
Ober be	fehl	nm	supreme command, high command
an emp	fehl	en	recommend
weiter emp	fehl	en	recommend
be	fehl	ig en m	command, be in command of, have under one's command, lead

	Feier	nf	rest; holiday; celebration; ceremony; festival; party
	feier	lich	solemn; festive; ceremonious
	Feier	lich keit	solemnity; ceremoniousness; ceremony
	feier	n	celebrate; observe; commemorate; honor, praise
ab	feier	n s	idle away
Nach	feier	nf	subsequent celebration, later celebration; after-celebration
nach	feier	n	hold a subsequent celebration, celebrate s.t. later
Vor	feier	nf	precelebration

Feil	e	file; rasp
feil	en	file
ab feil	en	file off; polish
aus feil	en	file, file out; give the finishing touches to s.t.
'durch feil	en	file through; polish, give the last finish to

fein	a	fine; delicate, dainty; minute; graceful; distinguished
Fein	heit	fineness, delicacy, daintiness; grace, gracefulness; elegance
un fein	a	indelicate; unmannerly, unrefined, coarse
über 'fein er	n	overrefine
Ueber fein er	ung	overrefinement
ver fein er	n	refine; improve
Ver fein er	ung	refinement

Feind	nm	enemy
feind	lich	hostile, enemy
Feind	lich keit	enmity, animosity, hostility; hatred; feud, strife
Feind	schaft	enmity, animosity, hostility; hatred; feud, strife
an feind	en	bear ill will to s.o., be hostile to s.o.; persecute s.o.
An feind	ung	hostility, persecution
Erz feind	nm	archfiend
sich ver feind	en	make an enemy, fall out with

fern	a	far; far off, distant, remote
Fern	e	distance, remoteness
fern er	a	further; farther
ent fern	en	remove; take away, put aside; clear away; take out spot
sich ent fern	en	go away, withdraw, absent o.s.; deviate, depart from

ent fern t a	remote, distant; far away
Ent fern ung	removal; distance, remoteness
un fern p	not far from, near
so fern	so far as

fert ig	ready; finished, done; complete; skilled, dexterous; accomplished
fert ig en	manufacture, make, fabricate, produce
Fert ig keit	dexterity; skill, art, facility; proficiency; fluency; practice
Fert ig ung	manufacture, production, fabrication; output
un fert ig	not ready, unfinished, incomplete; immature
ab fert ig en	dispatch; clear; forward, expedite; serve, deal with
Ab fert ig ung	dispatching; clearance; expedition; service
an fert ig en	make, manufacture, fabricate; prepare, draw up
An fert ig ung	making, manufacture; preparation
aus fert ig en	dispatch, expedite; draw up a document, execute; exemplify, issue
Aus fert ig ung	dispatch; drawing up; making out
unter 'fert ig en	sign, execute
unter fert ig te	the undersigned
ver fert ig en	make, manufacture, fabricate, prepare, compose
Ver fert ig ung	making, manufacture, fabrication, preparation
recht fert ig en	justify, warrant; vindicate, exonerate, exculpate

fest a	firm
Fest nn	festival, celebration; holiday
fest ig en	secure; strengthen, fortify; establish, consolidate power
Fest ig keit	firmness, solidity, compactness
fest lich	festive; solemn; splendid
Fest lich keit	festivity; solemnity; splendor
Fest ung	fortress; fort; citadel
be fest ig en	fix, fasten, make s.t. fast, attach, clamp; protect, stabilize
Be fest ig ung	fixing, fastening; fortification, entrenchment; pavement, paving
ver fest ig en	solidify, strengthen, reinforce, stiffen; solidify, consolidate
sich ver fest ig en	solidify, rigidify, become firm, become rigid, become inflexible
Ver fest ig ung	solidification; reinforcement; consolidation; rigidification

fett a	fat, corpulent; greasy; grimy, oily; fertile, rich
Fett nn	fat; grease; drippings; shortening
fett arm	poor in fats
fett en	grease, lubricate; compound oil
Fett heit	fatness
fett ig	fatty; greasy
Fett ig keit	fatness; greasiness
ein fett en	grease; oil

ent fett en	remove the fat from, degrease, scour
Ent fett ung	removal of fat, scouring
Ver fett ung	fatty degeneration, adiposis

feucht a	moist, damp
Feucht e	moisture, dampness; humidity; clamminess, dankness
feucht en	moisten, dampen
Feucht ig keit	moisture, dampness; humidity; clamminess, dankness
an feucht en	moisten, wet, dampen
be feucht en	moisten, dampen, wet; humidify
Be feucht ung	moistening, dampening
durch 'feucht en	wet thoroughly, soak

Feuer nn	heat; fire
feuer n	make a fire, light a fire
ab feuer n	fire off, discharge; shoot
an feuer n	fire, heat; pep s.o. up; cheer s.o. on, root for
An feuer ung	heating; incitement, stimulation
Be feuer ung n	lighting
ver feuer n	use up for fuel; use up, fire s.t.

Film nm	film, thin coating
film en	film s.t., shoot a film, make a film
film isch	pertaining to film; filmy
Bei film nm	supporting film, short film
ver film en	film; screen a film
Ver film ung	filming, screening; film version, screen adaptation

find en	find; meet with; discover, chance upon, come across; think, consider
Find er	finder
find ig	resourceful, ingenious, clever
Find ig keit	resourcefulness, ingenuity, cleverness
Find ling t	foundling
ab find en	pay off, satisfy, settle; put up with, be resigned
Ab find ung	arrangement, settlement, agreement, compromise
auf find en	find out, locate; spot, discover, detect
aus find ig	make out; locate, track down
be find en	find; consider, think
Be find en nn	health; opinion
sich be find en	be, be located
be find lich	be found; present, contained in
sich 'durch find en	find one's way through
sich ein find en	be present; appear, turn up; arrive
emp find bar	perceptible, sensible
emp find en	be sensible of, feel, experience
emp find lich	sensible to, sensitive, delicate, touchy
Emp find lich keit	sensibleness, irritability, touchiness, sensitivity
emp find sam	sentimental, sensitive
Emp find sam keit	sentimentality

Emp find ung	feeling, sentiment; sensation, perception
emp find ung s los	insensible, unfeeling
er find en	find out, invent, contrive, devise; discover
Er find er	inventor, contriver; discoverer
er find er isch	inventive, ingenious
Er find ung	invention, device, contrivance
vor find en	find, meet with, come upon
zurück find en sich	find one's way back
zusammen find en	find together; meet
un auf find bar	undiscoverable; not to be located
her aus find en	discover, find out, trace
sich dar ein find en s	put up with s.t., submit to
sich hin ein find en	become familiar with, understand
mit emp find en	feel for, sympathize with
nach emp find en	sympathize with, enter into s.o.'s feelings
über emp find lich	oversensitive, touchy
Ueber emp find lich keit	hypersensitiveness
un emp find lich	insensible, cold, indifferent to
Un emp find lich keit	insensibility, indifference to
un er find lich	undiscoverable; incomprehensible
statt find en	take place; be held, be staged; happen, occur
Emp find el ei	sentimentality

Fisch nm	fish
fisch en	fish; angle
Fisch er	fisherman
Fisch erei	fishing; fishery
fisch ig	fishy
fisch reich	abounding in fish, fishy
ab fisch en	fish off, empty of fish
auf fisch en	fish up; pick up

flach a	flat; plain, level, even
Fläch e	surface
Flach heit	flatness
ab flach en	flatten, level; truncate thread
Innen fläch e	inner surface
Ober fläch e	surface
ober fläch lich	superficial; shallow; perfunctory, cursory; rough
Ober fläch lich keit	superficiality, shallowness
ver flach en	flatten

Flämm chen	little flame
Flamm e	flame
flamm en	flame, blaze, flare
flamm ig	flame-like
auf flamm en	blaze up, burst into flames, flare up; flame out
ent flamm en	set ablaze; inflame, kindle; incense s.o.
ge flamm t	watered; waved

Fleck nm	spot, place; patch of leather; blot, spot, smudge, stain

Fleck chen	nn	fleck, speck; place, spot
Fleck en	nm	spot, place; patch of leather; blot, spot, smudge, stain
fleck en		spot artillery; patch shoe
fleck en los		spotless
fleck ig		spotted, speckled; stained, smudgy
be fleck en		stain, spot, soil; tarnish, sully, besmirch
Be fleck ung		tarnishing, staining
ge fleck t		spotted, speckled; freckled
un be fleck t		unsullied, spotless, undefiled, immaculate

Fleisch	nn	flesh; meat
Fleisch er		butcher
Fleisch erei		butcher's shop
fleisch ig		fleshy; meaty
fleisch lich		carnal, sensual
fleisch los		fleshless
zer fleisch en		mangle, lacerate; rend, tear to pieces, slash
ein ge fleisch t		incarnate; inveterate, engrained, dyed-in-the-wool

flick en		mend, patch up, repair
Flick en	nm	patch
Flick erei		patching, patchwork
Flick erin		patcher, mender
an flick en		patch on
aus flick en		patch up
ein flick en		patch in; add, insert
zusammen flick en		patch up

Flieg e		fly; imperial beard; bow tie; traveller, runner
flieg en		fly; stream, flutter; pilot a plane
flieg end		flying
Flieg er		flyer, airman, aviator, pilot
Flieg erei		flying, aviation
Flieg erin		air woman, aviatrix, woman pilot
flieg er isch		flying, piloting, aeronautical
ab flieg en		fly off; start, take off
an flieg en		fly against, come flying; land at, approach, touch
auf flieg en		fly up, soar, ascend; take off
aus flieg en		leave the nest, run away; go on a trip
be flieg en		fly regularly between, fly over a course
durch 'flieg en		fly through; hurry over a letter, glance through
'durch flieg en		fly through; hurry over a letter, glance through
ein flieg en		make test flights; enter by air
Ein flieg er		test pilot
ent flieg en		fly away
fort flieg en		fly away, take off
über 'flieg en		fly over, glance over, skim through
um 'flieg en		fly around
'um flieg en s		fall over; fly a round-about way
ver flieg en		fly off, vanish, disappear, evaporate
sich. ver flieg en		lose one's bearings

weg flieg en	fly away
weiter flieg en	continue the flight
zu flieg en	fly to; slam, bang
her aus flieg en	fly out
vor bei flieg en	fly past
her um flieg en	fly around
da von flieg en	fly away
aus ein	
ander flieg en	fly apart, fly asunder; be scattered

flieh en	flee, escape, run away; avoid, shun
ent flieh en	flee, escape, run away

fliess en	flow, run; pour, gush, stream, inflow; blot
ab fliess en	flow away; ebb; run off, drain off
aus fliess en	flow out; emanate from, issue from
'durch fliess en	flow through
durch 'fliess en	flow through
ein fliess en	flow in, flow into
'über fliess en	flow over, overflow
um 'fliess en	flow around
ver fliess en	flow off; elapse, pass, expire
zer fliess en	dissolve, melt
zu fliess en	flow to, flow into; flow towards
zurück fliess en	flow back, recede; ebb
zusammen fliess en	flow together; meet
her aus fliess en	flow out; issue
vor bei fliess en	flow past

floss: siehe fliess	
Floss nn	raft, float
flöss en	float, raft
ein flöss en	instill; administer; inspire with

flucht: siehe flieh	
Flucht nf	flight; escape
flucht art ig	hasty, hurried, headlong
flucht en	align
flücht en	flee
flücht ig	fugitive, absconding, runaway; fleeting, passing; hasty, careless
Flücht ig keit	fleetingness, transitoriness; hastiness; carelessness, cursoriness
Flücht ling	fugitive, runaway
ab flucht en	align
Aus flucht nf	evasion, subterfuge; shift; excuse, pretext
Zu flucht nf	refuge, shelter, resort
ver flücht ig en	volatilize
sich ver flücht ig en	evaporate; make o.s. scarce, vanish

flug: siehe flieg	
Flug nm	flight, swarm, flock; air travel

Flüg el	wing; blade, vane, fin; side piece; grand piano; flank
flüg el los	wingless
flüg el n h	wing
flüg ge a	fledged
flug s av	quickly, swiftly; in a jiffy, at once, instantly
Ab flug nm	take-off; start, departure
An flug nm	flight, approach; touch, tincture
Aus flug nm	flight, flying out; excursion trip
Aus flüg ler nm	excursionist
Ein flug nm	approach; raid
Fern flug nm	long-distance flight
Rück flug nm	return flight
Weiter flug nm	continuation of a flight
be flüg el n	wing, give wings to; accelerate, increase the speed of
Be flüg el ung	acceleration, quickening the pace
Ge flüg el nn	fowl; poultry
ge flüg el t	winged; wing-bearing; aliferous; dictum, saying
Neben flüg el nm	side wing, lateral wing
über 'flüg el n	outflank, surpass, outdo
Ueber flüg el ung	outstripping s.o., outdoing s.o., leaving s.o. behind

fluss: siehe fliess	
Fluss nm	river, stream, creek; flowing; melting, fusion
Flüss chen	rivulet, streamlet, creek
flüss ig	fluid, liquid; molten, melted; available, ready
Flüss ig keit	fluid, liquid; liquor, liquidity; fluidity
Ab fluss nm	drain, flowing off; outlet
Aus fluss nm	flowing out, discharge; outlet; secretion; result
Ein fluss nm	influx, influence
Neben fluss nm	tributary, affluent
Rück fluss nm	reflux, backward flow; regurgitation
Ueber fluss nm	plenty, abundance, surplus, excess; overflow
über flüss ig	useless, superfluous; unnecessary, surplus
Zu fluss nm	influx; supply; tributary; admission
Zusammen fluss nm	confluence, junction; conflux, fusion
be ein fluss en	influence s.o., affect; lobby for s.t.
Be ein fluss ung	influence, exertion of influence
un be ein fluss t	unaffected by; unprejudiced, not influenced
ver flüss ig en	liquefy; thin, dilute; increase the liquidity of
sich ver flüss ig en	become liquid
Ver flüss ig er	liquefier
Ver flüss ig ung	liquefaction, condensation; thinning

Flut nf	flood; high tide, flood tide
flut en	flow, flood; swell, surge
be flut en	flood
durch 'flut en	flow through, run through; flood, pervade
'über flut en	overflow; inundate, flood
über 'flut en	overflow; inundate, flood

um 'flut en	flow around s.t.; be surrounded by the sea
zurück flut en	flow back, flood back; sweep back

Folg e	sequence, succession; continuation, sequel; edition; series
folg en	follow; succeed; ensue; obey
folg end er mass en av	as follows, in the following manner, like this
folg e richt ig	logical, consistent
Folg e richt ig keit	logical consistency, logic
folg er n	infer, deduce, conclude, gather
Folg er ung	inference, deduction, conclusion
folg e wid r ig	illogical; inconsistent, inconsequential
Folg e wid r ig keit	inconsistency
folg lich c	consequently; therefore, hence, thus, so
folg sam	obedient; docile, submissive, unresisting
Folg sam keit	obedience; docility
Ab folg e	succession; sequence
aus folg en	deliver up, hand over; pay up
be folg en	follow, take advice; obey, observe, comply with rules
Be folg ung	following, observance; compliance, adherence
bei folg end	enclosed; annexed, attached
Er folg nm	result, outcome, issue; consequence, effect
er folg en	ensue, follow, result; happen, occur; be forthcoming
er folg los	unsuccessful, ineffective, vain, unavailing, fruitless, abortive
Er folg s los ig keit	unsuccessfulness, failure
Ge folg e nn	suite, retinue; train, entourage, followers
Ge folg schaft	following, adherents
in folg e p	in consequence of, as a result of, due to
Nach folg e	succession
nach folg en	follow; succeed; emulate, follow the example of s.o.
Nach folg er	follower; successor
Nach folg erin	follower; successor
un folg sam	disobedient; wayward
Un folg sam keit	disobedience
Ver folg nm c	course; progress; in the course of
ver folg en	pursue; persecute; prosecute; track, trail, shadow s.o.
Ver folg er	persuer; persecutor
Ver folg ung	persuit; persecution; persuance
zu folg e p	as a result of, due to; according to; by virtue of
ver ab folg en	deliver, hand over; give; provide, serve food
dar auf folg end a	ensuing, subsequent, following
Miss er folg nm	failure, fiasco, flop
zurück ver folg en	retrace the way, trace back
Auf ein ander folg e	succession, series
auf ein ander folg en	succeed one another

Förder er	furtherer, patron
förder lich	conductive; useful, profitable; effective; beneficial
forder n	demand, require; call for, ask for, exact
förder n	further, advance, promote; encourage; stimulate; aid, assist
Forder ung	demand; call for; claim; debt, debt claim
Förder ung	furtherance, promotion, advancement; encouragement; assistance
ab forder n	demand s.t. from s.o, claim s.t., exact s.t.
an forder n	demand, claim, call for; request; requisition
An forder ung	demand, claim, call; requirement
auf forder n	ask, request; bid, order; urge; challenge; summon
Auf forder ung	call, request; order; urging; invitation; challenge
Be förder er	convey, carry; transport
be förder n	convey, carry; transport, haul; forward; consign, ship
Be förder ung	carriage, conveyance; transportation
ein forder n	call in, demand payment of, call s.t. in; collect taxes
Ein forder ung	calling-in, demand; collection
er forder lich	necessary, requisite, required
er forder n	require, demand; exact; call for, necessitate
Er forder nis	requirement; necessity, requisite
Gegen forder ung	counterclaim
nach forder n	demand extra, charge extra; claim subsequently
Nach forder ung	extra charge; afterclaim
Rück forder ung	counterdemand; reclamation
über 'forder n	overcharge; overtax
Ueber forder ung	overcharge; overstrain, overwork
zurück forder n	claim back, reclaim
Zurück forder ung	reclamation
Her aus forder er	challenger
her aus forder n	ask for the return of; challenge, defy, provoke
Her aus forder ung	challenge, provocation
weiter be förder n	forward on, send on; redirect
Weiter be förder ung	reforwarding; further transportation
hin auf be förder n	carry up, hoist up
un auf ge forder t	unasked, unbidden

Form nf	form; shape; appearance, figure; style, cut of dress
form al	formal, technical
form en	form, model, fashion
Form er	former, molder
form ier en	form; array; line-up
förm lich	formal; ceremonious; punctilious; literal, veritable, regular
Förm lich keit	formality; ceremoniousness; ceremony
form los	formless, shapeless, amorphous; unceremonious; unpolished, rude
Form los ig keit	formlessness, shapelessness; informality; crudeness, rudeness
Form ung	formation; forming, shaping, molding

ab form en	mold, model; copy; shape
'um form en	remodel, recast, transform; redesign; convert
Um form er	electrical converter, transformer
un förm ig	misshapen, deformed; shapeless; monstrous; bulky; clumsy
Un förm ig keit	shapelessness; deformity; monstrosity; clumsiness
un förm lich	informal, unceremonious
Un förm lich keit	informality
Ur form nf	original form
ver form en	deform; work, shape
Ver form ung	working; shaping

Forsch a s	vigorous, energetic, enterprising; dashing; breezy, brisk
forsch en	inquire after; search for, seek; investigate for
Forsch er	inquirer, seeker, investigator; researcher, scientist; explorer
Forsch ung	investigation, research, research work
aus forsch en	search out, explore; investigate, inquire into
durch 'forsch en	search through, investigate, scrutinize; explore country
Durch forsch ung	search, investigation, scrutiny; exploration
er forsch en	explore land; inquire into, investigate, study
Er forsch er	explorer; investigator
Er forsch ung	exploration; investigation; fathoming
nach forsch en	investigate, make inquiries, conduct an investigation
Nach forsch ung	investigation, inquiry, search
un er forsch lich	impenetrable; inscrutable

Frag e	question
frag en	ask; question, interrogate; inquire after s.o.
Frag er	questioner, interrogator
frag lich	questionable, doubtful, problematic, uncertain; in question
frag los	unquestionable, indisputable
frag würd ig	questionable, dubious, shady
ab frag en	question s.o. about s.t.
An frag e	inquiry, question; application
an frag en	inquire, ask; apply
aus frag en	interrogate, question, quiz; sound out, draw out; cross examine
be frag en	question, interview; take a poll; examine, consult
Be frag ung	inquiry, interview
'durch frag en	ask one's way through
sich 'durch frag en	ask one's way through
er frag en	ascertain
Gegen frag e	counterquestion
Nach frag e	inquiry
nach frag en	inquire about, ask after
Neben frag e	side issue
Rück frag e	further inquiry, return question

rück frag en		inquire again, make a query
über 'frag en		ask too much, stump s.o.
Um frag e		general inquiry, opinion poll
Vor frag e		preliminary question
un ge frag t		without being asked
her um frag en	s	make inquiries, ask around

frass:	siehe fress	
Frass	nm	food, feed, chow; eating away; damage, destruction
ge fräss ig		greedy, gluttonous, voracious, wolfish, gourmand; ravenous
Ge fräss ig keit		greed, gluttony, voracity, wolfishness; ravenousness

frei	a	free from, independent; exempt; frank, open, candid
Frei e	nm	freeman, freewoman, free-born citizen
frei en		court s.o; make love to; woo
Frei er		suitor, wooer
Frei heit		liberty, freedom; exemption
frei heit lich		liberal, free
frei lich		certainly, to be sure, quite so
frei will ig		voluntarily, spontaneous
Frei will ig e		volunteer
Frei will ig keit		voluntariness, spontaneity
be frei en		free, deliver, liberate; release, rescue; exempt; strip
sich be frei en		free o.s. from, rid o.s. of; shake off, disentangle o.s.
Be frei er		liberator
Be frei erin		liberator
Be frei ung		deliverance, liberation, release; exemption
Ge frei ter		army private
un frei	a	unfree, not free; constrained, self-conscious
Ober ge frei ter		private first class

fremd	a	strange; foreign; alien; exotic; extraneous
fremd art ig		strange, heterogeneous; odd, outlandish, exotic
Fremd art ig keit		heterogeneity; strangeness, oddness
Fremd e		foreign country, foreign parts
Fremd e		stranger; foreigner, alien; tourist; guest, visitor
Fremd ling		stranger
Be fremd en	nn	astonishment, surprise; displeasure
be fremd en		astonish, surprise, appear strange to
be fremd lich		strange, surprising, disturbing
ent fremd en		estrange, alienate
Ent fremd ung		estrangement, alienation
Ueber fremd ung		foreign infiltration, foreign control

fress en		eat, feed; devour
Fress en	nn	feed, feeding, food

	Fress er	glutton, gormandizer, guzzler
ab	fress en	eat off; graze down; browse on; corrode; erode
an	fress en	gnaw at; peck; corrode, eat into
auf	fress en	devour, eat up
aus	fress en	clear, empty; erode; corrode
'durch	fress en	eat through; corrode
sich ein	fress en	penetrate s.t., corrode s.t., eat into s.t.; gnaw into s.t.
zer	fress en	eat away, gnaw; corrode

	Freu de nf	joy, gladness; pleasure; delight, glee
	freu d ig	joyful, joyous; glad; enthusiastic, keen
	Freu d ig keit	joyousness; enthusiasm, keenness, willingness
	freu d los	joyless, cheerless
	freu en	be glad, be pleased
sich	freu en	be glad, be pleased; look forward to
er	freu en	gladden, please, give pleasure to; delight, gratify
sich er	freu en	delight in s.t., find pleasure in s.t.
er	freu lich	delightful, pleasing, agreeable; glad, fine, pleasant
sich mit	freu en	rejoice with s.o., share one's joy
Vor	freu de	anticipated joy
un er	freu lich	unpleasant

	Freund nm	friend, boyfriend
	Freund in	friend, girlfriend
	freund lich	friendly, kind; amiable, pleasant, genial; obliging; cheerful
	Freund lich keit	friendliness, kindness; amiability; affability; pleasantness
	Freund schaft	friendship
	freund schaft lich	friendly, amicable
sich an	freund en	become friends, fraternize
sich be	freund en	become friends, make friends with one another
un	freund lich	unfriendly, unkind; disobliging; gruff, inclement, cheerless
Un	freund lich keit	unfriendliness, ill-feeling; inclemency

	Fried e nm a	peace; harmony; tranquility, peace of mind
	Fried en nm	peace; harmony; tranquility, peace of mind
	fried fert ig	peaceable, pacific
	Fried fert ig keit	peaceableness
	fried lich	peaceable, peaceful, untroubled, tranquil
	Fried lich keit	peaceableness; peacefulness
	fried los	peaceless, without peace
be	fried en	pacify, bring peace to
Be	fried ung	pacification
ein	fried en	enclose; hedge in, wall in, fence in
um 'fried en	enclose, fence in
Um	fried ung	enclosure, fence
Un	fried e nm	discord, dissension, strife
zu	fried en a	contented, satisfied; pleased, gratified
Zu	fried en heit	contentment, satisfaction, contentedness

un zu fried en a	dissatisfied, discontented, malcontent
Un zu fried en heit	dissatisfaction, discontent
be fried ig en	satisfy, please; appease, gratify; meet, answer
be fried ig end	satisfying, satisfactory
Be fried ig ung	satisfaction, appeasement; gratification
ein fried ig en	enclose; hedge in, wall in, fence in
Ein fried ig ung	enclosure
um 'fried ig en	enclose, fence in
Um fried ig ung	enclosure, fence
un be fried ig end	unsatisfactory

frier en	freezing, congelation; chill, shivering
ab frier en	freeze off, be bitten off by cold
an frier en	freeze on
'durch frier en	freeze through, chill through
ein frier en	freeze, freeze in
er frier en	freeze to death, die from cold, be killed by frost
Er frier ung	death from exposure; frostbite
ge frier en	freeze, congeal
zu frier en	freeze up, freeze over

frisch a	fresh, new; recent; vigorous; cool, chilly; brisk, lively; alert
Frisch e	freshness; coolness, chill; briskness, liveliness; vigor
frisch en p	refine, reduce a lead; revive copper; reclaim oil
Frisch ling	young wild boar
auf frisch en	renovate, refurbish; refresh, brighten up; touch up a picture
sich auf frisch en	freshen up, refresh; touch up; varnish, do up; renew, regenerate
er frisch en	refresh, freshen; cool; give new life to, revive
Er frisch ung	refreshment

fror: siehe frier	'
Ge fror nis nf	permafrost
ver fror en a	feel cold very easily; be chilled through
un ver fror en a	bold, audacious; forward, outspoken; impudent, impertinent
Un ver fror en heit	boldness, audacity; forwardness, insolence, freshness

Frucht nf	fruit; corn
frucht bar	fruitful
Frucht bar keit	fruitfulness; fertility, fecundity, productivity
Frücht chen	small fruit
frucht en	bear fruit; be of use, have an effect
frucht los	fruitless
Frucht los ig keit	fruitlessness
be frucht en	fertilize, fructify; pollenate; impregnate
Be frucht ung	fertilization, fructification, pollination; impregnation

un frucht bar	unfruitful, barren, sterile
Un frucht bar keit	unfruitfulness; barrenness, sterility

Fug e	joint; seam; slit; rabbet, groove; mortise
fug en	joint; groove; point
füg en	decree, ordain, dispose
füg en	yield to, submit to, comply with; resign o.s. to, put up with
füg lich	conveniently, rightly, justly, very well
füg sam	pliant, supple; tractable, manageable, docile; obedient
Füg sam keit	pliancy; docility; obedience
Füg ung	dispensation, providence, decree; coincidence; fate
an füg en	join, attach; add, annex; affix one's signature
An füg ung	addition, annex, attachment
be fug en i	empower, authorize, entitle
Be fug nis	authority, power, right; privilege
bei füg en	add, join; enclose, annex to letter; attach
Bei füg ung	addition; attribute; enclosure
ein fug en	dovetail, rabbet
ein füg en	put in, fit in; insert, sandwich in
sich ein füg en	fit in well; adapt o.s., fall in with others
Ein füg ung	fitting in, insertion; interpolation; adaptation
Ge füg e nn	joints
ge füg ig	pliable, supple, flexible; pliant, docile, submissive
Ge füg ig keit	pliancy, flexibility; docility, submissiveness
Un fug nm	mischief, nuisance; shenanigans
ver füg bar	available
ver füg en	decree, order; enact a law; proceed to; have at one's disposal
Ver füg ung	decree, order; instruction
zu füg en	add; do, cause; inflict
zusammen füg en sich	join together, unite; fit into one another; assemble
zusammen füg en	unite
un be fug t	unauthorized; incompetent
hin zu füg en	add; enclose, attach; append, annex
an ein ander füg en	join
in ein ander füg en	fit into each other, join

---

fühl bar	sensible; tangible, palpable; perceptible, noticeable; distinct
fühl en	feel; have a sense of, sense; perceive; be aware of
sich fühl en	feeling
Fühl er	feeler, antenna; tentacle
fühl los	unfeeling
Fühl ung	touch, contact
an fühl en	feel, touch
be fühl en	feel, touch, handle
sich ein fühl en	feel one's way into; acquire an insight into
Ge fühl nn	feeling, sentiment, emotion; sense
ge fühl los	numb; insensible, impossible; unfeeling, callous, heartless

Ge fühl los ig keit	unfeelingness, callousness, brutal act
ge fühl voll	full of feeling; sensitive; tender; sentimental, melodramatic
mit fühl en	sympathize with s.o. in s.t., feel for s.o.
nach fühl en	sympathize with s.o.; understand one's feelings
vor fühl en s	put out one's feelers
her aus fühl en	feel, sense
Mit ge fühl nn	sympathy
Voll ge fühl nn	full consciousness, full awareness
Vor ge fühl nn	presentiment

Fuhr e	conveyance, carriage; carting; cartload
führ en	lead, direct, take to; conduct, guide; command; result in
Führ er	leader, chief, head, conductor; commander; driver
Führ erin	leader, chief, head, conductor; commander; driver
führ er los	without a leader, guideless; driverless, pilotless
Führ er schaft	leadership, leaders
Führ ung	leadership; conduct; direction, management; command, control
Ab fuhr nf	carrying away, removal; transportation
ab führ en	lead off, deliver; remove, take away
ab führ end	purgative, cathartic
Ab führ ung	transport, clearing; purgation
An fuhr nf	carriage, conveyance; supply
an führ en	lead, command; quote, allege; adduce
An führ er	leader, commander, chief
An führ ung	direction, leadership, command; quotation
auf führ en	raise, build, construct; perform, represent; act
sich auf führ en	behave
Auf führ ung	construction; performance; behavior
Aus fuhr nf	export, exportation
aus führ bar	exportable, practicable, performable
Aus führ bar keit	feasibility, practicability
aus führ en	lead out, export; carry out, perform
aus führ lich	detailed, full, extensive, extended
Aus führ lich keit	fullness, completeness of detail
Aus führ ung	execution, performance; design, construction; statement
Durch fuhr nf	passage, transit
durch führ bar	feasible, practicable
Durch führ bar keit	practicability
'durch führ en	carry out, bring about; conduct; accomplish
Durch führ ung	execution, performance, accomplishment
Ein fuhr nf	import, importation
ein führ bar	importable, admissible
ein führ en	bring in; introduce; import; install; lead in
ein führ en	introduce; set a fashion; initiate measures
Ein führ ung	initiation, establishment; insertion; introduction, presentation
ent führ en	abduct, carry off, kidnap; elope with
Ent führ er	abductor, kidnapper

Ent führ ung		abduction, kidnapping; rape; elopement
fort führ en		lead away, convey; continue, carry on
Fort führ ung		conveyance; continuation; pursuit
her führ en	s	lead, bring here
hin führ en		take there, take to, lead to
mit führ en		carry along with
Rück führ ung		repatriation
'über führ en		carry over, transport, transfer, transmit; convict
Ueber führ ung		transportation; conveyance, viaduct, overpass; conviction
Unter führ er	m	subordinate commander
Unter führ ung		underpass
ver führ en		lead astray, mislead; seduce; bribe; tempt
Ver führ er		seducer, corrupter
ver führ er isch		seductive, tempting, alluring; fascinating, charming
Ver führ ung		seduction, enticement, allurement; temptation; bribing
voll 'führ en		execute, carry out; accomplish
vor führ en		bring forward; produce; present; demonstrate, project
Vor führ er		projectionist
Vor führ ung		bringing forth; demonstration; presentation, performance
Zu fuhr	nf	supply; addition; provisions; importation; conveyance
zu führ en		lead to; supply; convey; procure, deliver
Zu führ ung		supply, provision, conveyance; lead, feed
zurück führ en		lead back; reduce; attribute to, refer to, ascribe
zusammen führ en		bring together
her auf führ en		show up, lead up
ur auf führ en		premiere
Ur auf führ ung		first performance
un aus führ bar		impracticable, not feasible, impossible
her bei führ en		bring on; lead near; bring about, cause; induce
un durch führ bar		impracticable, not feasible
her ein führ en		show in, see in, usher in
wieder 'ein führ en		reintroduce, reestablish
Wieder ein führ ung		reintroduction, reinsertion, restoration, reestablishment
an ge führ t		cited, mentioned; imposed upon; led
her um führ en		lead around, take around; show over
un aus ge führ t		not carried out, unexecuted; open

Füll e		fullness, plenty, wealth, abundance, stoutness, corpulence
füll en		fill; inflate; stuff, cram; load, charge; replenish
sich füll en		foal; colt; filly
füll ig		full; well-rounded, plump
Füll ung		filling
Füll sel		stuffing; stopgap
ab füll en		fill; decant; draw off, bottle

an füll en	fill up, cram, stuff; charge	
auf füll en	fill up; refill, replenish, restock	
aus füll en	fill out, stuff, pad; fill in, stop; fill a position; absorb	
Aus füll ung	filling in; padding; rubble	
ein füll en	fill into s.t., pour into s.t., bottle s.t.	
er füll en	fill; inspire with; fulfill; accomplish task; meet condition	
sich er füll en	be fulfilled, materialize, come true	
Er füll ung	fulfillment, accomplishment; performance, compliance; realization	
nach füll en	fill up, refill, replenish	
Ueber füll e	superabundance, profusion	
über 'füll en	overfill, cram, overload, overcrowd, jam; overstock	
Ueber füll ung	overfilling, overloading; cramming; glut, surfeit	
'um füll en	decant; transfuse	
'voll füll en	fill up	
un er füll bar	unrealizable, unattainable	
Un er füll bar keit	unattainability	
un aus ge füll t	blank, not filled out	

---

fund: siehe find	
Fund nm	finding, discovery, find

Fuss nm	foot
fuss el n	make small steps, toddle; play footsie
fuss en	rest upon, rely upon, be based upon
fuss fäll ig	prostrate
fuss frei	ankle-length
fuss ling	foot of stocking
Bei fuss nm	mugwort, motherwort, artemesia
Gegen füss ler nm	antipode
Hinter fuss nm	hindfoot
Vorder fuss nm	forefoot

Futter nn	food
fütter n	feed
Fütter ung	feeding, foddering, forage
ab fütter n	feed
auf fütter n	feed up, rear
aus fütter n	line; fur; pad, upholster
'durch fütter n s	feed through the winter; feed, support
über 'fütter n	overfeed
ver fütter n	feed

Unter futter nn	lining
unter 'fütter n	line underneath
Zwischen futter nn	interlining

---

gab: siehe geb	
Gab e	gift, present, donation, gratuity
Ab gab e	delivery, levy; duty, rate, tax; social duty

An gab e		declaration, instruction, statement; showing off; denunciation
Auf gab e		handing in, dispatch; booking; task, assignment
Aus gab e		expense, outlay, cost; delivery; distribution; issue
be gab en		endow, bestow upon
Be gab ung		ability, capacity, endowment; gift; talents
Bei gab e		addition, supplement; free gift
Ein gab e		petition, memorial, application, address; presentation
Gegen gab e		present in return
Hin gab e		delivery; devotion; resignation, surrender
Rück gab e		return, restoration, reinstatement
Ueber gab e		delivery, surrender, handing over, transfer, submitting
Vor gab e		odds given, allowance, handicap
Weiter gab e		retransmission, forwarding
Wieder gab e		restitution, return; reproduction; rendering; reading
Zu gab e		addition, adjunct; surplus, extra, supplement
Zurück gab e		return, restitution, restoration, giving back
Her aus gab e		giving up, giving back, return, restitution; publication
Neben aus gab e		incidentals
ver aus gab en		spend, pay out
sich ver aus gab en		exhaust o.s., run short of money
un be gab t		untalented

---

	gang:	siehe geh	
	Gang	nm	going, walking, pace; motion, movement; hall, gangway, aisle
	gang bar		practicable, passable; saleable, marketable; popular
	gäng ig		swift
Ab	gang	nm	departure; starting; exit; loss; emission; retirement; death
ab	gäng ig		missing, deficient; saleable, marketable
an	gäng ig		admissable; possible, feasable, practicable
Auf	gang	nm	rising, ascent; rise, growth, increase; staircase, steps, stairway
Aus	gang	nm	going out, exit; result, issue; end
Durch	gang	nm	passing through, crossing, passage, transit
Durch	gäng er	s	absconder; runaway horse
durch	gäng ig	s	usual, general, generally, as a rule
Ein	gang	nm	entrance; introduction, preface, prologue; arrival; receipt
ein	gang s	av	in the beginning
Fort	gang	nm	departure; progress, success; continuation
Her	gang	nm	course of events; proceedings; details
Hin	gang	nm	passage; decease, death
Nieder	gang	nm	descent, decline
Rück	gang	nm	drop, decline, decrease, falling-off, reduction, recession

rück	gäng	ig	retrograde, retrogressive, dropping, declining
Ueber	gang	nm	passage, going over, transition; change, transfer, crossing
Um	gang	nm	convolution, rotation; acquaintance; relations with, association
um	gäng	lich	sociable, companionable, jolly
Um	gäng	lich keit	sociableness, affability
Unter	gang	nm	setting, decline, fall; sunset; destruction, extinction
ver	gang	en a	past, last, bygone; faded, withered
Ver	gang	en heit	past, background; past tense
ver	gäng	lich	transitory, fleeting; perishable
Ver	gäng	lich keit	transitoriness; perishableness
Vor	gang	nm	occurrence, event, incident; phenomenon; process, procedure
Vor	gäng	er	predecessor
Weg	gang	nm	going away, departure
Zu	gang	nm	access, approach, entry, entrance; increase
zu	gäng	lich	accessible, available, affable; approachable, open
Neben ein	gang	nm	side entrance
un um	gäng	lich	indispensable, imperative
un ver	gäng	lich	imperishable, immortal
un zu	gäng	lich	inaccessible, reserved
Spazier	gang	nm	stroll, walk; promenade

	gar	a	well-done; dressed leather; refined steel
	gar	av	quite, entirely, very; even
	Gar	e	mellowness, friable condition of soil
	gär	en	ferment; effervesce
	Gär	ung	fermentation
ober	gär	ig	top-fermenting
ver	gär	en	ferment
so	gar		even

	Gas	nn	gas
	gas en	s	develop gas
	gas förm	ig	gaseous
Ab	gas	nn	waste gas
ent	gas	en	remove gas; remove air; decontaminate
Ent	gas	ung	degassing
ver	gas	en	gasify; vaporize, gas, carburate
Ver	gas	er	carburetor
Ver	gas	ung	gasification; carburetion; gassing
Voll	gas	nn	full throttle

	geb en	give; hand over to, present, bestow, confer
	Geb er	giver, donor
ab	geb en	give up, hand over; deposit; resign; sell
sich ab	geb en	associate with
an	geb en	declare, specify, inform; suggest; pretend
An	geb er	author, informer, denouncer; braggart
An	geb erei	denunciation

an geb lich		pretended, supposed, alleged, nominally
auf geb en		commission, order; assign; give up, surrender
aus geb en		give out, distribute, issue; spend
sich be geb en		go, set out for, proceed to; happen, occur
Be geb en heit		occurrence, happening, accident, affair, event
Be geb ung		negotiation of a bill; issue
bei geb en		add, attach
'durch geb en		transmit
ein geb en		give, present; hand in, deliver; inspire
Ein geb ung		inspiration; suggestion
er geb en		yield, produce; prove, show; amount to
er geb en	a	devoted, attached to; humble, obedient; addicted to
sich er geb en		surrender to; be attached to; devote o.s. to; result from
Er geb en heit		devotion, attachment; submission, resignation
Er geb nis		result, issue, yield, output; outcome, consequence
er geb nis los		without result, futile
Er geb ung		surrender, resignation, submission
ge geb en en falls	av	in that case, if need be, if necessary
Ge geb en heit		reality; given fact, factor
her geb en		deliver, let have, hand over, give up
hin geb en		give away, abandon, give up, sacrifice
los geb en		release, set free
mit geb en		give along with, bestow upon
nach geb en		give in, yield to, give way; decline; indulge s.o.
über 'geb en		deliver up, hand over, offer, present; transfer
sich über 'geb en		vomit, throw up
um 'geb en		surround; put around
Um geb ung		surroundings, neighborhood, society, background, environment
unter 'geb en		subject, inferior, under a person's control
Unter geb ene		subordinate
ver geb en		give away; commission, confer; forgive; bestow on
ver geb ens	av	in vain, vainly
ver geb lich		idle, futile, fruitless, vain
Ver geb lich keit		uselessness
Ver geb ung		pardon, forgiveness; giving, placing; conferring
vor geb en		give an advantage to; allege, pretend
vor geb lich		pretended, so-called, ostensible
weiter geb en		pass on, forward; retransmit, relay
zu geb en		add; allow; confess, admit; recognize
zurück geb en		give back, return, restore
zusammen geb en		join in wedlock, marry
dar an geb en		give up
her aus geb en		give up, give back; edit, publish
Her aus geb er		editor, publisher
sich zurück be geb en		return, go back
Zwischen er geb nis		provisional result
da hin geb en		abandon, sacrifice
her um geb en		hand around; pass; deal

Mit her aus	geb er		co-editor
sich hin auf			
be	geb en		go up
acht	geb en		pay attention to; look out, be careful

	gegen	p	towards; against; opposed to; in the face of; about, nearly
	Gegen d	nf	region, country; district, area; locality; quarter
	gegen wärt ig		present
	Geg n er		opponent, adversary, antagonist; enemy, foe; rival, competitor
	geg n er isch		of the enemy, hostile
	Geg n er schaft		opposition; antagonism, hostility, rivalry
da	gegen	c	on the contrary, but then; whereas, while
da	gegen	av	against it, against that
ent	gegen	av	in opposition to, contrary to; in the face of; against
ent	gegen	p	towards, against
hin	gegen	c	however, on the contrary; on the other hand, whereas
zu	gegen	a	present
Um	gegen d	nf s	environs
be	geg n en		meet s.o.; run into; happen upon; encounter; happen to
Be	geg n ung		meeting, encounter
ent	geg n en		reply, return; retort
Ent	geg n ung		reply; retort, repartee

	geh en		go
	Geh en	nn	going, walking
	Geh er		walker
ab	geh en		go away; start; branch off; resign, leave
an	geh en		begin, open; catch fire
an	geh end		commencing, beginning, incipient, future
auf	geh en		rise; break up; come up; open
aus	geh en		go out, come to an end; fall out; run short
be	geh en		walk on, traverse, pace off, tread; commit
Be	geh ung		traversing; inspection; celebration; commission, perpetration
'durch	geh en		walk, go, pass through, cross; pierce
durch	geh ens av s		generally, throughout
ein	geh en		go in, enter, arrive; shrink, die; stop, decay
ein	geh end		detailed, thorough, exhaustive; exact
ent	geh en		escape, avoid; get off; elude
Er	geh en	nn	state of health, condition; luck; way of living
er	geh en		be published; be passed; come out, issue
sich er	geh en		submit to, endure; take, stand for, take a walk
fort	geh en		go away, withdraw; continue, advance
her	geh en		go here, walk along, proceed; fall upon, go on; happen
hin	geh en		go to, go there; pass away
hinter	geh en	s	deceive, fool, cheat; impose

los geh en			come off, loosen; go off, begin, start
mit geh en			accompany, go along
nach geh en			follow; attend to; pursue; investigate; be slow
nieder geh en			go down, set; fall
über 'geh en			leave out, omit; pass over, overlook
'über geh en			pass over, cross; go over, change into; overflow
'um geh en			go a round-about way, by-pass; circulate
um 'geh en			go around, outflank, evade, circumvent, by-pass
um geh end			by return mail; immediately
Um geh ung			circuit, flank-movement, detouring, by-passing, evasion
'unter geh en			sink, founder, perish; set
Ver geh en	nn		fault, trespass, sin, offence, crime, misdemeanor
ver geh en			pass, elapse; wear away; disappear, fade
sich ver geh en			commit an offence, offend, injure s.o., assault
vor geh en			advance, go before, go forward, occur
weit geh end	a		far-reaching, extensive, wholesale, sweeping
weiter geh en			go on, continue, walk on
zer geh en			dissolve, melt; dwindle
zu geh en			go on; shut; happen, take place
zurück geh en			go back, fall back; originate in; subside
zusammen geh en			go together, close; match; diminish, shrink
dar an geh en			set to work
her an geh en			go near, go up to, approach
vor an geh en			go on ahead, take the lead, precede
hin auf geh en			go up, go upstairs; rise
her aus geh en			go out of, vanish, come out
hin aus geh en			go out, leave; surpass, exceed; result in
vor aus geh en			go before, precede, walk in front, lead the way
vor bei geh en			pass by, go past, walk along; cease, stop
hin durch geh en			pass through, transit
hin ein geh en			go in; hold, contain, accommodate
ent gegen geh en			go to meet; face, encounter
ein her geh en			walk along
um 'her geh en			walk around
vor her geh en			precede s.o.
da hin geh en			walk along, pass
da hin geh end	av		to the effect that
da neben geh en			miscarry, go amiss
hin über geh en			go over, cross
vor über geh en			pass, pass over, pass by; neglect; stop
her um geh en	s		walk around, walk here and there
her unter geh en			decline, fall; drop, descend
hin unter geh en			go down, walk down, step down
da von geh en			go off
her vor geh en			go forth, come off; arise, result from
hin weg geh en			go away
aus ein ander geh en			part, break up; differ, be divided
spazier en geh en			go for a walk, take a walk
zu grund e geh en			go to ruin, perish

	Geld nn	money; coin; capital; currency
	geld lich	pecuniary, financial, monetary
An	geld nn	earnest money
Auf	geld nn	premium, agio

	gelt en	be worth
	Gelt ung	worth, value; validity
ab	gelt en	meet; discharge, compensate
Ent	gelt nn	equivalent; consideration, remuneration, compensation; reward
ent	gelt en	atone for, pay for
ent	gelt lich i	against payment
ver	gelt en	repay, requite, return; reward; retaliate, pay back
Ver	gelt ung	requital, return; reward
un ent	gelt lich	gratuitous, free, gratis

	gieb: siehe geb	
aus	gieb ig	extensive; substantial; ample, through, comprehensive; abundant
Aus	gieb ig keit	extensiveness, substantiality, ampleness; thoroughness; abundance
er	gieb ig	economical, profitable, productive, rich; abundant, plentiful
Er	gieb ig keit	yield, productivity; richness; profitableness, usefulness
nach	gieb ig	yielding, unresisting; soft, flexible, pliable, acquiescent
Nach	gieb ig keit	yieldingness, softness; flexibility, pliability, acquiescence
un er	gieb ig	unproductive, poor; unprofitable; sterile
Un er	gieb ig keit	unproductiveness, poorness, unprofitableness; barrenness
un nach	gieb ig	unyielding, unbending, inflexible, rigid; stubborn, adamant
Un nach	gieb ig keit	unyieldingness, unbendingness, inflexibility; rigidity, stubbornness

	giess en	pour
	Giess er	caster; founder, molder
	Giess erei	foundry; casting, molding
ab	giess en	pour off; decant; spray a toxic agent; cast
auf	giess en	pour; infuse; make
aus	giess en	pour out; empty; spill; fill up
Aus	giess ung	pouring-out; effusion
be	giess en	water, sprinkle; pour over; baste meat; wet s.t.
'durch	giess en	pour through; filter, strain
ein	giess en	pour into, infuse; pour out; cast in
er	giess en	pour out, gush forth
sich er	giess en	pour into s.t., flow into s.t.; flood s.t., pour over
nach	giess en	fill up, refill; add
über	'giess en	pour over; spill
'über	giess en	pour over; spill

'um	giess en	decant; refound, recast
ver	giess en	shed blood; spill, cast
'voll	giess en	fill up
zu	giess en	add, pour on; fill up
her unter	giess en	pour down; down a beer
hin unter	giess en	pour down; gulp down a drink

	Gift	nn	poison
	gift ig		poisonous, venomous
	Gift ig keit		poisonousness, virulence
ent	gift en		detoxicate; decontaminate; clear the atmosphere
Ent	gift ung		detoxification
Gegen	gift	nn	antidote
Mit	gift	nf	marriage portion, dowry
ver	gift en		poison; contaminate
Ver	gift ung		poisoning

	Glanz	nm	brightness; lustre
	glänz en		glance, gleam, shine; glitter, glisten, scintillate
	glänz end	a	bright, lustrous, brilliant, gleaming, radiant, shiny
	glanz los		dull, mat, dim, without lustre
	glanz voll		splendid, brilliant, resplendent, magnificent, glorious
Ab	glanz	nm	reflection; reflected glory, reflected splendor
er	glänz en		shine forth; gleam, sparkle

	Glas	nn	glass; tumbler; eyeglasses
	glas art ig		vitreous, glasslike
	Gläs chen		little glass, small glass
	Glas er		glazier
	Glas erei		glazier's work shop
	gläs er n	a	glass, glassy, vitreous
	glas ier en		glaze, gloss; varnish, enamel
	glas ig		glassy, vitreous; glazed
	Glas ur	nf	glazing, glaze, gloss
	glas weise	av	in glasses, by glassfuls
Fern	glas	nn	binocular
über	'glas en		glaze
ver	glas en		glaze, vitrify; glass in a room

	Glaub e	nm	faith, belief; creed; religious belief, religion
	glaub en		believe; give credence to; believe, think, suppose
	glaub haft		credible; authentic
	gläub ig	a	believing, faithful; pious, devout
	Gläub ig e		creditor, guarantor; mortgagee; follower, believer
	Gläub ig keit		full belief, full confidence
	glaub lich		credible, believable; likely
	glaub würd ig		credible; authentic, reliable; trustworthy
	Glaub würd ig keit		credibility; authenticity; reliability; trustworthiness
Un	glaub e		unbelief
un	gläub ig		incredulous, disbelieving; unbelieving
un	glaub lich		incredible, unbelievable

be glaub ig en		confirm, corroborate; attest, certify, verify; notarize
Be glaub ig ung		attestation, certification; legalization, authentication

---

gleich a		like, same; identical, equal; even, level
gleich art ig		of the same kind, homogeneous; similar, analogous
Gleich art ig keit		homogeneousness, homgeneity; similarity; uniformity
gleich en		equal, be equal to; be similar to, resemble; be like
gleich er mass en	av	in like manner, likewise
gleich er weise	av	in like manner, likewise
gleich fall s	av	also, likewise, as well, too, in the same way
Gleich heit		equality; sameness, identity
gleich mäss ig		proportionate, symmetrical; even, equable; uniform, regular
Gleich mäss ig keit		evenness, equableness; uniformity, regularity, continuity
Gleich nis	nn	image
Gleich nis haft		allegorical, parabolical; symbolic
gleich sam	av	as it were, so to speak, almost
gleich seit ig		equilateral
Gleich ung		equation
gleich wert ig		equivalent to, of the same value
Gleich wert ig keit		equivalence
ab gleich en		equalize, adjust, balance; level; match, align
an gleich en		assimilate to; adapt, adjust, approximate to
An gleich ung		assimilation; approximation
Aus gleich	nm	agreement, settlement, arrangement; balance; compensation
aus gleich en		make even; equalize; make up for, compensate; balance, adjust
Aus gleich ung		leveling, settlement; compensation; liquidation; balance
be gleich en		balance, pay, settle
Be gleich ung		settlement, payment
ob gleich	c	although, though
un gleich	a	unequal, different; uneven; unlike; varying; odd
Un gleich heit		inequality, irregularity; diversion, variation
Ver gleich	nm	comparison, simile; arrangement; compromise
ver gleich bar		comparable
ver gleich en		compare; liken to; check; collate texts; adjust, settle
Ver gleich ung		comparison, simile
zu gleich	av	at the same time; together
un ver gleich lich		incomparable, peerless, unrivaled; unique
so gleich		right away, at once, immediately

---

gleit: siehe leit	
ab gleit en	glide off, slip off, glance off; lapse into trivialities; stray

aus gleit en	slip, slide
be gleit en	accompany s.o.; attend s.o. as a servant; escort s.o.
Be gleit er	companion; attendant; escort; musical accompanist
Be gleit erin	lady companion, chaperone; escort; musical accompanist
ent gleit en	slip from one's hands, grow away from s.o., drift away from s.o.
her ab gleit en	slide down, slip off; glide down
hin be gleit en	accompany s.o. there
zurück be gleit en	accompany s.o. back, escort s.o. back
hin auf be gleit en	accompany s.o. up there, show s.o. up there
hin aus be gleit en	see s.o. out, see s.o. to the door, accompany s.o. outside
hin unter be gleit en	accompany s.o. downstairs, see s.o. downstairs

glich: siehe gleich	
un be glich en a	outstanding, unsettled, unpaid, due
aus ge glich en a	well-balanced, balanced; poised; steady, equable; harmonious
Aus ge glich en heit	balance, poise, equableness
un aus ge glich en a	unstable; moody, of uneven temper; unbalanced, unharmonious
Un aus ge glich en heit	emotional instability; moodiness, uneven temper, imbalance

Glied nn	limb, member; joint
glied er n	articulate, joint; arrange, dispose; organize
Glied er ung	articulation; segmentation; arrangement, pattern; structure
Mit glied nn	member
Zwischen glied nn	connecting link
an glied er n	link up with, join; affiliate with, incorporate in
An glied er ung	affiliation, incorporation; annexation
auf glied er n	split up, subdivide, break down; analyze; specify, itemize
Auf glied er ung	subdivision, breakdown; analysis; structure
ein glied er n	incorporate, integrate; classify into, assign to; enroll
Ein glied er ung	integration, incorporation, annexation; enrollment
Rück glied er ung	re-incorporation
zer glied er n	dismember; dissect; analyze
Zer glied er ung	dismemberment; dissection; analysis

Glück nn	fortune; luck, chance, stroke of luck; happiness, success
glück en	succeed, be successful, come off well
glück lich	fortunate; happy, blissful; lucky; prosperous, auspicious
glück lich er weise av	luckily, fortunately, happily, mercifully, by a lucky chance
be glück en	make happy; fill with happiness, delight; bless

miss glück en	fail, not succeed, miscarry
über glück lich	extremely happy, overjoyed
Un glück nn	misfortune, disaster, accident; misery
un glück lich	unfortunate; unhappy; unlucky, ill-fated; wretched, miserable
ver un glück en	meet with an accident; perish; miscarry, go wrong

glüh en	glow, to be redhot; be incandescent
aus glüh en t	cease glowing, cool down
'durch glüh en	make red hot; anneal thoroughly; burn out a bulb
durch 'glüh en p	inflame, inspire
er glüh en	glow; blush, flush

Gnad e	grace; clemency; mercy
gnad en reich	gracious; merciful; charitable
gnäd ig	gracious, favorable, kind, merciful, condescending
Un gnad e	disgrace, disfavor
un gnäd ig	ungracious, unkind; ill-humored, cross
Un gnäd ig keit	ungraciousness; unkindness
be gnad ig en	pardon, reprieve; amnesty
Be gnad ig ung	pardon, reprieve, clemency

gor: siehe gar	
un ver gor en a	unfermented

goss: siehe giess	
Goss e	gutter, runnel; sewer; hopper
an ge goss en a	fit like a glove, be a perfect fit
hin ge goss en a s	lying there completely relaxed

Gott nm	God
Gott heit	deity, divinity; god, goddess; godhead
Gött in	goddess
gött lich	divine, godlike; heavenly
Gött lich keit	divinity; godliness
gott los	godless, ungodly; irreligious; impious, sinful, wicked
Gott los ig keit	ungodliness, irreligion; impiety; wickedness
gott voll s	heavenly; splendid, priceless; most funny
Ab gott nm	idol
Ab gött erei	idolatry
ab gött isch	idolatrous
ver gött er n	deify; idolize, worship, adore
Ver gött er ung	deification; idolatry, adoration

Grab nn	grave, tomb; sepulchre
grab en	spade; cut ditches; dig trenches, trench, dig for s.t.
Grab en nm	ditch
Gräb er nm	digger, ditcher
ab grab en	dig off, dig away; level; drain off a river
auf grab en	dig up

aus grab en	dig out, unearth; exume, disinter a corpse; excavate
Aus grab ung	exhumation
be grab en	bury; inter, entomb
Be gräb nis	burial, interment; funeral
ein grab en	dig into; bury, hide in the ground; engrave
sich ein grab en	burrow into; dig in, entrench o.s.
'um grab en	dig up, turn up a field; break up soil
unter 'grab en	sap, undermine; corrupt
ver grab en	hide in the ground, bury s.t.

grad ig: siehe rad 1	
be grad ig en	straighten a street, straighten a line; align s.t.
Be grad ig ung	straightening, regulation, correction, alignment

greif bar	available, ready, on hand; tangible, palpable; obvious
greif en	seize, grasp, catch hold of; touch; put one's hand into
Greif er	claw, grab; excavator; gripper, lug; bloodhound
ab greif en	wear a book at edges; plot map; wear out by constant handling
an greif bar	assailable, open to attack, vulnerable
an greif en	handle, take hold of; attach, assault; weaken, exhaust; set about
An greif er	attacker, assailant
auf greif en	seize, pick up
aus greif en	step out
be greif en	feel, touch, handle; understand, comprehend
be greif lich	comprehensible, conceivable, understandable, natural
'durch greif en	put one's hand through; proceed without ceremony
ein greif en	engage; gear into, mesh; take action, step in; intervene
er greif en	seize, grasp, grip; pick up; apprehend, arrest, avail o.s. of
Er greif ung	seizure, capture
'über greif en	overlap, encroach on, infringe
sich ver greif en	mistake, touch by mistake
vor greif en	anticipate, forestall
zu greif en	make a grab; grasp s.t.; help o.s.; fall to s.o.
zurück greif en	fall back upon reserves; go back to s.t.
un an greif bar	unassailable
her aus greif en	pick out; select, choose; cite examples
ein be greif en	include, contain, comprise
un be greif lich	inconceivable, incomprehensible
'wieder er greif en	reseize, recapture
Wieder er greif ung	reseizure
in ein ander greif en	work into each other; gear, mesh; cooperate

Grenz e	boundary; frontier, border; extremity; edge, verge

grenz en	border on, touch; be bounded by
grenz en los	boundless, unlimited; infinite; immense
Grenz en los ig keit	boundlessness, immensity
ab grenz en	mark off, delimit; demarcate, differentiate, define
Ab grenz ung	demarcation, delimitation; definition
an grenz en	border on s.t., adjoin s.t.
be grenz en	mark off, delimit; bound, border; limit, determine, define
Be grenz t heit	limitation
Be grenz ung	bounds, limit, limitation
un be grenz t	unlimited, boundless
Un be grenz t heit	boundlessness
an ein ander grenz en	be adjacent, border on each other

griff: siehe greif	
Griff nm	grip, grasp, hold; snatch, clutch; hold, handhold
Griff el	style; slate; pencil; pistil
griff ig	granular; handy, wieldy; gripping well, non-skid
An griff nm	attack, aggression, assault; undertaking
Be griff nm	idea, notion; understanding, perception, term
be griff lich	abstract; notional, theoretical; conceivable
Ein griff nm t	operation; manipulation; gearing
er griff en a	struck, seized with, moved, touched, affected
Er griff en heit	emotion, shock
Miss griff nm	mistake, blunder; break
Rück griff nm l	recourse
Ueber griff nm	encroachment, infringement, inroad
Unter griff nm t	undersnatch, single flange
ver griff en a	bought up, out of stock, out of print, exhausted
Vor griff	anticipation
Zu griff nm	grip, clutch
Gegen an griff nm	counterattack
ein be griff en a	included, inclusive
In be griff nm	substance, essence, embodiment; contents
in be griff en a	included, inclusive of; implied
Ober be griff nm	superimposed concept
ab ge griff en a	well-thumbed, worn
an ge griff en a	affected, attacked, corroded; exhausted

gross a	great; large, big; bulky, voluminous; spacious; vast, extensive
gross art ig	great, grand; lofty, sublime; excellent, wonderful
Gross art ig keit	grandeur; loftiness; magnificence, splendor
Gröss e	size, largeness; height; tallness; stature; dimensions
über gross a	outsized, oversized; immense, huge, colossal
ver gröss er n	enlarge, extend, increase, augment, expand
sich ver gröss er n	enlarge; magnify; expand, widen; increase, add to; aggravate
Ver gröss er ung	enlargement

Grund nm	ground; soil

	gründ en		found, establish; institute, set up, organize
	Gründ er		founder; creator, originator
	gründ lich		thorough; careful, solid; exhaustive; complete; profound
	Gründ ling		groundling, gudgeon fish
	grund los		bottomless, unfathomable
	Grund los ig keit		groundlessness
	Gründ ung		foundation, creation
Ab	grund	nm	abyss: precipice
ab	gründ ig		abysmal
be	gründ en		establish, found, constitute; give reasons for, prove, motivate
Be	gründ er		founder, initiator, originator
Be	gründ ung		foundation, establishment; initiation; argument, substantiation
er	gründ en		fathom; penetrate, get to the bottom of; explore, probe
Gegen	grund	nm	counterargument, argument against
Hinter	grund	nm	background; rear
hinter	gründ ig		enigmatical, cryptic, profound; subtle, sly
Unter	grund	nm	underground
Vorder	grund	nm	foreground
zu	grund e	av	perish, go to ruin; take s.t. as a basis, form the basis of s.t.
un be	gründ et		unfounded, unbased, groundless
un er	gründ lich		unfathomable, bottomless; inscrutable
Un er	gründ lich keit		unfathomability, bottomlessness

	Grupp e		group, cluster
	grupp en weise	av	in groups
	grupp ier en		group, arrange in groups, range
	Grupp ier ung		grouping, arrangement in groups
Unter	grupp e		sub-group
'um	grupp ier en		regroup; reshuffle
Um	grupp ier ung		regrouping; reshuffling

	Gruss	nm	salutation, greeting; bow
	grüss en		greet
be	grüss en		greet, salute, receive; welcome, hail
Be	grüss ung		greeting, salutation, welcome
'wieder	grüss en		return a bow, return a salute

	guck en		peep, peek, peer; stare, gaze, look at
ab	guck en		learn s.t. by watching s.o.; copy s.t. from s.o.
an	guck en		look at, peek at
Aus	guck	nm	lookout
zu	guck en	s	watch s.o. doing s.t., look on
her aus	guck en		peek out

	Gunst	nf	favor; kindness; partiality, patronage; favorableness
	günst ig		favorable; auspicious; opportune, encouraging, beneficial

	Günst	ling	favorite
Miss	gunst	nf	ill-will; envy, jealousy
miss	günst	ig	envious, jealous; unfriendly, spiteful
Un	gunst	nf	disfavor; ill-will
un	günst	ig	unfavorable; disadvantageous, adverse, untoward
zu	gunst	en p	in favor of, for the benefit of; to the credit of
zu un	gunst	en p	to the disadvantage of
be	günst	ig en	favor; promote, foster, encourage; benefit; patronize; prefer
Be	günst	ig ung	promotion, encouragement; preference, patronage
Ver	günst	ig ung	privilege, favor; benefit, allowance

	guss:	siehe giess	
	Guss	nm	gush, jet; shower, heavy shower, downpour, icing, frosting
Ab	guss	nm	cast, casting, molding; pouring; decanting, decantation
An	guss	nm	metal lug; break of a letter in printing
Auf	guss	nm	infusion; cast-on mount
Aus	guss	nm	kitchen sink; drain, outlet; nozzle; lining; spout, beak
Ein	guss	nm	sprue, feeder; downgate, ingate; grouting
Er	guss	nm	discharge, flood, torrent; outburst, effusion, gush

	gut	a	good; kind; capable, efficient; favorable; advantageous
	Gut	nn	treasure; property, possession, goods; estate, farm
	gut art	ig	good-natured, harmless
	Gut art	ig keit	good nature; harmlessness
	Güt	e	goodness, kindness; generosity; charitableness; excellence
	güt	ig	good, kind, kindly; benevolent; indulgent
	güt	lich	amicable, friendly
un	gut	a	have misgivings about s.t.; ominous; strained
ver	güt	en	reimburse, refund; idemnify; compensate for; improve, refine
Ver	güt	ung	compensation, allowance; reimbursement
zu	gut	e av	make allowances for s.t.; be of benefit to s.o.; give s.t. to s.o.
rück ver	güt	en	refund, reimburse, repay
Rück ver	güt	ung	refund, reimbursement, repayment
be	güt	er t	rich, wealthy, well-to-do; propertied
be	güt	ig en	soothe, calm, appease, placate

	Haar	nn	hair
	haar	en	lose one's hair
	haar	ig	hairy, hirsute
	haar	los	hairless; bald
	Haar los	ig keit	hairlessness, lack of hair, baldness
ent	haar	en	remove hair; depilate
wider	haar	ig	cross-grained, refractory
un be	haar	t	hairless, bald; smooth

	Hab e		property; personal belongings, effects, goods
	hab en		have; possess, be in possession of, own, hold
	Hab en	nn	credit side of ledger, item of credit
	hab haft	av	get hold of, secure; catch, seize
ab	hab en	s	have a share of, want a bit of s.t.
an	hab en		have clothes on; wear, be dressed in
auf	hab en		have on, wear; have the door open; have homework to do
be	häb ig		sedate; phlegmatic, comfort-loving; portly
Be	häb ig keit		portliness; sedateness
er	hab en	a	raised, elevated
Er	hab en heit		elevation
Ge	hab e nn	a	behavior, affectation, mannerism
Ge	hab en	nn	behavior, conduct
sich ge	hab en	a	behave
her	hab en	s	have gotten s.t. from
In	hab er		possessor
In	hab erin		possessor
inne	hab en		hold, possess; fill; hold a record; occupy a town
'über	hab en	s	have coat on; have s.t. left over
'um	hab en	s	have on
vor	hab en	a	have on; intend, mean, propose, plan; be busy with
Vor	hab en	nn	intention, purpose
weg	hab en	s	have received one's share
'wieder	hab en		have back, have again
her aus	hab en	s	have solved; know s.t.; understand thoroughly
vor aus	hab en		have the advantage of s.t. over s.o.
Mit in	hab er		co-owner

	Hack e		hoe, mattock; pick axe
	hack en		hack, hoe; chop, cut, cleave; mince; peck, hack
	Häck er ling		chaff, chopped straw
	Häck sel	nm	chaff, chopped straw
ab	hack en		chop off, cut off; chop words
auf	hack en		hoe up; cut open
aus	hack en		hew out; grub up, hoe up
Ge	hack tes	nn	chopped meat, mincemeat
'um	hack en		hoe up; cut down, fell a tree
zer	hack en		hack to pieces, cut into pieces; mince, chop; slash
her um	hack en	s	find fault with s.o., carp at s.o.

	Hafen	nm	port; harbor; haven
Aussen	hafen	nm	outer harbor
Vor	hafen	nm	outer harbor
Flug	hafen	nm	airport

	Häk chen		hooklet, crochet
	Hak en	nm	hook; peg; clasp, hasp
	hak en		hook
	Häk elei		crochet work
	häk el n		crochet

	hak ig	hooked
ab	hak en	unhook; tick off, check off
an	hak en	hook on, hitch on
auf	hak en	unhook, undo
aus	hak en	unhook
ein	hak en	hook into, fasten
sich ein	hak en	link arms, take one's arm
Wider	hak en nn	barbed hook; barb
zu	hak en	hook up

	halb a	half; by halves, half
	halb fert ig	half-done
	halb ier en	halve, cut in half, divide into halves
	Halb ier ung	halving
	Halb heit	incompleteness, imperfection; half-measure
	halb voll	half-full
	halb weg s av	half-way, midway; tolerable, middling; to a certain extent

ausser	halb p	out of, outside; beyond
inner	halb p	within, inside of
ober	halb p	above
unter	halb p	below, underneath
ausser	halb av	outside, outside of; out of town
wes	halb av	why

	half: siehe halb	
	Hälf te nf	half

	halt imp	stop, halt, don't move, don't go
	halt av	just, you know, to be sure
	Halt nm	hold, foothold; pause; support, mainstay; steadiness, firmness
	halt bar	durable, lasting, permanent; stable, strong; solid, imperishable
	Halt bar keit	durability, stability; service; rugged design
	halt en	hold, keep; take in; support, maintain; stop, halt; endure
	Halt er	holder, legal owner; user; support, clip, bracket, rack
	halt ig	containing
	halt los	without support, untenable, unfounded, baseless; unstable
	Halt los ig keit	instability, unsteadiness; laxity, untenableness
	Halt ung	bearing, carriage; attitude, posture; position, stance, style
ab	halt en	keep off, hold, hold out; hinder, restrain
Ab	halt ung	hindrance, prevention; holding
An	halt nm	support, hold, prop; indication; protection; fact
an	halt en	stop, arrest; accustom; continue; discontinue
auf	halt en	keep open, hold open; stop, check; delay
sich auf	halt en	stay, stop; reside

aus halt en	endure, suffer, stand, bear; last, persevere
be halt en	keep; retain, remember
Be hält er	holder, receptacle, box, bin, case, container; vessel, trough, tank
'durch halt en	hold out; see s.t. through
Ein halt nm	stop, check
ein halt en	stop, check, cease; observe, adhere to
ent halt en	contain, hold, comprise; include, embody
sich ent halt en	refrain from, abstain from, forbear
ent halt sam	abstinent, moderate, frugal, temperate, continent
Ent halt sam keit	abstinence, moderation, continence, temperance
Ent halt ung	abstention, forbearance, abstinence
er halt en	receive, get; save; maintain, support
Er halt er	preserver, maintainer, supporter
er hält lich	obtainable, available, procurable
Er halt ung	preservation, maintenance, upkeep
fern halt en	keep s.o. at a distance
Ge halt nm	contents; value, merit; proportion; strength; capacity
Ge halt nn	salary, emoluments, pay
ge halt en pp	bound, obliged
ge halt los	empty, worthless
Ge halt los ig keit	emptiness
ge halt voll	solid, rich, of great value; substantial, nutritious
her halt en	hold forth, tender; suffer; pay
hin halt en	hold out; tender money
Hinter halt nm	ambush, trap
hinter hält ig	reserved, underhand, insidious, sly, malicious
In halt nm	contents, capacity; space, volume; meaning, substance; summary
in halt lich	in substance, in its contents
in halt s los	meaningless, empty
in halt s voll	significant, important, momentous, weighty
inne halt en	keep to; stop, pause
mit halt en s	take part in; hold jointly with
nach halt ig	lasting, enduring, protracted, permanent; persistent
nieder halt en	supress, keep down; immobilize, pin down
Rück halt nm	support, stay, reserve
rück halt los	unreserved, frank, openly, plainly
un halt bar	untenable; not durable, frivolous
Unter halt nm	support, subsistence; livelihood, maintenance, upkeep
'unter halt en	hold under
unter 'halt en	maintain; amuse, enjoy, entertain; feed
unter halt sam	amusing, entertaining
Unter halt ung	amusement, entertainment; conversation; upkeep, support
ver halt en	keep back, stop, hold in, supress, restrain
Ver halt en nn t	behaviour, conduct, attitude
sich ver halt en	behave, act, conduct o.s.
Ver hält nis	relation, proportion, rate, ratio; situation, condition

Vor halt nm t	deflection in marksmanship; suspension in music
vor halt en	hold before; reproach, rebuke; last, hold out
Vor halt ung	remonstrance, reproach
zu halt en	close, keep closed
Zu hält er	souteneur, procurer
Zu hält erei	pandering
zurück halt en	hold back, keep back, retain; inhibit; detain
Zurück halt ung	reserve, modesty, discretion, restraint, holding back
Zusammen halt nm	holding together, consistence, union, unity, agreement
zusammen halt en	hold together; compare; collate; confront; stick together
sich dar an halt en s	stick to s.t.
un auf halt bar	irresistible, incessant, continual, impetuous
un auf halt sam	irresistible, incessant, continual, impetuous
an be halt en	keep on
auf be halt en	keep on, keep open
bei be halt en	keep up; retain; maintain
Bei be halt ung	retention
ein be halt en	keep back, withhold, detain; stop
übrig be halt en	keep; spare
'um be halt en s	keep on
Vor be halt nm	reservation, reserve, proviso
vor be halt en	reserve
vor be halt lich	with the reservation of, on condition that, subject to
vor be halt los	unconditional
zurück be halt en	keep back, retain
Auf ent halt nm	stay, residence, seat, domicile; stop
vor ent halt en	keep back, withhold from s.o.
Vor ent halt ung	withholding, detention
'wieder er halt en	retrieve, recover
da für halt en	be of opinion, think
un ge halt en a	angry, indifferent; unfulfilled
da gegen halt en	oppose to; compare with, contrast
ent gegen halt en	contrast with; object
Miss ver hält nis	disproportion, incongruity
aus ein ander halt en	keep apart, distinguish
gegen ein ander halt en	compare together
fest halt en	hold s.t. tight; detain s.o.
sich fest halt en	hold on tight to, cling to
Haus halt nm	household, housekeeping; budget

Hand nf	hand; handwriting
Hand fert ig keit	manual skill, dexterity
hand lich	handy, wieldy; manageable, easy-to-use; compact
Hand lich keit	handiness, manageableness
ab hand en av	go astray, be mislaid
Hinter hand nf	hind quarter

Ober hand nf	back of the hand
Rück hand nf	tennis backhand
un hand lich	unwieldy; clumsy, bulky
Vor hand nf t	lead in cards; forehand in tennis; first option in business
vor hand en a	present, at hand; available, on hand, in stock; existing
Vorder hand nf t	forehand
aus händ ig en	hand s.t. over; deliver up, surrender
Aus händ ig ung	surrender, delivery, handing over
ein händ ig en	hand over to, deliver to
aller hand av	all kinds of; quite a thing, something

Handel nm	trade, trading in; commerce
handel n	act; proceed; take action
Händ l er	trader, dealer, merchant; storekeeper; vendor
Hand l ung	act, action, deed; plot of story; religious rite; store
hand l ung s fäh ig	capable of acting; capable of incurring liabilities
ab handel n	get s.t. out of s.o. by bargaining; treat a subject thoroughly
aus handel n	bargain for; negotiate, settle
Aussen handel nm	foreign trade
be handel n	treat, deal with; handle, manage; manipulate; process
ein handel n	purchase, buy; trade in, barter; get, obtain; chisel out
er handel n	get by bargaining; buy, purchase
miss handel n	ill-treat, maltreat, abuse, brutalize; maul, manhandle
unter 'handel n	negotiate, treat; hold a parley
ver handel n	negotiate, treat; parley, deliberate, confer; try in court
Zwischen handel nm	intermediate trade, commission business; wholesale trade
vor be handel n	pre-treat
ent gegen handel n	act against
zu wider handel n	act contrary to, counteract; contravene, violate, offend against
Zu wider handel nde	offender, trespasser
Ab hand l ung	treatise, essay; dissertation, article, paper
Be hand l ung	treatment
Miss hand l ung	ill-treatment, maltreatment, cruelty
Neben hand l ung	underplot, episode
Unter händ l er	negotiator
Unter hand l ung	negotiation
Ver hand l ung	negotiation, discussion, deliberation; conference, talks
Zwischen händ l er	middleman, intermediary, commission agent
Nach be hand l ung t	after-treatment, subsequent treatment
Vor be hand l ung	preliminary treatment
Zu wider hand l ung	contravention, violation, offense

Hang	nm		slope, declivity, incline, hang; propensity, tendency; disposition
hang en	a		great anxiety
häng en			hang, be suspended; adhere, cling; catch, attach, fix, fasten
Ab hang	nm		slope, declivity
ab häng en			take down; detach; hang off; uncouple, disconnect
ab häng ig			inclined, dependent
Ab häng ig keit			dependence, dependency, subordination
An hang	nm		appendix, supplement; amendment; annex; followers; endorsement
an häng en			hang on, hang up; append, annex, add
an hang en			cling to; be attached to, stick to, adhere to
An häng er			adherent, follower, disciple; tie-on label
An häng er schaft			following, adherents
an häng ig			adhering, cleaving; pending
an häng lich			attached; faithful to
An häng lich keit			attachment, adherence; fidelity
An häng sel	nn		appendix, appendage; label
auf häng en			hang up; suspend
Auf häng er			hanger, suspender, suspensor
Auf häng ung			hanging, suspension
Aus hang	nm		poster, placard; notice; display, show
aus häng en			hang out; mark for sale
Be hang	nm		flounce, fringe; drapery, hangings
be häng en			hang with, drape with
Durch hang	nm		sag
ein häng en			hang in, put in; replace; restore
sich er häng en			hang o.s.
Ge häng e	nn		slope, declivity; garland, festoon
hin häng en			hang up
nach häng en			follow; give way to; be addicted to
Ueber hang	nm	a	surplus money; overhanging rock, projecting ledge
'über häng en			hang over; impend, project
Um hang	nm		wrap, cape, shawl
'um häng en			hang in another place; put on; take up
ver häng en			cover, cover over; curtain off; decree, proclaim; impose
Ver häng nis			fate, destiny; disaster
ver häng nis voll			fatal, fateful; disastrous
Vor hang	nm		curtain, shade, drapery
vor häng en			hang before
weg häng en			hang away
zu häng en			hang over; cover with a curtain
Zusammen hang	nm		connection, coherence; relation; consistency; association
zusammen häng en			cohere; hang together, be connected with
zusammen hang los			disconnected, incoherent; loose, disjointed
Zusammen hang los ig keit			incoherence, disconnectedness; inconsistency
un ab häng ig			independent of; self-contained
Un ab häng ig keit			independence

un zusammen häng end	incoherent, disjointed, disconnected; detached; desultory
an ein ander häng en	stick together

har: siehe haar	
aus här en	remove hair, depilate

harr en	wait for, await; hope for; tarry, stay
aus harr en	persevere; hold out, endure to the end
be harr en	persevere, continue; stand firm, persist
be harr lich	persevering, persistent, unwavering; constant, steady, stubborn
Be harr ung	perseverance, persistence, patience, determination
ver harr en	persevere, hold out; persist in, abide by, stick to

hart a		hard; firm, solid
Härt e		hardness
härt en		harden; grow hard
Hart ung	nm	January
Härt ung		hardening
ab härt en		harden against, toughen up against, inure to
Ab härt ung		inurment to; robustness, hardness
ent härt en		soften
er härt en		harden, set; bear out, confirm, corroborate, substantiate
Er härt ung		confirmation, substantiation, consolidation; lithification
ver härt en		harden, indurate
Ver härt ung		hardening; bitterness; scleroma, sclerosis

hau en		hew, chop; cut; strike out at, lash out at
Hau er	h	hewer, cutter
Häu er		hewer, cutter; tusk, fang
ab hau en		cut off, chop off, cut down
an hau en		accost s.o.; molest s.o.
aus hau en		clear, thin a wood; hew, chisel out, carve
be hau en		rough hew; trim, dress; square; chisel, cut stone
'durch hau en		cut through; cleave, split; cut in two; flog
sich 'durch hau en		hack one's way through
ein hau en	s	strike s.o. with one's fists; dig into one's food; carve into
hin hau en	s	do a job in a haphazard manner, knock off
sich hin hau en	s	hit the ground; turn in, go to bed
nieder hau en		cut down, fell
'um hau en		fell, cut down; bowl over
Ver hau	nm	entanglement; mess, jumble
ver hau en		thrash, flog, beat up; spank; make hash of
sich ver hau en	s	make a blunder
zer hau en		cut asunder, cut to pieces
zu hau en		rough-hew stones; slam a door; punch s.o. hard
zusammen hau en		smash to pieces, dash to pieces; beat s.o. up

un be hau en	a		unhewn, uncut; unsquared
da neben hau en			miss; miss one's guess, be very wrong
her unter hau en	s		chop s.t. off, cut a branch off

Häuf chen			small heap
häuf el n			heap, pile, hill
Hauf en	nm		accumulation, cluster, mass; stack
häuf en			heap up, pile up; accumulate
hauf en weise	av		in heaps; in crowds
häuf ig			frequent; repeated; continual; numerous; copious, abundant
Häuf ig keit			frequency
Häuf lein	p		small heap; handful of men
Häuf ung			heaping, accumulation
an häuf en			heap up, pile up, accumulate; amass money; hoard
sich an häuf en			accumulate, aggregate, accrue
An häuf ung			piling-up; accumulation, increase; aggregation
auf häuf en			heap up, pile up, accumulate, amass
Auf häuf ung			accumulation
über 'häuf en			overwhelm; swamp with; overstock, glut the market
zu hauf	av	p	together
auf ein ander häuf en			pile up, heap up

Haupt	nn	p	head
Haupt ling	nm	t	chief, leader; chieftain
be haupt en			maintain, hold
sich be haupt en			hold one's own, weather the storm, remain steady, hold firm
Be haupt ung			assertion, statement, declaration, contention, allegation
ent haupt en			behead, decapitate
Ent haupt ung			beheading, decapitation; execution
Hinter haupt	nn		back of the head, occiput
Ober haupt	nn		chief, head; party leader
über haupt	av		generally, on the whole; actually, altogether; after all

Haus	nn		house
Häus chen			small house; cottage, cabin; lodge
haus en			dwell, live, reside
haus ier en			hawk, peddle
Haus ier er			hawker, pedlar; door-to-door salesman
Häus ler			cottager
häus lich			domestic, household; economical, thrifty, sparing; domesticated
Häus lich keit			family life, domesticity, domestication
Be haus ung			housing, accommodation; lodging, dwelling
Ge häus e	nn		case, box
Hinter haus	nn		back of the house
Neben haus	nn		adjoining house

Unter	haus	nn	lower house of congress; House of Commons
zu	haus e	av	at home
Zu	haus e	nn	home
Gast	haus	nn	inn, guesthouse
Kauf	haus	nn	department store
Krank en	haus	nn	hospital
Rat	haus	nn	city hall

	Haut	nf	skin; hide
	Häut	chen	thin coating
	häut	en	strip off the skin, flay
sich	häut	en	shed one's skin
	häut	ig	skinny
	Häut	ung	skinning
ab	häut	en	skin, flay
Aussen	haut	nf	outer skin, hull plating
ent	häut	en	skin, flay
Ober	haut	nf	epidermis
Vor	haut	nf	foreskin, prepuce

	Heb el	nm	lever, handle
	heb en		lift, heave, elevate, raise, pick up; improve
sich	heb en		rise, improve, begin to thrive; neutralize
	Heb er		lever; syringe; levator
	Heb ung		lifting, raising; heaving, elevation; improvement, removal
ab	heb en		take off, lift off; remove; take out
sich ab	heb en		detach o.s., stand out against
an	heb en		lift up; begin
auf	heb en		raise, hold up, lift up, pick up; keep; cancel
Auf	heb ung		abolition, annulment, suspension, repeal, cancellation
aus	heb en		heave off; unhinge; raise, lift out
Aus	heb ung		enlistment, draft, recruiting, conscription
be	heb en		remove; repair, correct; clear away
Be	heb ung		settling, removal, adjustment, servicing
ent	heb en		relieve of, exempt from; free from, deliver from
er	heb en		heave up, lift up; raise an objection
sich er	heb en		rise, stand up, get up; arise, start up
er	heb lich		considerable, important
Er	heb lich keit		importance
Er	heb ung		elevation, promotion; rising ground, peak, point
über	'heb en		exempt from, spare, save, relieve from
sich über	'heb en		strain o.s.; be overbearing; be proud of
über	heb lich		overbearing, presumptious
Ueber	heb lich keit		arrogance, presumption
Ur	heb er		author, founder, originator, creator
Ur	heb er schaft		parentage, authorship
sich ver	heb en		hurt o.s. by lifting
sich weg	heb en	p	lift away
her aus	heb en		lift out; lay stress on; set off
sich her aus	heb en		stand out

un er heb lich	trifling, irrelevant, insignificant
her vor heb en	make prominent, feature, stress, emphasize
ab heb er n	draw wine off; siphon off a liquid
aus heb er n	siphon, siphon s.t. out
Aus heb er ung	siphonage

Heft nn	handle, haft; copy-book
heft en t	fasten, attach, fix to
an heft en	attach, fasten, affix; tack on; pin on; stitch, baste
ein heft en	sew into, stich into; file
zu heft en	stitch up
zusammen heft en	stitch together a book; tack together

heil a	unhurt, uninjured, unscathed, safe and sound
Heil nn	welfare; well-being
Heil and nm	Savior, Redeemer
heil bar	curable, healable, remediable
Heil bar keit	curability, healability
heil en	heal, cure
heil ig	holy; sacred; hallowed; saintly, godly, pious; solemn; venerable
heil ig en	hallow, sanctify
Heil ig e	saint
Heil ig keit	holiness, saintliness, sanctity, sacredness
Heil ig tum nn	sanctuary
Heil ig ung	hallowing, sanctification
heil los a	unholy
heil sam	wholesome, salutary; salubrious
Heil ung	cure, healing, successful treatment
ab heil en	heal up
an heil en	heal on, heal up
aus heil en	heal up; cure completely
Un heil nn	mischief, harm; ruin, disaster, calamity
un heil bar	incurable; irreparable
Un heil bar keit	incurability; irreparability
ver heil en	heal up
zu heil en	heal up, close, cicatrize
zusammen heil en	heal up, heal over, heal closed
ent heil ig en	profane, desecrate
Ent heil ig ung	profanation, desecration

heim av	home; homeward
Heim nn	home
Heim at nf	home, native place
heim at lich	native, home; homelike, homy, vernacular
heim at los	homeless, without a home; outcast
Heim chen	house cricket
heim el ig	homy, homelike; snug, cosy, comfortable
heim isch	native, indigenous; national, domestic
heim lich	secret; hidden, concealed; clandestine; snug, cosy
Heim lich keit	secrecy, secret; furtiveness, stealth; underhandedness

	heim wärt s	av	homeward
da	heim	av	at home; at one's house; in one's own country, back home
Da	heim	nn	home
ein	heim isch		native; indigenous; home, domestic, inland, home-made
ge	heim	a	secret; confidential, private; concealed, hidden; mysterious
Ge	heim nis		secret
ge	heim nis voll		mysterious, mystical; hidden, dark, obscure
un	heim lich	a	uncanny, weird, unearthly; sinister; tremendous, terrific
un	heim lich	av	dreadfully, awfully
Un	heim lich keit		uncanniness; weirdness
ins ge	heim	av	in secret, secretly
be	heim at et		domiciled
an	heim el n		remind s.o. of home, make s.o. feel at home
an	heim el nd		homelike, homey; cozy, snug
ver	heim lich en		hide, conceal from, suppress, hold back
Ver	heim lich ung		concealment, dissimulation, suppression
ein	heim s en		reap; pocket, rake in

	Hei-rat	nf	marriage; wedding; match
	hei-rat en		marry; wed, lead to the altar; get married
	hei-rat s fäh ig		marriageable
	Hei-rat s fäh ig keit		marriageability, marriageable age, eligibility for marriage
Ein	hei-rat	nf	marriage into
ein	hei-rat en		marry into
Miss	hei-rat	nf	unsuitable match, misalliance
ver	hei-rat en		marry, give in marriage, wed
Ver	hei-rat ung		marriage
an ge	hei-rat et		related by marriage
un ver	hei-rat et		unmarried, single
'wieder ver	hei-rat en		remarry
Wieder ver	hei-rat ung		remarriage

	heiss	a	hot; torrid
	heiss en		call, name; order; be called; signify; hoist a flag
Ge	heiss	nn	order, command, bidding
ver	heiss en		promise
Ver	heiss ung		promise
ver	heiss ung s voll		promising, auspicious

	heiz bar	heatable, heating
	heiz en	heat, fire up; make a fire
	Heiz er	stoker
	Heiz ung	heating, firing; central heating; radiator
an	heiz en	heat up
be	heiz en	heat
ein	heiz en	make a fire, light a fire; heat a stove; make it hot for s.o.

Fern heiz ung		district heating
über 'heiz en		overheat; superheat
ver heiz en		fire, use up fuel; send troops to glory
un ge heiz t		unfired; cold

helf en		help; lend a hand, give a hand; promote; be of use
Helf er		helper, assistant
Helf erin		woman assistant, helper
ab helf en		help, remedy; redress, correct; supply
auf helf en		help s.o. up
aus helf en		help out, assist; supply, fix s.o. up
Be helf	nm	expedient
sich be helf en		manage
'durch helf en		help through; see through; help out of a difficulty
fort helf en		help s.o. to get away; help s.o. on
mit helf en		assist in, help with
nach helf en		help on, assist, give s.o. a lift up
ver helf en		help s.o. to s.t., help s.o. to get his due; help s.o. find s.o.
her aus helf en		help s.o. out of
her unter helf en	s	help s.o. down

hell	a	clear, sonorous
Hell e		brightness, clearness; luminousness; transparency
Hell ig keit		brightness; luminousness; brilliancy
auf hell en		clear, brighten, light up; enlighten, throw light upon
sich auf hell en		brighten, clear up
ein hell ig		unanimous
Ein hell ig keit		unanimity
er hell en		light up; illuminate; clear up, elucidate
miss hell ig		dissonant, dissentient, disagreeing
Miss hell ig keit		discord, dissension, unpleasantness
be hell ig en		bother, molest, importune
Be hell ig ung		trouble, bother, molestation
un be hell ig t		unmolested

Hemd	nn	shirt; chemise
Ober hemd	nn	shirt, outer shirt
Unter hemd	nn	undershirt

her	av	hither, here; from; ago
da her	c	therefore, for that reason; accordingly; as a result
da her	av	from there, from that place, thence; from this, hence
fern her	av	from afar
hinter her	av	behind; after, afterwards, subsequently; with hindsight
nach her	av	after that, afterwards; then, subsequently; later on
neben her	av	by his side, by her side, beside
vor her	av	before, previously, in advance, beforehand

vor	her ig		preceding, previous, foregoing; former
weit	her	av	from afar
zwischen	her	av	meanwhile, in the meantime
wo	her		how; where from, whence

	Herr	nm	master, lord
	Herr chen		young gentleman, little master; dandy, fop
	herr en los		without a master
	Herr in		mistress, lady
	herr isch		imperious, domineering, masterful; commanding; arrogant
	herr lich		grand, magnificent; wonderful, marvellous; excellent
	Herr lich keit		magnificence, grandeur, splendor; wonderful things
	Herr schaft		domination; rule; empire; government; reign; power
	Herr schaft en	np	master and mistress, Mr. and Mrs.
	herr schaft lich		belonging to a lord, manorial, high class, elegant
	herr sch en		rule over, be in power, control, dominate, govern
	Herr sch er		ruler; monarch, sovereign
	Herr sch erin		ruler; monarch, sovereign
Ober	herr schaft		supremacy
Vor	herr schaft		predominance; superiority
ver	herr lich en		glorify, exalt
Ver	herr lich ung		glorification
an	herr sch en		address s.o. gruffly, bark at s.o.
be	herr sch en		rule over, govern; dominate, command, control; master
sich be	herr sch en		control o.s., restrain o.s., keep one's temper
Be	herr sch er		ruler, sovereign
Be	herr sch erin		ruler, sovereign
Be	herr sch ung		rule, sway, domination, control
vor	herr sch en		predominate, prevail

	Herz	nn	heart
	Herz chen		darling
	herz en		press to one's heart, embrace, hug; caress, fondle, cuddle
	herz haft		courageous, plucky; bold; hearty
	herz ig		dear, lovely, charming, sweet
	herz lich		cordial, hearty; heart-felt; affectionate, loving
	Herz lich keit		heartiness, cordiality, warmth; sincerity
	herz los		heartless, unfeeling
	Herz los ig keit		heartlessness
be	herz t		courageous, brave, determined
Be	herz t heit		courage, gameness
weit	herz ig		broad-minded
be	herz ig en		take to heart, bear in mind
barm	herz ig		compassionate, merciful

---

hieb: siehe heb

	Hieb	nm	blow, stroke; hit, cut, slash, gash; whipping, beating
An	hieb	nm	at first attempt
Aus	hieb	nm	lunge, thrust; extraction; felling, cutting; tunneling
Durch	hieb	nm	breakthrough, cutting through; thinning, culling

	hilf:	siehe helf	
	Hilf e		help; assistance; aid, cooperation; relief, rescue; support
	hilf los		helpless, defenceless, destitute; clumsy, shiftless
	Hilf los ig keit		helplessness, destitution
	hilf reich		helping; charitable, benevolent; helpful
	hilf s be dürf t ig		in need of help; needy, indigent
	hilf s be reit		helpful; helping
Ab	hilf e		remedy; remedial measures
Aus	hilf e		temporary assistance, stopgap; temporary helper
be	hilf lich		helpful, lend a hand
Ein	hilf e		aid, assistance, grant in aid; abetment in crime
Ge	hilf e	nm	assistant; helper, underling; clerk; journeyman; accomplice
Ge	hilf in		assistant, helper; underling; clerk; accomplice
Mit	hilf e		assistance, help, cooperation
Nach	hilf e		assistance, help, boost

	hin	av	there, thither; along; towards
da	hin	av	there, to that place, thither
fern	hin	av	to a great distance
fort	hin	av i	from now on, hereafter, henceforth
mit	hin	av	consequently, therefore; thus, so, then
neben	hin	av	by the side, at the side
vor	hin	av	a little while ago, just now
weiter	hin	av	further on, in the future; furthermore, moreover
dar auf	hin	av	after that, thereupon; as a result, in answer to it
wo	hin		where to, where, whither

	hinder lich		hindering, impeding; obstructive; troublesome, embarrassing
	hinder n		hinder, hamper, handicap, impede
	Hinder nis	nn	obstacle, barrier; hindrance
be	hinder n		hinder, hamper; handicap, impede; restrain, obstruct
Be	hinder ung		hindrance, handicap, impediment, obstacle
ver	hinder n		prevent; hinder, stop
Ver	hinder ung		prevention; hindrance, obstacle
un be	hinder t		unhindered, unhampered, unimpeded, free
un ge	hinder t		unhindered

	hitz:	siehe heiz	
	Hitz e		heat, hot weather
	hitz frei		high fever; heatedly, hotly, passionately
	hitz ig		high fever; hot-tempered; hasty; passionate, violent

er hitz en	heat; make hot; pasteurize; inflame; fire the imagination
sich er hitz en	get hot; become heated; be aroused; work up a rage
Er hitz ung	heating
über 'hitz en	overheat; superheat

ho: siehe hoh	
Ho heit	sublimity
ho heit s voll	majestic; dignified; imperious

hoch: siehe hoh	
hoch a	high
Hoch nn	cheer, hurrah; toast
höch lich av	highly, greatly
höch st av	highest, uppermost, topmost
höch st ens av	at the most, at best, at most
hoch wert ig	high-grade, of high quality, high-class
zu höch st av	right at the top, at the very top; extremely, highly

Hof nm	courtyard, yard; backyard
hof fäh ig	presentable at court
hof ier en	court s.o., flatter, fawn upon
höf lich	polite, civil, courteous; gallant; obliging
Höf lich keit	politeness, civility, courtesy
Höf ling	courtier
Ge höf t nn	farmstead
Hinter hof nm	backyard
un höf lich	uncivil, impolite; rude
Un höf lich keit	incivility, impoliteness, rudeness
Vor hof nm	vestibule, front court, outer court
Bahn hof nm	railroad station, train station

Höh e	height
Höh er	higher; superior
An höh e	rise, height, hill
er höh en	raise, lift; elevate; increase, augment; intensify; heighten
Er höh ung	raising; elevation
über 'höh en	surmount; superelevate, raise excessively, send up prices
Ueber höh ung	superelevation; bank; increase, excess

hohl a	hollow; dull
Höhl e	cave, cavern; hole; grotto
Höhl ung	excavation; hollow; cavity
aus höhl en	hollow out, excavate; groove out; sap, undermine, erode
Aus höhl ung	groove; excavation
unter 'höhl en	undermine, hollow out from below
ver hohl en	hidden, secret, surreptitious
un ver hohl en a	unconcealed; unreserved, frank

hol en	fetch, get; go for, come for
ab hol en	fetch; call for, come for, pick up
Ab hol ung	fetching, pick-up; collection
auf hol en	have up; bring close to wind; make up
aus hol en	swing back; strike out
bei hol en	haul aft
ein hol en	bring in, collect; go to meet; haul down, fetch; overtake
sich er hol en	recover, get better, recuperate; rally, come round; rest; relax
er hol sam	restful
Er hol ung	recovery, recuperation, convalescence
her hol en s	get here, fetch here
nach hol en	fetch afterwards, bring up; make good, make up for
nieder hol en	haul down, lower a flag
'über hol en	fetch over, ferry over
über 'hol en	pass, overtake; outdistance, outrun; outpace, outstrip; overhaul
Ueber hol ung	overhaul, reconditioning
ver hol en	haul, tow
weg hol en	take s.t. away, call s.o. away from s.t.
'wieder hol en	repeat, say over again; recapitulate, sum up
wieder 'hol en	repeat, say over again; reiterate; recapitulate, sum up
Wieder hol ung	repetition, reiteration; recapitulation
zurück hol en	fetch back; call s.o. back
her aus hol en	get out, extricate; extract from, elicit
her bei hol en	fetch, go for
her ein hol en	fetch in; canvass orders
her über hol en	fetch over
her unter hol en	fetch down, get down; bring down, shoot down
weit her ge hol t	far-fetched

holf: siehe help	
un be holf en a	impractical, helpless; awkward, clumsy, heavy-handed
Un be holf en heit	impracticality; helplessness, awkwardness, clumsiness

Holz nn	wood; timber
holz en	cut wood, fell timber
Holz erei s	fight, brawl
hölz ern a	wooden, of wood; timber
holz frei	woodfree paper
holz ig	woody, ligneous
ab holz en	clear of timber, cut down, deforest
Ge hölz nn	wood, copse, thicket
Nieder holz nn	undergrowth, underwood
Unter holz nn	underwood, brushwood, copse
Streich holz nn	match

hör bar	audible, within earshot
Hör bar keit	audibility
hör en	hear, listen, overhear; give a hearing to
Hör er	hearer, listener; receiver, earpiece, earphones
Hör er schaft	audience
hör ig	be in bondage to, be a person's slave
Hör ig e	bondman, serf, vassal, slave
Hör ig keit	serfdom, bondage
ab hör en	listen to a recitation; interrogate; intercept, pick up, overhear
an hör en	listen to, give an ear to
auf hör en	leave off, stop, quit, cease, discontinue
Be hör de	authority, board, magistrate; government
be hör dlich	official
er hör en	hear; grant
Er hör ung	granting; hearing
Fern hör er	telephone receiver
Ge hör nn	hearing, audience; ear, attention
ge hör en	belong to; be necessary for; be included, be affiliated to
ge hör ig	belonging to; suitable, necessary
ge hör los	deaf
Ge hör los ig keit	deafness
Ge hor sam nm	obedience, duty
ge hor sam	obedient, submissive, dutiful; obsequious
mit hör en	listen in, monitor, overhear
über 'hör en	miss, not hear; ignore
un hör bar	inaudible
Ver hör nn	examination, trial, hearing, interrogation
ver hör en	examine, hear, try, interrogate, question
'wieder hör en	hear again
zu hör en	listen to, attend to
Zu hör er	auditor, hearer, listener
un auf hör lich	incessant, continuous, endless, interminable
Zu be hör nn	accessories, fixings, mountings; belongings
un er hör t	unheard of, unprecedented, outrageous, shocking
an ge hör en	belong to, be related to, be affiliated with
an ge hör ig	attached to, related to
An ge hör ig e	relatives, dependants
un ge hör ig	undue, improper, impertinent
Un ge hör ig keit	impropriety
Un ge hor sam nm	disobedience, insubordination
un ge hor sam	disobedient
zu ge hör en p	belong to; appertain to
zu ge hör ig a	belonging to, appertaining, accompanying, inherent; respective
Zu ge hör ig keit	membership, affiliation, relationship
zusammen ge hör en	belong together, be the same kind, match, be correlated
zusammen ge hör ig	belonging together, homogeneous, correlated

Zusammen
ge hör ig keit		solidarity, unity, homogeneousness, correlation
da zu ge hör ig		belonging to

horch en		listen, hearken; strain one's ears; eavesdrop
Horch er		eavesdropper
ab horch en		sound, listen, auscultate
auf horch en		prick up one's ears, listen to
aus horch en		sound s.o. out, pump s.o. for information
be horch en		overhear
ge horch en		obey, respond
her um horch en	s	go eavesdropping, spy around

Hüll e	wrapper, covering; envelope; jacket; case; coat; veil; bandage
hüll en	wrap up; cover, envelop; veil
ein hüll en	wrap up, envelop in; cover; encase, sheathe, coat
ent hüll en	uncover, bare; unveil; reveal, disclose, divulge; expose
Ent hüll ung	uncovering, unveiling
um 'hüll en	wrap up; cover, envelop with; veil, cover, sheathe
Um hüll ung	wrapping, wrapper, covering; envelope
ver hüll en	cover, veil, wrap up; drape
Ver hüll ung	cover, veil; disguise
un ver hüll t	unveiled; bare, undisguised, open

huls: siehe hull	
Hüls e	hull, husk; shell; pod; capsule
aus hüls en	husk, hull, shuck; shell
ent hüls en	husk, hull, shuck; shell

Hunger nm	hunger, appetite
hunger n	hunger, starve, go hungry; starve o.s.; fast; diet
hung r ig	hungering; ravenous; starving, famished
aus hunger n	starve out
ver hunger n	die of hunger, starve

Hut nm	hat
Hut nf	care, charge, keeping; protection, guard
hüt en	guard, keep, take care of, look after; protect
Hüt er	guardian, keeper; custodian; warden; herdsman
Hüt erin	female guardian, protector
be hüt en	look after, watch over; guard, keep, protect, preserve
be hut sam	cautious, careful, wary; gentle
Be hut sam keit	caution, carefulness
Be hüt ung	bound; encircle; enclose; circumscribe, limit
Nach hut nf	rear-guard
Ob hut nf	care, guard; protection, keeping, custody
ver hüt en	prevent, avert, obviate, ward off
Ver hüt ung	prevention
Vor hut nf	vanguard

inn e av	in, at; with; within; during
in p	within
inn en av	within, on the inside; indoors
inn ig	hearty, heartfelt, warm; tender, affectionate; sincere
Inn ig keit	closeness, intimacy; heartiness, sincerity; tenderness, affection
Inn ung	guild, corporation
dar in av	in it, in them, in that, in those; there; in this; at it

inner a	interior; inner, central; inward, internal; from within
Inner ei en np	innards, offals
inner halb p	within, inside of
inner lich	mental, spiritual; physical; contemplative; sincere, heartfelt
Inner lich keit	introspection, inwardness, introversion; sensitivity, cordiality
Inner st es nn	the innermost part; center
er inner lich	present to one's mind, recallable
er inner n	remind s.o. of s.t., recall s.t.
sich er inner n	remember, recall, recollect, call to mind
Er inner ung	remembrance, recollection; reminder; memory
sich zurück er inner n s	remember, recollect
ver inner lich en	spiritualize; intensify, deepen
Ver inner lich ung	spiritualization; intensification

irr e a	stray, off the right way, on the wrong track
Irr e nf	erring
Irr e nm	lunatic, insane person, madman
irr en	err, go astray, lose one's way, wander
sich irr en	be crazy, be delirious
Irr tum nm	error, mistake; oversight, slip; misunderstanding
irr tüm lich	erroneous; mistaken, false
ab irr en	lose one's way, go astray; err, deviate
Ab irr ung t	deviation
be irr en	confuse, mislead; disconcert, fluster; divert
durch 'irr en	wander through, rove through
sich ver irr en	go astray, lose one's way
Ver irr ung	aberration; error, mistake
un be irr bar	imperturbable, unwavering
un be irr t	unperturbed, unswerving, unflustered; staunch
um 'her irr en	wander around, rove about

Jag d nf	hunting, shooting; chase, pursuit
jag d bar	huntable, able to be hunted
Jag d bar keit	s.t. that can be hunted; fair game
jag d ge recht	huntsmanlike
jag en	hunt; drive; chase, give chase to, pursue; hound
Jag en nn	hunting, shooting; chase, pursuit; rush; forest section

Jäg er		hunter, huntsman, sportsman; ranger, game keeper
Jäg erei		hunting, shooting
ab jag en		override, overdrive horse; rush around
sich ab jag en		wear o.s. out, tire o.s., exhaust o.s.; rush like mad
auf jag en		start, raise game in hunting
durch 'jag en		hunt through, hunt across
'durch jag en		rush through, race through s.t.
ein jag en		frighten s.o., throw a scare into s.o.
er jag en		hunt down; catch, secure, lay hold of s.o.
fort jag en		turn away; turn s.o. out, kick s.o. out; expel
nach jag en		chase, pursue
ver jag en		drive away, chase away; banish
weg jag en		drive away, chase away; expel
hin aus jag en		chase out, drive out, expel
aus ein ander jag en		scatter

jagd:	siehe jag	
Nieder jagd	nf	small-game shooting, hunting

Jahr	nn	year
sich jähr en		it is a year today since
jähr ig		a year old; lasting a year, of one year
jähr lich		yearly, annual; every year
Jähr ling		yearling
be jahr t		aged, elderly
Miss jahr	nn	bad year, bad harvest
ver jähr en		become prescriptive; come under the statute of limitations
Ver jähr ung		limitation by lapse of time, statute of limitations
voll jähr ig		of full age; having reached one's majority
Voll jähr ig keit		full age, majority
Vor jahr	nn	preceding year
vor jähr ig		of last year, last year's
un ver jähr bar		imprescriptable, not subject to the statute of limitations
Früh jahr	nn	spring, springtime
Leb en s jahr	nn	year, year of one's life
Schul jahr	nn	school year

kalt	a	cold; frigid
Kält e		cold; chill; frostiness; frigidity
kält en		chill, refrigerate
er kält en		get cold, cool down; cool off
sich er kält en		catch cold
Er kält ung		cold, chill, catarrh

Kamm	nm	comb
kämm en		comb
ab kämm en		comb off; card wool; comb
aus kämm en		comb out; card wool, comb wool

'durch kämm en — comb thoroughly; comb out

Kampf nm	fight, combat; action, battle; struggle
kämpf en	fight, combat
Kämpf er	fighter; battler, campaigner; impost; abutment
kämpf er isch	fighting, militant, combative; aggressive
kampf fäh ig	fit to fight; fit for action
kampf los	without a fight
kampf un fäh ig	disabled; out of action
an kämpf en	struggle, battle, combat
aus kämpf en	fight out
be kämpf en	fight against, combat; resist, struggle against; oppose
Be kämpf ung	fight, combat, struggle; control
'durch kämpf en	fight through; fight a matter through to the end
sich 'durch kämpf en	fight one's way through
er kämpf en	gain by force, force
mit kämpf en	join in the combat, take part in a struggle
Mit kämpf er	combatant, comrade-in-arms
nieder kämpf en	subdue, overcome; overpower, put s.o. out of action
Vor kämpf er	champion, protagonist, pioneer
Vor kämpf erin	champion, protagonist, pioneer
ab ge kämpf t	worn out, spent, weak and weary

kann: siehe kenn	
be kann t	well known; famous, noted; familiar; acquainted
Be kann te	acquaintance, friend; lover
Be kann t heit	notoriety, publicity, familiarity; close acquaintance
be kann t lich	as is well known, as everybody knows
un be kann t	unknown, unfamiliar, strange; obscure; unknown, unidentified
an er kann t	acknowledged, recognized; established; approved; lawful, legal
un er kann t	unrecognized, unidentified; incognito

kau en	chew, masticate; bite
'durch kau en	chew through; ruminate over; belabor a point
vor kau en	chew; chew food for s.o.; spoon-feed s.t. to s.o.
'wieder käu en	ruminate, chew the cud
Wieder käu er	ruminant
zer kau en	chew well, masticate thoroughly

Kauf nm	purchase
kauf en	buy, purchase
Käuf er	buyer, purchaser; customer; bidder
käuf lich	purchasable; for sale; marketable; by purchase
Käuf lich keit	venality
ab kauf en	buy s.t. from s.o., purchase s.t.
An kauf nm	buying, purchase
an kauf en	buy, purchase
An käuf er	rise, height; hill

auf kauf en	buy up; corner goods on the market, discount a bill of exchange
Auf käuf er	wholesale buyer; buying agent; speculative buyer
Ein kauf nm	purchase; bargain
ein kauf en	buy, purchase, shop for; procure; stock supplies
Ein käuf er	purchaser, buyer; shopper
er kauf en	buy, purchase
los kauf en	buy off, redeem; ransom
Rück kauf nm	repurchase, redemption
Ver kauf nm	sale, selling; realization
ver kauf en	sell; dispose of, realize
sich ver kauf en	sell well, sell badly; sell o.s.
Ver käuf er	seller, retailer; salesman, salesclerk
Ver käuf erin	seller, retailer; salesman, salesclerk
ver käuf lich	for sale; saleable, marketable; negotiable
Ver käuf lich keit	saleableness
Wieder kauf nm	repurchase
zurück kauf en	buy back, repurchase; redeem a pawned item
Aus ver kauf nm	selling off; clearance sale; seasonal sale; bargain sale
aus ver kauf en	sell out; sell off, clear off the stocks, close out
un ver käuf lich	unsalable; not for sale
Vor ver kauf nm	advance sale
Weiter ver kauf nm	resale
'wieder ver kauf en	resell
Wieder ver käuf er	reseller; retailer, retail dealer

---

kenn en	know, be acquainted with; understand; be aware of
Kenn er	connoisseur, judge; expert, specialist; authority
kenn t lich	recognizable; distinguishable; conspicuous; marked
Kenn t nis nf	knowledge; acquaintance; awareness
kenn t nis reich	well-informed, very learned, experienced
sich aus kenn en	know one's way around a place; be versed in; know all about s.t.
be kenn en	admit; confess, acknowledge
Be kenn er	confessor
Be kenn t nis	confession; creed, denomination, religion
er kenn bar	recognizable; perceptible, discernable; identifiable
Er kenn bar keit	recognizability
er kenn en	recognize; perceive, discern; detect, diagnose; know, realize
er kenn t lich	perceptible; grateful
Er kenn t lich keit	thankfulness, gratitude
Er kenn t nis nf	knowledge, perception; realization, understanding, recognition
Er kenn ung	recognition, identification; detection
un kenn t lich	unrecognizable
Un kenn t lich keit	unrecognizable condition
Un kenn t nis	ignorance, unawareness
ver kenn en	misunderstand, misjudge; undervalue; fail to appreciate s.o.

Vor kenn t nis se np	previous knowledge, previous experience; basic knowledge
ab er kenn en l	deny s.o. s.t., deprive s.o. of a right; dispossess s.o.; disallow
Ab er kenn ung	denial
an er kenn en	acknowldege, recognize; accept; appreciate; approve
An er kenn ung	acknowledgement, recognition
un er kenn bar	unrecognizable
'wieder er kenn en	recognize
Wieder er kenn ung	recognition
zu er kenn en	award; confer on; award, adjudge, adjucate
Zu er kenn ung	award; adjudication
un ver kenn bar	unmistakable; obvious

Kern nm	kernel; nucleus
kern ig	full of pips
kern los	seedless
aus kern en	take out the pips of apples; stone; shell pulse
ent kern en	remove core from

Kett e	chain
kett en	fasten with a chain
an kett en	fasten with a chain
los kett en	unchain
ver kett en	chain up; interlink; link together, concatenate
Ver kett ung	interlinkage; concatenation, enchainment
zusammen kett en	chain together

Kirch e	church; divine service
kirch lich	ecclesiastical; sacred; ritual; spiritual; religious, devout
un kirch lich	unclerical; secular, worldly

Klag e	complaint; lament; grievance, charge, accusation
klag en	complain; lament, wail, moan
Kläg er	plaintiff; complainant
Kläg erin	female plaintiff, suitor, libelant, complainant
kläg lich	lamentable, deplorable; distressing, piteous
Kläg lich keit	deplorableness, wretchedness
An klag e	indictment
an klag en	accuse, charge; indict; impeach; arraign
An kläg er	accuser
be klag en	lament, deplore; bewail, bemoan; pity
sich be klag en	complain, make complaints about
Be klag te	defendant
ein klag en	sue for, file suit for, take legal proceedings to recover s.t.
Gegen klag e nf	countercharge, cross action
Gegen kläg er	bringer of a countercharge
Mit kläg er	co-plaintiff
Neben klag e l	incidental action

Neben	kläg er	l	accessory prosecutor
ver	klag en		accuse, inform against; sue; take legal proceedings against
Wider	klag e		counteraction, counterclaim
Wider	kläg er		defendant counter-claiming, bringer of a countercharge
An ge	klag te		defendant

	klar	a	clear; bright; transparent, limpid; pure
	klär en		clear up; clarify; purify; percolate
	Klar heit		clearness; brightness; transparency
	Klär ung		clarification
ab	klär en		clarify, clear; decant, filter
Ab	klär ung		clarification
auf	klär en		clear up, clarify; throw light on, enlighten s.o.; inform, instruct
sich auf	klär en		clear up
Auf	klär er	m	enlightener; pioneer of progress; reconnaissance plane
Auf	klär ung		clearing-up; enlightenment
er	klär bar		explainable, explicable
er	klär en		explain; interpret; define; illustrate, demonstrate; declare
sich er	klär en		declare o.s, speak one's mind
er	klär lich		understandable; evident, obvious
Er	klär ung		explanation, definition; reason; comment; declaration
un	klar	a	not clear; muddy; misty; indistinct; vague, obscure
Un	klar heit		lack of clearness; vagueness, obscurity
ver	klär en		transfigure; illumine
Ver	klar ung		ship's protest, sea protest
Ver	klär ung		transfiguration; radiance, ecstasy
un er	klär lich		inexplicable, unaccountable, mysterious
Un er	klär lich keit		unaccountability, mysteriousness
ab ge	klär t		detached, mellow, wise
auf ge	klär t		enlightened
Auf ge	klär t heit		enlightenment
un ge	klär t		unsettled,unclear; open to question
aus	klar ier en	n	clear out

	kleb en		adhere to, stick to, cling to; glue, paste, stick
	Kleb er		gluten in meal; glue, gum, adhesive
	kleb r ig		adhesive, sticky; tacky; glutinous; viscid; clammy
an	kleb en		stick on; paste on, glue on; post
auf	kleb en		stick on, paste on, glue on; affix, put stamp on
be	kleb en		paste s.t. over s.t.; label; paper, line
ein	kleb en		paste in
über	'kleb en		paste over
ver	kleb en		paste s.t. over, plaster over; stick together, cement, glue
zu	kleb en		paste up, glue up; seal a letter
zusammen	kleb en		stick together

	Kleid nn	garment, dress
	kleid en	clothe, dress, attire o.s.
sich	kleid en	clothe s.o., dress s.o.
	kleid sam	becoming
	Kleid ung	garments; dress, costume, garb; attire
an	kleid en	dress
sich aus	kleid en	take off one's clothes; line, coat, plate
be	kleid en	clothe, dress; attire, array; drape
Be	kleid ung	clothing, clothes; dress, attire, wearing apparel; draping
ein	kleid en	clothe; issue clothing to, fit out; couch thoughts
ent	kleid en	undress s.o., take clothes off; divest s.o. of s.t.
Ent	kleid ung	undressing, removing one's clothes
Ober	kleid ung	outer garments, outer wear
über	'kleid en	cover s.t. over
Ueber	kleid ung	outer wear, outer garments
'um	'kleid en	change one's clothes
um	'kleid en	clothe, cover
Unter	kleid nn	undergarment; slip
Unter	kleid ung	underwear, underclothing
ver	kleid en	disguise; make up as, dress up as; line, face s.t.; plank s.t.
sich ver	kleid en	disguise o.s.; make up as, dress up as
Ver	kleid ung	disguise
Ober be	kleid ung	outer garments, outer wear
un be	kleid et	unclothed, undressed, with nothing on

	klein a	little, small; minute, diminutive, tiny, short; trifling
	Klein e	little boy, little girl
	Klein heit	littleness, smallness; minuteness
	Klein ig keit	little thing; petty matter, bagatelle, trifle
	klein lich	petty, paltry; pedantic, punctilious, fussy
	Klein lich keit	meanness, ungenerosity; pettiness; pedantry; fussiness
	Klein od nn	jewel, gem
ver	klein er n	make smaller, reduce, scale down; diminish, lessen; depreciate
Ver	klein er ung	reduction, diminution, belittling, detraction
zer	klein er n	reduce to small pieces, mince; grind, pulverize
Zer	klein er ung	cutting to bits; mincing, chopping; crushing

	Klett erei	climbing
	Klett erer	climber
	klett er n	climb; scale
er	klett er n	climb up; ascend a mountain; rise on a scale

	Kling e	blade; sword
	Kling el nf	bell
	kling en	sound
ab	kling en	die away, fade away; subside, ebb
an	kling en s	suggest s.t., remind s.o. of s.t.; be heard

auf	kling en	resound, ring out
aus	kling en	die away, fade away; end
er	kling en	resound, ring out, be heard
mit	kling en	resonate
nach	kling en	echo, resound, linger in one's ear
ver	kling en	die away

	klingel:	siehe kling	
	klingel n		ring the bell
ab	klingel n		ring off
an	klingel n		call s.o., telephone s.o.
Ge	klingel	nn	tinkling, jingling
her aus	klingel n		ring up

	klopf en	knock; beat
	Klopf er	knocker, rapper; meat mallet; carpet beater
ab	klopf en	beat off, knock off; dust off; knock at, test by knocking, rap
an	klopf en	knock on door; sound s.o. out about s.t.
aus	klopf en	beat out; scale boiler; dust clothes, knock out pipe
Aus	klopf er	beater; switch, carpetbeater
be	klopf en	tap; percuss
zer	klopf en	knock to pieces, pound, smash

	klopp:	siehe klopf	
	Klöpp el		clapper, tongue; hammer; lace bobbin; beater
	Klöpp el ei		bobbin making, lace making, pillow making; piece of bobbin lace
	klöpp el n		make bobbin lace, make pillow lace; make s.t. on bobbins
	Klöpp l erin		bobbin lace maker, pillow lace maker
ver	klopp en	s	give s.o. a hiding, wallop s.o.; thrash, flog; sell s.t.

	klug	a	clever, intelligent; wise; sensible, judicious; prudent
	Klüg elei		sophistry
	klüg el n		be oversubtle, split hairs
	Klug heit		intelligence, wisdom, cleverness; good sense, prudence, shrewdness
	klüg lich		wisely, prudently
über	klug	a	overwise, too clever
un	klug	a	unwise, imprudent, ill-advised
aus	klüg el n		puzzle out; contrive

	Knie	nn	knee
	knie fäll ig		on one's bended knees
	knie frei		above the knee
	knie n		kneel, be on one's knees; kneel down
nieder	knie n		kneel down
sich hin ein	knie n	s	get down to s.t.

	Knopf	nm	button; stud, pommel; push-button

Knöpf chen	small button
ab knöpf en	unbutton
an knöpf en	button on
auf knöpf en	unbutton
vor knöpf en s	take s.o. to task, rebuke s.o.
zu knöpf en	button up
zu ge knöpf t	reserved, uncommunicative, silent

knupf: siehe knopf	
knüpf en	tie; knot; braid; weave; attach, fasten; join, unite, knit
ab knüpf en	untie, undo
an knüpf en	tie, fasten, knot s.t.; lengthen; form contacts; refer to s.t.
auf knüpf en	unknot; untie, undo; tie up; hang s.o.
ein knüpf en	knot s.t. in
ver knüpf en	knot s.t. together, bind s.t. together, combine, connect
Ver knüpf ung	connection, association
zusammen knüpf en	knot together, tie things together
wieder 'an knüpf en	renew, reestablish

Koch nm	cook; chef
koch en	be cooking; cook, boil; make
Koch er	cooker
Köch in	cook
ab koch en	boil down; decoct; scald
auf koch en	boil up
aus koch en	boil out; decoct, extract juice; scald vessels
ein koch en	boil down, thicken by boiling; make jam, make preserves
'über koch en	boil over
ver koch en	boil away; blow over
zer koch en	cook too long, overcook, cook to a pulp
aus ge koch t s	hardboiled, out and out; seasoned

Kohl e	coal
kohl en	char; carbonize; coal
Köhl er	charcoal burner
Köhl erei	charcoal works
ent kohl en	decarbonize
ver kohl en	carbonize, char; hoax, pull one's leg, fool s.o.

komm en	come, arrive; approach, draw near; come to pass, happen
ab komm en	come off; lose one's way
Ab komm en nn	settlement, agreement, deal
Ab komm en schaft	not wanted, unneccessary, free
ab kömm lich	dispensable; available; able to be spared
Ab kömm ling	descendant, offspring
an komm en	arrive, come, get to
An kömm ling nm	newcomer, new arrival, stranger

auf komm en		get up; recover, rise; prosper; come into use
Auf komm en	nn	recovery; introduction; spread; origin, rise
Aus komm en	nn	livelihood, subsistence
aus komm en		come out, manage; have enough of
aus kömm lich		sufficient
be komm en		get, receive, obtain
be kömm lich		wholesome, beneficial; digestible
bei komm en		come at, come up to, reach; dare
'durch komm en		come through, get through; come off, manage
ein komm en		come in, enter
Ein komm en	nn	income, rent, revenue
ent komm en		escape from; get off
fort komm en		get away, escape; prosper, succeed
Her komm en	nn	custom, usage, practice, routine, tradition; descent
her komm en	s	come near, approach, advance; be derived from
her kömm lich		traditional, customary, usual, conventional
hin komm en		come to, arrive at, get there
los komm en		come off, get away, get off
mit komm en		come along with, be able to follow, keep up with
Nach komm e	nm	descendant, offspring
nach komm en		come after, come later; comply with, fulfill
Nach komm en schaft		descendants, posterity, issue
Nach kömm ling		descendant
nieder komm en		lie in, be confined
über 'komm en		obtain, receive, befall, happen to
'um komm en		perish, die spoil, go bad, go to waste
Unter komm en	nn	dwelling, housing space, accommodation, employment
'unter komm en		find lodgings; find employment
ver komm en		perish, be ruined; decay, degenerate
Ver komm en heit		depravity, degeneracy
voll komm en	a	perfect, accomplished
Voll komm en heit		perfection
vor komm en		be found; prevent; happen, occur
Vor komm en	nn	occurrence, presence, existence; deposit
Vor komm nis		occurrence, event
weg komm en		get away, come off
weiter komm en		get ahead, make progress, advance
'wieder komm en		come back
zu komm en		come to s.o.; belong to s.o.; be due to; be suitable to s.o.
zurück komm en		come back, return; recur to
zusammen komm en		meet, assemble, come together
her ab komm en		come down, descend; dismount; sink down
un ab kömm lich		indispensable, reserved; keyed
her an komm en		come near, draw near, approach; come up to
vor an komm en		get on, make
her auf komm en		come up, get up
her aus komm en		come forth, get out; be published, appear
hin aus komm en		come out; amount to
ab be komm en		get share of, participate in, get damaged
auf be komm en		get open; have a lesson to do

mit be komm en	s		get at the same time; receive when leaving; get as dowry
weg be komm en	s		get away; get the knack of
'wieder be komm en			get back, recover
zu be komm en	s		get in addition
zurück be komm en			get back, recover, retrieve
her bei komm en			approach, come near
vor bei komm en			go past, go by, call, look in, come by
her ein komm en			come in, enter, drop in
Neben ein komm en		nn	additional income
Ueber ein komm en		nn	agreement, understanding, settlement, compromise
über 'ein komm en			agree, come to an agreement
ent gegen komm en			come to meet
Ent gegen komm en		nn	kindness, courtesy, fair terms
da hinter komm en	s		discover, find out
hin über komm en			get over
her um komm en	s		come around, travel around, get around; become known
her unter komm en			come down, decline, fall off, get low
un voll komm en	a		imperfect, defective, incomplete
Un voll komm en heit			imperfection
da von komm en			get off
her vor komm en			come forth, appear, come out of
zu vor komm en			anticipate, forestall; come first; prevent
zu vor komm end			obliging, complaisant, polite, courteous
Zu vor komm en heit			complaisance, civility, politeness
da zu komm en			arrive unexpectedly; happen
hin zu komm en			come up to, drop in by chance; be added
da zwischen komm en			come between, intervene, prevent
her aus be komm en			get back; get out; get change
her ein be komm en			get into; receive
her um be komm en	s		get over; talk over
ver voll komm n en			improve; perfect; round off, refine
Ver voll komm n ung			improvement; perfection; refinement

könn en			be able, be capable; possibility, likelihood; know
Könn en		nn	ability, faculty, power; skill, efficiency; knowledge
Könn er			very able man; master, expert
mit könn en	s		be able to come along
weiter könn en			be able to go on
zurück könn en	s		be able to return, be able to recede

Korn		nn	grain; seed; corn, cereals; wheat; rye; harvest
Körn chen			little grain, granule
körn en			run to seed; granulate; grain
Körn er			center punching tool
körn ig			granular, grainy; gritty
Körn ung			granulation; grain
an körn en			center-punch, countersink
ent körn en			shell, gin
ge körn t			granulated

voll körn ig	full-grained

Körp er	body
Körp er chen	small body, particle, corpuscle
körp er lich	bodily, physical; corporeal, substantial, material
körp er los	bodiless, incorporeal
Körp er schaft	corporate body, corporation, corporate entity
Ober körper nm	upper part of the body
un körper lich	incorporeal, immaterial; disembodied, spiritual
Unter körper nm	lower part of the body
ver körper n	personify, embody; represent; impersonate; typify
Ver körper ung	personification, embodiment; incarnation; impersonation

kost bar	precious, valuable; costly, expensive; splendid, luxurious
Kost bar keit	costliness, preciousness; precious object, treasure
kost en	cost
Kost en np	costs; expenses; charges; fees
kost en frei	free of cost
kost en los	free of charge, gratuitous
Neben kost en np	extra cost, extra expenses; extras, incidentals
Un kost en np	costs, expenses, charges

Kost nf	food, fare; board; diet, formula
köst lich	delicious, dainty, savory, tasty; charming, delightful; wonderful
aus kost en	enjoy to the full
'durch kost en	taste one after the other
Zu kost nf	vegetables, trimmings; preserves
be köst ig en	board, feed
Be köst ig ung	boarding, food; maintenance, keep
ver köst ig en	board, feed

Kraft nf	strength; force; power; might; efficacy; vigor; energy
kraft p	by virtue of; on the strength of
kräft ig	strong, robust, sturdy
kräft ig en	strengthen, invigorate, harden, fortify; refresh, restore
Kräft ig keit	strength, vigor, energy
Kräft ig ung	strengthening; invigoration; restoration
kraft los	without strength; powerless, faint; feeble, weak; limp; languid
Kraft los ig keit	weakness, feebleness, exhaustion, limpness; asthenia
kraft voll	strong, vigorous, powerful; athletic; energetic; pithy
ent kräft en	weaken, enfeeble, debilitate; enervate, exhaust; refute an argument
Ent kräft ung	weakening, debilitation; enervation; exhaustion
Gegen kraft nf	counteracting force, reaction

Ur kraft nf	original force; primitive strength
ver kraft en	bear, handle; cope with, meet
Voll kraft nf	full vigor
be kräft ig en	confirm, affirm; substantiate, ratify
Be kräft ig ung	confirmation, affirmation

Kreis nm	circle; ring
Kreis el	spinning top
kreis el n	spin the top; spin, whirl around
kreis en	move in a circle, spin around; revolve, rotate, gyrate
ein kreis en	encircle, envelop, outflank, surround; isolate
Ein kreis ung	encirclement
Um kreis nm	circumference, circuit
um 'kreis en	circle around s.t., revolve around s.t.

kreuz av	in all directions, this way and that, criss-cross
Kreuz nn	cross; crucifix
kreuz en	cross, traverse, intersect
Kreuz er	cruiser
kreuz ig en	crucify
Kreuz ig ung	crucifixion
Kreuz ung	crossing, intersection; crosswalk
kreuz weise av	crosswise, crossways, across
an kreuz en	check off
be kreuz en	make the sign of the cross upon s.o.
durch 'kreuz en	thwart, foil, frustrate
sich be kreuz ig en	cross o.s., make the sign of the cross

kriech en	creep, crawl; drag o.s. along
Kriech er	cringer, toady, sycophant
Kriech erei	cringing, grovelling; toadyism
kriech er isch	cringing, grovelling, servile, sneaking
aus kriech en	come forth; be hatched
'durch kriech en	creep through, crawl through
durch 'kriech en	crawl through, creep through
sich ver kriech en	hide; crawl away; creep into a hole

Krieg nm	war, armed conflict; warfare; feud; strife, quarrel; hostilities
krieg en s	catch, seize, catch hold of; get
Krieg er	warrior; fighter, combatant
krieg er isch	warlike, bellicose, martial; militant
ab krieg en	get one's share, come in for one's share
auf krieg en	get a door open, undo a knot, be given s.t. to do
be krieg en	make war upon, wage war against, fight
los krieg en	get loose
mit krieg en s	receive s.t. on one's way; receive s.t. as dowry; understand s.t.
'unter krieg en s	get s.o. down, bring s.o. to heel, get the better of s.o.
her aus krieg en	get s.t. out of s.t.; get change; make s.t. out, decipher s.t.

her um	krieg en	s	get s.t. around s.t.
Welt	krieg	nm	world war

	kühl	a	cool, chilly
	Kühl e		coolness
	kühl en		cool; freshen; refresh; chill, refrigerate
	Kühl er		cooler
	Kühl ung		cooling; refrigeration; coolness
ab	kühl en		cool off, cool down, chill
sich ab	kühl en		cool down; refresh o.s.
Ab	kühl ung		cooling
sich ver	kühl en	s	catch cold
Ver	kühl ung	s	cold, head cold

	Kumm er		grief, sorrow, affliction; trouble, worry
	kümm er lich		miserable, wretched, pitiful; poor, paltry, meager
	Kümm er ling		stunted plant; dying tree; undersized animal
	kümm er n		grieve, afflict; trouble, worry; attend to, mind, look after
sich	kümm er n		attend to, look after, take care of, meddle with
	Kümm er nis	nf	grief, sorrow, affliction; trouble, worry
	kumm er voll		sorrowful, grievous, sad
be	kümmer n		afflict, grieve; trouble, alarm, distress; concern
Be	kümmer nis		affliction, grief; distress, trouble
ver	kümmer n		become stunted, atrophy; waste away; pine away; starve
un be	kümmer t		unconcerned, careless; brisk; reckless
Un be	kümmer t heit		carelessness

	kund	av a	known
	künd bar		terminable; subject to being fired
	Kund e		knowledge, information, news, tidings; science
	Kund e	nm	customer, client, patron
	künd en	p	announce, make known; tell the story; bear witness
	kund ig		knowing, skillful
	künd ig en		give a notice; recall, call in
	Künd ig ung		notice, warning
	Kund schaft		customers, clients; custom, clientele; patronage; intelligence
	kund schaft en		reconnoiter, scout, spy out
	Kund schaft er		scout, spy; emissary
be	kund en		state; testify, depose; manifest, demonstrate, reveal, show
er	kund en		explore, spy out; reconnoiter, scout
Er	kund ung		reconnaissance
un	künd bar		irrevocable, binding; irredeemable; perpetual; permanent
un	kund ig		ignorant, unacquainted with, not knowing
Ur	kund e		document, deed, legal instrument; record; title, charter
ur	kund lich		documentary; authentic

be ur kund en	attest, certify; authenticate, verify; legalize, notarize; witness
Be ur kund ung	certification, authentication
an künd ig en	announce, proclaim; publish, advertise; herald
An künd ig ung	announcement, notification, proclamation; advertisement
auf künd ig en	cancel a treaty, denounce an agreement; break off a friendship
er kund ig en	inquire, ask, make inquiries
Er kund ig ung	inquiry
ver künd ig en	announce, make known; publish, proclaim; predict, prophesy
Ver künd ig er	harbinger, herald; prophet
Ver künd ig ung	announcement, proclamation; pronouncement; promulgation; preaching
aus kund schaft en	explore, spy out, ferret out; scout, reconnoiter

kunft:	siehe komm		
künft ig			future, next
kunft ig	av		future
künft ig hin	av		from now on, henceforth, in the future
kunft hin	av		from now on, henceforth, for the future
Ab kunft	nf		descent; parentage, lineage; extraction, origin, birth
An kunft	nf		arrival
Aus kunft	nf		information, particulars, intelligence
Aus kunft ei			inquiry office; private detective's office
Ein künft e	np		proceeds, receipts; profit; income
Her kunft	nf		descent, origin, extraction, provenance, derivation
Nieder kunft	nf		confinement, delivery, childbirth
Rück kunft	nf		return
Unter kunft	nf		dwelling, housing space, accommodation; employment
Wieder kunft	nf		return, coming back
Zu kunft	nf		future, time to come; future tense
zu künft ig			future, prospective, next; in future, for the future
Zusammen kunft	nf		meeting, gathering, assembly, convention, reunion
Neben ein künft e	np		additional income, casual earnings
Ueber ein kunft	nf		agreement, understanding, settlement; compromise, arrangement
Da zwischen kunft	nf		intervention, interference

kurz	a		short
Kürz e			shortness, brevity
Kürz el	nn		grammalogue, shorthand contraction
kürz en			shorten, abridge, condense; reduce; curtail
kürz lich	av		lately, recently, not long ago, the other day
Kürz ung			shortening; abridgment, condensation
ab kürz en			shorten; curtail; reduce, abridge, condense; abbreviate
Ab kürz ung			shortening, short-cut
ver kürz en			shorten, foreshorten; clip, abridge, curtail; while away the time

sich ver kürz en	become shorter, shorten
Ver kürz ung	shortening

läch el n	smile, grin
Lach en	laugh
Lach er	laughter
läch er lich	laughable, ridiculous; ludicrous, comical; funny; absurd
Läch er lich keit	ridiculousness; trivial matter, farce
lach haft s	laughable, ridiculous
an lach en	smile at, give s.o. a smile
auf lach en	burst out laughing, give a laugh
aus lach en	laugh at, jeer at, deride s.o.
be lach en	laugh at, laugh over s.t.
Ge läch ter nn	laughing, laughter; laughing-stock
los lach en	laugh out
ver lach en	laugh at, deride, snap one's finger at
an läch el n	smile at, give s.o. a smile
be läch el n	smile at
zu läch el n	smile at, give a smile; smile upon

Lad e	case, chest, box; drawer
lad en	load; invite, ask
Lad en nm	shop
Lad ung	loading, lading; load, freight
ab lad en	unload, discharge; dump
Ab lad er	unloader
auf lad en	load, laden; boost, supercharge; charge
aus lad en	discharge, unload; clear, lighten; disembark
Aus lad er t	unloader, stevedore
Aus lad ung	unloading, discharge, landing
be lad en	load, freight, charge; burden
ein lad en	load in; ship, embark; entruck; entrain; emplane
ein lad end	inviting; enticing, tempting; appetizing
Ein lad ung	invitation
ent lad en	unload, dump goods
sich ent lad en	burst, break, go off, explode, detonate; pour out one's anger
Ent lad ung	unloading; discharge; explosion
Hinter lad er	breech-loader
Rück lad ung	return cargo
über 'lad en	overload; overfreight; overcharge
Ueber lad ung	overloading; overcharge
'um lad en	reload, shift; transsship
Um lad ung	reloading, transshipment
ver lad en	load, ship; entrain, consign, forward; embark, emplane
Ver lad er	shipping agent, carrier
Ver lad ung	loading, shipping, shipment; entraining
vor lad en	summon, serve a summons on, cite; subpoena
Vor lad ung	summons, citation, subpoena
Vorder lad er	muzzle loader

lag:	siehe	lieg
Lag e		situation
Ab lag e		place of deposit; warehouse, depot; cloak-room
An lag e		laying-out, construction; installation
Auf lag e		imposition, levy; tax; direction, instruction; condition
Aus lag e		expenses
Be lag	nm	cover; coat; lining; flooring, planking
Bei lag e		addition; enclosure
Ein lag e		accompanying documents; padding; insole; investment; inserted song
Ge lag e	nn	feast, banquet; drinking-bout
Nieder lag e		defeat; rout; beating, licking
Rück lag e		reserve, reserve fund
Um lag e		special fee; apportionment
Unter lag e		base support, bed, rest
Ver lag	nm	publication; publishing house
Vor lag e		copy; pattern
Zu lag e		additional allowance
ver an lag en		assess
Ver an lag ung		assessment
ver aus lag en		lay out, disburse; advance
Wieder vor lag e		renewed submission
Grund lag e		basis, base, foundation; fundamentals, rudiments

---

lager:	siehe	lieg
Lager	nn	couch; bed, bedstead
Lager ist	nm	store-clerk
Lager ist in		store-clerk, stockkeeper
lager n		lie down, rest; lay down
Lager ung		storage, warehousing; seasoning
ab lager n		deposit rock, deposit sediment; age wood; mature; store tobacco
Ab lager ung		sediment, geological deposits, sedimentation, alluvium
an lager n		combine with chemicals, unite with, add on; accumulate
An lager ung		chemical adsorption; accumulation, deposit; adding on, combining
aus lager n		evacuate; take s.t. out of store; age, harden, settle
Aus lager ung		evacuation
Be lager er		besieger
be lager n		besiege, beleaguer, invest, lay siege to
Be lager ung		siege, besieging, beleaguering
Bei lager	nn	consummation of marriage
ein lager n		store s.t. up, lay s.t. in, stockpile s.t.; deposit
Ein lager ung		storage, embedment; inclusion, occlusion; interstratification
Ge läger	nn	dregs, sediment
über 'lager n		superimpose, overlay; overlie; overshadow, mask, conceal
Ueber lager ung		superimposition; disguise; psychic overtone

'um lager n		restore; redirect; rearrange
ver lager n		switch s.t. over, shift, move; displace, transpose, dislocate
Ver lager ung		shift, switch; displacement, dislocation; misalignment
Wider lager	nn	abutment

Land	nn	land; soil, ground; arable land; country; territory
land en		land
Länd erei		landed property, land, estate
Länd ler		country waltz
länd lich		rural; rustic, countrylike, bucolic; countrified
Land schaft		landscape, scenery; province, district, region; countryside
land schaft lich		provincial, rural; scenic
Land ung		landing; alighting; debarkation, disembarkation; arrival
Aus land	nn	foreign country
Aus länd er		foreigner, alien
aus länd er isch		foreign, external, alien; exotic; outlandish, strange
Ge länd e	nn	tract of land, area; country; ground, terrain; lot
Hinter land	nn	hinterland, interior of a country
In land	nn	native country; interior; inland
In länd er		inlander; native
In länd erin		inlander; native
Nieder land e	np	The Netherlands, The Low Countries
Nieder länd er	nm	Dutchman, citizen of The Netherlands
nieder länd isch	t	Dutch
Ober land	nn	upland
Unter land	nn	low land, low country
Vor land	nn	foreland
zu land e	av	in our country
Zwischen land ung		intermediate landing, stop
Deutsch land	nn	Germany

land er:	siehe lad	
Ge länd er	nn	railing, handrail; banister; stanchions, taffrail

lang a		long, tall; a long time
lang e	av	long, long ago; for a long time
Läng e		length, tallness; size; longitude; quantity; long
lang en		suffice, be sufficient, be enough
läng en		lengthen, extend, elongate
läng lich		longish, elongated, oblong
läng s	p	along, alongside of
lang sam		slow, leisurely, unhurried; tardy, sluggish; heavy
Lang sam keit		slowness, leisureness; tardiness, sluggishness, slackness
läng st	av	long ago, since
läng st ens av s		at the longest, at the latest, at the most
an lang en		arrive; concern, relate, regard
aus lang en		suffice; raise one's arm

Be lang nm	importance, concern; interest; meaning
be lang en	pursue; sue at law; indict for
be lang los	unimportant, of no interest, insignificant
Be lang los ig keit	insignificance, irrelevance
Be lang ung	prosecution, legal action
ent lang av	along
er lang en	reach, attain; obtain, get, acquire
Er lang ung	reaching; acquisition
ge lang en	arrive at, come home to; reach, attain; acquire
hin lang en	reach
hin läng lich	sufficient, competent, requisite, adequate
un läng st	lately, recently, not long ago, the other day
ver lang en	demand, require; desire, want; claim
Ver lang en nn	demand; request; claim; desire, wish, aspiration; eagerness
zu lang en	stretch out one's hands; help o.s.
zu läng lich	adequate, sufficient
Zu läng lich keit	adequacy, sufficiency
an be lang en	relate to, concern, regard
'wieder er lang en	recover, get back, retrieve
ab ver lang en	ask s.t. from s.o.
nach ver lang en	order additionally; claim afterwards
un ver lang t	unsolicited
zurück ver lang en	reclaim, demand back
un zu läng lich	insufficient, inadequate
Un zu läng lich keit	insufficiency, inadequacy; shortcomings
ver läng er n	lengthen, extend, prolong; renew; retain; stretch s.t.
Ver läng er ung	lengthening, extension, elongation, prolongation
ver lang sam en	retard, slow down, dampen
stund en lang av	for hours, for a long time
Zeit lang nf	a while, some time

---

lass a	weary, indolent
lass en	let, allow, yield; order; cause; leave, abandon; abstain from
läss ig	lazy, idle, indolent; careless, negligent
Läss ig keit	laziness, indolence
läss lich	pardonable, venial
Ab lass nm	drain; indulgence
ab lass en	leave off, cease; drain; abandon, let off
An lass nm	occasion, cause, motive, inducement
an lass en	start, set going; keep on, leave on
An lass er	starter
an läss lich	occasionally, on the occasion of
auf lass en	leave open; convey, surrender, cede property to
aus lass en	let out, omit, leave out; melt; eliminate, skip a line
Aus lass ung	omission, expression, remark, utterance
be lass en	leave s.t. in a condition, leave things as they are
Durch lass nm	allow to pass, let through; filter, strain
durch läss ig	permeable, pervious, penetrable
Durch läss ig keit	permeability, perviousness

Ein lass nm	admission, entrance, inlet
ein lass en	let in, admit; insert, put in
sich ein lass en	engage in, meddle with
ent lass en	dismiss s.o., discharge; drop, discard
Ent lass ung	dismissal, discharge, firing, removal, suspension
Er lass nm	remission; decree, ordinance; abatement; proclamation
er lass en	issue, publish, promulgate; enact a law; pardon
er läss lich a	remissable, dispensable
Er lass ung	publication; remission
fort lass en	let off; omit; allow to go
Ge lass nn	room, space
ge lass en a	composed, patient, calm, quiet, self-possessed
Ge lass en heit	calm, composure, patience; self-possession
her lass en s	allow to come
hin lass en s	let go to a place, admit
hinter lass en	leave behind; leave word; bequeath s.t. to s.o.
Hinter lass en schaft	inheritance, estate
los lass en	let go, let off, let loose; set free
Nach lass nm	remission, inheritance, estate, assets; statement, reduction
nach lass en	leave behind, reduce, remit; temper; slow down
Nach lass en schaft	inheritance, estate
nach läss ig	negligent, neglectful, careless, sloppy
Nach läss ig keit	negligence, carelessness, idleness
nieder lass en	let down, lower
sich nieder lass en	sit down, take a seat; settle, establish o.s.
Nieder lass ung	settling, settlement, colony; branch, establishment
über 'lass en	let have, leave, give up, entrust, yield
Ueber lass ung	leaving, transfer, cession; surrender, abandonment
übrig lass en	leave over, leave
Unter lass nm	intermission
unter 'lass en	omit; fail; neglect, abstain from
Unter lass ung	omission, neglect
Ver lass nm	reliance
ver lass en	leave, quit, forsake, abandon, desert; rush away
ver lass en a	forsaken, abandoned, deserted, desolate
Ver lass en heit	abandonment, solitude, loneliness, dereliction
ver läss lich	reliable, be relied on
vor lass en	give precedence, give access to, show in
weg lass en	let go, omit, leave out
zer lass en	dissolve, melt, liquefy
zu lass en	leave shut; admit, allow; permit, let, license
zu läss ig	allowable, admissible, permissible, permitted, safe
Zu lass ung	admission, permission, licence, approval
zurück lass en	leave, leave behind, abandon
her ab lass en	let down, lower
Her ab lass ung	condescension
un ab läss ig	incessant, continual, constant, uninterrupted
ver an lass en	cause, make, give rise to; arrange
Ver an lass er	causer
Ver an lass ung	occasion, cause, inducement, motive, reason, instigation

her auf lass en	s	send for
her aus lass en	s	let out
sich her bei lass en		condescend
vor bei lass en		let pass
un durch läss ig		impenetrable, impermeable, inscrutable
Un durch läss ig keit		impenetrability
her ein lass en	s	admit, let in
un er läss lich		indispensible
aus ge lass en	a	unrestrained, loose, wanton, boisterous, frisky, frolicsome
Aus ge lass en heit		unruliness, exuberance, wantonness
hin über lass en	s	let cross over
her unter lass en	s	let down, lower
zu ver läss ig		reliable, authentic, certain, sure; trustworthy, dependable
Zu ver läss ig keit		authenticity, certainty, reliability, trustworthiness
un zu läss ig		inadmissable, unallowable, prohibited; undue
un zu ver läss ig		unreliable, treacherous, uncertain, precarious
Un zu ver läss ig keit		untrustworthiness, unreliability
ver nach läss ig en		neglect, disregard, leave out, omit, slight
Ver nach läss ig ung		neglect, omission, oversight

Last	nf	load; burden, weight, charge; tonnage
last en		weight on, press on
Last er	nn	vice; depravity
Läst er er		calumniator, slanderer, backbiter, blasphemer
last er haft		vicious, wicked; depraved, corrupt
Last er haft ig keit		viciousness, profligacy, dissoluteness, depravity
läst er lich		slanderous, calumnious, abusive; blasphemous; disgraceful
läst er n		slander, calumniate, defame; abuse, revile, run down
Läst er ung		calumny, slander, abuse, blasphemy
läst ig		burdensome, cumbersome, troublesome, tiresome; inconvenient
Läst ig keit		burdensomeness, troublesomeness, irksomeness, inconvenience
aus last en		balance, equalize loads; employ to capacity
be last en		burden; load, charge; stress; weight
ent last en		unburden, take the weight off, ease; relieve
Ent last ung		relief; discharge; exoneration
Fern last er		long-distance truck
hinter last ig		tail-heavy, stern-heavy
ober last ig		top-heavy
über 'last en		overload, overcharge; overburden, overtax
Ueber last ung		overload, overcharge; overwork, pressure of business
vorder last ig		nose-heavy
'über be last en		overload
Ueber be last ung		overload
un be last et		unencumbered; carefree, light-hearted
vor be last et		handicapped

Vor be last ung		handicap; preloading
be läst ig en		molest, annoy; trouble, bother, inconvenience; pester
Be läst ig ung		molestation; annoyance, bother, nuisance

Lauf	nm	course, pace; running, operation; race; flight of stairs
Läuf chen		small leg of an animal
lauf en		run, walk; go, work; extend; flow; leak; pass, go by
lauf end		running, current; present; consecutive
Läuf er		runner; carpet strip; bishop in chess, armature, rotor; stretcher
Läuf erei		running around, running about
läuf ig		dog in heat; ruttish
Läuf ig keit		dog heat
Ab lauf	nm	flowing off; drain; expiration; outlet, sink, gutter
ab lauf en		run off; stop, expire, fall due
An lauf	nm	start, run; onset, attack; dash, rush
an lauf en		run, rush upon; put into a port; become dim, tarnish
Auf lauf	nm	crowd, mob, rush, riot; soufflé
auf lauf en		swell, increase, run up; accumulate, accrue
Aus lauf	nm	running out; sailing; finish; landing run, runway
aus lauf en		run out, depart; sail; run over, leak; project
sich aus lauf en		have a good run
Aus läuf er		runner, errand-boy; branch, spur
sich be lauf en		total, amount to, figure up, come to
bei läuf ig		by the way; occasional, incidental, casual
durch 'lauf en		run through, flow through, run all over; glance over
Ein lauf	nm	inlet; influx, intake; arrival; entry; enema
ein lauf en		run in
ent lauf en		run away, escape, run free; run on, last
ge läuf ig		current; ready; fluent
Ge läuf ig keit		currency; readiness; fluency, ease
gegen läuf ig		countercurrent; contrarotating
her lauf en s		run up
Hinter lauf nm h		hindleg
Mit läuf er		follower, hanger-on
nach lauf en		run after; go behind, lag
Ober lauf	nm	upper course
Rück lauf	nm	return movement; reversing stroke; gun recoil
Rück läuf er		dead letter
rück läuf ig		retrograde, recurrent, dropping
Ueber lauf	nm	overflow
'über lauf en		run over, flow over, desert
Ueber läuf er		deserter, runaway, turncoat
Um lauf	nm	turning, circulation, rotation; currency; revolution
'um lauf en		run down; circulate, revolve, rotate; run around
Unter lauf	nm	lower course, lower river
'unter lauf en		run under, slip in; occur

Ver lauf	nm	lapse; course; progress; process; run; curve; flow
ver lauf en		pass; elapse, proceed; take a course, develop
sich ver lauf en		lose one's way; disperse, scatter
Vor lauf nm t		start, preliminary round, eliminating race
vor lauf en		run before, outrun
Vor läuf er		forerunner, pioneer, precursor; spur; sign, clue
vor läuf ig		preliminary, preparatory, tentative, temporary, for the present
Vorder lauf nm h		foreleg
weg lauf en		run off
weit läuf ig		extensive, lengthy, wide, distant, spacious; detailed
weiter lauf en		go on, continue
zer lauf en		melt, dissolve
Zu lauf	nm	run, crowd, concourse; feed, supply, intake
zu lauf en		run up to, run on, run faster; crowd, flock
zurück lauf en		return, run back, recoil
Zusammen lauf	nm	concourse, riot, mob
zusammen lauf en		run together, come together, crowd together, flock
her aus lauf en		run out
hin aus lauf en		run out; come up; amount to
vor aus lauf en		run on ahead
her bei lauf en		come running along
vor bei lauf en		run past
her ein lauf en		run in
hin ein lauf en		run in, flow in
ent gegen lauf en		run to meet; oppose, be repugnant to
hinter her lauf en		run after
hin über lauf en		run across; go across, walk across
her um lauf en s		run, stroll about
hin unter lauf en		run down
da von lauf en		run away
zu wider lauf en		run counter to, be contrary to
aus ein ander lauf en		run here and there; disband, diverge
'durch ein ander lauf en		run around in confusion

---

laut	p	in accordance with; in pursuance of; according to
Laut	nm	sound
laut	a	loud
laut bar		become known, become public knowledge; be noised abroad
laut en		sound
läut en		ring
laut er	a	pure, unalloyed
Laut er keit		pureness, clearness; transparency
läut er n		purify
Läut er ung		purification; clarification, rectification; refining
laut ier en		spell phonetically, read phonetically
laut lich		phonetic

laut los		soundless; noiseless; silent; mute
Laut los ig keit		soundlessness, noiselessness, silence, hush, stillness
Ab laut	nm	vowel gradation, ablaut
ab läut en		ring off
ab laut en		change the radical vowel
An laut	nm	initial sound, anlaut
an läut en	s	ring a bell for
an laut en		begin
Aus laut	nm	final sound, terminal sound
aus laut en		terminate, end
aus läut en		cease ringing
ein läut en		ring in
Ge läut	nn	ringing, peel of bells; chime
Ge läut e	nn	ringing, peel of bells; chime
In laut	nm	medial sound
Mit laut nm g		consonant
Um laut	nm	vowel mutation; mutated or modified vowel, umlaut
un laut er	a	impure; shady, unfair to competition
ver laut en		be reported, be disclosed; transpire
vor laut	a	forward, pert
er läut er n		explain, elucidate, expound, comment upon; exemplify
Er läut er ung		explanation, elucidation, illustration; commentary
ver laut bar en		divulge, make known, disclose
Ver laut bar ung		announcement, report, statement, disclosure; bulletin

---

leb en		live, be alive, exist; reside, dwell; stay; live on
sich leb en		live
Leb en	nn	life, existence; being; living creature, living being; vitality
leb end ig		living
leb en s fäh ig		viable
Leb en s fäh ig keit		viability, vitality
leb en s voll		full of life
leb haft		lively, vivacious; ardent, fervent; animated, active
Leb haft ig keit		liveliness, vivacity, brightness, briskness, vividness, animation
leb los		lifeless, inanimate; dull
Leb los ig keit		lifelessness, deadness, inanimateness, unconsciousness, dullness
ab leb en		die, pass away
Ab leb en	nn	death
auf leb en		revive, come to life again; liven up
sich aus leb en		enjoy life to the full; sow one's wild oats
be leb en		enliven, liven up, animate, stimulate; invigorate; brighten
be leb t		animated; busy, bustling, frequented, crowded
Be leb ung		animation, stimulation; variegation
durch 'leb en		go through, live through, experience

sich ein	leb	en	accustom o.s.; settle down, acclimatize; become familiar with
er	leb	en	live to see, experience; pass through, meet with; live through s.t.
Er	leb	nis	experience; event, occurrence, episode
fort	leb	en	live on; survive
nach	leb	en	live up to, observe, conform to
Nach	leb	en	nn	after-life; after-effect of an idea
über	'leb	en	survive, outlive
sich über	'leb	en	outlive one's usefulness
ver	leb	en	spend, pass
ver	leb	t	dissipated; worn out; decrepit
vor	leb	en	exemplify s.t. to s.o. through one's own life
Vor	leb	en	nn	former life, past life; antecedents
Zusammen	leb	en	nn	living together, companionship; corporate life
sich			
zusammen	leb	en	adapt to each other
wieder 'auf	leb	en	revive
un be	leb	t	inanimate; unfrequented, quiet; dull, slack, dead
'wieder be	leb	en	restore to life; revive, reanimate, revitalize
Wieder be	leb	ung	revival, reanimation
mit er	leb	en	see, witness, be witness of
ab ge	leb	t	decrepit, effete
da hin	leb	en	vegetate

	Leder	nn	leather
	leder	n	of leather; leathern, leathery, tough
ab	leder	n	wipe with chamois skin
Ober	leder	nn	upper leather of shoe
Unter	leder	nn	sole leather

	leg	en	lay, put, place, lay down; pin to the floor
	Leg	er	easy, informal
ab	leg	en	take off, give up; lay down, discard, cast off
Ab	leg	er	shoot; layer; scion; branch
an	leg	en	put, lay on, put on; construct; land
auf	leg	en	put on, lay on, impose; fine; print
aus	leg	en	lay out; exhibit for, display; advance; explain
Aus	leg	er	interpreter, commentator
Aus	leg	ung	interpretation, comment, exegesis
Be	leg	nm	proof, evidence; document, deed; record, receipt
be	leg	bar	provable, attestable
be	leg	en	overlay, cover; inflict upon; fine; prove
bei	leg	en	add; enclose; confer; settle, impose upon
Bei	leg	ung	addition, attribution, settlement
dar	leg	en	lay open, show, explain, expose; state, point out
Dar	leg	ung	statement, exposition, explanation
ein	leg	en	lay in, insert, put in; enclose; put on, deposit
Ein	leg	er	depositer, investor; feeder
ent	leg	en	a	distant, remote, far away
Ent	leg	en heit	distance, remoteness
er	leg	en	kill; shoot down

Ge leg e nn		nest of eggs
ge leg en	a	situated, located; opportune, convenient
Ge leg en heit		occasion, opportunity, chance, opening
ge leg ent lich		occasional, casual, accidental, incidental, on occasion
her leg en	s	lay down here
hin leg en		lay down, put down
hinter leg en		deposit, place on deposit; give in trust
Hinter leg er		depositer
Hinter leg ung		deposition
los leg en	s	begin, start
nach leg en		make up the fire; put on more wood
nieder leg en		lay down, deposit; abdicate, resign, retire from
sich nieder leg en		lie down, go to bed
Nieder leg ung		laying down; abdication, resignation; strike
'über leg en		lay over
über leg en	a	superior; prevalent
über 'leg en		reflect upon, think over, consider
Ueber leg en heit		superiority preponderance
Ueber leg ung		reflection, consideration
'um leg en		put on, lay around; apply, shift; kill; transfer
Um leg ung		transfer, shifting
unter leg en	a	overcome, beaten
'unter leg en		put under
Unter leg ene		underdog
Unter leg en heit		inferiority
ver leg en	a	embarrassed, self-conscious; confused
ver leg en		mislay, misplace; displace, transport, transfer, relocate
Ver leg en heit		embarrassment, predicament, difficulty
Ver leg er		publisher
Ver leg ung		transfer, removal; postponement, adjournment; publication
vor leg en		put before, serve with; help to; submit, present
Vor leg er		mat, rug
weg leg en		put away, lay aside, discard
wider leg bar		refutable
wider 'leg en		disprove, refute, confute
wider leg lich		repugnant, disgusting, disagreeable, repulsive, loathsome
Wider leg ung		refutation, rebuttal
zer leg bar		collapsible, detachable, decomposable
zer leg en		part, separate, divide; cut up, analyze
Zer leg ung		carving, splitting up, dissection, dismantling
zu leg en		cover, shut; add, increase
zurück leg en		lay aside; save; traverse; attain
zusammen leg bar		foldable, collapsible
zusammen leg en		lay together; fold up; combine, consolidate; centralize, integrate
Zusammen leg ung		consolidation, integration; merger, fusion; centralization
her ein leg en		let s.o. down; take s.o. in

hin ein leg en	put in, take in
auf er leg en	impose, inflict
ab ge leg en	remote, out of the way; retired
an ge leg en a	important
An ge leg en heit	concern, affair, matter
an ge leg en t lich	urgent, earnest, pressing
auf ge leg t	disposed, inclined
un ge leg en a	inconvenient, inopportune, untimely
Un ge leg en heit	inconvenience, trouble
Vor ge leg e nn	back-gearing; arrangement
un über leg t	inconsiderate, unwise, thoughtless, ill-advised
Un über leg t heit	thoughtlessness
vor ver leg en	advance; lift fire
un wider leg bar	irrefutable; conclusive
fest leg en	establish, lay down; set a date for
grund leg end	fundamental, basic; elementary

Lehn e	support, rest, prop; armrest, backrest
lehn en	lean
sich lehn en	lean, prop, rest
ab lehn en	decline, refuse; reject; turn down
Ab lehn ung	refusal; rejection; disapprobation, objection
an lehn en	leave ajar
An lehn ung	contact
auf lehn en	lean, rest
sich auf lehn en	lean
Auf lehn ung	rebellion, revolt, mutiny; opposition, resistance
zurück lehn en	lean back
sich zurück lehn en	lean back
sich hin aus lehn en	lean out

be lehn en	invest with a fief, enfeoff
Be lehn ung	enfeoffment
ent lehn en	borrow

Lehr e	rule, precept, hint, lesson, warning; instruction, tuition
lehr en	teach, instruct; show
Lehr er	teacher; instructor; tutor
Lehr erin	woman teacher, instructress; governess
lehr haft	instructive; didactic
Lehr ling	apprentice; novice, beginner
lehr reich	instructive, informative
be lehr en	instruct; advise, apprise; enlighten
Be lehr ung	instruction, information, advice; correction
ge lehr ig	docile, teachable; clever, intelligent
Ge lehr ig keit	docility, teachability
Ge lehr sam keit	erudition, learning
ge lehr t	learned, erudite; scholarly
Ge lehr ter	learned man, scholar, savant
un be lehr bar	unconvincable
un ge lehr ig	indocile, unteachable, slow

un ge lehr t a	unlearnt, illiterate

Leib nm	body; belly
Leib chen	bodice; waist; vest
leib en	the very image of him, his very self
leib haft ig	corporeal; personified; embodied; living, in person
leib lich	bodily, of the body; corporeal
be leib t	stout, fat, portly, corpulent
Be leib t heit	corpulence, stoutness, portliness
bei leib e av	by no means, on no account, not by a long shot
sich ent leib en	commit suicide, kill o.s.
Hinter leib nm	hind quarters
Unter leib nm	abdomen, belly
ein ver leib en	incorporate; embody in; annex land to
Ein ver leib ung	incorporation, inclusion; annexation

leid a	I am sorry, I regret; I cannot help it
Leid nn	injury, harm; wrong; misfortune; sorrow, grief, pain
leid lich	bearable, tolerable; passable, middling
leid en	suffer; be afflicted with, be subject to
Leid en nn	suffering; affliction, trouble; complaint, ailment, malady
Leid en schaft	passion for, powerful emotion
leid en schaft lich	passionate; impassioned; ardent
Leid en schaft lich keit	passionateness, ardor, fervor; vehemence; impulsiveness
leid en schaft s los	dispassionate; impassive, cool, detached
leid er av	unfortunately
leid ig	tiresome, unpleasant, disagreeable; confounded, accursed
leid voll	sorrowful, full of grief
aus leid en	one's suffering is over
Bei leid nn	condolence, sympathy
er leid en	suffer, endure, bear; sustain, incur; suffer death
Mit leid nn	compassion
Mit leid en schaft	implication, involvement; damage, impairment
mit leid ig	compassionate, pitiful; sympathetic
mit leid los	pitiless, merciless
un leid lich	intolerable, insufferable
ver leid en	disgust s.o. with s.t.
zu leid e av	hurt s.o., do s.o. harm
be mit leid en	pity, commiserate, be sorry for
be leid ig en	offend, injure, hurt; insult, defame, libel, slander
Be leid ig er	offender, insulter
Be leid ig ung	insult, injury; affront

Leist e	ledge, border, strip; slat; groin
leist en	do; perform; carry out, execute; fulfill
sich leist en	treat o.s. to s.t.; afford s.t.
Leist en nm	last; boottree, block
Leist ung	performance; achievement, feat, stunt; accomplishment

leist ung s fäh ig	productive
Leist ung s fäh ig keit	efficiency
ab leist en	fulfill, perform; pass time of service; serve one's time
Gegen leist ung	return; equivalent
Vor leist ung	advance payment

---

leit en	lead, guide
Leit er	leader
Leit er nf	ladder
Leit erin	leader
leit fäh ig	conductive
Leit fäh ig keit	conductance, conductivity
Leit ung	leading, conducting, guidance; control, management, direction
ab leit en	lead off, turn aside; drain off water; shunt, abduct
Ab leit ung	diversion; drainage; derivation, deduction
an leit en	guide; instruct, school, train
An leit ung	guidance, instruction, direction; textbook, primer; introduction
ein leit en	start; initiate, introduce; launch; open talks
Ein leit ung	introduction, preface, preamble
Fern leit ung	long-distance telephone line; transmission line; pipeline
Ge leit nn t	conduct
ge leit en	accompany, conduct, escort
her leit en	conduct here; derive; deduce from, infer
hin leit en	lead to, steer to; call attention to
Ober leit ung	supervision
Rück leit ung	electrical return line
'über leit en	lead over, conduct over; transfuse blood
'um leit en	divert, by-pass, reroute traffic
Um leit ung	by-pass, diversion, detour
ver leit en	mislead, lead astray; seduce; induce
Ver leit ung	misleading; seduction; inducement; subornation
weiter leit en	forward, transmit; refer
zu leit en	let in; supply, pipe in, feed; conduct to; impart to; channel
Zu leit ung	supply; conduction, transmission
zurück leit en	lead back, return; feed back
zurück ge leit en	lead back, conduct back, escort back
Wasser leit ung	water pipes, water installation

---

lern en	learn; study; practice
sich lern en s	teach, learn; acquire, master
an lern en	train, instruct, school; break s.o. in
An lern ling	trainee
aus lern en	finish learning, complete one's apprenticeship
er lern bar	learnable
er lern en	learn, acquire, master
'um lern en	learn anew
ver lern en	unlearn, forget

zu lern en s	learn in addition, add to one's stock of knowledge
un ge lern t s	unskilled worker
kenn en lern en	make the acquaintance of s.o., meet s.o.; get to know s.o.

les bar	legible; decipherable; readable, worth reading
Les bar keit	legibility, readability, readableness
Les e	gathering; gleaning; vintage
les en	read; decipher
sich les en	reading; lecturing; gathering
Les er	reader
Les erin	reader
les er lich	legible, easy to read
Les er lich keit	legibility
Les er schaft	readers
Les ung	reading
ab les en	gather; pick off; read off a speech
an les en	acquire by reading
auf les en	gather, pick up
Aus les e	sorting; choice, selection
aus les en	select, choose, pick out; sort, grade; finish a book
be les en a	well-read
Be les en heit	extensive reading
'durch les en	read through, read over, peruse
sich ein les en	read o.s. into; familiarize o.s. with; read up on a subject
er les en a	select; choice, exquisite
er les en	acquire by reading; select, choose, pick
mit les en	read; be a joint subscriber to; control
Nach les e	gleaning; gleanings
nach les en	glean; read, look up in a book
über 'les en	read s.t. over, peruse; overlook
ver les en	read out; call over names; pick s.t.
sich ver les en	read wrong, make a mistake in reading
Vor les e	early vintage
vor les en	read aloud
Vor les er	reader; lecturer
Vor les erin	reader; lecturer
Vor les ung	reading
zer les en	well-thumbed
hin ein les en	read s.t. into s.t.
aus er les en a	chosen, hand-picked; exquisite, choice
un les er lich	illegible

Leucht e	light
leucht en	give light, emit light, shine forth; gleam, sparkle
Leucht er	candlestick; chandelier, lustre; sconce
ab leucht en	pass a light over, light off
auf leucht en	flash, light up
be leucht en	light up, illuminate; throw light on, illustrate
Be leucht er	lighting technician, theater electrician
Be leucht ung	lighting; illumination, lights

'durch leucht en	shine through; come to light, become apparent, show
durch 'leucht en	flood with light; x-ray s.t., investigate, analyze; clear up
Durch leucht ung	illuminations
ein leucht en	be clear, be obvious, be evident
er leucht en	light up, illuminate; enlighten
Er leucht ung	illumination; enlightenment
her vor leucht en	shine forth, shine out; come forth, manifest o.s.

licht a	light
Licht nn	light; brightness; illumination, lighting; luminary
licht en	clear
Licht ung	clearing, opening; glade
licht voll	illuminating
be licht en	irradiate; expose
Be licht ung	illumination
Fern licht nn	full headlight beam, high beam
Ge licht er nn	lot, rabble, riffraff
Gegen licht nn	opposite light
Ober licht nn	skylight
Rück licht nn	rear light, tail lamp; rear reflector
'über be licht en	overexpose
Ueber be licht ung	overexposure
un be licht et	unexposed
'unter be licht en t	underexpose
Unter be licht ung t	underexposure

lieb a	dear, beloved; kind, good, sweet
Lieb chen	love, sweetheart
Lieb e	love
Lieb elei	flirtation, amour, dalliance
lieb eln	flirt with, dally with; make love to; philander
lieb en	love, be in love with; cherish; like, be fond of
lieb en s wert	lovable, amiable, charming
lieb en s würd ig	kind, obliging; affable
lieb en s würd **ig er weise kindly**
Lieb en s würd ig keit	amiability; kindness; kind words, compliment
lieb er av	more willingly; rather, sooner
lieb e voll	loving, affectionate, kind hearted, tender
lieb lich	lovely, charming, sweet; delightful; smooth
Lieb lich keit	loveliness, charm, sweetness; delightfulness
Lieb ling	darling, pet; favorite
lieb los	unloving, unkind, cold
Lieb los ig keit	unkindness, uncharitableness, coldness; unkind words
lieb reich	loving, affectionate, tender; kind, amiable, benevolent
Lieb schaft	love affair, amour; liaison
Lieb st er	darling, sweetheart
Be lieb en nn	will, pleasure, discretion
be lieb en	deign, choose

be lieb ig		whatever you chose; optional, arbitrary, discretionary
be lieb t		liked, favorite; popular; sought-after
Be lieb t heit		popularity
Ge lieb te	nf	lover; sweetheart, darling; mistress
Ge lieb ter	nm	lover; sweetheart, darling
Gegen lieb e		unreturned love
miss lieb ig		unpopular, not in favor, odious
un lieb	a	disagreeable
un lieb sam		disagreeable, unpleasant
sich ver lieb en		fall in love with s.o., fall in love with s.t.
Ver lieb t heit		amorousness
Vor lieb e		predilection, preference, partiality
zu lieb e	av	do s.t. for one's sake
un be lieb t		disliked; unpopular
Un be lieb t heit		unpopularity

Lief er ant	nm	supplier, purveyor; contractor; caterer; distributor
lief er bar		to be delivered, deliverable; available; marketable, salable
lief er n		deliver
Lief er ung		delivery
lief er ung s weise		in serial parts
ab liefer n		deliver goods; deliver up, turn in, hand in; surrender
Ab liefer ung		delivery, handing over; surrender
an liefer n		deliver goods, deliver to the door
An liefer ung		delivery
auf liefer n		consign; dispatch
aus liefer n		turn over, hand over, deliver; extradite; supply; distribute
Aus liefer ung		surrender; extradition; delivery, supply; distribution
be liefer n		supply customers, furnish with, cater for hotels
Be liefer ung		supply, supplying, catering
ein liefer n		take; hand in, submit; deliver s.t. up, deposit; send s.t.
Ein liefer ung		admission; commitment, committal; delivery, deposit
nach liefer n		supply s.t. subsequently, deliver s.t. later; repeat the supply of
Nach liefer ung		subsequent delivery, later supply, repeated supply
über 'liefer n		hand s.t. down, pass s.t. on, transmit, bequeath; surrender
Ueber liefer ung		tradition; record

Lieg e		couch; chaise lounge
lieg en		lie, be lying; repose, rest
Lieg en schaft		immovables, real estate
ab lieg en		lie at a distance, be far off
An lieg en	nn	request, desire, wish; preoccupation; matter, affair
an lieg en		lie close to, border on, be adjacent to

An lieg er		adjoining owner, abutter
auf lieg en		lie, rest; weigh on; be laid out; be exposed for sale
sich auf lieg en		get bedsore
aus lieg en		be displayed, be exhibited, be on show
bei lieg en		be enclosed; lie to
bei lieg end		attached, appended, added; enclosed letter
da lieg en		lie there
'durch lieg en		get bed-sore
er lieg en		succumb; fall victim to
fern lieg en		be far from, not occur to, be far from one's mind
in lieg end		enclosed
ob lieg en		apply o.s. to s.t.; devolve on s.o., be one's duty
um lieg end	a	surrounding, neighboring
unter 'lieg en		be overcome, be defeated; succumb to
vor lieg en		a chain on the door; be present, be known; be a cause for worry
zurück lieg en		date back; belong to the past
da nieder lieg en		be laid up; languish, stagnate
gegen über lieg en		be opposite, lie opposite, face
her um lieg en	s	lie around, lie around s.t., laze around

Lin ie	nf	line; lineage, descent
lin ier en		rule, line
Lin ier ung		ruling
Neben lin ie		parallel line
un lin ier t		unruled

Lob	nn	praise; commendation; fame; eulogy, applause, approval
lob en		praise, commend, speak highly of; laud, eulogize, extol
lob en s wert		praiseworthy
löb lich		laudable, commendable
Aus lob ung	l	public reward
sich ent lob en		break off one's engagement
Ent lob ung		disengagement
ge lob en		promise solemnly, vow, pledge
Ge löb nis		promise; pledge, vow
ver lob en		engage
sich ver lob en		become engaged, become betrothed
Ver löb nis		betrothal, engagement
Ver lob ung		betrothal, engagement
be lob ig en		praise, commend
Be lob ig ung		praise, commendation

Lohn	nm	wage, wages; pay, payment; earnings, salary, remuneration
lohn en		reward, recompense, compensate, repay; pay; be worth
sich lohn en		be worth, be worthwhile, be rewarding, repay itself

	löhn en	pay wages to, pay soldiers
	Löhn ung	payment of wages, soldiers' pay
ab	lohn en	pay off, dismiss
be	lohn en	reward
Be	lohn ung	reward
ent	lohn en	pay s.o. off
Ent	lohn ung	paying s.o. off, pay, remuneration
ver	lohn en	be worthwhile, be worth the trouble
un be	lohn t	unrewarded

	los	av	go on, get going, get started
	Los	nn	lot, lottery, ticket; fate, destiny; portion, share
	los en		cast lots, draw lots
	Los ung		password, watchword, countersign; motto, political slogan
aus	los en		draw lots for; toss for
ver	los en		dispose of by lot; draw lots for, raffle
Ver	los ung		lottery, raffle

	lös bar		solvable, resolvable; soluble; separable, severable
	Lös bar keit		solvability, solvableness, solubility
	los e	a	loose, free; be rid of s.t.; be the matter
	Los e	nn n	slack of a rope, bight on a line
	lös en		loosen, unloose; untie, undo, unfasten, unbind; separate, detach
sich	lös en		loosen, come loose; separate, sever, come off; resolve itself
	lös lich		soluble, dissolvable, dissoluble
	Lös lich keit		solubility, dissolubility
	Lös ung		solution to a problem; unravelment of a plot; chemical solution
ab	lös en		loosen, take off, detach
sich ab	lös en		relieve one another, alternate, take turns
Ab	lös ung		loosening, detaching
auf	lös bar		solvable
auf	lös en		loosen, untie; disentangle; dissolve, melt; disintegrate; decompose
Auf	lös ung		loosening; disentanglement
aus	lös en		loosen, release
Aus	lös er		release
ein	lös en		redeem; withdraw from circulation; collect; convert
Ein	lös ung		redemption; withdrawal; payment; discharge
Er	lös	nm	proceeds
er	lös en		redeem, save; deliver, release, free; realize, net, get
Er	lös er		Redeemer, Savior
Er	lös ung		redemption
los	lös en		loosen, detach; sever
nach	lös en	t	take a supplementary ticket, pay for ticket on train
un	lös bar		unsolvable; inseparable
un	lös lich	t	insoluble

Zwischen lös ung	interim solution
un ab lös lich	irredeemable; consolidated; perpetual
un auf lös bar	indissoluble
un auf lös lich	indissoluble

Lösch e	slack; breeze; culm, charcoal dust
lösch en	put out a fire, turn off a light; quench thirst; blot ink; delete
Lösch er	fire extinguisher; ink blotter
Lösch ung	extinguishing a fire; turning off a light; quenching thirst
ab lösch en	extinguish, put out; chill; quench; temper steel; wipe off
aus lösch en	extinguish, put out; switch off, turn out; erase, delete
er lösch en	be extinguished, go out; become extinct, die out
ver lösch en	extinguish; efface writing
un aus lösch lich	inextinguishable; indelible; lasting
un ge lösch t	unquenched; unslaked lime

lub: siehe lob	
Ge lüb de nn	vow, solemn promise

Luft nf	air; atmosphere; breeze; breath; slackness
lüft en	air, ventilate; aerate; bleed of air
Lüft er	ventilator, fan
luft ig	airy, aerial; breezy; flimsy; vaporous, hazy; flighty
Lüft ung	airing; ventilation; aeration; bleeding of air
Ab luft nf	exhaust air
aus lüft en	air, ventilate
'durch lüft en	air, ventilate
ent lüft en	evacuate the air from; de-aerate; bleed air from; ventilate
Ent lüft er	air exhauster
Ent lüft ung	evacuation of air; ventilation

Aus lug nm n	porthole

Lug nm	falsehood
Lüg e	lie, falsehood, untruth
lüg en	lie, tell a lie, tell a fib
lüg en haft	lying, deceitful, untrue, fabricated, false
Lüg en haft ig keit	deceitfulness, mendacity; falsehood
Lüg ner	liar
Lüg nerin	liar
lüg ner isch	lying, deceitful, mendacious
an lüg en	tell s.o. a lie
be lüg en	lie to
er lüg en	invent, fabricate
Erz lüg ner nm	arch-liar
sich her aus lüg en	lie o.s. out of s.t.

Lust nf	pleasure, delight; enjoyment; gaiety; joy; lust, inclination
Lust bar keit	div~rsion, amusement; entertainment; festivity, fete
lüst ern a	desirous, greedy; lewd, lascivious, lecherous, lustful
Lüst ern heit	greediness; lasciviousness, lewdness, concupiscence
lust ig	merry, gay, jolly, cheerful; amusing, funny, ludicrous
Lust ig keit	gaiety, merriment, mirth; jollity, cheerfulness; fun
Lüst ling	voluptuary, debauchee, libertine, lecher, rake
lust los	listless, spiritless, unenthusiastic; lifeless, inactive; dull
Lust los ig keit	listlessness; dullness, slackness
Ge lüst nn	craving, appetite, desire, lust
ge lüst en	have a strong desire for, have a craving for
Un lust nf	listlessness; dislike for s.o., aversion to s.o.
un lust ig	listless; morose; reluctant
Ver lust nm	bereavement; damage; waste
ver lust ig	forfeit s.t., be deprived of s.t., lose s.t.
be lust ig en	amuse, divert, entertain
Be lust ig ung	amusement, entertainment

mach en	make, manufacture; produce, effect, procure; do, perform; cause
sich mach en	come about, happen; appear; do well
Mach er	maker, manufacturer
ab mach en	take off, detach; adjust; settle; arrange
Ab mach ung	loosening, settling, arrangement; stipulation
an mach en	bind, attach, tie; fix; dress
auf mach en	open, unlock, undo, unbutton; put up
sich auf mach en	run away, be off, set out for, make for; make up
Auf mach ung	outward appearance; make-up, lay-out
aus mach en	put out, switch off; figure out; locate; matter, amount to
'durch mach en s	go through, pass through, live through, experience, suffer
ein mach en	preserve, pickle, bottle, can
fort mach en s	make haste, go on
ge mach a	slowly, by degrees, gently
Ge mach nn	room, apartment
ge mäch lich	soft, slow, comfortable, slowly, conveniently
Ge mäch lich keit	slowness, ease
sich her mach en	tackle, fall upon s.o.; to delete; to set about
los mach en s	unfasten, make loose, release, free; cast off
mit mach en	join in, take part in, be in on, chip in
nach mach en	imitate, conterfeit, mimic, duplicate, copy
nieder mach en	cut down, wipe out; kill, slay, massacre
über 'mach en	send, bequeath; transmit
ver mach en	bequeath
'voll mach en	fill up, complete; dirty

vor mach en			put before; show s.o. how to do s.t.; impose upon s.o.; deceive
weg mach en	s		remove, take out spots
weiter mach en			carry on, continue; as you were
zu mach en	s		shut, close, fasten; fold; seal, stop up
sich dar an mach en	s		go at it
sich her an mach en	s		edge near; set to work, undertake; make a pass at a girl
her aus mach en	s		take out
sich her aus mach en	s		get on; blossom out; improve
ab ge mach t			agreed, all right, o.k.
aus ge mach t			decided, perfect, settled
Ein ge mach tes			preserved fruits, preserves, jam, sweetmeats, pickles
Un ge mach	nn	p	discomfort, hardship, trouble
her unter mach en	s		run down; cut up; upbraid
sich da von mach en	s		slip away, clear out, make off
irre mach en			confuse s.o., disconcert s.o., bewilder s.o.

Macht	nf		power, force, energy; strength, might; influence, control
mächt ig			powerful, mighty, strong; thick, wide, high; very much
Macht ig keit			mightiness; thickness
macht los			powerless
Macht los ig keit			powerlessness
macht voll			powerful
ent macht en			deprive s.o. of his power
Ueber macht	nf		predominance, superiority, superior force
über mächt ig			predominant, overwhelming, too powerful, paramount
Ver mächt nis			legacy, bequest, testament, will
Voll macht	nf		full power, power of attorney, authority, warrant, proxy
Vor macht	nf		leading power
sich be mächt ig en			get hold of, take s.t. over, seize
ent mächt ig en			deprive s.o. of civil rights, deprive s.o. of political power
er mächt ig en			empower, authorize
Er mächt ig ung			authorization, authority; warranty, power, faculty
be voll mächt ig en			authorize, invest s.o. with powers; empower; accredit
Be voll mächt ig te			authorized person, lawful agent, representative; private attorney
Be voll mächt ig ung			authorization, warrant, mandate, power of attorney

---

Mahl	nn	meal, repast; feast, banquet
mahl en		grind, mill; pulverize; crush, bruise; beat
aus mahl en		grind up, extract
zer mahl en		grind, pulverize

Ge mahl nm i	consort, husband
Ge mahl in	wife, spouse, consort
ver mähl en	wed, marry
Ver mähl ung	wedding, marriage
un ver mähl t p	unmarried

mahn en	remind; warn, admonish; urge
Mahn er	admonisher, monitor, warning voice; dunner
Mahn mal nn	memorial
Mahn ung	admonition, warning; reminder, dunning
er mahn en	admonish, exhort; expostulate; urge; caution, warn
Er mahn ung	admonition, exhortation
ge mahn en	remind s.o. of, put s.o. in mind of
ver mahn en	admonish, exhort, warn
Ver mahn ung	admonition, exhortation, warning

mal en	paint, portray; draw, sketch, represent, depict
Mal er	painter; artist
Mal erei	painting
Mal erin	painter; artist
mal er isch	pictorial, painting; picturesque
ab mal en	paint, portray
an mal en	paint
aus mal en	paint; illuminate, color
be mal en	paint; decorate
Ge mäl de nn	painting, picture; portrait
nach mal en	copy
über 'mal en	paint over
unter 'mal en	prime, ground, paint the background
Unter mal ung	incidental music

mal av	multiply by; once, at one time; formerly; for a change
Mal nn	mark, sign; boundary; monument
da mal ig	then, of that time
da mal s av	then, at that time; in those days
nach mal ig	subsequent
nach mal s av	afterwards; later on
vor mal ig	former
vor mal s av	formerly; erstwhile, onetime
zu mal c	the more so as, especially since
da zu mal av	at that time, in those days
Denk mal nn	monument, memorial
manch mal av	sometimes
Merk mal nn	peculiarity, characteristic; mark of identification

Mann nm	man, soldier, enlisted man; husband
mann bar	marriageable
Mann bar keit	manhood, puberty; marriageable age
Männ chen	little man, hubby; male bull
mann haft	manly; brave, stout, valiant; resolute

	Mann haft ig keit	manliness, stoutness, courage
	Mann heit	masculinity, manhood; virility
	männ lich	male; masculine; manly, virile
	Männ lich keit	manliness, virility
	Mann schaft m	body of men, personnel; team; crew; party; troops
be	mann en	man
Be	mann ung	manning; crew
ent	mann en	castrate; unman
Ent	mann ung	castration, emasculation
sich er	mann en	take heart, pluck up courage; pull o.s. together
Hinter	mann nm	rear-rank man
Neben	mann nm	next man
Ob	mann nm	chairman; steward, shop steward, spokesman
über	'mann en	overpower, overwhelm, overcome
un	männ lich	unmanly, effeminate
Un	männ lich keit	unmanliness
Vor	mann nm	foreman
Vorder	mann nm	man in front
un be	mann t	unmanned
ver	männ lich en	masculinize
jeder	mann pn	everybody
Kauf	mann nm	business man, merchant
Schutz	mann nm	policeman

	Marsch nm	march
	marsch ier en	march; stride
Ab	marsch nm	departure, marching off, start
An	marsch nm	approach
Auf	marsch nm	marching-up; line up
Aus	marsch nm	marching out, departure
Durch	marsch nm	passage, march through
Ein	marsch nm	march-in, entry
Rück	marsch nm	march back, retreat
Vor	marsch nm	advance
Vor bei	marsch nm	marching past
an	marsch ier en	approach, advance, march against, march towards
auf	marsch ier en	draw up, form up; assemble, deploy
aus	marsch ier en	march out, depart
'durch	marsch ier en	march through
ein	marsch ier en	march into, enter
los	marsch ier en	march off
vor bei	marsch ier en	march past, file by

	Mass nn	measure; measurement; proportion, rate; extent, size; quantity
	Mass e	mass; bulk; substance
	mass en haft	numerous, an abundance of, large quantities of
	mass en weise	in masses, in large numbers; wholesale
	mass ig	massy, bulky, voluminous; solid
	mäss ig	moderate; frugal; temperate; reasonable; mediocre; middling
	mäss ig en	moderate; soften; mitigate, temper; lessen, abate

Mäss ig keit	moderation, frugality; temperance, sobriety; restraint
mass iv a	solid, massive; heavy, powerful
Mass iv nn t	massif
mass los	boundless; immoderate, excessive; extravagant
Mass los ig keit	boundlessness; immoderateness; excess; extravagance
mass voll	moderate, temperate; discreet
sich an mass en	assume, usurp; pretend to, presume, have the impudence
an mass end	arrogant, presumptuous; overbearing; impudent
An mass ung	assumption; usurpation, assertiveness; presumption; arrogance
Aus mass nn	measurement, dimension, size; extent; scale; degree
ge mäss ig t a	moderate; temperate
Ueber mass nn	oversize; excess, excessive amount; transport; immoderation
über mäss ig	excessive, immoderate; undue, unjustified; extreme; too much
Un mass nn	immensity, excess
un mäss ig	immoderate, unreasonable, extravagant, boundless; excessive
Un mäss ig keit	immoderation, unreasonableness, extravagance; excess
Unter mass nn i	undersize
Ur mass nn	standard gauge
ver mass en	lose one's individuality
Ver mass ung	stereotyping
er mäss ig en	abate, reduce, lower; mark down
Er mäss ig ung	reduction, lowering

ge mäss p	according to, in agreement with, in compliance with
ge mäss a	appropriate
Ge mäss heit	conformity

Mauer nf	wall
mauer n	make a wall, lay bricks; risk nothing
Mau r er	bricklayer, mason
aus mauer n	wall up, brick up; line with
ein mauer n	wall in, immure; fix in a wall
Ge mäuer nn	ruins, decayed walls
hinter mauer n	back
um 'mauer n	wall in, wall around
unter 'mauer n	underpin; bolster, corroborate
Unter mauer ung	ground work
ver mauer n	wall up, wall in
zu mauer n	wall up; brick

meid en	avoid, shun, keep clear of
ver meid en	avoid; evade, dodge, steer clear of; shun

ver meid lich	avoidable
Ver meid ung	avoidance
un ver meid lich	inevitable, unavoidable, unfailing

meld en	inform s.o. of s.t., report s.t. to s.o.; announce
sich meld en	enter; signal; announce o.s., report; answer the telephone
ab meld en	give notice of one's leaving
Ab meld ung	notice of departure; leaving certificate
an meld en	announce, notify; report; advise; give notice of appeal
An meld ung	announcement, notification; report; registration
ver meld en p	announce; mention; inform, notify
sich zurück meld en	report back
un an ge meld et	unannounced

Meng e	quantity; amount; volume; aggregate, set; multitude; crowd
meng en	mix, blend
meng en mäss ig	quantitative
Meng sel nn	medley, hodgepodge, mess
bei meng en	mix s.t. with s.t., admix s.t. to s.t.
ein meng en	mix in, intermix, add
sich ein meng en	interfere, intervene, meddle with, butt in
Ge meng e nn	mixture; scuffle, brawl
Ge meng sel nn	medley, hodgepodge
Un meng e	enormous quantity
unter 'meng en	intermingle, intermix
ver meng en	mix up, mingle, blend; confuse s.o.

Mensch nm	human being; man; person, individual, fellow
mensch en würd ig	worthy of a human being
Mensch heit	mankind, humanity, human race
mensch lich	human; humane; tolerable
Mensch lich keit	human nature; humaneness, humanity
ent mensch t	inhuman, brutish
Mit mensch nm	fellow-man
Ueber mensch nm	superman
über mensch lich	superhuman
Un mensch nm	monster, brute
un mensch lich	inhuman, brutal; degrading; superhuman; tremendous, awful
Un mensch lich keit	inhumanity, brutality
Ur mensch nm	primitive man
ver mensch lich en	represent in a human form, humanize
Ver mensch lich ung	humanization

merk bar	perceptible, noticeable; retainable
merk en	pay attention to, listen to
merk lich	perceptible, noticeable; considerable; distinct, marked
Merk mal nn	mark, sign; characteristic, feature; distinctive mark, character

merk würd ig	noteworthy, remarkable; strange, odd curious, funny
merk würd ig er weise	strange to say, oddly enough
Merk würd ig keit	remarkableness; curiosity; sight; peculiarity; oddness
an merk en	mark; jot down, write down, make an annotation
An merk ung	observation, remark; comment; note, footnote
auf merk en	attend to, pay attention to
auf merk sam	attentive; watchful, vigilant, keen; obliging, courteous, kind
Auf merk sam keit	attention, attentiveness; watchfulness, alertness, vigilance
be merk bar	observable, perceptible; noticeable
be merk en	perceive, observe, notice, note
Be merk ung	remark, observation, comment; note, annotation
un merk lich	imperceptible
Ver merk nm	note, notice; entry; endorsement
ver merk en	note down, record; remark, observe; make a note of; enter
vor merk en	note down, make a note of, mark down; reserve s.t.
Vor merk ung	note, entry; booking, reservation
un auf merk sam	inattentive; distracted, absent-minded; careless, thoughtless
Un auf merk sam keit	inattention; thoughtlessness
un be merk bar	imperceptible
un be merk t	unnoticed, unseen
Vor be merk ung	preliminary remark; preamble
Zwischen be merk ung	incidental remark; interruption

---

mess bar	measurable
mess en	measure s.t., meter s.t., gauge s.t.; sound s.t.; time s.t.
sich mess en	measure; contain
Mess er	knife; razor; dagger; blade; scalpel; cutter
Mess ung	measurement; gauging; surveying; testing; sounding
ab mess en	measure off; survey; gauge time; measure a proportion
Ab mess ung	measurement; dimension, gauge; proportion
an mess en	take the measure for
aus mess en	measure out; survey land; gauge a vessel
Aus mess ung	measuring, measurement; survey; gauge
be mess en	proportion; time; dimension; rate; adjust; estimate, measure
Be mess ung	proportioning, dimensioning, design; rating
bei mess en	ascribe s.t. to s.o., credit s.o. with s.t.
'durch mess en	traverse, pass over; cover, travel a distance, walk
durch 'mess en	traverse, pass over; cover, travel distance
Durch mess er	diameter
er mess en	estimate; calculate; judge; weigh, consider; conceive

Er mess en nn	estimate, judgement
ge mess en a	measured; formal; strict; grave, solemn
Ge mess en heit	measuredness; formality; gravity
nach mess en	measure again, remeasure, check
un mess bar	immeasurable
ver mess en	survey, measure, take a measurement of
ver mess en a	daring, presumptuous; impudent, insolvent
sich ver mess en	measure wrong; dare, presume, have the impudence to
Ver mess en heit	presumption
Ver mess er	surveyor
Ver mess ung	measurement; survey of land
zu mess en	measure out; apportion, allot, mete out
un er mess lich a	immeasurable, immense, vast
ab ge mess en a	measured
an ge mess en a	suitable, appropriate, fit; reasonable, fair; adequate; proper
un an ge mess en a	unsuitable; improper; inadequate; incongruous

Miet e	lease; hire; rent; tenancy; stack, rick
miet en	lease, rent; hire; charter
Miet er	tenant; lodger, roomer; lessee; hirer; charterer
Miet erin	tenant; lodger, roomer; lessee; hirer; charterer
Miet ling	hireling, mercenary
ab miet en	hire; rent a house
Ab miet er	tenant, lessee
ein miet en	take lodgings, take rooms; pit, stack up; silo grain
sich ein miet en	take lodgings, rent a room
Unter miet e	sublease
Unter miet er	subtenant; lodger, roomer
ver miet en	rent; hire out; lease, let
Ver miet er	letter; landlord; hirer
Ver miet ung	letting; leasing; renting out
ab ver miet en	sublet
'unter ver miet en	sublet
Unter ver miet er	sublessor
weiter ver miet en	sublet

un militär isch	unmilitary
vor militär isch	premilitary
ent militar isier en	demilitarize
Militär nm	military man, soldier
Militär nn	the military; armed forces; army; military service
militär isch	military; soldiery, martial
militär isier en	militarize
Militär isier ung	militarization
Militär ist	militarist
militär ist isch	militaristic

mind er a	lesser; smaller; minor; inferior
Mind er heit	minority
mind er n	diminish, lessen, decrease; reduce, lower, abate

Mind er ung	decrease, diminution; reduction, abatement; depreciation
mind er wert ig	inferior, of inferior quality; low-grade, cheap
Mind er wert ig keit	inferior value, inferiority; inferior quality; lower valence
mind est ens av	at least, no less than, not under minority
zu mind est av	at least
ver mind er n	diminish, decrease, lessen
sich ver mind er n	diminish, decrease, lessen, decline; impair, reduce, curtail
Ver mind er ung	diminution, decrease, lessening; reduction, cut
un ver mind er t	undiminished
misch bar	miscible, mixable
Misch bar keit	miscibility
misch en	mix, mingle; blend; alloy; combine; compound; adulterate
Misch ling	hybrid, mongrel, cross-breed; half-caste, half-breed
Misch ung	mixture; blend; combination, composition; alloy; adulteration
bei misch en	mix s.t. with s.t., admix s.t. to s.t.
Bei misch ung	admixture, addition; impurity
ein misch en	interfere, meddle, butt in; mix in, intermix
Ein misch ung	interference, meddling
ent misch en	disintegrate, decompose
Ge misch nn	mixture
ge misch t	mixed, diffused
unter 'misch en	intermingle, intermix
ver misch en	mix up, mingle, blend; interbreed; adulterate; alloy
sich ver misch en	mix, blend; interbreed
Ver misch ung	mixture, blending; interbreeding, crossing
un ver misch t	unmixed; unblended, unalloyed
Mit-tag nm	midday, noon; south
mit-täg lich	midday, noon day; meridian, southern
mit-tag s av	at noon; at lunchtime
Nach mit-tag nm	afternoon
nach mit-tag s av	in the afternoon
Vor mit-tag nm	morning, forenoon
vor mit-tag s av	in the morning
Mittel nn	means; medium; instrument, tool; device; measure; average
mittel bar	mediate, indirect
mittel los	without means, impecunious, destitute
Mittel los ig keit	lack of means, destitution
mittel mäss ig	middling, indifferent; mediocre; moderate, average
Mittel mäss ig keit	mediocrity
mitt l er a	middle, central; intermediate; average, medium, mean

Mitt l er	mediator, intercessor, peacemaker
aus mittel n i	form the average; identify, determine
be mittel t	well-off, well-to-do
er mittel n	determine; ascertain, establish; investigate; find out, discover
Gegen mittel nn	remedy, antidote
über 'mittel n	transmit, convey
Ueber mittel ung	transmission
un mittel bar	immediate, direct
Un mittel bar keit	immediateness, immediacy, directness
ver mittel n	mediate; arrange, adjust, settle; reconcile; procure, obtain
ver mittel s p	by means of, through
un be mittel t	without means, impecunious
un ver mittel t	abrupt, sudden, unheralded
Er mitt l ung	ascertainment; scientific discovery, findings
Ver mitt l er	mediator
Ver mitt l ung	mediation, agency; settlement, adjustment; negotiation; intervention

Möbel nn	piece of furniture; furniture
möb l ier en	furnish
ver möbel n	thrash, flog, wallop, beat s.o. up, lay into s.o.
un möb l ier t	unfurnished

mög en	be willing; like s.t.
mög lich	possible; practicable, feasible; likely; eventual; potential
mög lich en fall s	av if possible, possibly; perhaps; it is possible that
mög lich er weise	av if possible, possibly; perhaps; it is possible that
Mög lich keit	possibility; eventuality; practicability, feasibility; chance
un mög lich	impossible
Un mög lich keit	impossibility, impractibility
ver mög e p	by virtue of, on the strength of; by dint of; owing to
Ver mög en nn	ability; power, capacity
ver mög en	be able to
ver mög end	wealthy, rich, well-to-do; well off
Un ver mög en nn	inability, incapacity; impotence
un ver mög end	unable, incapable; impotent, powerless; impecunious
er mög lich en	make possible, make feasible; enable s.o. to do s.t.

müd e a	weary, tired, fatigued, exhausted; weak and weary
Müd ig keit	weariness, fatigue, exhaustion; lassitude
er müd en	tire, fatigue, make s.o. weary; become weary
Er müd ung	fatigue
Ueber müd ung	overfatigue
un er müd lich	indefatigable, untiring, unflagging, unremitting
Un er müd lich keit	indefatigableness

Müh e	trouble, pains, labor, toil; exertion, effort; difficulty
müh e los	effortless, easy, without trouble
Müh e los ig keit	ease, easiness, facility
sich müh en	take pains; work hard, toil, exert o.s.
müh e voll	troublesome, hard; laborious
sich ab müh en	strive hard, sweat and strain, labor
be müh en	trouble
sich be müh en	endeavor, take pains, strive, exert o.s., try hard
Be müh ung	trouble, pains; effort, endeavor, exertion
her be müh en	trouble to come here
hin be müh en	trouble to go there
her auf be müh en	trouble to come up
sich her auf be müh en	trouble to come up
sich her ein be müh en	take the trouble of coming in

Mund nm	mouth; muzzle; opening, orifice; stoma
mund en	taste good, be delicious
münd en	lead to, end in; flow into; run into
mund ge recht	palatable
münd ig	of full age, of majority
münd lich	oral, verbal; personal
Münd ung	mouth; estuary; orifice; muzzle of gun
aus münd en	fall into; open into
ein münd en	discharge into
Ein münd ung	mouth, estuary; junction
fern münd lich	telephonic, by telephone
voll mund ig	full-bodied

Münd el nn	ward
Münd ig keit	full age, majority
un münd ig	under age, not of age, minor
Un münd ig e	minor
Un münd ig keit	minority
Vor mund nm	guardian
Vor mund schaft	guardianship, tutelage
vor mund schaft lich	tutelary, of a guardian
be vor mund en	keep in tutelage; patronize
Be vor mund ung	tutelage, patronizing; regimentation
ent münd ig en	put under tutelage; incapacitate
Ent münd ig ung	legal incapacitation

Muss e	leisure; spare time
müss en	have to; be obliged to; be bound to
müss ig	idle; superfluous; useless, futile, vain
'durch müss en s	be obliged to pass
ge müss ig t	feel obliged to do s.t.
her müss en s	have to come, be obliged to come
mit müss en s	be obliged to go along
weg müss en s	be obliged to go

| zurück müss en | s | be obliged to return, have to go back |
| be müss ig t | | feel obliged to do s.t. |

Muster	nn	model; type; pattern, design; specimen, sample
muster haft		exemplary, model, standard; ideal, perfect, excellent
Muster haft ig keit		exemplariness, model behavior
muster n		examine critically; inspect, pass in review
Muster ung		examination, inspection; scrutiny; review of troops
ab muster n	m	pay off
an muster n	n	enlist; enroll
aus muster n		discard, reject; scrap; discharge as unfit
Aus muster ung		rejection; discharge
be muster n		supply samples of, sample goods; send samples to s.o.

Mut	nm	courage; spirit, daring; gallantry, valor, fortitude
mut ig		courageous, game, daring; gallant
mut los		discouraged, disheartened; despondent
Mut los ig keit		discouragement; despondency, dejection; despair
Mut ung		claim
An mut	nf	grace; charm, loveliness, sweetness
an mut en		seem to s.o., appear to s.o.
an mut ig		graceful, charming, lovely, winsome
Ge müt	nn	mind; feeling; nature, disposition, temperament
ge müt lich		sociable, genial, jovial, good-natured; comfortable, cosy, snug
Ge müt lich keit		geniality, joviality, good nature; comfort, cosiness
ge müt los		unfeeling, heartless
ge müt voll		warm-hearted, emotional, full of feeling
Miss mut	nm	ill-humor; discontent
miss mut ig		ill-humored; cross, discontented; morose, sullen
Ueber mut nm a		wantonness; high spirits; sportiveness; insolence
über müt ig		wanton; in high spirits; sportive, rollicking, playful; insolent
Un mut	nm	ill-humor, displeasure, annoyance
un mut ig		annoyed
ver mut en		suppose, assume, guess; conjecture, expect; suspect
ver mut lich		presumable, supposed; probable, likely
Ver mut ung		presumption; guess; idea; conjecture; speculation
zu mut e	av	feel good, feel bad
zu mut en		expect s.t. of s.o., demand s.t. from s.o.; overtax o.s.
Zu mut ung		exacting demand, exaction; suggestion
un ge müt lich		uncomfortable; cheerless, dreary; unpleasant, nasty
Un ge müt lich keit		uncomfortableness; cheerlessness
un ver mut et		unexpected, unforeseen
ent mut ig en		discourage, dishearten
Ent mut ig ung		discouragement; damper
er mut ig en		encourage; hearten, embolden

Er mut ig ung	encouragement

Nacht nf	night
nächt ig en	spend the night
nächt lich	nightly, nocturnal
nacht s av	during the night, at night, by night
über 'nacht en	spend the night, stay overnight
über nächt ig	fatigued from lack of sleep, worn out, haggard
Ueber nacht ung	passing the night; overnight accomodation
um nacht et	clouded, benighted; demented
Um nacht ung	mental derangement
Weih nacht en nn	Christmas

Nagel nm	nail; peg; spike; tack; stud
nagel n	nail to; spike; tack
an nagel n	nail on
auf nagel n	nail down
ver nagel n s	nail up; nail down
ver nagel t s	dense, blockheaded
zu nagel n	nail up; nail down a lid

näh en	sew, stitch; suture up
Näh erei	sewing, needlework
Näh erin	seamstress
Nah t nf	seam; suture
nah t los	seamless
ab näh en	sew edgewise; tuck
Ab näh er	tuck
an näh en	sew on
auf näh en	sew; tuck
ein näh en	sew in, sew up in
ver näh en	sew up
zu näh en	sew up

nah e a	near, close; nearby; impending, forthcoming; imminent
Näh e	nearness, proximity; vicinity, surrounding; neighborhood
nah en	approach; draw near
näh er a	nearer, closer; more specific, more detailed, further
näh er n	near, approach to
Näh er ung t	approach; approximation
bei nah av	almost, nearly; all but
un nah bar	inaccessible, unapproachable; exclusive
Un nah bar keit	inaccesibility, haughtiness, reservedness
her an nah en	approach, draw near
an näh er n	approach, draw near
an näh er nd	approximate
An näh er ung	approach
Wieder an näh er ung	rapprochement

nahm: siehe nehm	
Ab nahm e	taking away; administering; decay, loss
An nahm e	acceptance, reception; adoption, admission; assumption
Auf nahm e	taking up; reception, admission, enrollment, photography
Aus nahm e	exception
aus nahm s los	without exception
Ein nahm e	reception; acceptance; conquest; receipts, income
Ent nahm e	taking, drain, extraction; drawing, withdrawal
Mit nahm e	carrying, taking
Nach nahm e	cash on delivery
Rück nahm e	taking back; revocation, withdrawal, repeal
Ueber nahm e	taking over, taking possession of, acceptance; undertaking
Vor nahm e	undertaking; taking in hand, taking up
Weg nahm e	seizure, confiscation, capture
Zu nahm e	increase, growth, rise, increment; progress, advance
Zurück nahm e	taking back, withdrawal, revocation, retraction
Fern auf nahm e t	long-range photograph, telephotograph
Innen auf nahm e	interior photograph; indoor stage set
Wieder auf nahm e	resumption, retake, reopening
Neben ein nahm en np	extra income; casual emoluments, perquisites
ver ein nahm en	receive
Vor weg nahm e	anticipation; prior art
Mass nahm e	step, measure, action, move

nähr en	nourish, feed; nurse, breast-feed; foster, harbor
nahr haft	nutritious, nourishing, substantial; productive; lucrative
Nahr haft ig keit	nutritiousness
Nahr ung	food, nourishment, diet; feed; livelihood, subsistence
er nähr en	nourish, feed; keep, support, maintain
Er nähr er	breadwinner
Er nähr erin	breadwinner
Er nähr ung	feeding; food, nourishment
unter er nähr t	underfed, undernourished
Unter er nähr ung	underfeeding, malnutrition

Nam e nm	name; title; designation; reputation
nam en los	nameless, anonymous; unspeakable, unutterable
nam en s p	in the name of, on behalf of
nam ent lich	nominal, by name, individually; especially, particularly
nam haft	notable, noted, renowned; considerable, substantial
näm lich	namely, that is to say
Vor name nm	**first name, Christian name**
Zu name nm	surname, last name

	nann:	siehe nenn	
zu be	nann t		called, surnamed
un ge	nann t		anonymous, unnamed
so ge	nann t	a	so-called, self-styled

	Natur	nf	nature; temperament, temper, disposition, character
	Natur al ien	np	natural produce; value in kind; natural history specimens
	natur al is ier en		naturalize
	Natur al is ier ung		naturalization
	Natur al is mus	nm	naturalism
	Natur al ist	nm	naturalist
	natur al ist isch		naturalistic
	Natur ell	nn	natural disposition, nature, temperament
	natur ge mäss		natural, according to nature
	natür lich		natural; normal; genuine; native, innate; unaffected, artless
	Natür lich keit	nf	naturalness; unaffectedness, artlessness; simplicity
	natur reich		kingdom of nature
	natur wid r ig		contrary to nature, unnatural; abnormal
über	natür lich		supernatural
Un	natur	nf	unnaturalness, abnormality
un	natür lich		unnatural; affected; forced
Un	natür lich keit		unnaturalness
wider	natür lich		unnatural, perverse
Wider	natür lich keit		perversity

	nehm en		take, seize, grasp; accept, receive; capture; negotiate
	Nehm er		taker, buyer, purchaser
ab	nehm en		take s.t. from, take off, shorten, remove, decrease
Ab	nehm er		buyer, customer, purchaser, consumer
an	nehm bar		acceptable, admissible, reasonable
an	nehm en		take, accept, receive; admit, adopt; suppose, allow
sich an	nehm en		take care of; interest o.s. for; assist s.o.
An	nehm lich keit		charm, pleasure, convenience, advantage, agreeableness
auf	nehm en		absorb; list; contain; borrow, photograph; pick up
aus	nehm en		take out, draw; except, exempt, exclude
sich aus	nehm en		form an exception; look; show up
aus	nehm end		exquisite, extraordinary; exceedingly, exceptionally
be	nehm en		take away, remove, deprive
Be	nehm en	nn	demeanor, behavior, conduct, manners
sich be	nehm en		behave o.s., conduct o.s., act
'durch	nehm en		go over; censure; lecture
ein	nehm en		take medicine; occupy; receive; collect; charm
Ein	nehm er		receiver, collector
ent	nehm en		take from, remove, infer from; withdraw, borrow
ge	nehm	a	agreeable, acceptable, convenient, suitable; welcome

her	nehm	en		get from, take from, draw; lecture
hin	nehm	en		take, accept, receive; bear, suffer
mit	nehm	en		take along with; take s.o. to; wear out, exhaust; affect
Mit	nehm	er		catch, cam, nose clutch, gripper
nach	nehm	en		collect on delivery
'über	nehm	en		take over, seize, take possession of; accept; enter
sich über	'nehm	en		overwork; overeat
'um	nehm	en		take about; put on
'unter	nehm	en		undertake s.t.; attempt, venture, risk, hazard
unter	'nehm	en		enterprise, undertaking; firm; operation, venture
Unter	nehm	en	nn	enterprise, undertaking
unter	nehm	end		enterprising, bold
Unter	nehm	er		manager, contractor, entrepreneur
Unter	nehm	er tum		business, free enterprise
Unter	nehm	ung		enterprise, undertaking
ver	nehm	bar		audible, perceptible, distinct
ver	nehm	en		perceive, distinguish; understand, hear; interrogate
ver	nehm	lich		perceptible, audible
Ver	nehm	ung		examination, trial, interrogation, hearing, question
vor	nehm	a		noble, select, distinguished; elegant, exclusive
vor	nehm	en		take before s.o.; put on; undertake s.t.; conduct; deal with
Vor	nehm	heit		distinction, high rank, distinguished bearing
vor	nehm	lich		chiefly, especially, particularly
weg	nehm	en		take away, seize, confiscate
zu	nehm	en		grow larger, increase; improve, progress
zurück	nehm	en		take back, withdraw, revoke
zusammen	nehm	en		take together, gather; control o.s., restrain o.s.
sich				
zusammen	nehm	en		make an effort
un an	nehm	bar		unacceptable
Un an	nehm	lich keit		annoyance, inconvenience, trouble, difficulty
wieder 'auf	nehm	en		resume s.t.
her aus	nehm	en		take out, draw out, pull out, extract
vor aus	nehm	en		anticipate
un ein	nehm	bar		inexpugnable; impregnable, invincible
an ge	nehm			pleasant, agreeable, nice
ent gegen	nehm	en		accept, receive
ein ver	nehm	en	ch	understanding, agreement
vor weg	nehm	en		anticipate, forestall
aus ein				
ander	nehm	en		disassemble, dismantle, take apart
un an ge	nehm	a		disagreeable, unpleasant, distasteful, undesirable, troublesome
ge	nehm	ig en		assent to, approve of, accept, grant
Ge	nehm	ig ung		approval, agreement, permit; permission, authorization
teil	nehm	en		participate in; share
wahr	nehm	en		observe, notice, perceive; take advantage of s.t.

Neig e		slope; decline; dregs
neig en		bend, incline; bow down; tilt
Neig ung		inclination; slope; propensity; liking; leaning; tendency, trend
Ab neig ung		disinclination, reluctance, unwillingness
ge neig t		sloping, inclined; well-disposed towards s.o., gracious
Ge neig t heit		inclination; kind disposition, benevolence
hin neig en		incline, lean
sich hin neig en		incline, lean; tend, gravitate toward
sich ver neig en		bow, curtsy
Ver neig ung		bow; curtsy
zu neig en		lean towards, incline to
Zu neig ung		affection, attachment
ab ge neig t		disinclined, unwilling, averse to; loath to do s.t.
Ab ge neig t heit		aversion, dislike, disinclination

---

nenn bar		mentionable
nenn en		name; call, designate; mention; quote; nominate
sich nenn en		be named, be called, go by the name of
nenn en s wert		worth mentioning, considerable
Nenn er nm t		denominator
Nenn ung		naming; mentioning; designation; nomination
be nenn en		name, call; designate, denominate, term; fix a day
Be nenn ung		naming, denomination; name, designation, term
er nenn en		nominate, appoint, constitute
Er nenn ung		appointment, nomination, designation
un nenn bar		inexpressible; unnamable, unutterable

---

nicht av		not
nicht ig		vain, idle, empty; futile; transitory; flimsy; invalid
Nicht ig keit		vanity, futility; nothingness; nullity, voidness
Nicht s nn t		nothingness; non-entity; void; trifle
nicht s pn		nothing, naught
nicht s würd ig		infamous, base; contemptible
Nicht s würd ig keit		worthlessness, infamy, villainy
mit nicht en av		by no means, not at all, in no way
ver nicht en		annihilate; destroy, exterminate, eradicate; dash, shatter hopes
Ver nicht ung		anihilation, destruction; extermination
zu nicht e av		shatter, wreck, ruin, destroy; thwart plans; dash hopes

---

nick en		nod one's head
Nick er chen		nap
ein nick en		fall asleep, nod off to sleep
Ge nick nn		neck, nap of the neck
zu nick en		nod to

---

nied: siehe nieder		
da nied en av p		down here, here below

---

	nied er	av	low; down
	Nied er ung		lowland; depression, low ground, valley
	nied r ig		low; lowly, humble; mean, base; inferior; moderate
dar	nieder	av	down, downwards
her	nieder	av p	down
er	nied r ig en		degrade; humble, humiliate; reduce, lower prices
er	nied r ig end		abasing, humiliating, degrading, debasing
Er	nied r ig ung		degradation, abasement; humiliation

	nomm:	siehe nehm	
be	nomm en	a	benumbed, confused
Be	nomm en heit		numbness, dizziness
un be	nomm en	a	permitted
an ge	nomm en	a	supposing, hypothetical, accepted; fictitious, assumed
aus ge	nomm en	p	except, with the exception of
ein ge	nomm en	a	partial to, fond of; prejudiced against
Ein ge	nomm en heit		prejudice
vor ein ge	nomm en	a	biased, prejudiced
Vor ein ge	nomm en heit		bias, prejudice
un vor ein			
ge	nomm en	a	unbiased, unprejudiced, objective

	Not	nf	need; want; emergency; predicament, indigence, misery; necessity
	not dürf t ig		scanty; needy, poor; makeshift, temporary; rough-and-ready
	not fall s	av	if necessary, if need be, in case of need
	nöt ig		necessary, needed, required, requisite; indicated
	nöt ig en		force s.o. to do s.t.; compel s.o.; urge, press
	nöt ig en fall s	av	in case of need, in an emergency; if necessary, if need be
	Nöt ig ung		compulsion, constraint; pressing, urgent request; intimidation
	not wend ig		necessary, requisite; needful; urgent; essential; indispensable
	Not wend ig keit		necessity, needfulness; urgency; inevitability
un	nöt ig		unnecessary, needless; superfluous
von	nöt en	av	necessary, needful
ab	nöt ig en		extort from s.o.
be	nöt ig en		want, need, require

	Not ar	nm	notary; conveyancer
	Not ar iat	nn	notary's office
	not ar iell	a	notarial, certified by a notary
	Not e		note; annotation; banknote, bill
	not ier en		note down, make a note of, jot down; quote prices
	Not ier ung		noting; booking, entry; quotation
	Not iz	nf	note, memo; quotation; news item, notice
un	not ier t		unlisted, unquoted

	numer ier: siehe nummer	
	numer ier en	number, ticket
	Numer ier ung	numbering
	numer isch	numerical
'durch	numer ier en	number consecutively

	Nummer nf	number; copy, issue; size; event
be	nummer n	number

	Nutz nm	utility
	nutz bar	useful; utilizable; effective; profitable, productive
	Nutz bar keit	usefulness; profitableness
	nutz en	be useful; serve s.o.; benefit s.o.
	Nutz en nn	use, utility; profit, gain; advantage; benefit; yield
	nütz en	use, utility; profit, gain; advantage; benefit; yield
	nütz lich	useful, serviceable, helpful; advantageous, beneficial
	Nütz lich keit	usefulness; utility; advantage; profitableness
	nutz los	useless, unprofitable; needless; wasted
	Nutz los ig keit	uselessness; futility
	Nutz ung	using; utilization
ab	nutz en	use up, wear out
sich ab	nutz en	wear out, get worn out, be subject to wear
Ab	nutz ung	wear, abrasion
aus	nutz en	utilize fully, make the most of, take advantage of; exploit
Aus	nutz ung	utilization; exploitation
be	nutz en	use, make use of; employ, profit by, avail o.s. of
Be	nutz er	user, subscriber
Be	nutz ung	use, utilization
un	nütz a	useless, unprofitable; superfluous
zu	nutz e av	take advantage of s.t., profit from s.t.
mit be	nutz en	use s.t. jointly with others
un be	nutz t	unused, unemployed; idle; unoccupied
ab ge	nutz t	worn-out; used up
un ge	nutz t	unused, unemployed, unutilized, unimproved; waste an opportunity

	ober a	upper; higher; superior, senior, chief
	Ober nm	headwaiter
	ober halb p	above
	Ober in	mother superior; matron
	ober st a	uppermost, topmost, top; highest; chief, principal
	Ober st nm	colonel
	Ob r ig keit	the authorities; government; magistracy
	ob r ig keit lich	magisterial, official
Er	ober er	conqueror
er	ober n	conquer; capture, take
Er	ober ung	conquest, capture
zu	ober st av	at the top, uppermost, topmost
'wieder er	ober n	reconquer, recapture
zurück er	ober n	reconquer

offen a	open; public; frank, candid, sincere, exposed
offen bar	manifest, obvious, evident; clear; apparent; public
offen bar en	manifest; reveal, disclose, unveil; show
Offen bar ung	manifestation, revelation
Offen heit	openness, frankness, candor
öffen t lich	public
Öffen t lich keit	publicity; the general public; public opinion
öff n en	open; uncork; unlock; dissect, autopsy
Öff n er	opener
Öff n ung	opening, aperture; hole; gap; slot; inlet; outlet; vent
un ver öffen t lich t	unpublished
ver öffen t lich en	publish; make public, announce; promulgate a law; advertise
Ver öffen t lich ung	publication; announcement, promulgation
er öff n en	open; inaugurate
Er öff n ung	opening, inauguration; disclosure, information, notification

Öl nn	oil
öl en	oil, lubricate; anoint
Öl er	oiler, oil-can, lubricator
öl ig	oily, oleaginous, oily, unctuous
Öl ung	oiling, lubrication; anointment
ein öl en	oil, lubricate
ent öl en	free from oil, remove oil from, drain off oil

Orden nm	order; decoration, medal
orden t lich	tidy, neat, well-kept; orderly; regular; respectable, decent
ord n en	put in order, tidy, straighten up; arrange, organize; settle
Ord n er	organizer, supervisor, regulator; steward; monitor; filer
Ord n ung	order; arrangements; classification; system, regime; succession
ord n ung s ge mäss	regular, lawful, legal; orderly
ord n ung s mäss ig	orderly, regular, in due order; lawful
ord n ung s wid r ig	contrary to order, irregular; illegal
ausser orden t lich	extraordinary, unusual, exceptional, amazing, extreme; remarkable
un orden t lich	disorderly, careless; slovenly, unkempt; untidy
Un orden t lich keit	disorderliness, untidiness
ab ord n en	delegate, depute, deputize
Ab ord n ung	delegation, deputation
an ord n en	arrange, design; group; dispose
An ord n ung	arrangement; design, layout
bei ord n en	adjoin; coordinate; assign s.o., appoint s.o. as assistant to
Bei ord n ung	coordination; assignment
ein ord n en	arrange, file, classify; integrate, incorporate
'über ord n en	place s.o. over s.t.

Un ord n ung		disorder, confusion, disarray, mess
'unter ord n en		subordinate
Unter ord n ung		subordination
ver ord n en		ordain, decree; establish, order; prescribe
Ver ord n ung		decree; ordinance, regulation, order
zu ord n en		attribute s.t. to s.o., allocate s.t., assign s.t.
Ab ge ord n ete		deputy, delegate, representative
Bei ge ord n ete		assistant, deputy
un ge ord n et		unarranged, unsettled; disorderly
unter ge ord n et		subordinate, ancillary; of secondary importance, minor
ausser orden t lich		extraordinary

order:	siehe orden	
Order	nf	orders, command; injunction, direction
be order n		order, command, direct
Be order ung		order, command, direction
Gegen order	nf	counterorder
her be order n		order s.o. to come here

Ort	nm	place; site; spot, point; locality; village, town
ort en		orient s.o, take one's bearing, navigate
ört lich		local, topical; endemic
Ort schaft		place, locality; village
Ort ung		orientation, location, position, finding; navigation
Ab ort	nm	watercloset, lavatory, toilet, latrine
Vor ort	nm	suburb
er ört er n		discuss, debate, argue; discuss in detail
Er ört er ung		discussion, debate, argument

Pack	nm	pack; package, parcel; bundle; bale
Päck chen		small parcel, package
pack en		pack up, wrap up, package; pile up; seize, grip, grasp, thrill
Pack en	nm	large packet, large parcel, bundle; pile; bale
Pack er		packer; stevedore
Pack erei		packing-room
Pack erin		packer; stevedore
Pack ung		packing, stowage; package, packet
an pack en		lay hold of, seize, grasp; tackle
auf pack en		pack up, load
aus pack en		unpack; uncase
be pack en		pack, load weight
bei pack en		pack up with, add
ein pack en		pack up; wrap up; wrap s.o. up
Ge päck	nn	luggage
'um pack en		repack
ver pack en		pack up; package; wrap up
Ver pack ung		packing up
'voll pack en		pack s.t. full; load s.o. up
zu pack en	s	grip, clutch, grasp; work hard; lend a hand
zusammen pack en		pack up

un ver pack t	unpacked, loose

Partei nf	party; faction; side; tenant
partei isch	partial; biassed, prejudiced; one-sided, unfair
Partei lich keit	partiality, bias
partei los	impartial, neutral; independent, non-party
Partei los ig keit	neutrality; independence
Gegen partei nf l	party in opposition, opposite party
über partei lich	above party lines, non-partisan
un partei isch	impartial, unbiassed
Un partei ische	umpire
Un partei lich keit	impartiality

Pass nm	passage; pass, defile; amble; passport, papers
pass en	fit, fit in; become s.o.; suit, be convenient; harmonize
sich pass en s	be fit, be proper, be seemly
pass end	fit, suitable, suited; convenient
pass ier bar	passable, practicable
pass ier en	pass over, pass through, go through; clear
ab pass en	fit, adjust; watch for, wait for; waylay
an pass en	fit on, adapt, accomodate; adjust, tune; proportion; match
sich an pass en	adapt o.s., accomodate o.s., conform
An pass ung	adaptation, adjustment, accommodation; marching
auf pass en	take care of, watch, mind, pay attention to; adapt s.t.
Auf pass er	watcher, overseer, watchdog; spy
ein pass en	fit into
un pass end	unsuitable; inappropriate, improper; unseasonable, untimely
un päss lich	indisposed, unwell; poorly, out of sorts
Un päss lich keit	indisposition
ver pass en	miss a chance, miss a train; fit s.t. onto s.t.
zu pass av	come at the right time for s.o., come in handy for s.o.
zusammen pass en	fit into one another; adjust; match
un pass ier bar	impassable

Person nf	person; individual; personage; character, part, role
Person al nn	personnel, staff, employees; attendants, servants
Person al ien np	particulars, personal data
Person i fik ation	personification; embodiment
person i fiz ier en	personify, impersonate, embody
persön lich	personal; private
Persön lich keit	personality; personage
un persön lich	impersonal

Pfeif e	whistle; pipe; fife; organ-pipe; bird-call; tobacco pipe
pfeif en	whistle, blow a whistle; hiss; howl
Pfeif er	whistler; fife-player, piper

ab pfeif en		stop s.t. by blowing a whistle; blow the final wistle
an pfeif en		give the starting whistle; tell s.o. off, dress s.o. down
aus pfeif en		hiss off the stage; hoot, boo
ver pfeif en	s	squeal on

pfiff:	siehe pfeif	
Pfiff	nm	whistle; trick; style, swank
pfiff ig		smart, sharp, shrewd, clever, adroit, cunning
Pfiff ig keit		sharpness, cunningness; roguishness, impishness
Pfiff ikus	nm	cunning fellow, dodger, sly fellow
An pfiff	nm	starting whistle; telling s.o. off, dressing s.o. down

Pflanz e	plant
pflanz en	plant, set; pot
Pflanz er	planter; settler, colonist
pflanz lich	vegetable
Pflänz ling	seedling
Pflanz ung	plantation; settlement, colony
an pflanz en	plant, cultivate
An pflanz ung	planting, cultivation; plantation
auf pflanz en	set up; fix the bayonet
aus pflanz en	transplant, bed out; pop out
be pflanz en	plant
ein pflanz en	plant; implant
fort pflanz en	propagate; transmit, communicate; spread; reproduce, multiply
sich fort pflanz en	propagate; transmit, communicate; reproduce, multiply
Fort pflanz ung	propagation
über 'pflanz en	transplant
'um pflanz en	transplant
um 'pflanz en	surround s.t. with plants, plant trees around s.t.
ver pflanz en	transplant
Ver pflanz ung	transplanting

Pfleg e	care; grooming; nursing; child-care, cultivation; maintenance
pfleg en	attend to; nurse; cultivate; groom; conserve, preserve
sich pfleg en	take care of s.o., take it easy, pamper s.o.
Pfleg er	fosterer; male nurse; guardian, curator; trustee; promoter
Pfleg erin	fosterer; male nurse; guardian, curator; trustee; promoter
pfleg lich	careful
Pfleg ling	foster child; charge, ward
Pfleg schaft	guardianship; curatorship; trusteeship
ge pfleg t	well-groomed; cultivated, polished, refined
ver pfleg en	board; cater for; supply with rations, provision
Ver pfleg ung	board; catering; food supply
un ge pfleg t	uncared for, neglected; unkempt

Pflicht nf	duty; obligation, liability; responsibility; office
bei pflicht en	agree with s.o.; assent to, concur with an opinion; approve of
ver pflicht en	oblige; obligate, engage; sign up
Ver pflicht ung	obligation, liability; engagement, commitment
Gegen ver pflicht ung	approach, be under way; be on track

pflog: siehe pfleg	
Ge pflog en heit	habit, custom, practice

Pinsel nm	paintbrush
Pinsel ei	daubing, piece of daubing
pinsel n	handle the brush; paint; daub
an pinsel n	paint s.t. over
über 'pinsel n	paint s.t. over

Platz nm	place; spot, point; room, locality; site; position
Plätz chen	snug place; spot; patch of shade
platz en	burst, explode; crack, split, rupture; blow out
auf platz en	burst open, crack
los platz en s	burst out laughing; blurt out s.t.
Vor platz nm	place in front, forecourt
zer platz en	burst asunder, explode
her aus platz en s	burst out
her ein platz en s	burst into
Sport platz nm	playing field, area for sports

Polit ik nf	policy; politics
Polit ik er	politician; statesman, policy-maker
Polit ik um nn	political issue
polit isch	political; politic
polit is ier en	talk politics
Aussen polit ik nf	foreign policy
aussen polit isch	of foreign affairs, international
Innen polit ik nf	home politics; domestic policy
innen polit isch	concerning home affairs; domestic, internal
inner polit isch	relating to domestic affairs
un polit isch	non-political; impolitic

präg en	stamp; coin; emboss
Präg ung	stamping, coinage; character
auf präg en	impress, stamp
aus präg en	coin, stamp, mint
ein präg en	impress, imprint
sich ein präg en	impress itself on one's mind, sink into one's mind, sink in
ein präg sam	impressible, easily remembered; impressive
Ge präg e nn	impression; coinage
'um präg en	recoin
aus ge präg t	distinct, marked, pronounced

Press e	press; the Press, journalism; squeezer, juicer; lustre lustre

press en	press, squeeze; compress; force; strain; emboss leather
Press ling	pressed piece; molding
Press ung	pressing, pressure, squeeze, compression
ab press en	squeeze off
aus press en	press out, squeeze out; crush
'durch press en	press through, squeeze through; strain
ein press en	press into, squeeze into
er press en	extort; blackmail s.o.; squeeze money from s.o.
Er press er	extortioner, blackmailer
Er press ung	extortion, blackmail
zusammen press en	press together, squeeze together, compress; condense; clench
her aus press en	press out, squeeze out

Prob e		experiment; trial, test, probation, sample pattern; rehearsal
prob en		rehearse, go over
prob e weise	av	by way of trial, on probation; on approval
prob ier en		try; put to the test; taste food; attempt, experiment
An prob e		fitting, trying on
er prob en		try, test, prove; put to the test
Er prob ung		trail, test, try-out
Gegen prob e		checktest
an prob ier en		try on, fit on
auf prob ier en		try on
aus prob ier en		try out, put to the test; sample s.t., taste wine

Produkt	nn	product; produce; result, outcome
Produkt ion	nf	production; output; yield
produkt iv		productive
Produkt iv ität		productivity
Neben produkt	nn	by-product
Ueber 'produkt ion	nf	overproduction
un produkt iv	a	unproductive

prüf en	examine, test, examine, scrutinize; scan, inspect; investigate
Prüf er	examiner; tester, checker; inspector; assayer; auditor
Prüf ling	examinee; test specimen
Prüf ung	examination, test; scrutiny; investigation, analysis
'durch prüf en	examine, test thoroughly; scan, screen
nach prüf en	verify, make sure; check; investigate; inspect
Nach prüf ung	verification; check; inspection
über 'prüf en	reconsider, study; examine, investigate; screen; verify
Ueber prüf ung	examination, investigation; scrutiny, checking; audit, inspection
Vor prüf ung	previous examination; preliminary examination
Auf nahm e	

	prüf ung	entrance examination

	Pump nm	credit
	Pump e	pump
	pump en	pump; lend, loan, give on credit
an	pump en	touch s.o.
auf	pump en	pump up; blow up; inflate
aus	pump en	pump out, evacuate; exhaust, rarify
ver	pump en s	lend, loan

	Punkt nm	point; dot; full stop, period; spot, place, item, topic
	punkt ier en	dot, point; punctuate; stripple; puncture, tap
	pünkt lich	punctual, prompt, sharp; accurate, exact, precise, conscientious
	Pünkt lich keit	punctuality; diligence, conscientiousness; precision
aus	punkt en o	beat by points, outpoint
Neben	punkt nm	accessory point
un	pünkt lich	unpunctual
Un	pünkt lich keit	unpunctuality
Ge sicht s	punkt nm	point of view, viewpoint; angle, aspect, slant
Mitt el	punkt nm	center, central point, middle
Stand	punkt nm	point of view, standpoint
Zeit	punkt nm	moment, time

	Putz nm	dressing, millinery, apparel; finery, ornaments; plastering
	putz en	clean, scour, scrub; polish, furbish up; wipe, adorn, decorate
	Putz er	cleaner; batman
	putz ig	droll, funny
ab	putz en	clean off; wipe off; polish, rub down a horse
Auf	putz nm	finery, attire
auf	putz en	dress up, deck out, smarten up; clean up
Aus	putz nm	adornment; trimmings
aus	putz en	clean out; prune trees; trim vine; adorn, decorate
Aus	putz er	sweeper
Ver	putz nm	roughcast, plaster
ver	putz en	roughcast, plaster
her aus	putz en	dress o.s. up, spruce o.s. up, doll o.s. up
her unter	putz en s	run s.o. down, give s.o. a dressing down

	Quell e	spring; well; fountain head; origin; authority, informant
	quell en	gush, arise, spring; flow, swell; bulge; originate, emanate
	Quell ung	swelling; soaking
auf	quell en	well up; swell up, rise; bubble up
Ur	quell nm	primary source
vor	quell en	bulge out
her vor	quell en	well forth, spring forth; bulge out

	quem: siehe komm	
be	quem a	comfortable, easy; convenient, easy; indolent, lazy
sich be	quem en	bring o.s. to do s.t.; consent, condescend to do s.t.
be	quem lich	comfortable, easy; convenient, comfort-loving, lazy
Be	quem lich keit	comfort, ease, convenience; laziness, indolence
an be	quem en	accomodate o.s., adapt o.s.
un be	quem a	uncomfortable; inconvenient; awkward, embarrassing
Un be	quem lich keit	uncomfortableness, lack of comfort; inconvenience
	quer av	crossways, crosswise, athwart; diagonally
	Quer e	transverse, crossdirection; breadth
	quer en	traverse
durch	'quer en	pass through, cross, traverse
Durch	quer ung	crossing
über	quer av	across, crossways, diagonally
über	'quer en	cross, transverse
Ueber	quer ung	crossing
Ge	rad e nf	straight line
ge	rad e av	just the same, exactly the same thing
ge	rad e a	straighten
Gegen ge	rad e nf	back stretch
nach ge	rad e av	by this time, by now; gradually; really
un ge	rad e a	uneven, out of line; odd
	Rad nn	wheel; gear; trundle; impeller; bicycle, bike
	Räd chen	small wheel; caster
	räd el n	cycle, pedal, bike
	räd er n	brake on the wheel
	Rad ler s	cyclist, bicycle rider
	Rad ler in s	cyclist, bicycle rider
Hinter	rad nn	rear wheel, back wheel
Vorder	rad nn	front wheel
Fahr	rad nn	bicycle
Motor	rad nn	motorcycle
	Rahm nm	cream
	Rahm en nm	frame
	rahm ig	creamy
ab	rahm en	skim milk
ein	rahm en	frame
ent	rahm en	skim; separate
um	'rahm en	frame; surround, serve as setting to
	Rand nm	edge, brink; rim; brim of hat; margin; border; fringe
	ränd el n	rim, border
	ränd er n	rim, border
um	'rand en	border, edge, put a border around
Um	rand ung	border, edge, rim

sich ras ier en	shave
Ras ur nf	shave
ab ras ier en	shave off
un ras ier t	unshaven

Rat nm	advice, counsel; suggestion; recommendation; consultation
Rat e	installment; ratio, proportion; rate of growth
rat en	give advice; advise, counsel; guess, divine
rät lich	advisable, expedient
rat los	helpless, perplexed
Rat los ig keit	helplessness, perplexity
rat sam	advisable; wise, prudent; commendable; expedient
Rät sel nn	riddle, puzzle; enigma, mystery; problem
rät sel haft	puzzling; enigmatic, mysterious; cryptic
ab rat en	dissuade, advise against, warn
an rat en	advise; recommend
be rat en	advise, counsel; deliberate on, discuss, debate s.t.
Be rat er	adviser, counselor, consultant
Be rat erin	adviser, counselor, consultant
Be rat ung	deliberation, discussion, debate; conference, consultation
Bei rat nm	adviser, counselor; advisory board
ent rat en	do without, dispense with
er rat en	guess; hit upon the answer
Ge rät nn	tool, utensil, implement, gear; apparatus, instrument
ge rat en	come in, fall in, get into, happen upon
ge rat en a	successful; advisable, commendable, advantageous, profitable
miss rat en	fail, turn out badly
Un rat nm	rubbish; filth
un rät lich a	inadvisable
Ver rat nm	betrayal
ver rat en	betray, give a secret away; let out
Ver rät er	traitor, betrayer
ver rät er isch	treacherous, traitorous, treasonable; revealing; telltale
Vor rat nm	store, stock, supply, provision
vor rät ig	available, on hand, in stock, stocked
wider 'rat en	dissuade s.o. from s.t., advise s.o. against s.t.
zu rat en	advise
hin ge rat en s	get to, end up at
un ge rat en a	spoilt, undutiful
zusammen ge rat en	come together; have an argument
be vor rat en	stock up
Be vor rat ung	stocking, stockpiling, stocks, supplies
hin ein ge rat en	get o.s. into s.t.
an ein ander ge rat en	clash; fly at each other; come to blows
ent rät sel n	solve, unravel, puzzle out; decipher

Rauch	nm	smoke; steam, vapor; fume; soot
rauch	en	smoke; fume; smoke a cigarette
Rauch	er	smoker
räuch	er n	smoke meat; cure fish; fumigate, perfume
rauch	ig	smoky
rauch	los	smokeless
an rauch	en	blow smoke against; begin to smoke; season a pipe
aus rauch	en	finish smoking
ver rauch	en	go off in smoke; blow over
aus räuch	er n	fumigate; smoke out
ein räuch	er n	smoke; fill with smoke
ver räuch	er n	fill with smoke

Raum	nm	room; space
räum	en	remove, clear away; dredge; clean up; vacate, clear
räum	lich	of space, relating to space, three-dimensional; spatial
Räum	lich keit	spatiality; locality, room
raum	los	spaceless
Räum	ung	clearing, removal
Ab raum	nm	mining rubble, waste; overlay shelf
ab räum	en	clear away, remove
auf räum	en	remove, clear away; put in order; tidy up a room
aus räum	en	empty, evacuate, clear; remove, broach
ein räum	en	put furniture in a room; clear away; put in order; grant
Ein räum	ung	concession, allowance; admission
ge raum	a	a considerable length of time
ge räum	ig	spacious, roomy
Ge räum	ig keit	spaciousness, roominess
Innen raum	nm	interior
Neben raum	nm	offices; service rooms
'um räum	en	remove, rearrange, move
Vor raum	nm	anteroom; outer office
weg räum	en	clear s.t. away, remove s.t.
Zwischen raum	nm	interspace, interval; distance, clearance; interstice
an be raum	en	appoint, fix, schedule
auf ge räum	t	cheerful, jovial, in high spirits, expansive

Rechen schaft		account
rech n	en	reckon; calculate, work out
Rech n en	nn	reckoning; calculation, arithmetic
Rech n	er	calculator, computer; arithmetician
rech n er	isch	mathematically, arithmetically, by way of calculation
Rech n	ung	calculation, sum, reckoning; account, bill; invoice
be rechen	bar	calculable
un be rechen	bar	incalculable; dangerous; unpredictable
Un be rechen	bar keit	unpredictability
ab rech n	en	deduct, subtract
Ab rech n	ung	deduction, discount; allowance; settlement; account

an rech n en	charge to one's account, put to one's debit
An rech n ung	charge, debiting
auf rech n en	count up; charge, credit; balance, settle; compensate
Auf rech n ung	balancing, squaring
aus rech n en	calculate, compute; reckon out, figure out; do a sum
Aus rech n ung	calculation, computation
be rech n en	calculate, compute; figure out; sum up; estimate
be rech n end	calculating, selfish
Be rech n ung	calculation, computation; figure, estimate
'durch rech n en	count, calculate, go over, check
ein rech n en	include, reckon in, count in; allow for, take into account
er rech n en	reckon out, calculate, compute
Gegen rech n ung	control account, controlling account; counterclaim
mit rech n en	include in the account
nach rech n en	examine, check; calculate over again
über 'rech n en	count s.t. over; check
'um rech n en	convert
Um rech n ung	conversion
ver rech n en	reckon up; charge; set off; compensate
sich ver rech n en	miscalculate; make a mistake
Ver rech n ung	reckoning up; charging; settling, clearing; miscalculation
vor rech n en	reckon up, enumerate to s.o.
zu rech n en	add
Zu rech n ung	addition, inclusion
zusammen rech n en	add up, sum up, total up, reckon
aus ge rech n et p	just, exactly
un ge rech n et	uncounted; not included
Vor aus be rech n ung	precalculation; forecast

recht a	right, correct; just; due; lawful, legitimate; proper
Recht nn	right; privilege; title, claim; authority; law; justice
Recht e	right hand
recht en	dispute, argue
recht ens	lawfully, legally, by law
recht lich	legal, juristic; lawful, legitimate
Recht lich keit	legality, lawfulness, legitimacy, legitimateness
recht los	without rights; outlawed; unlawful; illegal
Recht los ig keit	absence of rights; outlawry; unlawfulness, illegality
recht mäss ig	lawful, legal; rightful, legitimate; fair
Recht mäss ig keit	lawfulness, legality, legitimacy; validity
recht s av	on the right; to the right
recht schaff en	honest, righteous, upright
Recht schaff en heit	honesty, probity, uprightness
recht s fäh ig	having legal capacity
Recht s fäh ig keit	legal capacity
recht s wid r ig	illegal, unlawful, illicit
An recht nn	right, title, claim; qualification, eligibility
auf recht a	upright, erect

ent recht en			deprive one of one's civil rights, disenfranchise
Ent recht ung			deprivation of rights
ge recht	a		just, righteous; fair, equitable, impartial; justified, legitimate
Ge recht ig keit			justice; righteousness, fairness, justification
Ge recht same	nf	a	right; franchise, privilege
Un recht	nn		wrong, injustice
un recht	a		wrong, unjust, unfair; improper; inopportune
Vor recht	nn		privilege, prerogative; priority, preference
wider recht lich			illegal, unlawful, wrongful
Wider recht lich keit			illegality, unlawfulness
zu recht	av		right, in order; to rights, rightly, with reason
un ge recht	a		unjust, unfair
Un ge recht ig keit			injustice
be vor recht en			privilege, grant privileges to
Be vor recht ung			privilege, prerogative; preference
be recht ig en			entitle s.o. to s.t.; authorize, empower; qualify to
be recht ig t			entitled, qualified, eligible; authorized; competent
Be recht ig ung			authorization; power, licence, qualification; justification
un be recht ig t			unauthorized, unfounded; unfair, unreasonable; unqualified

---

Red e		speech, address, oration; language
red en		speak, talk, converse, chat; discourse; discuss
red lich		upright, honest, sincere, candid
Red lich keit		uprightness, honesty, probity, integrity; sincerity
Red ner		speaker, orator, preacher, platform speaker
red ner isch		oratorical, rhetorical
Ab red e		agreement
An red e		address; harangue; salutation
an red en		speak to, address; accost; harangue
auf red en		talk s.o. into s.t.
Aus red e		evasion; pretence
aus red en		finish speaking
sich aus red en		exculpate o.s.; use evasions
be red en		speak of, talk over; persuade, induce to
sich be red en		deliberate, consult with, confer with
be red sam		eloquent
Be red sam keit		eloquence
be red t		eloquent
Ein red e		contradiction; objection; plea; defense
ein red en	l	persuade, talk s.o. into s.t., urge s.o. to do s.t.
Ge red e	nn	talk, talking; report; rumor, gossip
Gegen red e		contradiction; reply
mit red en		put in a word; join in conversation
Nach red e		epilogue; slander, gossip
nach red en		repeat; slander, speak ill of s.o.; speak well of s.o.
über 'red en		persuade to, prevail on, talk into
Ueber red ung		persuasion
un red lich		dishonest
Un red lich keit		dishonesty

sich unter 'red en	converse, confer with
Unter red ung	conference; conversation
Vor red e	preface, foreword, prologue, introduction, preamble
vor red en s	make s.o. believe s.t.; tell s.o. lies about
Vor red ner	previous speaker
Wider red e	contradiction; objection
zu red en	advise; coax, urge, encourage, persuade
ver ab red en	agree upon, concert
Ver ab red ung	appointment; agreement; engagement, date
sich her aus red en	make excuses, try to get off by evasions
vor bei red en	be at cross purposes
hin ein red en	interfere in
da her red en	talk nonsense, babble
'durch ein ander red en	talk simultaneously, speak all in a crowd

Regen nm	rain
reg n en	rain
reg n er isch	rainy
ein reg n en	be drenched by the rain; be detained by the rain
sich ein reg n en	settle in with rain
ver reg n en	spoil by raining
her ein reg n en	rain in; rain into the room

reib en	rub, give a rub; massage; wipe; grate
sich reib en	quarrel with s.o.
Reib erei s	friction, tiff, squabbling
Reib ung	rubbing, friction
reib ung s los	frictionless; smooth
ab reib en	rub off; give a rubdown; polish; pumice
Ab reib ung	rubbing off, abrasion; rubbing down, sponge-down
auf reib en	rub off, rub sore; broach; wear away; annihilate; exhaust
aus reib en	rub out; ream
'durch reib en	wear s.t. through, fray; rub s.t. sore, chafe s.t.
ein reib en	rub into
Ein reib ung	rubbing in; embrocation
ver reib en	grind down; spread by rubbing, rub in an ointment
zer reib en	rub to powder, grind down, pulverize

reich en	reach, pass, hand, give, present; administer; suffice; stretch
aus reich en	suffice, be sufficient; do, last
aus reich end	sufficient
Be reich nm	reach; area, region
dar reich en	reach, hand s.t. to s.o.
Durch reich e	hatch
'durch reich en	pass through
ein reich en	hand in, deliver; file, submit, send in, present

Ein reich ung	handing in; submittal, tender; presentation; filing
er reich bar	within reach, available
er reich en	reach; catch
Er reich ung	reaching; attainment, achievement
ge reich en	contribute to s.t., redound to s.t.
her reich en	reach, hand, pass
hin reich en	reach out
über 'reich en	hand s.t. over, present s.t.
Ueber reich ung	presentation
weit reich end	far-reaching
zu reich en	reach over, hand over; hold out
her an reich en	reach up to, touch, come close to
hin aus reich en	reach beyond
un er reich bar	unattainable; inaccessible
un er reich t	unequaled, unrivaled
her über reich en	hand over, reach over
hin über reich en	pass across; hand over
her um reich en	hand around
hin unter reich en	hand down
un zu reich end	insufficient

reich	a	rich, wealthy, opulent, ample, copious, abundant
Reich	nn	empire; realm
reich lich		ample, copious, plentiful, substantial
Reich tum	nm	riches; wealth, opulence, affluence; fortune; abundance; variety
über reich	a	too rich
über reich lich		superabundant
an reich er n		enrich; concentrate; amplify, augment
An reich er ung		enrichment, concentration; amplification, addition
be reich er n		enrich; enlarge
Be reich er ung		enrichment

reif	a	ripe; mature; mellow; fully developed
Reif e		ripeness, maturity
reif en		ripen, mature; grow ripe
reif lich		mature, careful
Reif ung		curing of cheese
aus reif en		ripen, mature thoroughly
be reif en		cover with frost, rime, frost over
be reif en		hoop a barrel; put a tire on a wheel
Be reif ung		tires
nach reif en		ripen in storage
über reif	a	overripe
un reif	a	unripe, immature, callow, raw
Un reif e		unripeness, immaturity
her an reif en		ripen, mature, grow up

Reih e	row; file; rank; line; series; succession; set; train
reih en	put in a row, place in line, range
an reih en	add; string; arrange in a series, align
sich an reih en	join, rank; form a line, line up

auf	reih en	string thread
ein	reih en	range, insert in; classify; enroll, enlist, incorporate

	rein a	pure; neat, tidy
	Rein heit	purity, pureness; cleanliness; clearness; neatness, innocence
	rein ig en	clean, cleanse
	Rein ig ung	cleansing
	rein lich	clean; cleanly; neat, tidy
	Rein lich keit	cleanliness; neatness, tidiness
un	rein a	impure, unclean; polluted; with flaws
Un	rein heit	impurity; uncleanliness
un	rein lich	uncleanly
Un	rein lich keit	uncleanliness
be	rein ig en	settle; validate; clear up, remove; smooth out
Be	rein ig ung	settlement
ver un	rein ig en	soil, dirty; infect, pollute
Ver un	rein ig ung	soiling, pollution, defilement

	Reis e	journey; voyage; travel; tour; trip; expedition
	reis e fert ig	ready to start
	reis en	travel, make a journey; go touring
	Reis end e	voyager; tourist; passenger
	Reis ig er	horseman, horse-soldier; knight on horseback
Ab	reis e	departure
ab	reis en	depart, leave; set out, start
Aus	reis e	departure, exit
be	reis en	travel, tour; visit
Durch	reis e	passage, transit
'durch	reis en	travel through, pass through
durch	'reis en	travel over, tour a country
Durch	reis ende	traveler
Ein	reis e	entry
fort	reis en	depart, leave, go away
her	reis en s	travel here, come here
Hin	reis e	outbound journey
hin	reis en	travel there, go there
mit	reis en	travel along
Mit	reis ende	fellow-traveler
nach	reis en	travel after, follow
Rück	reis e	return journey, journey back
ver	reis en	go on a journey
zurück	reis en	travel back, return
her um	reis en s	travel around

	reiss en	tear, rupture; tug; pull, jerk
sich	reiss en	break, snap; burst, rupture, split, crack
	reiss en d a	rapid; impetuous; torrential; accute, racking; rapacious
	Reiss er	box-office success; thriller
ab	reiss en	clear off, pull off; pull down building; wear out clothes

an	reiss	en	tear off
An	reiss	er	market tout; marking tool
auf	reiss	en	rip up; tear open; fling, open the door; open one's eyes wide
aus	reiss	en	tear out; uproot; pull out, extract teeth
Aus	reiss	er	fugitive, runaway, deserter
'durch	reiss	en	tear, get torn, break
ein	reiss	en	tear, rend; pull down, take down, demolish
ent	reiss	en	tear away, snatch away; wrench from; save from death
fort	reiss	en	tear s.t. away, sweep s.t. off; tear s.o. from s.t.
hin	reiss	en	carry off, sweep off; enrapture, thrill, fascinate
los	reiss	en	tear away; rip off, pull off
mit	reiss	en	drag along, carry along, carry away, electrify
nieder	reiss	en	tear down; pull down, demolish
'um	reiss	en	pull down; knock down
um	'reiss	en	outline
ver	reiss	en	pull to pieces
weg	reiss	en	tear away, pull off; snatch away, carry away, sweep away
zer	reiss	bar	capable of being torn, tearable
zer	reiss	en	tear, rip up; rend; disconnect, disrupt; dismember; shred; rupture
Zer	reiss	ung	rending, tearing; dismemberment
sich zusammen	reiss	en s	pull o.s. together
her aus	reiss	en	tear out; extricate, free, get out of
her unter	reiss	en s	pull down; pull to pieces, tear down
un zer	reiss	bar	untearable
Un zer	reiss	bar keit	untearability
aus ein ander	reiss	en	tear apart, tear asunder

	reit	en	ride, go on horseback, mount; riding, equitation
	Reit	er	rider, horseman, trooper; tab
	Reit	erei	cavalry, horsemen, mounted troops
	Reit	erin	horsewoman
ab	reit	en	set out on horseback; override a horse
aus	reit	en	ride out, take a ride
be	reit a		ready, prepared
be	reit	en	train a horse, ride over country; prepare, make ready; cause s.t.
Be	reit	er	horse trainer, riding master
be	reit	s av	already
Be	reit	schaft	readiness, preparedness; police squad
Be	reit	ung	breaking in a horse; dressing, washing
'durch	reit	en	ride through
durch	'reit	en	ride through, cross on horseback
sich 'durch	reit	en	ride o.s. sore, chafe o.s. by riding
ein	reit	en	break in a horse
sich ein	reit	en	ride on, ride away
über	'reit	en	run down; override a horse; outride s.o.

um 'reit en	ride around
'um reit en	ride down
vor reit en	ride before s.o.; ride a horse through its paces
zu reit en	break in a horse; ride up to; ride on, ride faster
zurück reit en	ride back
auf be reit en t	dress, wash ore
vor be reit en	prepare
Vor be reit ung	preparatory training, preparation
zu be reit en	prepare; cook food; mix drink
Zu be reit ung	preparation; cooking food; mixing drinks
vor bei reit en	ride past
her ein reit en	bring s.o. to grief, let s.o. down
her um reit en s	insist on s.t.; criticize, pester, annoy
un vor be reit et	unprepared

Reiz nm	charm; attraction, fascination, appeal; temptation; stimulation
reiz bar	irritable, excitable; sensitive, touchy; nervous, testy
Reiz bar keit	irritability; irascibility; sensitiveness, touchiness
reiz en	irritate; excite; provoke; needle; stimulate, entice, charm; attract
reiz los	unattractive; insipid; not worth one's while
Reiz ung	irritation; provocation; stimulation; incitement; enticement
reiz voll	charming, attractive; fascinating; graceful; seductive; tempting
An reiz nm	incentive, stimulus, impulse, incitement
an reiz en	incite, stimulate; induce; abet; energize, excite
auf reiz en	incite, provoke, stir up; instigate, egg on
Auf reiz ung	incitement, provocation, instigation
ge reiz t	irritated, nettled, irritable, testy, edgy
Ge reiz t heit	irritation
über 'reiz en	overexcite; overstrain nerves
Ueber reiz t heit	overexcitement, overstrain; overwrought state
Ueber reiz ung	overexcitement, overstrain, overwrought state

renn en	run; race, dash, rush, tear
Renn en nn	running; race; heat
an renn en	run against, jostle against
be renn en	storm, assault
'durch renn en	race through, dash through, run through
ein renn en	smash open, crash through, force a door
nach renn en	run after
über 'renn en	run over, run down; overrun
'um renn en	run down, knock down
sich ver renn en	get set on s.t., get stuck on s.t.

rett en	save, rescue, deliver, recover, retrieve, salvage
sich rett en	save o.s.; escape
Rett er	rescuer, deliverer
Rett erin	rescuer, deliverer

Rett ung	rescue; deliverance; escape; salvage
rett ung s los	irrecoverable, past help, beyond recovery
er rett en	save, rescue; deliver from
Er rett er	rescuer, savior
Er rett ung	rescue, deliverance
un rett bar	irrecoverable, past recovery; ruined

richt en	set right, arrange; adjust, fix; tidy, dress, straighten
Richt er	judge
Richt erin	judge
richt er lich	judicial, judiciary
richt ig	right, correct; accurate, exact; proper, suitable
Richt ig keit	rightness, correctness, exactness, accuracy; justness, fairness
Richt ung	direction; way, route; bearing, course; trend
ab richt en	teach, train; adjust, fit; straighten
An richt e	dresser, sideboard
an richt en	prepare, dress, serve; cause; do damage
auf richt en	set up, erect; lift up, support; comfort
auf richt ig	sincere, candid, true, honest, upright
Auf richt ig keit	sincerity, candor, genuineness
aus richt en	straighten; carry out, deliver; tell; obtain
Aus richt ung	alignment
Be richt nm	report, information, summary, minutes; statement
be richt en	report, give account, cover; reveal, disclose
ein richt en	establish, set up, install; adjust; furnish
sich ein richt en	establish o.s., plan
Ein richt ung	arrangement, setup; plant, equipment; furniture; device
ent richt en	pay, discharge, give
er richt en	erect, build; found, establish
Er richt ung	erection; establishment, foundation
Ge richt nn	dish, course
Ge richt nn	court of justice, law court; judgement
ge richt lich	judicial, legal, forensic
Ge richt s bar keit	jurisdiction
her richt en	prepare, get ready; set in order, arrange
hin richt en	direct toward; execute, put to death
Hin richt ung	execution
Nach richt nf	news, information, intelligence; report, account, notice
Ober richt er	chief justice
un richt ig	incorrect, wrong, erroneous
Un richt ig keit	incorrectness
Unter richt nm	instruction, lessons, school, education, teaching
unter 'richt en	instruct, teach, educate; inform of, advise
Unter richt ung	information
ver richt en	do, perform, execute
Ver richt ung	performance, achievement, work, duty; maintenance
vor richt en	prepare, fit up

Vor	richt ung		arrangement, preparation; appliance, device; equipment, mechanism
zu	richt en		prepare, get ready, finish; cook; dress
Zu	richt er		dresser; finisher
Zu	richt ung		preparation, dressing; adjustment, fitting, finishing
un auf	richt ig		insincere
Un auf	richt ig keit		insincerity
wieder 'auf	richt en		raise again
Vor be	richt	nm	preliminary report; advertisement; introduction, preface
Innen ein	richt ung		interior decoration
ausser ge	richt lich		extra-judicial, out of court
Bei ge	richt	nn	side-dish
Neben ge	richt	nn t	side-dish
Vor ge	richt	nn	first dish, entree
Fern unter	richt	nm	correspondence course, postal course
un ver	richt et		unperformed
be	richt ig en		correct, adjust, rectify, settle, pay, satisfy, calibrate
Be	richt ig ung		rectification, adjustment, amendment, correction
be nach	richt ig en		inform of, send word to, notify, advise
Be nach	richt ig ung		information, advice

---

	rieb:	siehe reib	
Ab	rieb	nm	abrasion, attrition, wear; abrasive dust, metal grindings

---

	Ring	nm	ring; circle; rings around the eyes
	Ring el chen		ringlet, circlet
	ring el n		ring; curl
sich	ring el n		curl; coil; wind, meander; wriggle; wreathe
	ring en		twist; wring laundry
	Ring en	nn	wrestling match
	Ring er		wrestler
	ring förm ig		annular, ring-shaped
	ring s	av	around
aus	ring en		wring out
sich 'durch	ring en		struggle through, fight one's way through
ent	ring en		wrest s.t. from s.o., wring s.t. from s.o.
sich ent	ring en		escape from s.o., break away from s.o.
er	ring en		obtain; achieve, gain fame; win the prize
ge	ring	a	little, small
nieder	ring en		overpower, get down; wear down
um 'ring en			ring around, throng around; surround; beset
ver	ring er n		diminish, decrease, lessen; reduce, cut back
Ver	ring er ung		diminution, decrease, reduction, cut

---

	riss:	siehe reiss	
	Riss	nm	tearing, rending; tear, breach, break, gap; cleft
	riss ig		full of cracks, cracked; threadbare, worn; fissured; rifted
Ab	riss	nm	outline, short survey, summary; abridgement; layout; demolition

Auf riss	nm	elevation, front elevation, front view; vertical projection; outline
Ein riss	nm	tear, slit, rent; score, cleft, crack; flaw
ge riss en a s		sly, shrewd, cunning, clever; wily, foxy, tricky
Ge riss en heit		shrewdness, cunning, craftiness; wiliness, foxiness, trickiness
Um riss	nm	outline, contour, profile, silhouette; skyline
zer riss en	a	torn, tattered, ripped, battered, rugged; disrupted
Zer riss en heit		disintegration
ab ge riss en	a	torn off, pulled down, demolished; shabby, threadbare; disconnected
hin ge riss en	a	be delighted with, be fascinated by; in raptures, in ecstacy

ritt: siehe reit		
Ritt	nm	ride, ride on horseback
ritt lings	av	astride, astraddle
Aus ritt	nm	horse ride; ride, outing on horseback
be ritt en	a	mounted
Ein ritt	nm	entrance on horseback
ritter: siehe reit		
Ritter	nm	knight, cavalier, gallant person
ritter haft		chivalrous, chivalric, gallant
ritter lich		chivalrous, chivalric, gallant
Ritter lich keit		chivalry, chivalrousness, gallantry
Ritter ling		edible fungus of tricholoma genus
Ritter schaft		knighthood, knights; rank of a knight
Ritter tum	nn	knighthood, chivalry; knights
un ritter lich		unchivalrous

Roll e	roll; roller, cylinder; coil; reel, spool
roll en	roll
sich roll en	roll; wheel s.t.
roll en förm ig	cylindrical
Roll er	scooter; motorscooter
ab roll en	roll off
auf roll en	roli up, wind up on a line; roll open; bring an affair up again
aus roll en	roll out dough; run out cable
ein roll en	roll up, roll in; curl
ent roll en	roll down
Ge röll	nn	pebbles; rubble
Neben roll e t	subordinate part, minor part
über 'roll en	overroll, sweep over
zusammen roll en sich	roll up, coil up
zusammen roll en	roll o.s. up

Rost	nm	rust; smut, mildew
rost en		rust, get rusty, oxidize
rost frei		rustless, rustproof; stainless steel
rost ig		rusty, corroded

'durch rost en		rust through
ein rost en		rust in, get rusty
ent rost en		remove rust, derust
ver rost en		get rusty, rust; corrode

ruck art ig		jerky; abrupt
rück en		move; shift; push away
rück weise	av	by jerks; by fits and starts
ab rück en		move away, remove
an ruck en		approach, draw near; advance
an rück en		approach, draw near
auf rück en		move up, advance
aus rück en		march out, depart
Aus rück er		disengaging gear, releasing lever
be rück en		captivate, charm, bewitch
ein rück en		insert, put in, publish
Ein rück ung		insertion, publication
ent rück en	p	remove, whisk off
her rück en	s	move near, draw near
nach rück en		move after, follow
ver rück en		displace, move, shift; disarrange
ver rück t		crazy, mad, batty, loony, nuts
Ver rück t heit		madness; foolish action, folly; craze
vor rück en		move forward, advance
zusammen rück en		move together
her an rück en		move near, pull up
her aus rück en		push out, move out
un ver rück bar		unremovable; steadfast, unshakable

Rück en	nm	back; dorsum; chine
rück fäll ig		revertible
rück ling s	av	backwards; from behind
rück wärt ig		rearward, at the back
rück wärt s		backwards, rearwards; retrograde; downhill; in retrospect
hinter rück s	av	from behind, from the back

Ruf	nm	call, cry, shout; summons; reputation, standing; fame
ruf en		call, cry, shout, call to, hail
Ab ruf	nm	call; recall
ab ruf en		call off; call away; remove
An ruf	nm	shout, calling; appeal; telephone call
an ruf en		call on telephone; implore
An ruf er		caller
Auf ruf	nm	calling up, call; proclamation, summons; appeal
auf ruf en		call up; proclaim
Aus ruf	nm	exclamation, interjection; proclamation
aus ruf en		proclaim; exclaim
Aus ruf er		public crier; proclaimer; auctioneer
Aus ruf ung		outcry, exclamation; proclamation
Be ruf	nm	profession; occupation, calling

be ruf en	call s.o.; convene, convoke an assembly
sich be ruf en	refer to s.t.; quote; rely on s.t.
be ruf lich	professional
Be ruf ung	vocation, calling; appointment to an office
'durch ruf en s	telephone through to s.o.
Fern ruf nm	telephone number; long distance telephone call
her ruf en	call to here
Nach ruf nm	obituary
nach ruf en	call after s.o.
Rück ruf nm	recall
Ver ruf nm	bad repute
ver ruf en	ill reputed, notorious
Wider ruf nm	revocation
wider 'ruf en	revoke, abolish
wider ruf lich	revocable; revocably, at will, at pleasure; on probation
Wider ruf ung	revocation
Zu ruf nm	call, shout; acclamation
zu ruf en	call to; applaud
zurück ruf en	call back; recall
zusammen ruf en	convoke, call together
Zwischen ruf nm	interruption by heckler
her aus ruf en	call forth; call before the curtain
ab be ruf en	call home, recall
Ab be ruf ung	calling home, recall
ein be ruf en	call up soldiers; convoke
Ein be ruf ung	conscription, draft call
Neben be ruf nm	additional occupation, avocation
neben be ruf lich	avocational; spare-time, sideline; as an extra occupation
un be ruf en a	uncalled for
zurück be ruf en	call back; recall
Zurück be ruf ung	recall; calling back
her bei ruf en	call in; hail a taxi
her ein ruf en	call in
her vor ruf en	call forth, cause
un wider ruf lich	irrevocable
Un wider ruf lich keit	irrevocability

Ruh e	rest, repose; sleep; quiet, silence, tranquility; calm, composure
ruh e be dürf t ig	in need of rest
ruh e los	restless; fidgety; disquieted
Ruh e los ig keit	restlessness
ruh en	rest, repose; sleep, idle; be at a standstill
ruh e voll	peaceful, quiet
ruh ig	at rest; quiet; still; silent; calm
aus ruh en	rest, take a rest, repose; relax, take a breath
be ruh en	be based on s.t., rest on s.t.
ge ruh en	condescend, deign to do s.t.
ge ruh sam	quiet, peaceful, tranquil; leisurely, comfortable, relaxed

Un ruh	nf	balance
Un ruh e		restlessness, uneasiness; trouble, agitation
un ruh ig		unquiet, restless; fidgety, nervous; troubled, alarmed, worried
be ruh ig en		quiet, calm; soothe, placate, modify; reassure, alleviate
sich be ruh ig en		calm down, reassure o.s., compose o.s., stabilize, abate
Be ruh ig ung		calming down; stabilizing
be un ruh ig en		disturb, trouble; harass; disquiet, worry, alarm
sich be un ruh ig en		be alarmed about, worry about
Be un ruh ig ung		disturbance, trouble, worry; anxiety, alarm

Ruhr	nf	dysentery
rühr en		stir, move
rühr en d	a	touching, moving; pathetic; heartstirring
rühr ig		active, busy; brisk, energetic, bustling, alert
Rühr ig keit		activity; enterprise; alertness; nimbleness
Rühr ung		emotion
an rühr en		touch, handle; mix, stir up; temper; touch upon
Auf ruhr	nm	rebellion, revolt, sedition, insurrection, mutiny; riot
auf rühr en		stir up, rouse, revive memories; inflame passions
Auf rühr er		rebel, insurgent, mutineer
auf rühr er isch		rebellious, insurgent, mutinous; seditious, inflammatory
be rühr en		touch; handle, finger; mention, concern
sich be rühr en		meet; come in contact with; graze; border on, meet
Be rühr ung		touching, touch, contact
'durch rühr en		stir thoroughly, mix thoroughly
ein rühr en		stir, mix in, mix with; beat up eggs
her rühr en		come from, derive from; originate from; be due to
'um rühr en		stir up
un be rühr t		untouched; virgin
un ge rühr t		unmoved, untouched, unaffected

rund	a	round; circular; spherical; cylindrical; rotund; plump
Rund e		round; circle; policeman's beat; party, company
rund en		round; round off
Rund heit		roundness
rund lich		round; rotund; plump, pudgy
Rund ung		roundness; swelling; curve
rund weg	av	plainly, flatly, pointblank
ab rund en		round off; chamfer teeth; blunt tread
Ab rund ung		curvature, rounding
auf rund en		round off
über 'rund en		outlap in sports
Vor rund e	o	preliminary round
Zwischen rund e	o	semi-final

rung: siehe ring	
Rung e	stake; stanchion
Er rung en schaft	acquisition, achievement, attainment; device, convenience

rüst en	prepare
rüst ig	vigorous, robust, strong; active; alert, spry
Rüst ig keit	vigor; activity; unimpaired strength
Rüst ung	preparations; armament; mobilization; implements
ab rüst en	take down scaffolding
Ab rüst ung	disarmament
auf rüst en	rearm; assemble
Auf rüst ung	armament
aus rüst en	furnish, provide, supply; fit out; arm, equip
Aus rüst ung	fitting out
ent rüst en	fill with indignation; anger, incense, provoke, shock
sich ent rüst en	become angry; flare up; be shocked
Ent rüst ung	indignation; anger; exasperation
Ge rüst nn	scaffold; trestle
zu rüst en	prepare; fit out, equip; make ready, get ready
Zu rüst ung	preparation; fitting-out, equipment
Wieder auf rüst ung	rearmament, rearming

sä en	sowing, seeding the land
aus sä en	sow
be sä en	sow, seed; stock a pond
ein sä en	sow
über 'sä en	strew

Sach e	thing, object; affair, matter, fact; point; issue; case
sach lich	real; relevant, pertinent, businesslike, realistic; factual
säch lich g	neuter
Sach lich keit	reality; relevance; realism; objectivity; functionalism
Neben sach e	minor matter; secondary consideration
neben säch lich	subordinate; incidental; unimportant; not essential; irrelevant
Neben säch lich keit	triviality
un sach lich	not objective, personal; irrelevant, not pertinent
Ur sach e	cause, reason; occasion; motive
ur säch lich	causal, causative
Wider sach er nm	adversary; antagonist, opponent
ver ur sach en	cause, occassion; produce, create; give rise to; entail
ver sach lich en	render factual
Haupt sach e	the main thing
haupt säch lich	main, principal, essential, primary
Tat sach e	fact
tat säch lich	actual, real, factual; true

Sag e	legend, myth; fable, tradition
sag en	say, tell
sag en haft	legendary, mythical, fabulous, incredible
Ab sag e	refusal, excuse
ab sag en	countermand, renounce, refuse; call off, cancel
An sag e	declaration, announcement; bidding
an sag en	declare, announce, notify
An sag er	announcer
auf sag en	recite; repeat
Aus sag e	declaration, statement; evidence, testimony
aus sag en	say, state, declare; give evidence; predicate
be sag en	say; purport, prove; indicate, mean, signify
be sag t	said; above-mentioned
ent sag en	give up; turn away from, renounce; abdicate, resign
Ent sag ung	resignation, renunciation; abdication; abjuration
her sag en	recite; repeat
sich los sag en	renounce s.t., give up s.t.; part from
Los sag ung	renunciation
nach sag en	repeat mechanically; speak of, say of
un sag bar	unspeakable, ineffable, unutterable; immense
un säg lich	unspeakable, ineffable, unutterable; immense
unter 'sag en	forbid, prohibit from
Unter sag ung	interdiction, prohibition
ver sag en	deny, refuse; fail, break down
Ver sag er	breakdown, failure; unsuccessful person
vor sag en	tell to; rehearse to, prompt s.o.
weiter sag en	repeat, tell others
'wieder sag en s	repeat, tell again
Zu sag e	promise; acceptance; consent, assent
zu sag en	promise; accept; answer to; suit s.o., please s.o.; agree with
Gegen aus sag e	counter-evidence
her aus sag en	speak out
Vor aus sag e	prediction, prophecy; tip
vor aus sag en	predict, foretell, tell in advance
Vor aus sag ung	prediction, prophecy; tip
un ge sag t	unsaid
Vor her sag e	prediction, prophecy
vor her sag en	foretell, predict
so zu sag en	so to speak
Säg e	saw
säg en	saw
Säg er	sawyer
ab säg en	saw off
aus säg en	saw out
'durch säg en	saw through
zer säg en	saw up

Salz nn	salt
salz arm	saline
salz en	salt, season with salt, pickle

	salz	ig		salty, briny; brackish
	salz	los		salt-free
ein	salz	en		salt; cure meat
ver	salz	en		oversalt; spoil s.t.

	Sam	en	nm	seed; sperm, semen; germ; source, offspring
	Säm	erei en	np	seeds
be	sam	en		inseminate
Be	sam	ung		insemination

	sam	t	p	together with, along with, including
	säm	t lich	pn	complete, whole, entire; all, without exception
ge	sam	t	a	whole, entire, all, complete; total, aggregate; united
Ge	sam	t heit		total, whole, entire
mit	sam	t	p	together with
ins ge	sam	t	av	altogether, in all, all told; total

	sammel:	siehe sam 2	
	sammel	n	gather s.t.; pick flowers; collect stamps; harvest; accumulate s.t.
	Samm	l er	collector; gatherer; accumulator, storage battery
	Samm	l ung	gathering, collecting
an	sammel	n	collect; gather, assemble, concentrate; amass, hoard up
sich an	sammel	n	accrue, accumulate
auf	sammel	n	gather up, pick up, collect
ein	sammel	n	gather in, collect; win, reap
ver	sammel	n	assemble, rally; convoke, convene
An	samm	l ung	collection, accumulation; heap, pile; gathering, assembly
Ver	samm	l ung	assembly, meeting, gathering
Voll ver	samm	l ung	plenary meeting

	sammen:	siehe sam 2	
bei	sammen	av	together
mit	sammen	av	together
zu	sammen	av	together, jointly; at the same time

	sand:	siehe send	
Ge	sand	te	nm	envoy, diplomatic minister
Ge	sand	t schaft	legation, mission
Ver	sand	nm	dispatch, shipment
ver	sand	en	silt up; peter out, come to nothing
Ver	sand	ung	siltation
ab ge	sand	te	emissary, special envoy; messenger, courier

	sang:	siehe sing	
	Sang	nm	singing, chant, song
	sang	bar	singable, suitable for singing
	Säng	er	singer, vocalist; songster; poet, bard
	Säng	erin	chanteuse, female singer, singer, vocalist

	Säng	er	schaft	singers; choir
Ge	sang	nm		singing; song, hymn; voice; canto; book
ge	sang	lich		vocal
Vor	säng	er		precantor, principal singer, leading soloist; cantor, chanter
Ab ge	sang	nm		concluding part of a ternary strophe
Auf ge	sang	nm		the first two sections of a ternary strophe

	sass:	siehe sitz	
an	säss	ig	residing, resident, domiciled
An	säss	ig keit	residence, status of resident
auf	säss	ig	rebellious, hostile; refractory; recalcitrant
Auf	säss	ig keit	rebelliousness, refractoriness; recalcitrance, hostility
Bei	sass	e nm	person without full civil rights; small tenant farmer; cottager
Ge	säss	nn	buttocks, posterior, behind; seat
Hinter	sass	e nm	rear vassal
In	sass	e nm	occupant; passenger; inmate; inhabitant, dweller
In	sass	in	occupant; passenger; inmate; inhabitant, dweller

	satz:	siehe sitz		
	Satz	nm		sentence, phrase; period
	Satz	ung		statute, by-law; standing rule
	satz	weise	av	sentence by sentence; by leaps and bounds
Ab	satz	nm		intermission, stop; paragraph; sediment; heel; circulation
An	satz	nm		added piece; mouthpiece; onset, start; arrangement; estimation
Auf	satz	nm		top; center piece; essay, composition; article; fixture
Aus	satz	nm		leprosy; scab; lead
aus	sätz	ig		leprous
Aus	sätz	ig e		leper
Be	satz	nm		border, edge, trimming; braid; lace
Be	satz	ung		garrison, occupying forces, occupation troops; crew
Bei	satz	nm		admixture, alloy
Ein	satz	nm		putting in, insertion; container; filling; onset; deposit
Ent	satz	nm		relief, rescue, succor; relieving army
Er	satz	nm		compensation; indemnity, reparation; substitute, replacement
Fort	satz	nm		continuation; process; appendix
Gegen	satz	nm		contrast, opposite, contrary; opposition, disparity
gegen	sätz	lich		contrary, opposite; opposing, antagonistic
Nach	satz	nm		postscript; final clause; minor proposition
Neben	satz	nm	g	subordinate clause
Um	satz	nm		turnover, returns, receipts, sales, transactions; business
Unter	satz	nm		support, supporter; stand, base, pedestal; saucer
Ver	satz	nm		stowing, gobbing, paloning

Vor satz nm	design, purpose, intention, plan; resolution; attached device
vor sätz lich	intentional, deliberate, willful
Vorder satz nm	antecedent, premise
Zu satz nm	addition, alloy; dash; appendix; insert; postscript
zu sätz lich	additional, added, supplemental; extra, auxiliary
Zwischen satz nm g	parenthesis
un vor sätz lich	unintentional, undesigned; unpremeditated
Grund satz nm	principle; maxim; doctrine
grund sätz lich	fundamental, basic; on principle

sauer a	sour, acid; tart, acrid; acidulous
säuer lich	sourish; acidulous, sub-acid; wintry, sour
Säuer ung	leavening of bread, acidification, acidulation
Säu r e	sourness; acidity; acid; acrimony
säu r e frei	non-acid
an säuer n	leaven dough; acidify, acidulate
durch 'säuer n	make sour, acidify; leaven dough
ein säuer n	acidify; leaven bread; pickle meat; ensilage fodder
über 'säuer n	make too sour; overacidify
Ueber säuer ung	hyperacidity
un ge säuer t	unleavened

saug en	suck; suck up, absorb
säug en	suckle, nurse, give the breast to, breast-feed
Saug er	sucker; dummy teat; suction apparatus, suction cup
saug fäh ig	absorbent
Saug fäh ig keit	absorptive capacity
Säug ling	baby, infant
ab saug en	suck off, exhaust gas; vacuum a room
an saug en	suck in, aspirate, prime a pump
auf saug en	suck up, aspirate, absorb
aus saug en	suck out; suck; drain, exhaust
ein saug en	suck in; absorb, imbibe
sich 'voll saug en	suck o.s. full
ab säug el n	inarch in horticulture
Staub saug er	vacuum cleaner

schad e a	pity
Schad e nm	damage; injury, harm; infirmity; defect; ravages
Schad en nm	damage; injury, harm; infirmity; defect; ravages
schad en	damage, injure, harm, hurt; be injurious; prejudice
schad haft	damaged; defective; faulty; dilapidated, decayed
Schad haft ig keit	damaged state, defectiveness
schäd ig en	damage, impair, affect; wrong, hurt, injure; prejudice
Schäd ig ung	damage, impairment, injury; prejudice, detriment
schäd lich	harmful, injurious; noxious, poisonous; pernicious; prejudicial
Schäd lich keit	harmfulness, injuriousness; noxiousness, unwholesomeness

Schäd ling	noxious person, parasite
schad los	indemnified
un schäd lich	innocuous, harmless
Un schäd lich keit	harmlessness
un be schad et p	without prejudice to; irrespective of, notwithstanding
be schäd ig en	damage, injure, disable
Be schäd ig ung	damage, injury, hurt
ent schäd ig en	reimburse, remunerate, compensate s.o. for s.t.
Ent schäd ig ung	idemnification, making good
un be schäd ig t	uninjured, intact; undamaged, in good condition

schaff en	create, produce; call into being, organize; set up; do
Schaff n er	steward, manager; guard, conductor
Schaff n erin	stewardess, housekeeper; conductress
Schaff ung	creation; production; provision; organization, establishment
ab schaff en	abolish, discontinue; repeal, supress; do away with
Ab schaff ung	abolition, repeal; redress, removal; doing away with
sich an schaff en	supply o.s., provide o.s. with s.t.
An schaff ung	procurement, purchase, acquisition
be schaff en	procure, provide, make available; obtain, furnish, supply
be schaff en a	constituted, conditioned
Be schaff en heit	constitution
Be schaff ung	acquisition
er schaff en	create; produce, make
Er schaff er	creator
Er schaff ung	creation
fort schaff en	carry away, transport off; rush away; get rid of
her schaff en s	bring here, get here
hin schaff en	move there, transport there, convey there
ver schaff en	procure, get, provide, furnish, supply
zurück schaff en	convey back, take back, haul back; return s.t.
hin auf schaff en	switch off, break, disconnect, cut off; turn off
her aus schaff en	take out, move out, carry out
hin aus schaff en	take out, get out, remove
'wieder be schaff en	replace
her bei schaff en	bring here; move to the spot; supply, procure

Schal e	shell; peal, skin; husk, hull; peeling; bark, rind
schäl en	remove the shell from; husk; peel, pare; bark
Schal ung	form
ab schäl en	peel, pare; bark
aus schäl en	peel; shell
be schäl en	cover, serve
Be schäl er	stallion
ver schal en	plank, board, encase
Ver schal ung	planking; boarding, casing
her aus schäl en	knock out; lay bare; unfold, develop

Vor schäl er		accessory plowshare, forward plowshare

	schalt en		direct, rule
	Schalt er		sliding window; ticket office; switch, circuit breaker, cut-out
	Schalt ung		control; gear-change, gearshift, shifting
ab	schalt en		switch off; break, disconnect, cut off; turn off one's mind, relax
an	schalt en		switch on, turn on; connect, wire up
aus	schalt en	t	eliminate; dispose of s.t.; compensate for, correct; switch off
Aus	schalt er		circuit-breaker, circuit cut-out
Aus	schalt ung		elimination, exclusion, disposal
'durch	schalt en		shift the gears through full range; put s.t. through
ein	schalt en		insert, put in; interpolate; connect up; switch on, turn on
sich ein	schalt en		step in, intervene; engage in conversation, join in, cut in
Ein	schalt ung		insertion; interpolation
'um	schalt en	s	switch over, change over; shift
Um	schalt er		change-over switch, electrical commutator
Um	schalt ung	s	commutation
zurück	schalt en		change down, shift down into first gear
hinter ein			
ander	schalt en	t	connect in series
Hinter ein			
ander	schalt ung	t	series connection
neben ein			
ander	schalt en	t	connect in parallel
Neben ein			
ander	schalt ung	t	electrical parallel connection

	Scham	nf	shame; bashfulness, modesty
sich	schäm en		feel ashamed, be ashamed
	scham haft		bashful, modest; blushing; coy, prim; prudish
	Scham haft ig keit		bashfulness, modesty; coyness; chasteness
	scham los		shameless; impudent
	Scham los ig keit		shamelessness, unashamedness, indecency, lewdness, obscenity
be	schäm en		put to shame, embarass, confuse; eclipse
Be	schäm ung		humiliation, shame, confusion
ver	schäm t		bashful, shamefaced
un ver	schäm t		impudent, impertinent, insolvent, saucy
Un ver	schäm t heit		impudence, impertinence, insolence, effrontery

	schank:	siehe schenk	
Aus	schank	nm	sale of alcoholic drinks, beer on tap; bar, counter

	scharf	a	sharp; sharp-edged, cutting, keen; pointed, acute
	Schärf e		sharpness; keenness; severity, rigor, harshness; exactness
	schärf en		sharpen, whet; grind; point

ein schärf en	enjoin, impress s.t. on s.o., urge s.t. on s.o.
ent schärf en	disarm, unprime, de-cap; deactivate ammunition
un scharf a	blurred, fuzzy, poorly defined; unprimed ammunition
ver schärf en	add to, intensify, heighten; aggravate
Ver schärf ung	intensification, heightening; aggravation

Schatt en nm	shadow, shade
schatt en haft	shadowy, shadow-like; ghostly
schatt en los	shadowless, shadeless
schatt ier en	shade, tint; hatch
Schatt ier ung	shading; shade, tint, hue
schatt ig	shady, shadowy; shaded
be schatt en	shade, overshadow, dim, cast a gloom over
über 'schatt en	overshadow; cast a cloud over
um 'schatt en	shade

Schatz nm	treasure; rich store; find; rich source, bonanza
schätz bar	estimable
schätz en	estimate; value, assess; appraise, price, forecast; esteem
schätz en s wert	estimable, valuable
Schätz er	- expert valuer; appraiser
Schätz ung	estimate, valuation; computation; rating; assessment
schätz ung s weise av	approximately, roughly
ab schätz en	estimate; value, rate; appraise, evaluate, assess
Ab schätz er	appraiser; assessor
ab schätz ig	disparaging
Ab schätz ung	estimation; appraisal, valuation; assessment
ein schätz en	assess, appraise, estimate; value, rate; size s.o. up
über 'schätz en	overrate, overestimate
Ueber schätz ung	overestimation
un schätz bar	inestimable, invaluable
unter 'schätz en	undervalue; underestimate, underrate

Schau nf	view, inspection; show, exhibition; spectacle, review
schau en	see, perceive, view, behold, look
Schau er	shower; shudder, shiver; attack, fit, thrill
Schau er	shed, shelter
schau er lich	horrible, ghastly, gruesome
schau r ig	horrible, horrid, weird
an schau en	look at, view; consider s.t.
an schau lich	lively, graphic, descriptive
An schau lich keit	liveliness; vividness
An schau ung	contemplation; opinion, point of view
auf schau en	look up, lift one's eyes; look up to s.o.
Aus schau nf	be on the lookout for, watch for
aus schau en	look like, have an appearance; look out for s.t.
Be schau nf	examination, inspection
be schau en	examine, inspect

Be	schau	er	examiner, inspector; observer, onlooker
be	schau	lich	thoughtful, reflective; quiet, peaceful life
Be	schau	lich keit	reflection, quiet, contemplation
'durch	schau	en	look through
durch	'schau	en	see through s.o.; penetrate
her	schau	en	look here
nach	schau	en	look for s.t.; look up a word; look back after
Rück	schau	nf	retrospect, review, looking back
über	'schau	en	survey; overlook s.t.; have a general grasp of s.t.
Um	schau	nf	survey, review; looking around
sich 'um	schau	en	look back; look around for s.t.
Vor	schau	nf	film preview
zu	schau	en	look on, watch s.t.
Zu	schau	er	spectator, onlooker, bystander, observer
Zu	schau	erin	spectator, onlooker, bystander, observer
zurück	schau	en	look back
Zusammen	schau	nf	synopsis
her ab	schau	en	look down on s.t., despise s.t.
her aus	schau	en	look out of
hin aus	schau	en	look out
vor aus	schau	en	prospective, farsighted, long-range
her ein	schau	en	look into
um 'her	schau	en	look around
hin über	schau	en	look over to, look across to
her um	schau	en s	look around
hin unter	schau	en	look down upon
ver an	schau	lich en	make s.t. clear, illustrate s.t.
Ver an	schau	lich ung	demonstration, illustration
Welt an	schau	ung	world view, personal philosophy

	Schaufel	nf	shovel; scoop; paddle; palm; blade, bucket
	schaufel	n	shovel; dig
	Schauf l	er	buck with palmed antlers
aus	schaufel	n	shovel out
zu	schaufel	n	shovel up, fill up

	Scheid e	line of separation, borderline, parting; sheath; scabbard
	scheid en	separate; depart, leave; part, take leave of one another
sich	scheid en	separate, part; sever; divide; analyze, refine ore; divorce
	Scheid ung	separation, parting; divorce
ab	scheid en	separate, divide, part; decease, pass away
Ab	scheid er	separator
Ab	scheid ung	separation
aus	scheid en	eliminate, separate; remove, exclude, rule out
Aus	scheid ung	elimination, removal, separation
Be	scheid nm	answer, reply
be	scheid en a	modest, unassuming, shy, unpretentious, plain; reserved
be	scheid en	allot, assign, award; inform, notify s.o.; instruct; summon

sich be scheid en	moderate o.s., be content
Be scheid en heit	modesty
Ent scheid nm	decree, decision
ent scheid en	decide, determine, settle; decree, rule, adjudge
sich ent scheid en	be decided, be settled; decide, vote, make up one's mind
ent scheid end	decisive, conclusive; final; crucial
Ent scheid ung	decision, determination
hin scheid en p	pass away, depart this life
unter scheid bar	distinguishable, discernible
unter 'scheid en	distinguish, discriminate; discern, differentiate
Unter scheid ung	distinction, discrimination; difference
ver scheid en	pass away, expire
un be scheid en a	immodest; presumptuous; unreasonable
Un be scheid en heit	immodesty; presumption
Vor be scheid nm	preliminary decision
Zwischen be scheid nm	intermediate reply
Vor ent scheid ung	preliminary decision

Schein nm	shine; light; gleam
schein bar	seeming, apparent; false, fictitious
schein en	shine, give light, gleam
An schein nm	appearance, look, semblance; probability
an schein end av	apparently, seemingly
be schein en	shine upon; irradiate
'durch schein en	shine through
durch schein end	translucent, transparent, diaphanous
er schein en	appear; come along, turn up; put in an appearance
Er schein ung	appearance, phenomenon; spectacle; phantom; vision
un schein bar	insignificant; plain, homely; inconspicuous
Un schein bar keit	insignificance; plainness, homeliness
Vor schein nm	bring to light, bring forward, produce
Wider schein nm	reflection
'wieder er schein en	reappear; resume publication
be schein ig en	certify, attest; verify, authenticate
Be schein ig ung	certificate, certification
wahr schein lich	probable, likely

scheit: siehe scheid	
Scheit nn	piece of wood; log; billet; spade
Scheit el	top of the head, part in hair; apex, summit, maximum, top
scheit el n	make a part in one's hair
scheit er n	fail, founder; be frustrated; be shipwrecked, wreck, run aground
ge scheit a	clever, intelligent, bright; sensible; good, thorough
Ge scheit heit	cleverness, intelligence, smartness; intelligent remark

Schenk	nm	cupbearer; publican, inn-keeper
Schenk	e	public house, inn, tavern; roadhouse
schenk	en	give; grant, endow
Schenk	er	giver, donor
Schenk	ung	gift, donation
aus schenk	en	pour out; retail; sell liquor
be schenk	en	make s.o. a present, make a donation of s.t.
ein schenk	en	pour out, pour into
Ge schenk	nn	present, gift, donation; gratuity
ver schenk	en	give away
'voll schenk	en	fill up
Gegen ge schenk	nn	return present, present given for another present

Scher	e	scissors; shears; wire-cutters; plate-shears
scher	en	shear, clip; shave, trim; cut; clip, prune
ab scher	en	shear off; cut, crop
be scher	en	present to, bestow upon
Be scher	ung	giving of Christmas presents, Christmas presents

aus scher	en	leave formation, fall out

Schicht	nf	layer, bed
schicht	en	put in layers, pile up; stack; stow; stratify; classify
Schicht	ung	arrangement in layers; stratification; classification
schicht weise	av	in layers; in shifts
auf schicht	en	stack up, staple, arrange in layers
Ober schicht	nf	top layer; upper class
Ueber schicht	nf	extra shift
'um schicht	en	pile afresh
um schicht	ig	by turns, alternately
Um schicht	ung	regrouping, shifting
Unter schicht	nf	lower stratum

Ge schicht chen	nn	little story; anecdote
Ge schicht e	nf	story, narrative, tale; history, affair, business
ge schicht lich		historical; historic
Ur ge schicht e		early history
ur ge schicht lich		prehistoric
Vor ge schicht e		prehistory, early history
vor ge schicht lich		prehistoric

schick: siehe scheh		
schick	a	chic, stylish, smart, elegant
Schick	nm	chic, style, elegance
schick	en	send, dispatch, forward, communicate; transmit, remit
sich schick	en	happen, come to pass; chance
schick	lich	becoming, proper, seemly, decent, suitable, convenient
Schick lich keit		propriety, decorum, decency
Schick sal	nn	fate, destiny, lot, fortune
schick sal haft		fateful

	Schick ung	providence; divine dispensation, divine decree; affliction
ab	schick en	send s.t. away, dispatch s.t.
sich an	schick en	begin s.t.
aus	schick en	send s.o. out, dispatch s.o.
be	schick en	send goods to a fair; feed the stove; alloy metal
Be	schick ung	sending goods; feeding the stove; metal alloy
ein	schick en	send s.t. in
fort	schick en	send s.t. away
Ge	schick nn	fate, destiny; aptitude, knack, skill
Ge	schick lich keit	cleverness, skill, dexterity
ge	schick t	clever, skillful, dexterous
her	schick en s	send here
hin	schick en	send there, send to
mit	schick en	send s.t. with s.o.
nach	schick en	send s.t. after; forward letters
über	'schick en	send, consign to
un	schick lich	inappropriate, unseemly, unbecoming, improper
Un	schick lich keit	inappropriateness, impropriety, unseemliness
ver	schick en	send s.t. off, dispatch, forward s.t.; deport
Ver	schick ung	dispatching, forwarding; deportation
vor	schick en	send to the front; send forward
weg	schick en	send s.t. away
weiter	schick en	send on
zu	schick en	send s.t. to s.o; forward s.t.
zurück	schick en	send s.t. back
hin auf	schick en	send out
vor aus	schick en	send on before, send on ahead; presuppose
Miss ge	schick nn	misfortune, bad luck
Un ge	schick nn	misfortune, disaster
Un ge	schick lich keit	clumsiness, awkwardness
un ge	schick t	awkward, clumsy, gauche
ent gegen	schick en	send to meet

	schieb en	push, shove; move; thrust; slide, slip; wheel
	Schieb er	pusher, slide; damper; bolt, bar; profiteer
	Schieb ung	sharp practice, swindle, underhand dealings
ab	schieb en	push off; expel; evacuate; get rid of, send off
an	schieb en	push, give a shove
auf	schieb en	push open; put off; defer, postpone, delay; adjourn
ein	schieb en	shove in, push in, slip in; insert; interpolate; introduce
Ein	schieb sel nn	insertion; interpolation
Ein	schieb ung	insertion; interpolation
Ge	schieb e nn	shoving, pushing
'unter	schieb en	push under; substitute; attribute falsely to, foist on s.o.
Unter	schieb ung	substitution
ver	schieb bar	sliding, movable, adjustable
ver	schieb en	shift, remove; displace, put off, postpone; sell underhandedly

Ver	schieb ung	shifting, displacement; postponement
vor	schieb en	push forward, push on, advance; feed to s.o.
zu	schieb en	close, shut; push towards; impute to
zusammen	schieb en	push together; telescope
un auf	schieb bar	not to be delayed; urgent, imperative

	schied:	siehe scheid	
Ab	schied	nm	departure, parting, farewell; dismissal; resignation
ent	schied en	a	decided, determined, resolute; distinct; emphatic; peremptory
Ent	schied en heit		determination, resoluteness; peremptoriness
Unter	schied	nm	difference, distinction
unter	schied lich		different, differing, varied, variable
unter	schied s los		indiscriminate; without exception
ver	schied en	a	different, distinct, unlike, varied, diverse; deceased
Ver	schied en heit		difference, dissimilarity; diversity; variety
ver	schied en t lich		several; repeated
ver ab	schied en		dismiss, discharge; retire an officer
sich ver ab	schied en		take one's leave of s.o.; say goodbye to s.o.
Ver ab	schied ung		dismissal; passing
un ent	schied en	a	undecided; open, unsettled
ab ge	schied en	a	solitary, lonely, lonesome; deceased; separated, divided
Ab ge	schied en heit		solitude, loneliness, lonesomeness

	schiess en	shoot, blast, discharge a gun, open fire
	Schiess erei	gunfight, shooting
ab	schiess en	shoot off, discharge gun, shoot, fire, down s.t. by gunfire
an	schiess en	shoot first, crystallize; wound
auf	schiess en	open a breach; shoot up, spring up, grow tall
aus	schiess en	shoot out, shoot for; cast out, reject; sprout
be	schiess en	fire upon, bombard, shell, gun
Be	schiess ung	bombardment, shelling, shellfire
durch	'schiess en	shoot through
'durch	schiess en	interleave, space out, interline
ein	schiess en	batter down, shoot down; try, test; shoot; invest
sich ein	schiess en	practice shooting
er	schiess en	shoot dead
Er	schiess ung	shooting, execution
los	schiess en	fire off, fire away; start, begin
nieder	schiess en	shoot down, rush down
'über	schiess en	shoot over, fire beyond the target, exceed, overshoot
ver	schiess en	use up ammunition; fade, change color
vor	schiess en	advance, lend money
zer	schiess en	shoot to pieces
zusammen	schiess en	shoot down; knock out, batter down
hin aus	schiess en	overshoot the mark
vor bei	schiess en	miss the mark
da neben	schiess en	miss one's mark

	Schiff nn	ship, vessel; boat, craft; steamship, steamer
	schiff bar	navigable
	Schiff bar keit	navigability
	Schiff chen	small ship, small boat
	schiff en	navigate, sail
	Schiff er	mariner, sailor, navigator
aus	schiff en	disembark, debark, put ashore, land; discharge cargo
sich aus	schiff en	disembark, debark, put ashore, land; discharge a cargo
Aus	schiff ung	disembarkation, debarkation
durch	'schiff en	sail across, sail through; cross, traverse
ein	schiff en	embark, ship
sich ein	schiff en	embark, go on board
Ein	schiff ung	embarkation
Hinter	schiff nn	stern of ship
um	'schiff en	circumnavigate, sail around; double a cape
Um	schiff ung	transshipment, reshipment, passenger transfer
ver	schiff en	ship
Ver	schiff ung	shipment
Voll	schiff nn	full-rigged ship
Vor	schiff nn n	forecastle

	Schimpf nm	insult, affront, outrage, disgrace
	schimpf en	scold; grumble
	schimpf lich	insulting, abusive; disgraceful; dishonorable; outrageous
aus	schimpf en	scold s.o., berate s.o., tell s.o. off
be	schimpf en	insult, abuse, revile, swear at; disgrace, dishonor
Be	schimpf ung	insult, abuse, outrage, affront

	Schirm nm	umbrella, shade; cap visor; screen; protective shield, shelter
	schirm en	shield, guard, protect; shade
ab	schirm en	screen, shield, shade; protect, guard
Ab	schirm ung	protection, screen, cover, covering; security
be	schirm en p	shield, protect, guard, shelter
Be	schirm er	protector, guardian, defender
Be	schirm ung p	protection, guard, shelter
Regen	schirm nm	umbrella

	schlacht: siehe schlag	
	Schlacht nf	battle
	schlacht en	kill, slaughter; butcher, massacre
	Schlächt er	butcher
	Schlächt erei	butcher's shop; butchery, slaughter, massacre
	Schlacht ung	killing
ab	schlacht en	slaughter, butcher
Ab	schlacht ung	slaughter, butchering
aus	schlacht en	cut up, cut s.t. into pieces; salvage parts, exploit s.t., break up
Aus	schlacht ung	cannibalization; exploitation; capitalization

hin	schlacht en	slaughter, massacre, butcher
ober	schlächt ig	overshot
über	schlächt ig	overshot
unter	schlächt ig	undershot
un ge	schlacht a	bulky; uncouth; coarse, rude; uncivilized, barbaric

	Schlaf nm	sleep
	Schläf chen	doze, nap, snooze; catnap
	Schläf e	temple of head
	schlaf en	sleep, slumber, doze
	Schläf er	sleeper
	Schläf erin	sleeper
	schlaf los	sleepless
	Schlaf los ig keit	sleeplessness, insomnia
	schläf r ig	sleepy, drowsy
	Schläf r ig keit	sleepiness, drowsiness; dullness; indolence
aus	schlaf en	sleep one's fill
Bei	schlaf nm	cohabitation, coition, sexual intercourse
Bei	schläf er	bedmate; lover
Bei	schläf erin	bedmate, lover
ein	schlaf en	fall asleep, go to sleep; become numb; die, die out, fizzle out
ent	schlaf en	fall asleep; die, pass away
über	'schlaf en	sleep on s.t.
ver	schlaf en a	sleepy, drowsy
ver	schlaf en	miss by sleeping; forget, neglect; oversleep, sleep s.t. off
Ver	schlaf en heit	sleepiness, drowsiness
ein	schläf er n	lull to sleep; narcotize, put to sleep; lull into security
Ein	schläf er ung	lulling to sleep, induction to sleep; anesthetization; mercy killing

	Schlag nm	blow, knock, stroke, impact; hit, slap, punch
	schlag en	strike, beat, hit; punch, sock, knock, slug, slap
	Schlag er	hit song, smash hit, box office success
	Schläg er	brawler, rowdy; slugger, batsman; beater, bat
	Schläg erei	fighting, scuffle, brawl, free fight
Ab	schlag nm	deduction, decline, rebound; reduction
ab	schlag en	turn down; strike, rebound; sink; strike off
ab	schläg ig	denying; negative
An	schlag nm	stroke, touch; poster, bill, notice, announcement; design
an	schlag en	strike at, knock at; affix; take aim at
Auf	schlag nm	striking; surtax, surplus; advance; lapel, cuff
auf	schlag en	hit, strike; serve, consult, set up
Auf	schläg er	server
Aus	schlag nm	rash, eruption, breaking out; deflection; shoots
aus	schlag en	beat, knock out; decline; reject, refuse
Be	schlag nm	metal-work, mounting, fittings; deposit; moisture, damp
be	schlag en a	cover with; fit; get tarnished; sweat; dim

be schlag en		experienced
Durch schlag	nm	punch, piercer; opening; copy; screen, sieve, strainer
durch 'schlag en		beat through; strain; punch, pierce
sich 'durch schlag en		make one's way, beat one's way through
durch schläg ig		effective
Ein schlag	nm	cover, envelope; fold, impact; touch
ein schlag en		drive in, knock, break; wrap up; follow
ein schläg ig		belonging to; relative to, pertinent to; competent
sich ent schlag en		get rid of; give up, dismiss
er schlag en		slay, kill
Gegen schlag	nm	counter-blow
hin schlag en		fall down
los schlag en		knock off, knock down; strike; attack s.o.
nach schlag en		consult a book; take after
Nieder schlag	nm t	precipitation, rainfall; sediment, deposit; result
nieder schlag en		knock down, cast down; suppress; precipitate
Nieder schlag ung		settling; precipitation; depositing, deposition, suppression
Rück schlag	nm	backfire; recoil; reverse; setback; recession
Ueber schlag	nm	calculation, estimate; facing; somersault
'über schlag en		cross; flashover, sparkover
über 'schlag en		calculate roughly; consider; omit; turn over
über schlag en	a	lukewarm, tepid
sich über 'schlag en		tumble over one another; nose over; capsize
Um schlag	nm	envelope, cover; collar, cuff; change, alteration; turnover
'um schlag en		shift; knock down; turn over; fall down
Unter schlag	nm	embezzle; intercept; suppress
unter 'schlag en		cross one's arms
Unter schlag ung		embezzlement; interception; suppression
Ver schlag	nm	partition, box, booth; planking; compartment; shed
ver schlag en		partition, cross off; board
ver schlag en	a	cunning, crafty, sly, wily
Ver schlag en heit		cunning, craftiness, slyness
Vor schlag	nm	offer, proposal, proposition, suggestion, recommendation
vor schlag en		propose, suggest, recommend, offer
zer schlag en		beat to pieces, smash, shatter, batter
sich zer schlag en		come to nothing; be broken off
Zu schlag	nm	increase, addition, surcharge; adjudication
zu schlag en		strike hard, bang, slam
zurück schlag en		beat back, repel, strike back, hit back
zusammen schlag en		smash up, knock down; clap; clasp
her ab schlag en		beat down
ver an schlag en		value, rate, estimate, assess
Ver an schlag ung		estimate, valuation
Vor an schlag	nm	estimate, preliminary calculation
her aus schlag en		make profit, make money by; knock out
nieder ge schlag en	a	dejected, cast down, downhearted, depressed
Nieder ge schlag en heit		depression, dejection

her um	schlag en	s	wrap around
her unter	schlag en		beat down
Gegen vor	schlag	nm	counter-proposal
'über ein			
ander	schlag en		cross

---

	schlecht:	siehe schlag	
	schlecht	a	bad; poor; imcompetent; precarious, disadvantageous; nasty, wicked
	Schlecht ig keit		badness, rottenness; poorness, incompetence; evilness
Ge	schlecht	nn	sex; kind, genus, species; race; line
ge	schlecht lich		sexual, sex; generic; sexually
ge	schlecht s los		sexless, asexual, neuter, nonsexual; agamic, anandrous
Ge	schlecht s los ig keit		sexlessness, asexuality
un ge	schlecht lich		asexual, sexless; agamic, agamous

	Schliess e		fastening, catch, latch, clasp
	schliess en		shut, close, lock, bolt; close down
	Schliess er		doorkeeper, jailer; turnkey; latch
	Schliess ung		closing, shutting
ab	schliess en		lock up, close; separate, isolate; conclude
sich an	schliess en		attach, join
an	schliess end		adjacent, next, neighboring; subsequent, following
auf	schliess en		unlock, open; break up, disintegrate, decompose; develop
sich auf	schliess en		unfold, pour out one's heart
aus	schliess en		shut out, exclude, bar from; disqualify; suspend; lock out, expel
aus	schliess lich		exclusive
Aus	schliess lich keit		exclusion; excommunication; lock-out
Aus	schliess ung		exclusion; excommunication; lock-out
be	schliess en		end, finish, terminate, conclude, close; decide, resolve, decree
Be	schliess er		housekeeper
Be	schliess erin		housekeeper, wardrobe keeper
bei	schliess en		enclose
ein	schliess en		lock up, confine; surround, encircle, include
ein	schliess lich	av	inclusive; compromising
Ein	schliess ung		confinement, blockade
sich ent	schliess en		determine, resolve, make up one's mind; intend
Ent	schliess ung		resolution, decision
er	schliess en		open, make accessible
Er	schliess ung		opening up; developing
um	'schliess en		enclose, surround; clasp, embrace
ver	schliess bar		fitted with lock and key
ver	schliess en		shut, close, seal up, lock; keep aloof from
zu	schliess en		lock up, shut, close
zusammen	schliess en		join closely; link together, chain together, interlock

	schloss:	siehe schliess		
	Schloss	nn		lock; clasp; snap; belt buckle; castle, palace
	Schlöss	chen		small castle, chateau
	Schloss	e		sleet, hailstone
	Schloss	er		locksmith; motor mechanic; mechanic, fitter
	Schloss	erei		locksmith's workshop
	schloss	er	n	tinker, work
be	schloss	en	a	agreed, settled
ent	schloss	en	a	resolute, determined
Ent	schloss	en heit		determination, resoluteness; energy
ge	schloss	en	a	closed; compact; enclosed, self-contained, consistent; united
ver	schloss	en	a	closed, shut; locked up; taciturn, reserved, silent
Ver	schloss	en heit		reserve, taciturnity
un ent	schloss	en	a	irresolute, vacillating, wavering, hesitating
Un ent	schloss	en heit		irresolution
un er	schloss	en	a	undeveloped; untapped
auf ge	schloss	en	a	open, alert to; open-minded, free-minded; communicative
Auf ge	schloss	en heit		open-mindedness
aus ge	schloss	en	a	impossible, out of the question
un ver	schloss	en	a	unlocked; unsealed

	schluchz:	siehe schluck	
	schluchz	en	sob
	Schluchz	en nn	sob
	Schluchz	er	sob
auf	schluchz	en	give a sudden sob

	Schluck	nm	gulp, swallow; mouthful, sip, swig, draught
	Schlück	chen	sip, drop of liquid
	schluck	en	swallow; gulp down, absorb
	Schluck	en nm	hiccups
	Schluck	er s	starveling, poor fellow
hinter	schluck	en s	swallow, gulp down
ver	schluck	en	swallow up; slur over
sich ver	schluck	en	swallow the wrong way
hin unter	schluck	en	swallow s.t. down; swallow a pill whole; gulp down

	schluss:	siehe schliess	
	Schluss	nm	close, end; conclusion; unit of trade
	Schlüss	el	key
	schlüss	el fert ig	ready for occupancy
	schlüss	ig	resolved, determined; logical
Ab	schluss	nm	termination, conclusion, end; completion; settlement
An	schluss	nm	annexation, joining, union; supply; connection
Auf	schluss	nm	explanation, information
Aus	schluss	nm	exclusion, expulsion; exemption
Be	schluss	nm	decision, decree; determination, resolution; conclusion

Bei schluss	nm	enclosure; delivery, package
Ein schluss	nm	enclosure; parenthesis
Ent schluss	nm	resolve, resolution; decision; determination
Nach schlüss el	nm	master key, lock pick, skeleton key
Neben schluss	nm t	shunt
Rück schluss	nm	conclusion, inference
un schlüss ig		irresolute, undecided, wavering
Un schlüss ig keit		irresolution, indecision, hesitation
Ver schluss	nm	closing, fastening; breechlock; stopper; shutter; trap
Zusammen schluss	nm	union, federation, merger, fusion, consolidation, combination
Fern an schluss	nm	long-distance telephone connection
Neben an schluss	nm	telephone extension line
ver schlüss el n		encode, encipher
Ver schlüss el ung		coding, cryptography
auf schlüssel n		subdivide, break down; distribute costs, allocate
ent schlüssel n		decipher, decode

---

schmack: siehe schmeck	
schmack haft	savory, palatable, tasty; appetizing
Schmack haft ig keit	savoriness, fine taste, delicious flavor
Ge schmack nm	taste, flavor; palate; liking, fancy
ge schmack los	tasteless, insipid, flat; flavorless, crude, in bad taste
Ge schmack los ig keit	tastelessness
ge schmack voll	tasteful, in good taste; elegant, stylish
ab ge schmack t	insipid, tasteless, flat; absurd, vulgar; garish; corny
Ab ge schmack t heit	tastelessness, bad taste; tactlessness; silliness, absurdity
Bei ge schmack nm	taste, smack, tang, tinge; unpleasant taste
Nach ge schmack nm	aftertaste, lingering taste
Neben ge schmack nm	slight flavor, peculiar taste, smack, tang
Vor ge schmack nm	foretaste

---

schmeck en	taste, sample
ab schmeck en	taste
vor schmeck en	predominate in taste

Schmelz nm	glaze; bloom, flush, glow of youth, tooth enamel
schmelz bar	fusible, meltable
Schmelz bar keit	fusibility
Schmelz e	melting of snow; smelting, fusion; charge
schmelz en	melt, dissolve; liquefy; soften; melt away, dwindle
Schmelz erei	smelting-works; smeltery; foundry
ab schmelz en	melt off; fuse metal; smelt ore
aus schmelz en	melt out; fuse ore; render fat; try tallow
'durch schmelz en	melt, fuse
ein schmelz en	melt down
'um schmelz en	remelt; recast
ver schmelz en	melt into one another, fuse; amalgamate; blend into s.t.

Ver schmelz ung	fusion, amalgamation
zer schmelz en	melt away
zusammen schmelz en	melt down; fuse

Schmutz nm	dirt, filth; smut; mud, muck
schmutz en	soil, give off dirt; soil easily, get dirty
Schmutz erei	filth, smut
schmutz ig	dirty; filthy, muddy; soiled; grimy; smutty; sordid, shabby
Schmutz ig keit	dirtiness, filth, grime; smut
be schmutz en	soil, dirty; stain, smudge; bespatter, splash; sully
ver schmutz en	soil; pollute water; befoul s.t.

schnei: siehe schnee	
Schnee nm	snow
schnee ig p	snowy
schnei en	snow
ein schnei en	snow in
zu schnei en	be snowed in
her ein schnei en	it is snowing at the window; blow in, drop in, turn up unexpectedly

Schneid nm	dash, pluck, guts
Schneid e	edge; cutting edge, cutter; cutting blade; drill bit
schneid en	cut
Schneid er	tailor; ladies' tailor, dressmaker
Schneid erei	tailoring, tailor's business; dressmaking
Schneid erin	ladies' tailor, dressmaker
schneid er n	tailor, do tailoring, do dressmaking
schneid ig	plucky, spirited; dashing, resolute, energetic; snappy
Schneid ig keit	smartness, dash; terseness
ab schneid en	cut off, slice off, cut down, pare, trim; take a shortcut; intercept
Ab schneid er	cutter; cropper
an schneid en	begin to cut; raise a subject; aim at, get a bearing on
auf schneid en	cut up, cut open; carve; dissect; boast, brag
Auf schneid er	braggart, boaster, show-off
Auf schneid erei	bragging, boasting, exaggeration
auf schneid er isch	boastful, exaggerated
aus schneid en	cut out; cut off; excise, trim; cut s.t. low; stamp out
be schneid en	cut, clip, trim; curtail, reduce; cut to exact size; plough
Be schneid ung	curtailment, reduction; circumcision
durch 'schneid en	cut; intersect, cross, traverse; cleave, plough the waves
'durch schneid en	cut through, cut s.t. in two; saw through; interesect, sever
ein schneid en	cut into; slot, slit; groove, recess, notch; engrave
nach schneid en	cut some more, finish cutting; resize, retap

über 'schneid en	intersect; overlap; coincide, clash; collide
Ueber schneid ung	intersection; overlap; clash, collision
unter 'schneid en	intersect; undercut
Unter schneid ung	distinction; discrimination, differentiation; difference
ver schneid en	cut s.t. badly, cut s.t. wrong; blend; adulterate; emasculate
vor schneid en	cut s.t. up, carve; cut, slice; roughcut, rough out
weg schneid en	cut s.t. away, slice s.t. off; retrench; excise, cut s.t. off
zer schneid en	cut up, cut in two, cut to pieces; slice; shred; carve
zu schneid en	cut up; cut a suit to size
Zu schneid er	cutter
her aus schneid en	cut out; excise, snip out
hin ein schneid en	cut a hole into s.t.; make a cut in s.t.

schnell a	quick; fast; rapid; swift; fleet; speedy, abrupt; hasty
Schnell ig keit	quickness; fastness; swiftness; rapidity; promptness, speed
schnell st ens	as quickly as possible
ab schnell en	yank off, flip off
sich ab schnell en	jerk off, bound off, bounce off
auf schnell en	bound up
vor schnell a	rash, hasty, precipitous, precipitate
zurück schnell en	rebound, jump back

schnitt: siehe schneid	
Schnitt nm	cut, incision, notch, shape, form; pattern, style; intersection
Schnitt chen	sandwich; canape
Schnitt e	slice of bread, cut of bread; sandwich; steak
Schnitt er	cropper, reaper, harvester, mower, harvestman
schnitt ig	streamlined, stylish, racy, rakish
Ab schnitt nm	section, cutting, segment, division; passage in a book
An schnitt nm	first cut of bread; outside slice of meat; lead angle of a saw
Auf schnitt nm	cold cuts, slices of cold meats
Aus schnitt nm	neck; cutout; clipping; detail; extract, excerpt, section, facet
Be schnitt ener	circumcised
Durch schnitt nm	average, mean, arithmetic mean; section; cutting through
durch schnitt lich	average, mean, normal, ordinary; mediocre, middling
Ein schnitt nm	cut, incision; slot, slit, groove; recess, notch
Ver schnitt nm	scraps, waste pieces, waste; blend
Zu schnitt nm	cut; caliber, stature; pattern
aus ge schnitt en a	low-necked, low-cut; notched
un ver schnitt en a	unblended, pure, sheer

	Schnur nf	cord; string, twine; line; lace; tape; braid, piping
	schnür en	lace; tie with cord, tie up, strap
ab	schnür en	unlace, untie; constrict, strangulate
auf	schnür en	lace, tie; untie; unlace shoes; undo knots
ein	schnür en	lace; strangle; tie up
ver	schnür en	tie up, cord up; lace s.t.
zu	schnür en	lace up; cord up
zusammen	schnür en	lace up, cord up; choke, strangle

	schon av	already; before; by this time, so far; yet, ever; even
	schön a	beautiful; fair; pretty, nice; lovely; splendid; good, fine
	schon en	spare; take care of; preserve; save, husband strength
	schön en	brighten colors; gloss a color; clarify a wine
	Schon er	protector; antimacassar; covering; schooner
	Schön heit	beauty; fineness; nobleness; beautiful woman, beauty
	Schon ung	mercy, indulgence, forbearance; good care; protection
	schon ung s los	unsparing, merciless, pitiless, relentless
ob	schon c	although, though
un	schön a	unlovely, unsightly
ver	schon en	spare
ver	schön er n	embellish, beautify; improve; brighten
Ver	schön er ung	embellishment; improvement; face-lifting
be	schön ig en	color; gloss over, extenuate, find excuses for
Be	schön ig ung	palliation, excuse, extenuation
wunder	schön a	most beautiful

	Schopf nm	crown, top of the head; tuft, bob; mop of hair
	schöpf en	scoop, ladle; draw; bail
	Schöpf er	creator, maker, originator, author, framer
	schöpf er isch	creative, productive; original
	Schöpf ung	creation; the universe, production, work
ab	schöpf en	skim off
aus	schöpf en	scoop, ladle out, empty; bale out a boat; drain, exhaust
er	schöpf en	exhaust, wear out, drain, deplete; treat extensively
er	schöpf t	exhausted, spent, done in; run down
Er	schöpf ung	exhaustion, weariness, prostration; depletion
Ge	schöpf nn	creature
un er	schöpf lich	inexhaustible

	schor: siehe scher	
un ge	schor en a	remain untroubled; get away with s.t.; unshaven, unshorn

	schoss: siehe schiess	
	Schoss nm	shoot, spring, sprout
	Schoss nm	lap, womb; coattail, flap, skirt

Schöss ling	offshoot, sprout; scion
er schoss en a	shot dead; dead tired
Ge schoss nn	projectile, shell, bullet, dart; floor
Ober ge schoss nn	upper story
Unter ge schoss nn	ground floor, first floor

Schrank nm	cupboard
Schrank e	barrier; railroad gate; turnpike toll gate; railing, grating
schränk en	put crosswise, cross legs; fold arms
schrank en los	boundless, unlimited; licentious
Schrank en los ig keit	boundlessness; licentiousness
be schränk en	confine, limit, restrict; restrain, curb, narrow
be schränk t	limited, confined, restricted; narrow
Be schränk t heit	confinement, limitation; scantiness; narrowness
Be schränk ung	confinement, restriction, limitation
ein schränk en	restrict, confine, limit; reduce, curtail, cut down
Ein schränk ung	restriction; reduction, cut; qualification
ver schränk en	cross, fold arms or legs; stagger; set the teeth of a saw
un be schränk t	unrestricted; absolute; uncontrolled
un um schränk t	unlimited; absolute, autocratic
un ein ge schränk t	unrestricted, unlimited, uncontrolled; full, unqualified
Kühl schrank nm	refrigerator, icebox

Schraub e	screw; bolt
schraub en	screw
schraub en förm ig	screw-shaped, spiral, helical
ab schraub en	unscrew, screw off
an schraub en	bolt, screw on, fasten a screw
auf schraub en	screw on; unscrew
ein schraub en	screw in, screw into position
ge schraub t	screwed, bolted; stilted, affected
los schraub en	unscrew, screw off
ver schraub en	screw on
Ver schraub ung	screwed joint
zu schraub en	screw up, screw tight
zusammen schraub en	bolt together
hin auf schraub en	push up prices; step up, tune up, increase production

Schreck nm	fright, shock, terror; alarm; panic; fear; horror
schreck en	frighten, scare, terrify; dismay; alarm, startle; deter
schreck haft	easily frightened, fearful, timid, nervous
schreck lich	terrible, frightful, fearful, dreadful; horrible, awful
Schreck lich keit	terribleness, frightfulness; horror, atrocity
Schreck nis nn	horror
ab schreck en	scare away; frighten off; deter, discourage; chill, quench
Ab schreck ung	deterrance; intimidation

auf schreck en	startle, frighten; rouse up
er schreck en	frighten, scare, terrify, dismay; startle, shock, alarm
zurück schreck en	frighten away, deter
zusammen schreck en	jump from fright, start

Schrei	nm	cry; shout; yell; wail; scream; shriek; roar
schrei en		cry out, shout; yell; scream, shriek, screech, wail; roar
Schrei er		bawler; brawler
Schrei erei		bawler; brawler
an schrei en		shout at s.o., yell at s.o.
Auf schrei	nm	cry, yell, scream, shriek
auf schrei en		cry out, give a yell; scream, shriek, screech
Ge schrei	nn	shouting, yelling; shouts, cries, screams
nieder schrei en		shout s.o. down
über 'schrei en		cry down
sich über 'schrei en		overstrain one's voice
ver schrei en		decry, cry down

schreib en		write, inform
Schreib en	nn	writing; letter, note
Schreib er		writer, clerk, secretary, copyist
Schreib erei		writing, paperwork, scribbling
Schreib erin		female writer, clerk, secretary, copyist
Schreib er ling		writer, clerk, secretary, copyist
Schreib ung		spelling
ab schreib en		copy, write out; engross; imitate; write off
Ab schreib er		copyist, plagiarist
Ab schreib ung		transcription; writing off, depreciation
an schreib en		write down, credit to s.o.'s account
An schreib en	nn	cover note
auf schreib en		write down, record, put down, note
aus schreib en		write to the end, finish; copy, plagiarize; announce
Aus schreib ung		drawing up, abstract; making out; convocation; proclamation
be schreib en		write upon; describe, depict
Be schreib ung		description, specification; characterization, outline
bei schreib en		add a note on the margin, annotate
'durch schreib en		copy, make a copy
ein schreib en		book; write in; enrol, register
Ein schreib ung		entering; registration, matriculation, enrollment
Fern schreib er		teleprinter, teletypewriter
fort schreib en		project to subsequent dates; extrapolate
Ge schreib sel	nn s	scrawl, scribbling
hin schreib en		write down, write to
mit schreib en		take down, jot down, note down
nach schreib en		copy, write down, write from dictation
nieder schreib en		write down
Rück schreib en	nn	letter in reply, answer to a letter
über 'schreib en		address, label, entitle; transfer
Ueber schreib ung		transfer; superscription

um 'schreib en	circumscribe; paraphrase
'um schreib en	rewrite, transcribe; transfer, reindorse
Um schreib ung	description, paraphrase
Um schreib ung	transcription, transfer; rewriting
unter 'schreib en	sign; subscribe to
ver schreib en	use in writing; prescribe; write incorrectly
sich ver schreib en	make a slip in writing; devote o.s. to
Ver schreib ung	order, prescription; bond, obligation
vor schreib en	set a copy of; prescribe, order, command; direct
zu schreib en	attribute to; owe; blame s.o. for; transfer to
zurück schreib en	write back
zusammen schreib en	compile; scribble
un be schreib lich	indescribable
mit unter schreib en	add one's signature, countersign

schreit en	stride along, pace along, stalk along; walk, strut along
ab schreit en	pace off, step s.t. off; walk along; inspect a line of troops
aus schreit en	stride, step out
Aus schreit ung	outrage, excess; dissipation, dissoluteness, debauchery
be schreit en	walk along, go along, tread, take
durch 'schreit en	cross, traverse, ford
ein schreit en	intervene, step in; take action, take measures
fort schreit en	progress, advance, proceed; spread; march on, pass; progress
rück schreit end	retrogressive, retrograde
über 'schreit en	cross, go across; pass; exceed, go beyond, transcend; strain
Ueber schreit ung	crossing, going over
unter 'schreit en	fall below, fall short of, remain under; go below
vor schreit en	step forward, advance
zu schreit en	walk up to s.o.; step out well, put one's best foot forward
ein her schreit en	stalk along

schrieb: siehe schreib	
un be schrieb en a	blank
un ge schrieb en a	unwritten

schrift: siehe schreib	
Schrift nf	writing; handwriting, script; character, letter
schrift lich	written, in writing; by letter
Schrift tum	literature
Ab schrift nf	duplicate; transcript
ab schrift lich	copied; in duplicate
An schrift nf	address
Auf schrift nf	address, label; inscription; sign, name
be schrift en	inscribe, letter; mark, label
Be schrift ung	inscription, lettering, caption, legend
Durch schrift nf	copy, carbon copy

Gegen	schrift	nf	refutation, rejoinder, written reply
In	schrift	nf	inscription, legend, caption
Nach	schrift	nf	postscript; copy; transcript; dictation; notes
Nieder	schrift	nf	report, record; writing down; notes; manuscript
Ueber	schrift	nf	title, heading; headline, head; address
Um	schrift	nf	inscription on margin; legend of coin
Unter	schrift	nf	signature; caption
Ur	schrift	nf	original text, original copy
ur	schrift	lich	original, in the original
Vor	schrift	nf	prescription; order, command; direction; instruction
Zu	schrift	nf	letter; official communication
Gegen unter	schrift	nf	countersignature
Zeit	schrift	nf	magazine, periodical

	schritt:	siehe schreit	
	Schritt	nm	pace; stride; footstep, footfall
	schritt weise	av	gradual, progressive, step-by-step
Fort	schritt		progress, headway; advancement, improvement
Fort	schritt ler		believer in progress, progressionist, progressive person
fort	schritt lich		progressive, advanced; modern
Rück	schritt	nm	step backwards, regression; reaction
rück	schritt lich		reactionary
Fort ge	schritt ene		advanced student

	schrob:	siehe schraub	
ver	schrob en	a	eccentric, crotchety, odd, cranky
Ver	schrob en heit		eccentricity, crankiness; kink; crotchet, twist

	schrock:	siehe schreck	
er	schrock en	a	frightened, scared, terrified; with fright
Er	schrock en heit		fright, scare; alarm
un er	schrock en	a	undaunted, dauntless; intrepid, unflinching; fearless, unafraid
Un er	schrock en heit		dauntlessness, undauntedness, intrepidity; fearlessness

	schub:	siehe schieb		
	Schub	nm		push, shove; batch, baking; thrust; shear; push; drawer
	Schub er			cardboard booksleeve, book slipcase; slipcover
	Schub s	nm	s	push, shove
	schub s en			push, shove
	schub weise			in batches, gradually, by degrees, little by little
Auf	schub	nm		postponement, deferment, delay, procrastination; reprieve
Ein	schub	nm		insertion, interpolation, insert; inserted piece; false floor
Nach	schub	nm		supply, supplies; reinforcements
Vor	schub	nm		feed; assistance, furtherance, support, countenance

	Schuh nm	shoe
an	schuh en	shoe, tip with iron; lengthen
be	schuh en	shoe
Ueber	schuh nm	overshoe; galosh, rubbers
Hand	schuh nm	glove

	Schul e	school; schoolhouse
	schul en	train; school, discipline; teach, instruct; break s.o. in
	Schül er	schoolboy, pupil; student; disciple; novice
	schül er haft	schoolboy-like, boyish; unripe, immature
	Schül erin	schoolgirl, pupil; student, disciple
	Schül er schaft	the pupils, the student body
	schul frei	on a holiday
	schul ge recht	according to rule, in due style; methodical
	schul isch	scholastic, school
	schul mäss ig	orthodox
	Schul ung	training, schooling, instruction; practice; education
Ein	schul ung	enrollment
Mit	schül er	school fellow, classmate
Ober	schul e	secondary school
'um	schul en	retrain, convert
Um	schul ung	retraining, conversion
Vor	schul e	preparatory school
Mitt el	schul e	middle school, junior high school
Volk s	schul e	grade school, grammar school
Volk s hoch	schul e	adult education program

	Schuld nf	guilt; fault; wrong; sin; cause
	schuld en	owe s.o. s.t., be indebted to s.o. for s.t.
	schuld en frei	free from debt; unencumbered
	schuld ig	guilty, responsible; owing, due money; due respect
	Schuld ig er	guilty person, guilty party; culprit
	Schuld ig keit	duty, obligation
	schuld los	guiltless, innocent
	Schuld los ig keit	innocence, guiltlessness
	Schuld n er	debtor
	Schuld n erin	debtor
ent	schuld bar	excusable, pardonable
Ent	schuld ung	liquidation of s.o.'s indebtedness
Mit	schuld nf	complicity
mit	schuld ig	accessory to the crime; implicated
Mit	schuld ig e	accessory, accomplice
Ueber	schuld ung	heavy indebtedness, debt encumbrance
'um	schuld en	convert; fund
Un	schuld nf	innocence; purity; virginity
un	schuld ig	innocent, chaste, untouched, virgin; harmless
ver	schuld en	encumber with debts; be guilty of, be to blame for
Ver	schuld ung	indebtedness
zu	schuld en av	get on the wrong side of the law, make o.s. guilty

un ent schuld bar		inexcusable, unpardonable
un ver schuld et		undeserved; not in debt; unencumbered
an schuld ig en	l	accuse, charge with, incriminate
An schuld ig ung	l	accusation, charge, incrimination
be schuld ig en		accuse, charge with
Be schuld ig er		accused, defendant
Be schuld ig te		accused, defendant
Be schuld ig ung		charge, accusation, imputation
ent schuld ig en		excuse, pardon; justify
Ent schuld ig ung		apology; excuse, pretext
Gegen be schuld ig ung		countercharge
an ge schuld ig te		accused

---

schuss:	siehe schiess	
Schuss	nm	shot, round, report of a gun
Schuss el	s	clumsy person
Schüss el		bowl, basin; dish, pan; tureen
Ab schuss	nm	firing, discharge; launching; downing
ab schüss ig		steep, precipitous
Ab schüss ig keit		steepness, precipitousness, declivity
An schuss	nm	first shot, sighting shot; crystallization
Aus schuss	nm	refuse, waste, scrap; committee, board, panel
Be schuss	nm	test firing; bombardment, shelling
Durch schuss	nm	weaving weft; blank space, margin, space line; shot through
Ein schuss	nm	bullet entry hole, entry wound; invested capital; weaving weft
Ueber schuss	nm	surplus, carry-over; excess profit; remainder, margin
über schüss ig		surplus, remaining; excess, in excess
Vor schuss	nm	money advanced, advance; deposit
Zu schuss	nm	raise, extra pay, extra allowance; subsidy, contribution

---

schuster:	siehe schuh	
Schuster	nm	shoemaker; cobbler
schuster n		make shoes, cobble

---

auf schütt en	heap up; pour on; store up; charge, fill, feed; throw up
Auf schütt ung	accumulation, deposit; storage; embankment, barrier
aus schütt en	pour out, dump out; empty; spill; distribute, pay dividends
Aus schütt ung	atomic fallout
be schütt en	pour s.t. over s.o.; spill s.t. over o.s.
ein schütt en	pour into
über 'schütt en	cover; overwhelm
'um schütt en	pour out into another vessel, decant; spill, upset
ver schütt en	spill a liquid; fill up; block up; bury alive
weg schütt en	dump; pour away
zu schütt en	add; fill up

ab schüttel n	shake off, shake down; throw off, cast off a burden
auf schüttel n	shake up
aus schüttel n	shake out
'durch schüttel n	shake s.t. up thoroughly
her aus schüttel n	shake out
er schütt er n	shake s.t., rock s.t., stagger s.o.; shock s.o., upset s.o.
Er schütt er ung	concussion, shock, jolt; vibration; blow; emotion
un er schütt er lich	unshakable; imperturbable; stolid, firm

Schutz nm	shot
Schütz e nm	shot, marksman; huntsman; rifleman, private; gunner
schütz en	protect, guard; defend; secure, keep from, shelter
Schütz ling	protege, charge
schutz los	unprotected, defenseless
be schütz en	protect, guard, shelter from; watch over; escort
Be schütz er	protector, defender, protectress
Ge schütz nn	gun, cannon; heavy artillery
vor schütz en	give as an excuse, pretend
un ge schütz t	unprotected, unsheltered; exposed

schwang: siehe schwing	
Ueber schwang nm	rapture, exuberance, exultation

Schweb e	be in suspense, be undecided, tremble in the balance; be pending
schweb en	be suspended, be poised, hang in the air; float; hover
Schweb ung	vibration
ent schweb en	float away
vor schweb en	have s.t. in mind

schweig en	be silent; keep silence, say nothing, hold one's tongue
Schweig er	taciturn person, man of few words
schweig sam	silent, quiet; taciturn; discreet, closemouthed
Schweig sam keit	taciturnity; discretion
sich aus schweig en s	say nothing, persist in silence; be silent
ge schweig e c	not to mention, to say nothing of; let alone, much less
ver schweig en	conceal; keep secret, withhold, hide from
Ver schweig ung	concealment

schweng: siehe schwing	
Schweng el	handle, lever; clapper; swing bar, splinter bar; evener, pendulum
über schweng lich	rapturous, rhapsodic; effusive, gushing
Ueber schweng lich keit	effusion, effusiveness, gushiness, exuberance

schwer a	heavy; weighty; ponderous, clumsy; burdensome, difficult

Schwer e t	heaviness, weight; gravity; pregnancy
schwer fäll ig	heavy, ponderous; awkward, clumsy; sluggish; dull, slow-witted
Schwer fäll ig keit	heaviness, ponderousness
schwer lich av	hardly, scarcely
Be schwer de nf	burden, hardship, trouble; complaint; discomfort
be schwer en	burden, charge; weight; weigh on, be a load on
sich be schwer en	complain
be schwer lich	burdensome, fatiguing; inconvenient; heavy, difficult
Be schwer lich keit	difficulty; troublesomeness
Be schwer ung	load, loading; burden, burdening
er schwer en	render difficult, complicate; impede, obstruct; aggravate
Er schwer ung	impediment; complication, handicap; aggravation
un schwer a	not difficult, easy
un be schwer t	unencumbered, unburdened, free and easy; light, light-hearted

---

schwier: siehe schwer	
schwier ig	difficult, hard; tough; complicated, intricate; delicate
Schwier ig keit	difficulty; intricacy; awkwardness; crisis; obstacle, dilemma

---

schwieg: siehe schweig	
ver schwieg en a	withheld, supressed, concealed
Ver schwieg en heit	reticence, secrecy; discretion; closeness

---

schwimm en	swim; float, drift
Schwimm er	swimmer
Schwimm erin	swimmer
schwimm fäh ig	buoyant, floatable
an schwimm en	come swimming along; swim against the current; swim towards
'durch schwimm en	swim through; float across
durch 'schwimm en	swim through, swim across, cross; swim a distance
ver schwimm en	become indistinct, become blurred, dissolve; fade away
hin über schwimm en	swim across, swim over

Schwind el	vertigo; giddiness, dizziness; swindle; cheat, fraud, take-in
Schwind el ei s	white lie, fib; constant lying; swindling, cheat
schwind el frei	free from giddiness
schwind el haft	swindling, fraudulent, bogus
schwind el n	fib, tell fibs; cheat, swindle
schwind en	dwindle, wane, grow less, shrink, wither; fade away; vanish
schwind l ig	giddy, dizzy, vertiginous; staggering
ent schwind en	disappear, vanish, pass out of sight
ge schwind a	quick, fast, swift; rapid, speedy, hasty; prompt

Ge schwind ig keit	swiftness, speed, promptness, pace
hin schwind en	vanish away, dwindle away
ver schwind en	disappear, vanish; dissolve, fade away
da hin schwind en	melt away; pine away; fade
ab schwind el n	swindle s.o., cheat s.o. out of s.t.
an schwind el n	lie to a person; tell a person a white lie
be schwind el n	swindle, cheat; trick, bamboozle
er schwind el n	obtain by trickery, get by fraud
vor schwind el n	tell s.o. a lie, lie to s.o.

schwing en	swing; save; brandish, flourish; wield
sich schwing en	swing o.s.
Schwing er s	a haymaker, a powerful swing, a strong punch
Schwing ung	swinging; oscillation; vibration; pulsation; cycle
an schwing en	begin to swing, begin to vibrate
sich auf schwing en	fly up, soar; rise to s.t.; bring o.s. to do s.t.
aus schwing en	swing out, cease swinging; fade out, die away, die down; turn out
be schwing en	cheer, enliven, animate, elate, exhilarate
be schwing t	cheerful, sprightly, vivacious, lively, gay; winged
Be schwing t heit	cheerfulness, sprightliness, vivacity, liveliness, gaiety
ein schwing en	turn in; build up; onset impulses, initiate impulses
er schwing en	be able to afford s.t.
er schwing lich	attainable, within one's reach; reasonable, agreeable
mit schwing en	resonate, covibrate
sich her ab schwing en	swing down
sich hin auf schwing en	swing o.s. up; fly up, soar up
un er schwing lich	exorbitant, prohibitive; unattainable, beyond one's means

schwitz en	sweat, perspire
aus schwitz en	exude; sweat out
'durch schwitz en	soak with sweat
ver schwitz en	soak with sweat; forget all about s.t.

schwomm: siehe schwimm	
ver schwomm en a	blurred, vague, hazy, dim, foggy; woolly, muddy
Ver schwomm en heit	blurredness; vagueness, haziness, fogginess; dimness

schwör en	swear, take an oath
be schwör en	confirm s.t. by oath, swear to; conjure, exorcise, banish
Be schwör er	exorcist
Be schwör ung	conjuration; exorcism
Ge schwor ene	juror
ver schwör en	forswear
sich ver schwör en	conspire, plot
Ver schwör er	conspirator, plotter
Ver schwör ung	conspiracy, plot

her auf be schwör en   conjure up, evoke, call up; give rise to; provoke

schwung:	siehe schwing	
Schwung	nm	swinging motion, swing, turn; impulse, momentum, push, speed
schwung haft		booming, flourishing, roaring, sweeping; full of drive
schwung los		without drive, without impetus, without energy, without life
schwung voll		sweeping, full of drive, full of impetus, full of life
Ab schwung	nm	dismounting; follow-through; economic downward movement
An schwung	nm	initial impetus, first impulse; push-off
Auf schwung	nm	impetus, stimulation, stimulus; impulse; upswing, rise
Um schwung	nm	reversal, change, turnabout; vicissitudes; turn of the tide

Seel e	soul; mind; heart; bore of gun; core of cable
seel en los	soulless; inanimate, lifeless
seel en voll	soulful
seel isch	psychic, mental; spiritual; emotional
be seel en	animate; inspire; fill
be seel t	animated; inspired; soulful look
Be seel ung	animation
ent seel t	dead, lifeless
un be seel t	inanimate

seh en		see, look; behold, look at, notice, watch
Seh er		seer, prophet
Seh erin		female seer, prophetess
seh er isch		prophetic
ab seh bar		within sight; before long
ab seh en		turn one's eyes from; see, anticipate; refrain from
An seh en	nn	appearance, sight, look, aspect; consideration, respect
an seh en		look at, consider; examine; go to see, view
An seh ung		consideration of, in regard for
auf seh en		look up
Auf seh en	nn	sensation; attention
Auf seh er		overseer, inspector; attendant, superintendent
aus seh en		look, appear
Aus seh en	nn	look, air, face, exterior, appearance
be seh en		look at, view, inspect
'durch seh en		see through; revise; look over, peruse, examine; review
ein seh en		look into, examine; perceive; understand, realize
er seh en		see, learn; note from
Fern seh en	nn	television
fern seh en		televise, telecast
Fern seh er		television receiver, television set
her seh en		look here

hin	seh	en	look at, look towards
nach	seh	en	look after; check, revise; look up, consult
Nach	seh	en nn	go empty-handed, be left out in the cold
über	seh	bar	visible at a glance, surveyable
'über	seh	en	overlook; survey; miss, neglect
sich 'um	seh	en	look around, look back
Ver	seh	en nn	mistake, slip, error, oversight, negligence
ver	seh	en	perform, discharge, hold; fill; furnish with; neglect
sich ver	seh	en	make a mistake; expect s.t.; be aware of s.t.
ver	seh	en t lich	inadvertently, by mistake
vor	seh	en	foresee; consider; assign for; plan
sich vor	seh	en	take care, be careful
Vor	seh	ung	providence
weg	seh	en	look away, overlook
Wieder	seh	en nn	meeting again, reunion
'wieder	seh	en	see again, meet again
zu	seh	en	look on, watch, witness
zu	seh	ends av	visibly, noticeably, manifestly, obviously
zurück	seh	en	look back, reflect on the past
her ab	seh	en	look down upon
un ab	seh	bar	immeasurable, immense, unbounded
Ober auf	seh	er	supervisor, superintendent
vor aus	seh	en	foresee, anticipate
un be	seh	en a	unseen, unexamined; without hesitation
aus er	seh	en	choose, select, single out; doom
ab ge	seh	en a	apart from, setting aside, without regard to
an ge	seh	en a	esteemed, respected, distinguished
un ge	seh	en a	unseen
ent gegen	seh	en	look forward to; await, expect; look in the face
un über	seh	bar a	vast, immense, intricate, incalculable; incontrollable
un ver	seh	ens av	unexpectedly, unawares, by suprise
hin weg	seh	en	see over, look over s.t.; overlook
un vor her			
ge	seh	en a	unforeseen, unexpected
Fern	seh	en nn	television

sich	sehn en	long for, yearn for, crave for; grieve after; pine for
	sehn lich	longing, ardent; passionate; keen
an	sehn lich	imposing, stately; considerable, important; handsome
er	sehn en	long for, hanker for, crave
sich fort	sehn en	wish o.s. away
sich zurück	sehn en	long to return, wish o.s. back
un an	sehn lich	unsightly, mean-looking; plain; insignificant, trifling
Un an	sehn lich keit	unsightliness; plainness; insignificance, paltriness

	sehr av	very, most
ver	sehr en	hurt, injure; disable; damage
Ver	sehr ter	disabled person

un ver sehr t	uninjured; intact
Un ver sehr t heit	integrity

Seif e	soap; glacial deposit
seif en	rub with soap, soap s.t., lather s.t.
seif en art ig	soapy, saponaceous
seif ig	soapy, saponaceous
ab seif en	clean with soap, soap s.t.
ein seif en	soap; lather beard; dupe s.o., take s.o. in
ein seif en	soap s.t., lather s.t.
ver seif en	saponify, hydrolyze

sein v	be; exist, be there; live; take place, occur, happen
ab sein v	be off, be broken off; be far away; be exhausted
auf sein v s	be up; be open
da sein v	be there; be present; exist, be available
Da sein nn	life, existence; presence
hin sein v s	be broken; be ruined; be exhausted; be carried away
zurück sein v s	be back; be behind, be in arrears; be backward
Zusammen sein nn	meeting, gathering
hin aus sein v	be outside; have left; be past s.t.
da bei sein v	be there, be present, attend
her unter sein v s	be down, be run down, be low
hin weg sein v	be away, be off, be gone; have gotten over s.t.

seit p	since, for
Seit e	side; flank; face; page of book; aspect of a matter
seit en s p	on the side of, from the side of, on the part of; by
seit lich	lateral, side; at the side
seit wärt s av	sideways, sidewards, aside
ab seit s av	aside, apart; offside
Ab seit s nn o	aside, apart; offside
ab seit s p	aside of, off from the street
Aussen seit e	outside, exterior, surface, periphery
Aussen seit er	outsider, dark horse
Bei seit e	aside, apart
Gegen seit e nf	opposite side
gegen seit ig	mutual, reciprocal; bilateral
Gegen seit ig keit	reciprocity, mutuality
Hinter seit e nf	hind part, back; rear
Innen seit e	inner side
Ober seit e	top side, upper side
Rück seit e	back, reverse side
um seit ig	overleaf, on the reverse, on the next page
Unter seit e	underside, bottom side
Vorder seit e	front
be seit ig en	remove; abolish, do away with, get rid of; dispose of; conceal; cure
Be seit ig ung	removal, elimination, clearing; settlement
ander er seit s av jen	on the other hand

seit s av	on the other side
viel seit ig	versatile; from many sides

send en	send for s.o.; forward, communicate
Send er	sender
Send ung	sending; consignment, shipment; parcel
ab send en	send off, forward, dispatch, ship; mail; send s.o. out
Ab send er	sender, dispatcher, consignor, forwarder
Ab send ung	dispatching
aus send en	send out, dispatch; transmit radio message; emit
ein send en	send in; transmit; submit, file, hand in; net the ball
Ein send er	sender, transmitter
Ein send ung	sending in, transmittal; contribution; letter
ent send en	send off, dispatch
nach send en	send after; send on to, forward, redirect
Rück send ung	redelivery; return
über 'send en	send, forward, transmit, consign, ship goods; remit money
Ueber send ung	sending, transmission; consignment; remittance
ver send en	send, dispatch, forward; ship
Ver send ung	dispatch, shipment, forwarding
zu send en	dispatch s.t., send s.t. to s.o., mail s.t. to s.o.
zurück send en	send back; return s.t.

senk: siehe sink	
Senk e	depression, hollow; valley
Senk el	lace
senk en	sink; let down, lower; dip; lay; cast down, bow, reduce prices
sich senk en	sink, drop, go down
Senk er	sinker; layer; counterbore; core drill
senk recht	vertical, perpendicular
Senk ung	sinking; lowering, reduction, cut of price; hollow; incline
ab senk en	layer, sink a shaft
Ab senk er	cutting, slip; shoot, offshoot
ein senk en	sink in, let s.t. in
Ein senk ung	depression
Ge senk nn	die, forging die, swage
ver senk bar	concealable, lowerable; sinkable
ver senk en	sink; send ship to the bottom; countersink, counterbore
sich ver senk en	become absorbed in s.t., bury o.s. in s.t.
Ver senk ung	sinking
Ober ge senk nn	upper die
Unter ge senk nn	lower die in machining

sess: siehe sitz	
Sess el	easy chair, armchair; seat
sess haft	settled, established, stationary; resident; persistent

	Sess haft ig keit	settledness; stationariness
be	sess en a	possessed; obsessed with; frantic
Be	sess ene	possessed person; maniac
Be	sess en heit	possession; obsession; madness, frenzy
ver	sess en a	bent on, crazy about, mad about
Ver	sess en heit	craze
an ge	sess en a	settled, resident
ein ge	sess en a	resident, domiciled

---

	setz: siehe sitz	
	setz en	set, place; compose; erect, raise; put in; fix
sich	setz en	sit down, take a seat
	Setz er	compositor, typesetter
	Setz erei	composing room
	Setz ling	slip, layer, young plant, fry
ab	setz bar	removable; saleable, marketable
ab	setz en	put down, deposit; drop; take off; remove; deduct
sich ab	setz en	disengage o.s., retreat
an	setz en	set on, join; fasten; sew on; fix
auf	setz en	pile up; set up; put on; compose, draw up; touch down
sich auf	setz en	sit upright
aus	setz en	put out, set out, set; bequeath; postpone
	Aus setz ung	exposure; settlement; suspension; intermission; bequest
be	setz en	trim; set; occupy; man, fill
	Be setz ung	occupation, appointment; personnel; nomination, entry
bei	setz en	add, alloy; put beside; inter; spread
	Bei setz ung	burial
durch	'setz en	intersperse, intermingle, mix up
	'durch setz en	effect, carry through; enforce
sich 'durch	setz en	make one's way; succeed, have one's way
ein	setz en	set in, place in, put in; pledge; employ; begin
sich ein	setz en	stand up for, plead for; advocate s.t., champion s.t.
	Ein setz ung	institution; installation; appointment; insertion
	Ent setz en nn	fright, horror, amazement, alarm
	ent setz en	frighten; dismiss, suspend; depose
sich ent	setz en	be terrified, be shocked; shudder at
	ent setz lich	terrible, horrible, awful; tremendous
	Ent setz lich keit	frightfulness, terribleness
	Ent setz ung	removal, dismissal, deposition, suspension, relief
	er setz bar	reparable, renewable, replaceable
	er setz en	replace, substitute; reimburse, refund; compensate
	er setz lich	reparable, renewable, replaceable
	Er setz ung	supplying; reparation, compensation, replacement; renewal
fort	setz en	place farther away; continue, pursue
	Fort setz ung	continuation, pursuit, sequel; prosecution
	Ge setz nn	law, act, rule, commandment; bill; principle
	ge setz lich	lawful, rightful, legal, legitimate, statutory

Ge setz lich keit	lawfulness, legitimacy
ge setz los	lawless, illegal
Ge setz los ig keit	lawlessness, illegalness
ge setz t	quiet, sedate, calm, grave, serious
Ge setz t heit	sedateness, gravity
hin setz en	put down, set down
nach setz en	hunt after, pursue
nieder setz en	set down
über setz bar	translatable
über 'setz en	translate; gear; top; overcharge
'über setz en	pass over, cross, ferry over
Ueber setz er	translator, decoder
Ueber setz ung	translation; gear, transmission
um setz bar	marketable, saleable
'um setz en	transpose; sell, dispose of; realize; transform
Um setz ung	transposition; change, conversion; transformation; sale
'unter setz en	set under
Unter setz er	saucer; flowerpot stand
unter setz t	thick-set, square-built, squat, stocky; geared down
Unter setz ung	reduction gearing
ver setz en	remove, displace; move up; promote; shift
Ver setz ung	displacing, remove; transposition, promotion; pledging; transfer
vor setz en	put forward, place before, set before; serve; intend
weg setz en	put away
sich wider 'setz en	oppose, resist
wider setz lich	refractory; insubordinate
Wider setz lich keit	refractoriness; insubordination, obstinacy
zer setz en	decompose, dissolve, disintegrate, break up
Zer setz ung	decomposition, disintegration, splitting up; dissociation
zu setz en	add to; lose; press; attack; urge s.o.; wear out
zurück setz en	put back; set aside; replace; reduce; roll back
Zurück setz ung	disregard, neglect, slight; reduction, rollback
zusammen setz en	put together, compound, compose; make up, assemble
Zusammen setz ung	composition, combination, compound; synthesis, structure
her ab setz en	put down, lower; curtail; debase, degrade
Her ab setz ung	degradation; reduction, retardation; disparagement
dar an setz en	venture, risk, stake
her auf setz en s	raise
hin auf setz en	raise
hin aus setz en	put s.o. out
vor aus setz en	presume, presuppose; postulate
Vor aus setz ung	supposition, assumption, hypothesis; condition, stipulation
'um be setz en	recast, reshuffle
Um be setz ung	reshuffle, shake-up; change
un be setz t	unoccupied, vacant, free

'wieder be setz en	reoccupy
wieder 'ein setz en	replace, restore; reinstate, rehabilitate
Wieder ein setz ung	restoration, rehabilitation
un er setz lich	irreparable, irreplaceable, irrecoverable
fort ge setz t a	incessant, continuous
un ge setz lich	illegal, unlawful
Vor ge setz te	superior, chief, boss, senior officer
ent gegen setz en	oppose, contrast
hin über setz en	drive over
rück über setz en	retranslation
un über setz bar	untranslatable
zurück über setz en	retranslate
zurück ver setz en	put back, restore to a former state
sich zurück	
ver setz en	turn one's thoughts back, go back to a time
sich hin weg setz en	disregard, brush aside, make light of s.t.
hin zu setz en	add to, annex to
aus ein	
ander setz en	place apart; make clear; analyze, explain
Aus ein	
ander setz ung	explanation; discussion, dispute; settlement; composition
un aus ge setz t	continual, constant, uninterrupted
vor aus ge setz t	assuming that, provided that
ent gegen ge setz t	opposite, contrary, inverse; opposed, contrasted

sicher a	secure, safe; immune; certain, sure; definite
Sicher heit	security; safety; certainty; reliability, confidence, assurance
sicher heit s halb er	for safety; to be on the safe side
sicher lich av	surely, certainly, sure; for certain, undoubtedly, doubtless
sicher n	secure, safeguard; make safe, lock; protect; guarantee
Sicher ung	securing; safeguard; security, guaranty; protection
ent sicher n	unlock, release the safety catch of
un sicher a	insecure; unsteady; unsafe, precarious; uncertain, doubtful
Un sicher heit	insecurity, unsteadiness; precariousness; uncertainty
ver sicher n	assure, assert; protest, affirm
Ver sicher ung	assurance, affirmation; protestation; guarantee; insurance
zu sicher n	assure s.o. of s.t., guarantee s.t. to s.o.; promise s.t. to s.o.
Zu sicher ung	promise, assurance; guarantee, pledge
Gegen ver sicher ung	reciprocal insurance
nach ver sicher n	take out additional insurance; increase the sum insured
Nach ver sicher ung	additional insurance
rück ver sicher n	reinsure
Rück ver sicher ung	reinsurance

| 'über ver sicher n | overinsure |
| 'unter ver sicher n | underinsure |

sicht: siehe seh	
Sicht nf	sight; view; visibility
sicht bar	visible; perceptible; noticeable, conspicuous; evident, obvious
Sicht bar keit	visibleness, visibility; obviousness
sicht en	sight; sift wheat; bolt flour; examine; screen, sort over
Sicht ig keit	visibility
sicht lich	visible
Sicht ung	sighting; examination; sifting, screening
Ab sicht nf	intention, design; aim, object, end, purpose
ab sicht lich	intentional, deliberate, wilful
ab sicht s los	unintentional; without design
An sicht nf	sight, view; opinion, notion, outlook; drawing
an sicht ig	catch sight of s.o., set eyes on s.t.
Auf sicht nf	supervision, inspection, control; superintendence
Aus sicht nf	view, sight, prospect; look-out
aus sicht s los	hopeless, without prospects
Aus sicht s los ig keit	hopelessness, futility
aus sicht s voll	promising, rich in prospect
Durch sicht nf	view, looking over; perusal, revision; inspection, examination
durch sicht ig	transparent, clear, lucid; obvious
Durch sicht ig keit	transparency, clearness, lucidity
Ein sicht nf	insight, understanding, reason; examination, perusal
ein sicht ig	understanding, discerning, sagacious, perceptive
ein sicht s los	injudicious; unreasonable
ein sicht s voll	judicious, prudent; reasonable, sensible
er sicht lich	clear, obvious, evident
Fern sicht nf	prospect, perspective, panorama, distant view
fern sicht ig	longsighted, presbyopic
Ge sicht nn	face, sight, vision; aspect, look, appearance
Hin sicht nf	respect, view, regard; consideration; relation
hin sicht lich p	with regard to; concerning, regarding; relating to; as to
Nach sicht nf	forbearance, indulgence, leniency; inspection; respite
nach sicht ig	indulgent, forbearing; lenient, patient
nach sicht s voll	indulgent, forbearing; lenient, patient
Rück sicht nf	regard, consideration, respect; motive
rück sicht s los	inconsiderate, thoughtless; reckless; unfeeling, ruthless
Rück sicht s los ig keit	lack of consideration, thoughtlessness; recklessness, ruthlessness
rück sicht s voll	regardful, considerate, thoughtful; kind; gentle
Ueber sicht nf	survey, review, analysis; summary; control; perspective
über sicht ig	farsighted, hyperopic

Ueber sicht ig keit	farsightedness, hyperopia
über sicht lich	clear, distinct; clearly arranged, easily understandable
Ueber sicht lich keit	clearness, lucidity, perspicuity
Um sicht nf	circumspection, prudence, caution, discretion
um sicht ig	cautious, circumspect, prudent
un sicht bar	invisible
Un sicht bar keit	invisibility
un sicht ig	zero visibility, hazy
Vor sicht nf	caution, prudence, foresight; providence; precaution, care
vor sicht ig	cautious, careful, prudent
weit sicht ig	long-sighted; farsighted
Weit sicht ig keit	long-sightedness, presbyopia; far-sightedness, perspicacity
Neben ab sicht nf	secondary objective
un ab sicht lich	unintentional, undesigned, involuntary; accidental, inadvertant
Rück an sicht nf	back view, rear view
Vorder an sicht nf	front view, elevation
Ober auf sicht nf	superintendence
Vor aus sicht nf	foresight, prudence
vor aus sicht lich	prospective, probable, presumable; expected; estimated
un durch sicht ig	opaque, not transparent, diaphanous
Un durch sicht ig keit	opacity
An ge sicht nn	face, countenance
an ge sicht s p	in the presence of, in view of; considering, seeing that
un nach sicht ig	unrelenting, pitiless, strict, severe
Un nach sicht ig keit	strictness, severeness
un über sicht lich	badly arranged, difficult to survey; unmethodical; complex
Zu ver sicht nf	confidence, assurance, trust
zu ver sicht lich	confident, optimistic
Zu ver sicht lich keit	confidence, trust, self-assurance
un vor sicht ig	incautious; inconsiderate; imprudent, rash, careless
Un vor sicht ig keit	incautiousness, imprudence, carelessness
be sicht ig en	view, survey, look over; examine; inspect; visit
Be sicht ig ung	view, inspection, visitation; survey; sight-seeing
be ab sicht ig en	intend, mean, propose; contemplate, aim at doing
be auf sicht ig en	look after, control; supervise, inspect, superintend
Be auf sicht ig ung	supervision, inspection, control
un be ab sicht ig t	unintentional, undesigned; inadvertent, unwitting

---

siedel n	settle, colonize
Sied l er	settler, colonist; homecrafter, homesteader
Sied l ung	settlement; colony; housing-estate, suburban colony
an siedel n	settle, colonize; establish o.s.
sich an siedel n	settle, colonize; establish o.s.; place s.t.

aus	siedel n	evacuate, transfer compulsorily
Aus	siedel ung	compulsory transfer, evacuation
be	siedel n	colonize, settle; populate
'über	siedel n	remove; emigrate to
Ueber	siedel ung	removal; emigration
'um	siedel n	resettle
Um	siedel ung	resettlement; family relocation; evacuation
An	sied l er	settler, colonist
An	sied l erin	settler, colonist
An	sied l ung	settlement, colony, colonization
Be	sied l ung	colonization, settlement
Ueber	sied l ung	removal, emigration

Sieg	nm	victory, triumph; conquest
sieg	en	be victorious, conquer; gain victory over, win
Sieg	er	conqueror, victor, winner
Sieg	erin	conqueror, victor, winner
sieg	haft	triumphant
sieg	reich	victorious, conquering, triumphant; successful
be sieg	en	conquer, vanquish; defeat, beat, whip, lick; outdo
Be sieg	er	conqueror
Be sieg	te	defeated
Be sieg	ung	conquering, conquest
ob sieg	en	be victorious; triumph over s.o.
ver sieg	en	dry up, run dry; be exhausted
un be sieg	bar	invincible
un ver sieg	bar	inexhaustible, everflowing, unfailing

sing	en	sing, carol; chant; vocalize
ab sing	en	sing off, sing to the end
be sing	en	sing the praises of, celebrate
mit sing	en	join in the song
vor sing	en	sing s.t. to s.o.

sink	en	sink; go down, founder
ein sink	en	sink into; subside, cave in
ent sink	en	drop
hin sink	en	sink down; faint away
nieder sink	en	sink down, go down; drop down, collapse
'um sink	en	sink down; fall into a swoon
'unter sink	en	sink under; go down
ver sink	en	sink down; go under, founder; lapse
zurück sink	en	sink back, fall back; relapse
zusammen sink	en	sink down, collapse
her ab sink	en	sink down, descend; be degraded, fall

Sinn	nm	sense; mind; faculty; taste, liking; soul, heart; sense, meaning
sinn	en	meditate, reflect, think about; muse, ponder
sinn	fäll ig	obvious, striking
sinn	ge mäss	analogous, corresponding, equivalent
sinn	ier en	ponder, ruminate, brood

sinn ig	ingenious, clever; thoughtful, nice; apt, appropriate
sinn lich	sensuous; material; perceptible; sensual, voluptuous; carnal
Sinn lich keit	sensuousness; sensuality, voluptuousness
sinn los	senseless; meaningless; absurd, foolish; pointless, futile
Sinn los ig keit	senselessness; absurdity, foolishness, futility
sinn reich	ingenious, clever; witty
sinn voll	meaningful; wise, sensible; efficient
sinn wid r ig	absurd, preposterous
An sinn en nn	unfair demand, unreasonable request
Be sinn en nn	reflection, recollection
sich be sinn en	reflect, consider
be sinn lich	thoughtful, reflective, contemplative
Be sinn ung	reason; reflection, consideration, stock-taking; consciousness
be sinn ung s los	unconscious, insensible; insensate, senseless; blind
Be sinn ung s los ig keit	unconsciousness
sich ent sinn en	remember, recall, recollect
er sinn en	devise, contrive, think up; invent
ge sinn t	well disposed
Ge sinn ung	mind, sentiment; way of thinking; opinions
ge sinn ung s los	unprincipled, characterless; disloyal
Ge sinn ung s los ig keit	lack of principle
nach sinn en	muse, meditate, reflect
über sinn lich	transcendental
Un sinn nm	nonsense
un sinn ig	nonsensical; foolish, unreasonable; absurd; insane, mad
Un sinn ig keit	foolishness, unreasonability; absurdity, insanity
Wider sinn nm	nonsense
wider sinn ig	paradoxical, absurd, nonsensical, preposterous

Sitt e	custom; habit; tradition; usage, practice; fashion
sitt en los	immoral, licentious
Sitt en los ig keit	immorality, profligacy, licence
sitt en wid r ig	immoral; conflicting with national policy
sitt lich	moral, ethical; decent, respectable
Sitt lich keit	morality, morals
sitt sam	modest, demure; chaste, virtuous; well-behaved; decent
Sitt sam keit	modesty; chastity; good manners; decency
ge sitt et	civilized; moral; well-bred, polite, courteous
Ge sitt ung	civilization
Un sitt e	bad habit; abuse
un sitt lich	immoral, indecent
Un sitt lich keit	immorality
un ge sitt et	uncivilized; unmannerly
ent sitt lich en	demoralize, deprave, corrupt
Ent sitt lich ung	demoralization

Sitz nm	seat, chair, place, residence, domicile, headquarters
sitz en	sit, be seated; squat, be perched; live, stay, have its seat
Sitz er	seater
Sitz ung	meeting, conference, sitting, session, seance, hearing
ab sitz en	get off, dismount; serve a prison sentence, serve time
auf sitz en	sit on, sit up; perch; mount
Be sitz nm	possession; property, real estate, realty; personality
be sitz en	possess, be in possession of; have, own, hold; be provided with
Be sitz er	possessor, proprietor, owner
be sitz los	unpropertied
Be sitz tum	possession, property, estate
Be sitz ung	possession, property
Bei sitz nm	assession
bei sitz en	sit by
Bei sitz er	member of a committee; assistant judge; assessor
'durch sitz en	wear out by sitting
er sitz en	acquire by prescription
Er sitz ung	positive prescription
Hinter sitz nm	rear seat, backseat
nach sitz en	be kept in
Rück sitz nm	backseat, reserve seat
Voll sitz ung	plenary session
Vor sitz nm	presidency, chairmanship, the chair
Vor sitz ende	chairman, president
Vorder sitz nm	front seat
Mit be sitz nm	joint property
Mit be sitz er	joint proprietor
Voll be sitz nm	full possession

Sommer nm	summer
sommer lich	summer-like, summery
sommer n	summer is coming
sömmer n	sun, air; prune trees; sow fields with spring corn
Nach sommer nm	late summer, indian summer

sonder av	without
sonder bar	strange, odd, funny; extraordinary; peculiar
sonder bar er weise av	strange to say, oddly enough
Sonder bar keit	strangeness, oddity; singularity; peculiarity
sonder lich	special, peculiar, remarkable
Sonder ling	eccentric person, crank
sonder n	separate, sever, segregate; put asunder
sonder n c	but
Sonder ung	separation
ab sonder lich	peculiar, strange, odd, bizarre
Ab sonder lich keit	peculiarity, strangeness, oddity

ab sonder n	set apart, separate; detach; isolate, segregate; discharge
Ab sonder ung	separation, detachment; isolation, seclusion
aus sonder n	sort out, single out, select; separate
Aus sonder ung	selection; separation
Be sonder heit	particularity, characteristic, special quality
be sonder s av	especially, particularly, in particular; above all; chiefly
in sonder heit av a	in particular, particularly, especially
ins be sonder e av	in particular, particularly, especially, above all
ab ge sonder t	separate

---

sonn: siehe sinn	
be sonn en a	sensible, sober, level-headed; prudent, cautious; discreet
Be sonn en heit	considerateness, soberness; composure; prudence, caution
ge sonn en a	minded, disposed; have in mind; be inclined; intend to
ver sonn en a	thoughtful, meditative; dreamy, pensive; lost in thought
un be sonn en a	thoughtless, impudent; rash; reckless
Un be sonn en heit	thoughtlessness, rashness

Sorg e	care; sorrow; anxiety, concern; fear, vexation
sich sorg en	be anxious, be concerned; be apprehensive, worry
sorg en voll	full of cares, uneasy, anxious; worried, troubled
Sorg falt nf	solicitude; exactness, scrupulousness; circumspection
sorg fält ig	careful; attentive; exact; accurate; scrupulous, cautious
sorg lich	careful, solicitous
Sorg los ig keit	unconcern; carelessness; negligence; lightheartedness
sorg sam	careful, painstaking, particular; cautious
Sorg sam keit	care, carefulness, caution
be sorg en	apprehend, fear; get, procure, supply
Be sorg nis	apprehension, fear, alarm, concern
Be sorg t heit	anxiety, uneasiness; concern, solicitude
Be sorg ung	care, attention; procurement; handling, errand
Für sorg e	care, solicitude
Für sorg er	welfare officer, social worker
Für sorg erin	welfare officer, social worker
für sorg lich	careful, thoughtful, solicitous
ver sorg en	provide, supply, furnish; support, maintain, take care of
Ver sorg er	provider, supporter, breadwinner
Ver sorg ung	supply, provision, maintenance; subsistence
Vor sorg e	provision, providence; precaution
vor sorg en	provide; take care; provide for the future
vor sorg lich	provident; precautionary
un be sorg t	unconcerned

un ver sorg t	unprovided for, without means

Spann nm	instep
Spann e	span; short distance; short space of time
spann en	stretch; bend a bow, tighten; flex muscles
sich spann en	be tight; pinch
Spann er	stretcher, boot-tree; press for trousers
Spann ung	tension; stress; strain; pressure; span, stress; voltage
ab spann en	unbend, unhook; slacken; unharness, unyoke
Ab spann ung	unbending; relaxation; fatigue
an spann en	stretch; put to, harness up, hitch up
An spann ung	tension, strain, exertion
auf spann en	stretch; mount; fix, clamp s.t.; put up; pitch a tent
aus spann en	stretch, extend; spread; unharness horses; release, unclamp
aus spann en	take a rest, relax, take it easy
Aus spann ung	relaxation, recreation, rest
be spann en	put the horses to; string musical instrument
Be spann ung	team of horses; stringing, strings; fabric; lining
ein spann en	stretch; harness, clamp, chuck; make s.o. work
ent spann en	relieve the tension on; release; expand; relax, unbend
sich ent spann en	relax; ease
Ent spann ung	relaxation, rest, diversion
Ge spann nn	team; horse and carriage; turn-out
ge spann t	stretched, tight, tense; strained, eager, anxious
Ge spann t heit	tension; intensity, intentness; strained relations
Nieder spann ung	electrical low tension, low voltage
über 'spann en	span, traverse, vault, stretch; exaggerate one's claims
über spann t	extravagant, fantastic; eccentric
Ueber spann t heit	extravagance; eccentricity
Ueber spann ung	overstraining; exaggeration
um 'spann en	span, encompass; comprise, embrace; clasp
'um spann en	change horses
Um spann er	electrical transformer
ver spann en	brace, stay, guy
Ver spann ung	bracing, stays
Vor spann nm	team of horses; relay
vor spann en	harness horses; prestress concrete; link locomotive to train
ab ge spann t	exhausted, wary, run down, debilitated
Ab ge spann t heit	exhaustion, weariness
an ge spann t	strained, tense, hard

spar en	save money, save time, economize; spare
Spar er	saver; depositer
spär lich	scant, scanty; scarce; sparse; poor; meagre
Spär lich keit	scantiness; scarcity; sparseness; poorness
spar sam	saving, thrifty, economical, parsimonious
Spar sam keit	economy, thrift, thriftiness; parsimony; frugality, austerity

ab spar en	stint o.s.; put every penny aside for s.t.	
auf spar en	save; put s.t. by; keep in reserve, reserve s.t.	
aus spar en	leave open, leave vacant; recess	
Aus spar ung	recess, notch, cutout	
ein spar en	save up, economize	
Ein spar ung	saving; economizing, economies	
er spar en	save, put away money	
Er spar nis nf	saving	

Speis e	food, nourishment; victuals, eatables; dish	
speis en	eat, have a meal; take one's meals	
Speis ung	feeding; boarding, maintenance; supply, feed	
ab speis en	feed; put s.o. off	
ver speis en	eat up, consume	
Vor speis e	hors d'oeuvres, entree, appetizer	
Zu speis e	side dish, trimming	

Spiegel nm	looking-glass, mirror; reflector; surface; level, sea level	
spiegel n	shine, glitter, sparkle	
sich spiegel n	mirror, reflect, be reflected, look at s.o. in a glass	
Spiegel ung	reflection; mirage	
ab spiegel n	mirror, reflect	
be spiegel n	flash a mirror at s.o.; throw light on, illuminate	
Rück spiegel nm	rear-view mirror	
vor spiegel n	pretend	
Vor spiegel ung	pretense	
'wider spiegel n	reflect s.t.	

Spiel nn	play, playing; game; match; sport; gambling	
spiel en	play; gamble	
spiel end	easily, with effortless ease, just like that	
Spiel er	player; gambler	
Spiel erei	play, playing, sport, pasttime; trifle; child's play	
Spiel erin	player; gambler	
spiel er isch	playing, as a player; playful	
ab spiel en	play a record, play a song; play back; take place, happen	
sich ab spiel en	happen, occur, take place	
an spiel en	play first; kick off; have the lead; serve the ball	
An spiel ung	allusion, hint, insinuation	
auf spiel en	strike up	
sich auf spiel en	show off, put on airs	
aus spiel en	play to the end, finish; play a card; play for a prize	
Bei spiel nn	example, model; instance, illustration, demonstration	
bei spiel haft	exemplary; model	
bei spiel los	unexampled, unprecedented, unheard of; peerless, matchless	
'durch spiel en	play through, play over; play to the end	
ein spiel en	practice; balance out; realize, net	

sich ein spiel en		balance out; warm up
Ge spiel e	nm	playmate
Ge spiel in		playmate
Gegen spiel er		opposite number
mit spiel en		join in a game; play in a game, appear, be involved, play a part
Mit spiel er		partner
Nach spiel	nn	epilogue, afterpiece, musical postlude
über 'spiel en		pass one's opponent; outmaneuver s.o.; overact
um 'spiel en		pass the ball, dribble around
ver spiel en		lose; gamble away
Vor spiel	nn	prelude, overture
vor spiel en		play s.t. to s.o.; play s.t. before s.o.
Wider spiel	nn	contrary, reverse; counterpart
zu spiel en		play s.t. into one's hands, play one's way; pass the ball to s.o.
zurück spiel en		pass the ball back
Zusammen spiel	nn	team-work
her um spiel en		play around
Schau spiel	nn	play, theatrical performance
Schau spiel er		actor

spitz	a	pointed, peaked; acute angle; thin, poignant, biting
Spitz	nm	**Pomeranian dog, spitz**
Spitz e		point; peak, summit, top; tip; spire; vertex of triangle, apex; lace
Spitz el		spy, informer, stool pigeon; snooper
spitz el n		spy, snoop about; play the informer
spitz en		point; sharpen
Spitz er		pencil-sharpener
an spitz en		point, sharpen
über 'spitz en		subtilize; exaggerate, overdo
sich zu spitz en		taper off; become more critical, come to a head
be spitz el n		spy on s.o.

sprach: siehe sprech		
Sprach e		speech; language, tongue; vernacular; words; voice
sprach lich		of languages, linguistic; grammatical
sprach los		speechless
Sprach los ig keit		speechlessness
Ab sprach e		arrangement, agreement
An sprach e		address, speech
Aus sprach e		pronunciation, accent; talk, discussion; explanation
Für sprach e		intercession
Ge spräch	nn	talk, conversation, colloquy, discourse; discussion; dialog
ge spräch ig		talkative, communicative, chatty
Ge spräch ig keit		talkativeness; talking mood
Rück sprach e		discussion, consultation, conference
Fern ge spräch	nn	telephone conversation

	sprech en	speak, talk, say, utter
	Sprech er	speaker, talker; broadcaster, announcer, spokesman
ab	sprech en	contest, dispute, refuse
ab	sprech end	deprecatory, slighting
ab	sprech er isch	deprecatory, slighting
an	sprech en	address, speak to; interest s.o.; please
an	sprech end	pleasing, engaging, attractive
aus	sprech en	pronounce, articulate; speak to the end; declare, utter
sich aus	sprech en	speak one's mind, express o.s. about, talk over, unburden o.s.
be	sprech en	speak of; talk over, arrange; review; comment upon; record
Be	sprech ung	discussion; agreement; review; interview, consultation, negotiation
'durch	sprech en	talk over, discuss
ein	sprech en	encourage, comfort s.o.
ent	sprech en	correspond to; satisfy, comply with, conform to, answer to, suit
ent	sprech end	adequate to, appropriate, corresponding, suitable
Ent	sprech ung	equivalent, analogy; denotation
fern	sprech en	telephone, talk on the telephone
Fern	sprech er	telephone
Für	sprech er	intercessor, mediator; advocate
los	sprech en	absolve, acquit, free, declare free
mit	sprech en	join in; come into consideration
nach	sprech en	repeat
ver	sprech en	promise; pledge, become bound to
Ver	sprech en nn	promise
sich ver	sprech en	make a mistake in speaking, make a slip of the tongue; engage o.s.
Ver	sprech ung	promise
vor	sprech en	pronounce to s.o., teach s.o. pronounciation; call on, drop in
wider	'sprech en	contradict, gainsay; oppose
zu	sprech en	speak to; encourage, comfort; drink copiously
Zu	sprech ung	adjudication
un aus	sprech lich	unspeakable, inexpressible, unutterable
Vor be	sprech ung	preliminary discussion
dem ent	sprech end	accordingly

	Spreng el	district; diocese; parish
	spreng en	sprinkle, spray; water; force open, blow up, blast
	Spreng ung	explosion, blowing up, blasting; breaking, dispersion
ab	spreng en	blast off, blow off, cut off troops; sprinkle flowers
auf	spreng en	burst open, force open; blow up
aus	spreng en	blast out; spread
be	spreng en	sprinkle, spray
ein	spreng en	burst open; sprinkle; admix, interstratify, intersperse

los	spreng	en	blast off
ver	spreng	en	disperse, scatter
zer	spreng	en	break open, burst open; blow up; disperse, scatter a crowd

	spring	en	jump; leap; vault; hop, skip; spring; bounce, bound
	Spring	en nn	jumping, vaulting; diving
	Spring	er	jumper; diver
ab	spring	en	leap down; dismount; take off, jump off
an	spring	en	jump on, pounce on; leap against
auf	spring	en	jump up, leap up, bound up, spring to one's feet; land
aus	spring	en	snap out
bei	spring	en	hasten to one's aid; stand by s.o.; help s.o. out
ein	spring	en	jump into; catch, snap; shrink; help out, step into the breach
ent	spring	en	escape; rise from, spring from; arise, come from, originate
los	spring	en	jump off; snap off, burst off
'über	spring	en	leap over, flash across
über	'spring	en	jump, clear s.t.; overleap; skip
'um	spring	en	skip around
vor	spring	en	jump forward, leap forward; project, jut out
zer	spring	en	burst, break; crack; be splitting
zu	spring	en	jump at s.o.
zurück	spring	en	leap back, jump back; rebound; recede
her aus	spring	en	jump out, leap out
hin über	spring	en	jump, leap over
her vor	spring	en	leap, bound

	sproch:	siehe sprech	
aus ge	sproch	en a	decided, marked, outspoken

	spruch:	siehe sprech	
	Spruch	nm	saying, aphorism, maxim; text, passage; message, decision
An	spruch	nm	claim, demand; pretension, title
an	spruch s los		unpretending, unassuming, modest
An	spruch s los ig keit		modesty, unpretentiousness
an	spruch s voll		fastidious; pretentious; exacting
Aus	spruch	nm	utterance, saying; opinion, remark; decision, verdict
Ein	spruch	nm	objection, protest, reclamation, opposition
Fern	spruch	nm	telephone message
Wider	spruch	nm	contradiction, opposition, conflict; discrepancy; approval, praise
Zu	spruch	nm	consolation, encouragement; run of customers
be an	spruch	en	claim, demand s.t. from s.o.; engross; require
Be an	spruch	ung	claim; stress, strain; service; condition, load

	sprung:	siehe spring

	Sprung nm	leap, jump; spring; dash; crack, gap, flaw, fault
	sprung haft	precipitous; erratic; spasmodic, volatile; flighty
	sprung weise	in jumps, by leaps, in bounds
Ab	sprung nm	leap from a train; dismount; parachute, drop
Ein	sprung nm	preliminary jump; turn, return; angle of a wall, recess
Ur	sprung nm	origin; commencement, beginning; extraction; source, spring
ur	sprüng lich	initial, original, primary; first; natural, pristine, primal
Ur	sprüng lich keit	originality
Vor	sprung nm	projection; ledge; headstart, lead, advantage
Weit	sprung nm	broad jump; spread fence, spread obstacle

	spül en	wash against; rinse; flush
	Spül ung	rinsing; wash, irrigation; water flush; scavenging
ab	spül en	wash, rinse
aus	spül en	wash out, rinse; flush
be	spül en	wash, beat against; rinse
nach	spül en	rinse; flush again
um	'spül en	wash around
unter	'spül en	wash away, hollow land
weg	spül en	wash away

ab	spul en	unwind, reel off
auf	spul en	wind, spool, reel
'um	spul en	rewind

	Spur nf	trace; trail, scent; mark; track; footprint; wake; gauge
	spür bar	sensible; distinct, marked; considerable
	spur en	keep on the track; lay the course; toe the line
	spür en	feel; sense, be conscious of, perceive, notice; detect
	spur los	trackless, traceless
auf	spür en	hunt up, track down, trace out, ferret out
'durch	spür en	put up; fix; pin up; attach, slip on
nach	spür en	trace, track; spy on s.o.
ver	spür en	feel, perceive, sense, be conscious of
Voll	spur nf t	standard gauge, broad gauge
voll	spur ig t	standard gauge, broad gauge
weit	spur ig	wide tracked, broad gauged

	Staat nm	state; country, nation; government; colony
	staat en los	stateless
	staat lich	government; national, public; political
über	staat lich	supranational
ent	staat lich en	denationalize
Ent	staat lich ung	denationalization
ver	staat lich en	nationalize, transfer to state ownership; expropriate
Ver	staat lich ung	nationalization

	Stadt nf	town; city
	Städt chen	small town
	Städt er	townsman, city dweller
	städt isch	municipal; urban; metropolitan
Innen	stadt nf	downtown
Vor	stadt nf	suburb
vor	städt isch	suburban
ver	städt er n	urbanize
Ver	städt er ung	urbanization
Gross	stadt nf	big city, metropolis

	stall: siehe stell	
	Stall nm	stable, barn, cowshed; shed, outhouse
	Ställ chen	playpen
	stall en i	stale, urinate from a horse
be	stall en	install s.o. in an office, invest s.o. with an office
Be	stall ung	installation, appointment

	Stamm nm	stem; stalk; trunk
	stamm en	be descended from; originate from; spring from; come from a town
	stämm ig	sturdy, burly; brawny, husky, hefty; stocky
	stämm ig keit	sturdiness, brawn, huskiness
ab	stamm en	descend from, be descended from; come off; derive from
Ab	stamm ung	descent, extraction, birth, origin
ent	stamm en	be descended from; come from, come of, originate from
her	stamm en	descend; be a native of, come from, be born in
an ge	stamm t	ancestral, hereditary; innate

	stand: siehe steh	
	Stand nm	standing; standing position; stand, position; footing
	Stand ard nm	standard
	stand ard is ier en	standardize
	Stand ard is ier ung	standardization
	Stand art e	standard, banner; guidon
	Ständ chen	serenade
	Ständ er	stand; rack; post, pillar; support, mount; stator
	stand haft	steadfast, steady; firm; unyielding; resolute; staunch
	Stand haft ig keit	steadfastness; perseverance, constancy
	ständ ig	permanent; constant; continuous; fixed, established
Ab	stand nm	distance; space, spacing
An	stand nm	decency, propriety; hesitation, objection; delay, stand
an	ständ ig	decent; proper, respectable; reasonable, sufficient; generous
An	ständ ig keit	decency, propriety, respectability; fairness
an	stand s los	unhesitatingly, readily, promptly, without objection; freely

Auf stand nm	revolt, rebellion, insurrection, uprising; mutiny
auf ständ isch	insurgent, rebellious, mutinous
Aus stand nm	strike
aus ständ ig	on strike, striking; outstanding, in arrears
Aus ständ ig e	striker
Aussen ständ e np	outstanding debts, arrears; liabilities
ausser stand e av	be unable to, not be in a position to
Be stand nm	existence; continuance, duration; durability; consistence
be stand en a	successful, passed
be ständ ig	constant, steady; unchanging, invariable, lasting, settled
Be ständ ig keit	steadiness; invariability; permanence, durability; continuance
Bei stand nm	aid, help, support; assistant, standby; adviser
Ein stand nm	installation; deuce; footing
Ge ständ e nn	confessing
ge ständ ig	admitting one's guilt, pleading guilty
Ge ständ nis	confession; admission, avowal
Gegen stand nm	object, thing, item; subject, theme topic
gegen ständ lich	objective, concrete; graphic
gegen stand s los	without object, abstract; irrelevant, immaterial, invalid
im stand e av	able; be able to do s.t., be capable of s.t.
in ständ ig	urgent, earnest, pressing; instant
Miss stand nm	grievance, abuse; impropriety; inconvenience, nuisance
Rück stand nm	arrears; residue, sediment; remainder, waste
rück ständ ig	antiquated, backward, old-fashioned; undeveloped; in arrears
Rück ständ ig keit	backwardness
über ständ ig	stale, flat; decrepit, superannuated
Um stand nm	circumstance, condition, state; formalities; trouble
um ständ lich	circumstantial; minute, detailed; ceremonious; complicated
Um ständ lich keit	circumstantiality; formality; fussiness
un ständ ig	impermanent
Unter stand nm	shelter; dug-out
Ver stand nm	understanding, intelligence, intellect, mind, sense
ver ständ ig	intelligent; reasonable, sensible; judicious
Ver ständ ig keit	sensibleness, good sense; prudence
ver ständ lich	intelligible, distinct, clear; understandable
Ver ständ lich keit	clearness, articulation, distinct transmission
Ver ständ nis	intelligence, understanding, comprehension; agreement, sympathy
ver ständ nis los	uncomprehending, blank; unappreciative, unsympathetic
Ver ständ nis los ig keit	lack of comprehension
ver ständ nis voll	intelligent; understanding, appreciative, sympathetic; knowing
voll ständ ig	complete, whole, entire, total; integral
Voll ständ ig keit	completeness, entirety, totality; integrity

Vor stand nm	board of directors, head, director
Wider stand nm	resistance, drag; strength; opposition, hostility
wider stand s los	without resistance
Zu stand nm	condition, state, situation, position, circumstance
zu stand e av	manage s.t., succeed in doing s.t., achieve s.t.; materialize
zu ständ ig	competent; responsible; proper, appropriate; local; duly qualified
Zu ständ ig keit	competence, responsibility; power
be an stand en	object to; take exception to, complain of, contest, oppose; reject
Be an stand ung	objection, protestation, complaint, protest
un an ständ ig	indecent; obscene, unmannerly; shocking
Un an ständ ig keit	indecency; obscenity; unmannerliness
Fort be stand nm	continuance; survival; persistance
un be ständ ig	inconstant, unsteady, unstable; erratic, fickle, inconstant
Un be ständ ig keit	inconsistency, inconstancy, instability, fickleness
ab ge stand en a	stale, flat
Ein ge ständ nis	avowal, confession, admission
Zu ge ständ nis	admission, concession, compromise
Neben um stand nm	accessory circumstance
ein ver stand en av	agree, consent, be agreeable to
Ein ver ständ nis	accord, understanding, consent, collusion
miss ver ständ lich	misleading; erroneous
Miss ver ständ nis	misunderstanding; dissension, difference
Un ver stand nm	lack of judgement, injudiciousness; folly, stupidity
un ver stand en a	not understood; misunderstood
un ver ständ ig	unwise, injudicious, foolish
un ver ständ lich	unintelligible; incomprehensible, inconceivable
Un ver ständ lich keit	unintelligibility; inconceivableness
un voll ständ ig	incomplete, imperfect
Un voll ständ ig keit	incompleteness
un zu ständ ig	incompetent; having no jurisdiction
Un zu ständ ig keit	incompetence; lack of jurisdiction
Ur zu stand nm	primitive state, original condition
un be an stand et	not objected to, unopposed, uncontested
un miss ver ständ lich	unmistakable, unequivocable
ver ständ ig en	inform, notify, advise
sich ver ständ ig en	communicate with s.o., make o.s. understood to s.o.
Ver ständ ig ung	information, agreement, arrangement, communication, message
ver voll ständ ig en	complete, supplement
Ver voll ständ ig ung	completion
selbst ständ ig	independent
selbst ver ständ lich	obvious; of course, naturally

stark a	strong; robust, sturdy; stout, corpulent; thick; powerful; intense
Stärk e	strength, force; power; stoutness; concentration; intensity

stärk en	strengthen; invigorate, brace; fortify; starch laundry
Stärk ung	strengthening; invigoration; comfort; refreshment
be stärk en	confirm, strengthen, fortify; encourage, support s.o.
Be stärk ung	confirmation; strengthening; encouragement, support
er stark en	grow strong, gain strength, strengthen
Er stark ung	strengthening
ver stärk en	strengthen, reinforce; boost, amplify, intensify, increase
sich ver stärk en	grow stronger, strengthen, gain
Ver stärk er	radio amplifier
Ver stärk ung	strengthening, reinforcement
Zwischen ver stärk er	intermediate amplifier

statt:	siehe steh	
Statt	nf	place, stead
statt	p	instead of, in lieu of
Stätt	e	place, spot; scene; abode
statt haft		admissible, allowable; legal
statt lich		stately; handsome; impressive, splendid, magnificent; considerable
Statt lich keit		stateliness, portliness
ab statt en		pay, make, give, render
an statt	p	instead of, in the place of, in lieu of, in preference to
aus statt en		provide, furnish, equip, fit out, supply
Aus statt ung		equipment, outfit; provision, supply; furniture
be statt en		bury, inter; cremate
Be statt ung		burial, funeral, interment; cremation
er statt en		restore, return; repay, refund
Er statt ung		restitution, return, compensation; reimbursement, refunding
ge statt en		allow, permit; consent to
un statt haft		inadmissible, illicit
von statt en	av	take place, proceed
zu statt en	av	be useful to s.o.
Innen aus statt ung		interior decoration
Rück er statt ung		restitution; refund; reimbursement
'wieder er statt en		restore, return, restitute; refund, reimburse
Wieder er statt ung		restitution; repayment, refund, reimbursement
zurück er statt en		restore, return; refund, repay

Staub	nm	dust; powder; pollen
Stäub chen		particle of dust, mote, atom
staub en		give off dust, raise clouds of dust
stäub en		dust; spray
staub frei		dust-free
staub ig		dusty
ab staub en		dust; steal s.t.
aus staub en		wipe dust off, brush dust out of, shake out the dust from

be stäub en	cover with dust; dust, spray; pollinate
Be stäub ung	dusting; spraying
ein stäub en	dust, powder
ent staub en	free from dust
ver stäub en	dust s.t.
ver staub en	get dusty
zer stäub en	pulverize; spray, atomize; disperse, scatter
Zer stäub er	pulverizer; sprayer, atomizer, scent-spray

stech en	prick; sting; bite; pierce, puncture; stab; cut
Stech er	engraver, pricker; hair-trigger of gun; scoop for cheese
ab stech en	prick off; tap; drain a pond; draw off wine
Ab stech er	excursion, trip; detour
an stech en	prick; broach; tap a barrel
auf stech en	pierce open, prick open; puncture; lance a boil
aus stech en	dig; cut out; engrave, carve; prick out; slacken; outdo, eclipse
be stech en	bribe, corrupt, suborn witnesses
be stech lich	bribable, corrupt, venal
Be stech lich keit	corruptibility, venality
Be stech ung	bribery, corruption
'durch stech en	pierce through; perforate
durch 'stech en	pierce s.t. through; run s.o. through
Durch stech erei	underhand dealing
ein stech en	prick, puncture; stick a needle in; cut, recess; engrave
er stech en	stab
nieder stech en	stab down
zer stech en	prick all over, sting all over; bite; pierce
un be stech lich	incorruptible, unbribable; keen, unerring
Un be stech lich keit	incorruptibility, integrity
her vor stech en	stand out; be prominent, be salient, be conspicuous

steck en	stick; set, plant; put somewhere; insert; plug into
Steck er	plug
Steck ling	layer, slip, cutting
ab steck en	unpin; undo one's hair; plot a course; mark out, stake out
an steck en	stick on, pin on; put on a ring; set on fire; infect
an steck end	infectious, communicable, contagious, catching
An steck ung	infection, contagion
Be steck nn	setting of knife, fork, and spoon
be steck en	stick, prick; garnish; plant
'durch steck en	pass through, put through, stick through
ein steck en	put in, stick in; put in pocket, sheathe a sword; pocket money
'um steck en	pin differently; change; rearrange a dress
'unter steck en s	put under, stick under
Ver steck nn	hiding place, hide-out; ambush
ver steck en	hide, conceal

vor steck en		put before; pin before, stick before; stick out one's head
weg steck en		put away; hide
zu steck en		pin up
zurück steck en		put back
zusammen steck en		put together, join together
her aus steck en		put up flag
hin ein steck en		put into, slip into
da hinter steck en	s	be at the bottom of s.t.

steh en		stand, be somewhere; be written; be used, suit, become; have stopped
Steh er		stayer
ab steh en		stand off from; get stale; abstain from
an steh en		linger, hesitate; fit; last, remain; stand in line
auf steh en		be open; get up, stand up; recover; revolt
aus steh en		suffer, endure, bear
be steh en		be, exist; last; undergo; resist; encounter
bei steh en		aid, stand by, assist, help
ein steh en		answer for, be responsible for s.o.
ent steh en		arise from, begin, start, result from, happen
Ent steh ung		origin, rise, birth; formation
er steh en		to arise; purchase, buy; pick up
fern steh en		be a stranger to
ge steh en		confess, acknowledge, admit, avow
nach steh en		be behind s.o.; be inferior to s.t.; make way for
neben steh end		annexed; marginal, alongside
'über steh en		overcome; endure, survive, get over
um 'steh en		stand around
um steh end	a	standing around; on the next page
'unter steh en		stand below; find shelter
unter 'steh en		pertain; be subordinate to
sich unter 'steh en		dare, venture
sich ver steh en		understand one another
ver steh en		conceive, realize, envisage; understand
vor steh en		project, protude; precede; represent, manage
Vor steh er		director, manager, principal, chief, superintendent
wider 'steh en		resist, withstand, hold out; stand
zu steh en		be due to, become to, suit, belong to
zurück steh en		stand back; be inferior to
zusammen steh en		stand together, side with one another
un aus steh lich		insupportable, insufferable, intolerable
fort be steh en		continue to subsist
weiter be steh en		continue to exist, survive, go on
auf er steh en		rise from the dead
Auf er steh ung		resurrection
ein ge steh en	a	confess, avow, admit
zu ge steh en		admit, concede, grant
ent gegen steh en		opposed, stand opposite to
gegen über steh en		stand opposite, face, stand in front of
her um steh en	s	stand around, loiter around
miss ver steh en		misunderstand, mistake

be vor steh en		lie ahead, be near, be approaching
her vor steh en		project, stand out, be prominent
un wider steh lich		irresistible
Un wider steh lich keit		irresistibility
fest steh en		be certain, be definite

stehl en		steal, thieve, commit larceny
Stehl er		thief
be stehl en		rob, steal from
sich fort stehl en		steal away, sneak off
sich hin ein stehl en		sneak into

steif a		stiff; rigid; inflexible; fixed, firm; awkward, clumsy
Steif e		dressing, starch; strut; prop, stay
steif en		stiffen; starch, dress laundry; prop, stay s.t.
Steif heit		stiffness, rigidity; stability; workability; stiffness; awkwardness
ab steif en		underprop, support; strut
aus steif en		stay, strut, brace
ver steif en		strut, prop, brace
sich ver steif en		stiffen, harden

Steig nm		narrow path, footpath
Steig e s		ladder, steep stairs; ascent
steig en		go up, ascend, climb, rise, soar, mount
Steig er		climber, pit-foreman; riser gate
steig er n		raise, increase; augment, enhance, heighten; improve, better
sich steig er n		increase, rise, intensify, improve o.s.
Steig er ung		raising, rise, increase, aggravation, enhancement
Steig ung		rise, gradient, upgrade, slope; ascent; pitch, lead
ab steig en		descend; step out; get off one's horse; alight; put up at
an steig en		mount, ascend, rise; increase
auf steig en		rise, mount, ascend, climb; increase; swell; climb up
aus steig en		get out, step out; get off, step off, disembark; bail out
be steig en		climb, ascend; mount; board a ship, enplane
Be steig ung		ascent, accession
ein steig en		get into, get on, board
ent steig en		arise; emerge from
er steig en		ascend, scale, climb, mount
Er steig ung		ascent
nieder steig en		descend
Ober steig er t		foreman of a mine
über 'steig en		surmount, surpass, exceed; cross, pass; overcome
'um steig en		change trains, transfer
sich ver steig en		lose one's way; have the presumption to; go so far as
her ab steig en		come down, descend; dismount; sink down
hin ab steig en		climb down, go down

her auf steig en	ascend; approach
hin auf steig en	mount, ascend, step up
her ein steig en	step in, get in
un über steig lich	insurmountable, insuperable
über 'steig er n	force up; exaggerate, go too far with; outbid s.o.
Ueber steig er ung	exaggeration
Ver steig er er	auctioneer
ver steig er n	sell by auction, put up for sale
Ver steig er ung	auction, public sale
sich hin ein steig er n	get worked up about s.t.

Stein nm	stone, rock
stein ern a	of stone; stony
stein ig	stony, full of stones; rocky
stein ig en	stone
Stein ig ung	stoning
stein reich	rich in stones; very wealthy
aus stein en	stone, pit
ent stein en	stone s.t., remove stone from
Ge stein nn	rock, stone, mineral; rock stratum
ver stein er n	petrify, turn into stone
Ver stein er ung	petrification; petrifaction, fossil

Stell e	place, spot, stand; position, site; employment, job, post
stell en	put, place, set, stand, arrange, regulate
sich stell en	take one's stand, position o.s., place o.s.
stell en los	out of work, umemployed, jobless
Stell ung	position, situation, employment, job; place, post; status, rank
stell ung s los	out of work, unemployed, jobless
ab stell en	put down; stop; turn off, disconnect; abolish
an stell en	employ, appoint, hire; turn on; cause
sich an stell en	behave, set about doing s.t.; line up for
an stell ig	able, skillful, handy, clever
An stell ung	employment, appointment, place, post, position
auf stell en	put up, set up, raise; activate; prepare
sich auf stell en	run for
Auf stell ung	setting up, putting-up, arrangement; statement; table; erection
aus stell en	lay out; exhibit, show; issue; make out
Aus stell er	exhibitor, drawer
Aus stell ung	exhibition, display, show, exposition; objection
be stell en	order, subscribe to; appoint; reserve; cultivate; deliver
Be stell er	customer, client; orderer, buyer; deliverer
Be stell ung	order; subscription; arrangement; cultivation; delivery; message
dar stell bar	representable, suitable for the stage
dar stell en	exhibit; present, represent; describe; perform
Dar stell er	exhibitor; representer; performer, player, actor
Dar stell ung	exhibition; show, presentation; performance, acting

ein stell bar	adjustable	
ein stell en	stop, discontinue, quit; employ, enlist; strike, focus	
Ein stell ung	attitude; engagement; focussing; strike; enlistment; discontinuance	
ent stell en	disfigure, deform, distort, mutilate; falsify	
Ent stell ung	disfigurement, distortion, mutilation, misrepresentation	
er stell en	provide, make available, supply; erect, construct, build	
Ge stell nn	frame, stand, support, rack, shelf, pedestal	
Ge stell ung	presentation; muster; appearance	
her stell en	put over here; repair, restore; establish; manufacture	
Her stell er	manufacturer, maker, producer; concern	
Her stell ung	manufacture, production	
hin stell en	put down, place somewhere; represent; raise a building	
nach stell en	place behind, put back, regulate, adjust, pursue	
Nach stell ung	pursuit, persecution; ambush, snare; adjustment	
Neben stell e	extension, agency, branch	
Rück stell ung	reserve; release; replacement	
um 'stell en	put into a different place, rearrange; adapt, convert	
'um stell en	surround, encircle	
Um stell ung	change, adaptation, conversion; inversion	
'unter stell en	place under, put under cover	
unter 'stell en	place under the command; insinuate	
Unter stell ung	insinuation; subordination, putting under the command of	
ver stell bar	movable, adjustable, variable; controllable	
Ver stell bar keit	adjustability	
ver stell en	displace, remove; misplace; shift, adjust; disguise	
sich ver stell en	dissemble, feign, put on an act	
Ver stell ung	dissimulation, hypocrisy; adjustment; displacement	
vor stell en	put ahead; introduce, present; mean; explain; demonstrate	
vor stell ig	present a case to s.o.; protest	
Vor stell ung	performance; imagination; show; idea; introduction; demonstration	
zu stell en	deliver to, send, hand to; obstruct	
Zu stell ung	forwarding, sending on, delivery	
zurück stell en	put back, set back, replace; reserve; defer	
Zurück stell ung	putting back, deferment; exemption	
zusammen stell en	put together, compose; assort; classify; set up	
Zusammen stell ung	composition, arrangement, combination; inventory; assembly	
hint an stell en	set aside, postpone; slight, neglect, disregard	
her aus stell en	put out	
sich her aus stell en	turn out, appear, come to light; prove	
hin aus. stell en	put outside	
ab be stell en	discontinue, countermand, cancel, revoke, annul	

Ab be	stell	ung		revocation, cancellation, counter-order
her be	stell	en	s	ask to come, send for s.o., make an appointment with
nach be	stell	en		order subsequently, reorder, repeat an order
Nach be	stell	ung		additional order, second order
vor be	stell	en		order in advance, make reservations
Vor be	stell	ung		advance order, booking, reservation
An ge	stell	te		employee, clerk
Unter ge	stell	nn		undercarriage, base, underframe
ent gegen	stell	en		set against, oppose; contrast, compare
wieder 'her	stell	en		restore, cure, repair, rebuild, reconstruct
Wieder her	stell	ung		restoration, recovery, repair, reconstruction
da hin	stell	en		leave s.t. undecided, not go into s.t.
gegen über	stell	en		oppose, confront with; contrast
Gegen über	stell	ung		opposition; contrast; confrontation
fest	stell	en		find out; establish s.t., determine s.t.; point out, state s.t.
Fest	stell	ung		perception, observation; ascertainment, discovery; determination
Halt e	stell	e		bus stop, subway stop, streetcar stop
Schrift	stell	er		writer, author
Tank	stell	e		filling station, service station, gas station

	sterb	en	decease, pass away, expire; be killed
	sterb	lich	mortal
	Sterb	lich keit	mortality
ab	sterb	en	die away, die out; fade away, whither; get numb
aus	sterb	en	die out; become extinct; become deserted
er	sterb	en	die away, expire; fade away
hin	sterb	en	die away
un	sterb	lich	immortal, undying; awfully, dreadfully
weg	sterb	en	die off

	stet:	siehe steh	
un	stet	a	unsteady, inconstant, changeable; restless, vagrant; unsettled
Un	stet	ig keit	unsteadiness; inconstancy; restlessness; vagrancy

	stich:	siehe stech	
	Stich	nm	prick, stab, thrust; puncture; sting, bite; stitch; taunt
	Stich	el	single lip cutter; cutter bit
	Stich	elei	gibe, taunt
	stich	el n	gibe, taunt; sew with small stitches
	stich	ig	tainted
	Stich	l er	giber, taunter
	Stich	ling	stickleback
Ab	stich	nm	tapping of a melting furnace; wine racking; cutting of turf
An	stich	nm	top for a beer keg; fresh draft of beer; turning the first sod
Aus	stich	nm	wine of the first quality; railway cut

Durch stich	nm	cut s.t. through; roulette

stieg:	siehe steig	
Stieg e		staircase, stairs; crate; score
Ab stieg	nm	descent
An stieg	nm	ascent; gradient; rise, increase; progress
Auf stieg	nm	ascent, ascension, rise; take off; advancement
Aus stieg	nm	escape hatch
Ein stieg	nm	entrance, climbing into
ver stieg en	a	eccentric; high-flown

still	a	still, quiet; silent; peaceful, calm; lifeless; secret; dull
Still e		stillness, quietness, silence; peace, calm; lull; dullness
still en		quiet, calm, silence; stop, soothe pain; quench thirst; nurse
Still ung		staunching; quenching; appeasing; gratification; nursing
un still bar		unappeasable; unquenchable
un ge still t		unstilled; unappeased; unquenched

Stimm e	voice; vote; comment; part
stimm en	tune an instrument
Stimm er	tuner
stimm haft	voiced, vocal
stimm lich	vocal
stimm los	voiceless, unvoiced, breathed
Stimm ung	tuning; pitch, key
stimm ung s voll	full of genuine feeling; impressive; sentimental; idyllic
ab stimm en	tune; harmonize; vote
Ab stimm ung	voting, referendum; tuning radio; tuning music
an stimm en	tune up, strike up
be stimm bar	determinable, definable, ascertainable
be stimm en	designate, ascertain, fix, appoint; stipulate; estimate; calculate
be stimm t	appointed, fixed, stated, specified; precise, distinct, determinate
Be stimm t heit	determination, firmness; accuracy, precision; certainty; strictness
Be stimm ung	determination; statement; appointment, details, specifications
bei stimm en	agree with s.o.; concur with s.o.; assent to; fall in with
Bei stimm ung	agreement, assent, approval
ein stimm en	join in, agree with
Ein stimm ig keit	unanimity
Gegen stimm e t	counterpart
Miss stimm ung	discord, ill humor
nieder stimm en	vote down, outvote
Ober stimm e	treble, soprano

über 'stimm en	outvote, vote down
'um stimm en	tune to another pitch; make s.o. change his mind
Un stimm ig keit	discrepancy, inconsistency; disagreement, friction
ver stimm en	put out of tune; put out of humor; irritate s.o.
Ver stimm ung	discord, ill humor
zu stimm en	agree, consent, approve of s.t., acquiesce, endorse s.t.
Zu stimm ung	consent, assent, agreement; endorsement
zusammen stimm en t	harmonize, agree, match; tally
Ur ab stimm ung	plebiscite
mit be stimm en	share in a decision, have a say in a matter
Mit be stimm ung	legal co-determination, co-rule
un be stimm bar	indeterminable; undefinable
un be stimm t	indeterminate, vague, indefinite; uncertain; undecided
Un be stimm t heit	indetermination; indefiniteness, vagueness, uncertainty
über 'ein stimm en	agree with s.o.; correspond with s.o., be identical with s.t.
Ueber ein stimm ung	agreement; conformity, concurrence; harmony, unison
miss ge stimm t	ill-humored, in a bad humor
vor aus be stimm en	predetermine
Vor aus be stimm ung	predetermination
vor her be stimm en	determine beforehand, predetermine; preordain; predestine
Vor her be stimm ung	predetermination

Stock nm	stick; can; baton; beehive; story, floor; stock
stock en	stop, come to a standstill; slacken; make no progress
stock ig	moldy, fusty; mildewy; decayed
Stock ung	standstill, deadlock; interruption, delay; pause; traffic jam
auf stock en	add a story to a house; increase, accumulate money
ver stock t	hardened, callous, obdurate; impenitent
Ver stock t heit	obduracy
Zwischen stock nm	entresol

stohl: siehe stehl	
be stohl en a	robbed
Be stohl ene	person robbed
ver stohl en a	surreptitious, furtive, stealthy, sly

stopf en	stuff; cram; plug; fill; stop leak; patch up
aus stopf en	stuff
ein stopf en	stuff into, cram into
ver stopf en	stop up, plug; clog, obstruct; jam, choke up; constipate
Ver stopf ung	stopping, clogging, obstruction; jam, congestion
'voll stopf en	stuff, cram

zu stopf en	stop up, plug, stuff; mend, darn clothes

stör en	disturb; trouble; bother, annoy; irritate, interrupt
stör end a	disturbing; troublesome; inconvenient; awkward; intrusive
Stör ung	disturbing
stör ung s frei	undisturbed; interference-free; trouble-free
auf stör en	stir up; disturb
ent stör en	clear, dejam; remove a radio disturbance
Ent stör ung	radio interference suppression; fault-clearing
Ver stör t heit	distraction; bewilderment, consternation
zer stör bar	destructible
zer stör en	destroy, demolish; ruin, wreck, devastate, ravage
Zer stör er	destroyer
Zer stör ung	destruction, demolition; ruin, devastation, ravages
un ge stör t	undisturbed, uninterrupted, peaceful
un zer stör bar	indestructible
Un zer stör bar keit	indestructability

storb: siehe sterb	
ab ge storb en a	dead, numb; devitalized, necrotic
aus ge storb en a	extinct, dead, fossil

Stoss nm	rush, shove, thrust; blow, knock
Stöss el	pestle, tamping, ramming tool, plunger; valve tappet
stoss en	push, shove, thrust; kick, punch, jab, knock, strike
Ab stoss nm	push off; goal kick in football
ab stoss en	push off, get rid of s.t.; pay off debt; repel s.t.
ab stoss end	repulsive
An stoss nm	kickoff in football; collision; impulse, stimulus; annoyance
an stoss en	push against, nudge; strike; kick off, shock; adjoin
an stöss ig	annoying, offensive, shocking
An stöss ig keit	annoyance, offense, shock
auf stoss en	push open; it occurs to him; he belches
Aus stoss nm	output, production
aus stoss en	push s.o. out; banish; give vent to, breathe; manufacture goods
be stoss en	damage s.t. by knocking
Durch stoss nm	breakthrough
'durch stoss en	push through; pierce, penetrate, stab
durch 'stoss en	thrust, push, break through
ein stoss en	push s.t. in, smash s.t. in
fort stoss en	kick
Gegen stoss nm	counter stroke, counterattack
nieder stoss en	stab s.o., cut s.o. down
Rück stoss nm t	thrust back, repulsion; recoil
'um stoss en	throw s.t. down, knock down, tip over, overturn
Ver stoss nm	offense against s.t., violation of s.t.
ver stoss en	disown; divorce wife; offend against the law
Vor stoss nm	thrust forward, advance, attack; ledge, projection

vor stoss en	push forward; advance suddenly; project, protrude
weg stoss en	push away
zer stoss en	knock s.t. to pieces; bruise, crush, pound s.t.
zu stoss en	push forward; shut a door, slam a door; happen to s.o.
zurück stoss en	back up; push back, repel s.t.; repulse
Zusammen stoss nm	collision, clash, impact
zusammen stoss en	bump together, collide; clash; touch, border on
her ab stoss en	swoop down
Aus ge stoss ene	outcast
un um stöss lich	irrevocable, irrefutable
an ein ander stoss en	bump against; adjoin, border on each other
auf ein ander stoss en	collide, clash together; meet; hit upon by chance

straf bar	liable to prosecution, punishable, criminal; culpable
Straf bar keit	punishability, criminal nature; culpability
Straf e	punishment; penalty; fine; retribution; sentence
straf en	punish; penalize; chastise, correct
Straf frei heit	impunity; immunity from criminal prosecution
sträf lich	punishable, criminal; culpable; inexcusable, unpardonable
ab straf en	punish, chastise
be straf en	punish; sentence; penalize; chastise, castigate
Be straf ung	punishment, penalization
Neben straf e l	secondary punishment
un sträf lich	blameless
Vor straf e	previous conviction
vor be straf t	previously convicted, having a criminal record
un ge straf t	unpunished

Strahl nm	ray; beam; flash; stream; jet; radius
strahl en	emit rays, radiate; shine, flash, sparkle; be radiant
strahl en förm ig	radiate, radial
Strahl er	emitter; radiator; cathode heater
Strahl ung	radiation, rays
aus strahl en	irradiate, beam, broadcast; radiate
Aus strahl ung	radiation, emission, emanation
be strahl en	shine upon; irradiate
Be strahl ung	irradiation, exposure to radiation
Rück strahl er	rear reflector; cat's eye
Rück strahl ung	reflection
über 'strahl en	shine upon, irradiate; outshine, eclipse
um 'strahl en	bathe in light, irradiate
Zer strahl ung	annihilation of matter
zurück strahl en	reflect, reverberate
Zurück strahl ung	reflection, reverberation

Streb e	prop, stay, support; crossbeam, traverse; brace
streb en	strive after, struggle for, aspire to
Streb er	pusher, careerist, climber; place-hunter

Streb er tum	nn		pushing, ambition; place-hunting
streb sam			assiduous, active; zealous, pushing; eager; aspiring; ambitious
Streb sam keit			assiduity; zeal, push; ambition
ab streb en			strut, brace
an streb en			aim at, aspire to, strive for
auf streb en			rise, soar, tower up; aspire
be streb en			endeavor to, strive to
Be streb ung			endeavor, effort, attempt, aspiration
er streb en			strive after, aspire to; desire, covet
hin streb en			try to get to a place, head for a place; strive for s.t.
nach streb en			strive after, aspire to; emulate s.o.
ver streb en			strut, brace
Ver streb ung			strut, brace
Wider streb en	nn		resistance, opposition; reluctance
wider 'streb en			oppose; struggle against, be repugnant to
zu streb en			make for; aim at, strive for, tend towards

streck bar			extensible; ductile; malleable
Streck bar keit			extensibility, ductility, malleability
Streck e			stretch, route; distance; span, stage of journey
streck en			stretch, extend; spread; dilute; draw; straighten
streck en weise	av		in parts, here and there
Streck ung			stretching, extension; lengthening of supplies; rolling
aus streck en			stretch out
sich er streck en			extend, stretch, reach, range
hin streck en			hold out one's hand; fell, knock s.o. down
Neben streck e	t		railroad branch line
nieder streck en			stretch down, strike on the ground, fell, floor s.o.
voll streck bar			executable, enforceable
voll 'streck en			execute, enforce, carry out
Voll streck er			executor
Voll streck ung			execution
vor streck en			thrust out, stretch forward, extend; put forward, advance money
her aus streck en			put forth, put out
ent gegen streck en			hold out, stretch out

Streich	nm		stroke; blow; whiplash; joke, prank, trick
streich el n			stroke; caress, fondle; pat
streich en			stroke, rub gently, touch gently; sleek, smooth; spread butter
Streich er	np		the strings
Streich ung			cancellation; deletion; suppressed passage
ab streich en			wipe off
an streich en			paint, coat; whitewash; mark, underline; check off
An streich er			painter
auf streich en			brush on, coat on; spread
aus streich en			strike out, cross out; cancel, smooth down; paint; grease

be	streich	en		spread over, smear; coat, paint
'durch	streich	en		cross out, strike out, cancel
ein	streich	en		pocket money
über	'streich	en		paint s.t. over, coat
unter	'streich	en		underline, underscore
ver	streich	en		pass away, slip by, elapse; expire
weg	streich	en		strike out, take off, cancel
her aus	streich	en		extol, praise to the skies, eulogize
her um	streich	en		prowl, roam around, rove about

	Streit	nm		quarrel; difference, dispute, argument, controversy; combat; feud
	streit	bar		warlike, combative, fighting; militant; belligerent
	streit	en		contend for; fight, struggle for; combat
	Streit	er		fighter, warrior, combatant; disputant; champion
	streit	ig		contestable, debatable, disputable, controversial
	Streit	ig	keit	quarrel, dispute, argument, controversy; combat; feud
ab	streit	en		dispute, contest, deny
be	streit	bar		contestable, disputable, challengable
be	streit	en		contest, dispute, challenge; deny; doubt; pay for
Be	streit	ung		contestation, argument; defrayal, payment
un	streit	ig		incontestable, indisputable
Wider	streit	nm		opposition, antagonism
wider	'streit	en		conflict with, clash with, be contrary to
un be	streit	bar		incontestable, indisputable, unquestionable
sich her um	streit	en	s	quarrel persistently

	streng	a		severe, rigorous, stern; harsh; rigid; austere; strict
	Streng	e		severity, rigor, sternness; harshness; strictness; stringency
an	streng	en		exert; tax, try, exhaust, strain
an	streng	end		fatiguing, exhausting, strenuous, hard; trying; back-breaking
An	streng	ung		strain, stress, exertion, fatigue; effort
ge	**streng**	a	a	severe
über 'an	streng	en		overexert, overstrain
Ueber an	streng	ung		|overexertion

	strich:	siehe streich		
	Strich	nm		stroke; line; dash; stripe, streak; region, district
	strich	el n		mark with little lines; dot; hatch, shade
	strich	weise	av	by strokes, by lines; in parts, here and there
Ab	strich	nm		downstroke; deduction; curtailment, cut
An	strich	nm		painting, coating; whitewash; paint, color
Auf	strich	nm		upstroke; spread; coat, layer
Bei	strich	nm		comma

	Strick	nm		cord, line; rope
	strick	en		knit
	Strick	er		knitter
	Strick	erei		knitting

	Strick erin	knitter
be	strick en	ensnare; charm, fascinate, bewitch
um	'strick en	ensnare
ver	strick en	spend time in knitting; entangle, ensnare

	stritt:	siehe streit	
	stritt ig		contentious, controversial, disputable, contestable
um	stritt en	a	contested; disputed; debatable, controversial
un be	stritt en	a	uncontested, undisputed, unquestioned; undenied, unchallenged
un um	stritt en	a	undisputed, proven

	Strom	nm	stream, river; torrent; flood; current; power
	ström en		stream; flow, run; gush; pour; throng
	Strom er		tramp, bum; scamp, blackguard
	Ström ung		current; flow, flux
aus	ström en		stream forth, gush forth, escape, exhaust; radiate; effuse
'durch	ström en		flow through, run through; thrill through
durch	'ström en		flow through, run through; thrill through
ein	ström en		stream into, flow into
ent	ström en		flow from, stream; gush from; escape, issue from
Gegen	strom	nm	reverse current
Gegen	ström ung		countercurrent
hin	ström en		flock there, throng there, stream there
Rück	strom	nm	electrical reverse current
'über	ström en		overflow, run over
Unter	ström ung		undercurrent
Zu	strom	nm	influx
zu	ström en		stream towards, flow towards; throng towards
zusammen	ström en		flow together; flock together, crowd together
her aus	ström en		pour out; pour forth; gush out
her bei	ström en		flock here, crowd here, come in crowds
her ein	ström en		flood in

	Stück	nn	piece; bit; morsel; cut, part, portion; fragment, shred; slice
	stück el n		cut into pieces, cut to bits; divide into shares
	Stück el ung		denomination of shares
	stück en		piece together, patch up
	stück weise	av	piece by piece, piecemeal; by the piece, by retail
be	stück en		arm with guns
Be	stück ung		armament, guns
Gegen	stück	nn	counterpart, antitype; equivalent
Zwischen	stück	nn	intermediate piece, connection
zer	stück el n		cut up, cut into pieces, dismember; parcel out; disintegrate
Zer	stück el ung		cutting up; parcelling out; dismemberment
Früh	stück	nn	breakfast

	Stud ent	nm	student
	Stud ent en schaft		body of students

Stud ent in		woman student
stud ent isch		student-like, academic, collegiate
Stud ie nf		study; sketch, essay
stud ien halb er	av	for the purpose of studying
stud ier en		study; go to the university, go to college
Stud io nm		studio
Stud ium nn		study; studies, reading; research, investigation
Fern stud ium nn		correspondence course
ein stud ier en		study; rehearse, produce a play

student: siehe stud	
Fern student nm	student of a correspondence course

Stuf e	step; rung; interval; hue; phase; degree, standard; rank
stuf en förm ig	in the form of steps, by steps
stuf en weise av	by steps, by degrees, gradually; in stages
ab stuf en	form into steps, grade, graduate, gradate
Ab stuf ung	gradation, shade
ein stuf en	classify, grade, rate
Ein stuf ung	classification, rating
Ober stuf e	higher grade, senior class
Unter stuf e	lower grade
Vor stuf e	first step; elements
Zwischen stuf e	intermediate stage

Sturm nm	storm, hurricane, tornado, gust; assault, forward line
stürm en	storm; assault
Stürm er o	hotspur, forward
sturm frei m	sheltered from the storm; unassailable
stürm isch	stormy, squally; rough; uproarious; tempestuous, passionate
An sturm nm	assault, charge, onset, onslaught
an stürm en	assault, assail, charge, storm, rush
Aussen stürm er	wing forward, winger
be stürm en	storm, assail, assault
Be stürm ung	storming, assault
er stürm en	take by storm, assault, storm
Er stürm ung	taking by assault, storming
los stürm en	rush forth
vor stürm en	rush forward, dash forward
her ein stürm en	rush into

Sturz nm	fall, tumble; crash, dive; drop; collapse; ruin
Stürz e	dishcover, lid; bell of a wind instrument
stürz en	fall, tumble; crash into
sich stürz en	precipitate; throw, upset, overturn; overthrow
Ab sturz nm	fall, plunge
ab stürz en	fall down, be precipitated; go down, crash; descend steeply
be stürz en	dismay, startle, take a person aback

Be stürz ung		dismay, alarm, consternation
Ein sturz	nm	collapse, crash
ein stürz en		fall in, break down, tumble down, collapse; cave in
hin stürz en		fall down, tumble down
nach stürz en		rush after
über 'stürz en		hurry, rush, precipitate
sich über 'stürz en		act rashly, follow in rapid succession
Ueber stürz ung		precipitancy, hurry, rush
Um sturz	nm	overthrow, upheaval; subversion, revolution
'um stürz en		overthrow, upset, overturn; subvert
Um stürz ler		revolutionary
um stürz ler isch		subversive, revolutionary
zu stürz en		rush up to
zusammen stürz en		collapse; fall in
her ab stürz en		throw down, precipitate, push down
her aus stürz en		fall out; rush out, tumble out
hin aus stürz en		rush out, dash out
her bei stürz en		rush here, rush to the scene
her ein stürz en		rush into
ent gegen stürz en		rush towards
hin unter stürz en		gulp down, toss down a drink
her vor stürz en		rush forwards; burst forth

Such e		search, hunt for; tracking
such en		seek, search out; trace; want, desire
Such er t		seeker, searcher
Such t nf		sickness, disease; mania, passion, rage for; addiction to
süch t ig		addicted; craving; have a mania for, maniacal; sickly, diseased
ab such en		search all over; scour, comb; beat; sweep
An such en nn		request, application, petition
an such en		make a request to s.o. for s.t., solicit s.t., apply for funds
auf such en		seek out, search for, locate
aus such en		search; choose, select, pick out, single out
Be such nm		visit
be such en		go to see s.o., visit, pay a visit to; call on s.o.
Be such er		visitor, caller; guest; frequenter
durch 'such en		search all over; ransack, hunt; comb, scour; search, frisk
Durch such ung		search
er such en		call upon s.o. to do s.t,; entreat, beseech, request urgently
Er such en nn		request, petition
Ge such nn		request, petition, suit; applicant
ge such t		much sought after
Ge such t heit		affectation
nach such en		search for, look for
Nach such ung		search; inquiry; application, petition; request
unter 'such en		look into; examine, inspect, scrutinize; explore; overhaul

Unter such ung	examination, scrutiny; inquiry; analysis
Ver such nm	attempt
ver such en	attempt, try; endeavor, make an effort
Ver such er	tempter
Ver such ung	temptation
zusammen such en	gather; collect
her aus such en	choose, select, pick out
Gegen be such nm	return visit
aus ge such t	exquisite, choice; hand-picked; studied, exquisite
Vor unter such ung	preliminary examination
un ver such t	untried
her vor such en	search for s.t., rummage for s.t.; pick s.t. out
eifer sücht ig	jealous

sunk: siehe sink	
ver sunk en a	sunken, foundered; lost in oblivion; engrossed in s.t.
Ver sunk en heit	engrossment, absorption

Tag nm	day; date
tag en	dawn, break of day; hold a meeting, sit in conference
tag e weise	by the day, on certain days
täg lich	daily; everyday
Tag ung	meeting, conference, congress, convention; session
be tag t	aged, advanced in years
ver tag en	adjourn; prorogue parliament
Ver tag ung	adjournment
Vor tag nm	previous day, day before
zu tag e av	open to view, open to light
All tag nm	workaday routine, humdrum routine
Ge burt s tag nm	birthday
heut zu tag e av	nowadays

tan: siehe tu	
Unter tan nm	subject, underling
unter tän ig	subject, obsequious, submissive, humble
Unter tän ig keit	submission, humility
an ge tan	attired in, clad in; likely to; be pleased with, be taken with
zu ge tan	attached to, devoted to, fond of

Tanz nm	dance, dancing
tänz el n	dance, skip, frisk; amble
tanz en	dance
Tänz er	dancer
Tänz erin	dancer; dance partner
ab tanz en	dance through; wear shoes out by dancing
durch 'tanz en	spend the night dancing, dance through the night
Ein tänz er	gigolo; taxi-dancer
Ein tänz erin	gigolo; taxi-dancer

mit tanz en	join in the dance
vor tanz en	dance before s.o.; show s.o. how to dance s.t.; lead off the dance
Vor tänz er	leader of the dance, leading dancer
her um tanz en	dance around

tat: siehe tu	
Tat nf	act, action, deed, exploit; fear; crime, offence
tat en los	inactive, idle
Tät er	doer, actor; perpetrator, delinquent, culprit; author
Tät erin	doer, actress; perpetrator, delinquent, culprit; author
Tät er schaft	guilt
tät ig	active, busy, hard at work; efficacious
tät ig en	bring off, carry out, effect; transact, undertake a business
Tät ig keit	activity, action; occupation, business, job, profession
tät lich	violent
Tät lich keit	violence, physical violence, assault
Mit tät er	accomplice, accessory, joint offender
Mit tät er schaft	complicity
Un tat nf	crime
un tät ig	inactive, idle
Un tät ig keit	inactivity, idleness
Zu tat nf	ingredients, seasoning; addition, complement; findings
be tät ig en	practice; set in motion, operate; manifest, prove
sich be tät ig en	do some work, be active, busy o.s.; take part in s.t.
Be tät ig ung	practice, activity, participation; manipulation, operation, control

taub a	deaf to; hard of hearing
Taub heit	deafness; numbness; barrenness; emptiness
be täub en	deafen, din, stun, daze; drug; stupefy; benumb, narcotize
Be täub ung	deafening; stunning; state of insensibility
über 'täub en	stun, deafen; stifle

tauch en	dive, plunge; dip; swim under water; submerge
Tauch en nn	diving
Tauch er	diver
tauch fäh ig	submersible
auf tauch en	rise up, emerge; surface; appear suddenly, emerge, turn up
ein tauch en	dip into, immerse in; sop, steep in
'unter tauch en	dive; submerge
wieder 'auf tauch en	come to light again, reappear, turn up again

Tausch nm	exchange, barter, truck

	tausch	en	exchange for, barter for, swap
	täusch	en	deceive, fool, dupe; mislead, delude; hoax; disappoint
sich	täusch	en	deceive o.s., be mistaken in, be wrong
	Täusch	ung	deception; delusion; illusion; mystification; fallacy; fraud
Aus	tausch	nm	exchange
aus	tausch	en	exchange; interchange; barter, swap; substitute
ein	tausch	en	exchange, barter; trade in s.t.
ent	täusch	en	disappoint, let s.o. down; frustrate
Ent	täusch	ung	disappointment, let-down; disillusion
Um	tausch	nm	exchange, barter; conversion
'um	tausch	en	exchange; convert
ver	tausch	en	exchange; change places; substitute
Ver	tausch	ung	exchange
vor	täusch	en	feign, simulate, pretend, counterfeit
hin weg	täusch	en	blind s.o. to s.t., mislead s.o. with regard to s.t.

	Teil	nm	part, piece, portion, share; element, component; member, party
	Teil	nn	part, piece, portion, share; element, component; member, party
	teil	bar	divisible
	Teil	bar keit	divisibility
	Teil	chen	particle
	teil	en	divide, split; distribute; separate; share, take part in
	Teil	er	divider, sharer, divisor
	teil	haft ig	partaking of, sharing
	teil s	av	partly, in part
	Teil	ung	division, distribution, separation, partition; sharing; forking
Ab	teil	nn	compartment
ab	teil	en	separate, partition off; classify; portion out
Ab	teil	ung	division; section, department; partition, compartment
An	teil	nm	share; interest
an	teil	ig	proportionate
auf	teil	en	partition, apportion, distribute
Auf	teil	ung	partition, apportionment, distribution
aus	teil	en	distribute; give out orders; deal cards; share, divide
Aus	teil	ung	distribution, division; administration
ein	teil	en	divide, distribute, arrange, group, classify
Ein	teil	ung	division, distribution, arrangement, classification
er	teil	en	give, confer on; bestow on; grant
Er	teil	ung	conferral, bestowing; granting
Gegen	teil	nn	contrary, reverse
gegen	teil	ig	the contrary
Hinter	teil	nn s	back, back part; buttocks
mit	teil	en	inform, communicate
mit	teil	sam	communicative

Mit teil ung	communication, information, message, report
Nach teil nm	disadvantage; prejudice
nach teil ig	disadvantageous, derogatory, disparaging
Ober teil nm	upper part
un teil bar	indivisible
Un teil bar keit	indivisibility
Unter teil nn	lower part, base
unter 'teil en	subdivide; section, section off
Unter teil ung	subdivision, section
Ur teil nn	judgement, decision
ur teil en	judge; sentence
ver teil en	distribute; dispense, apportion, assign; disseminate
Ver teil er	distributor
Vor teil nm	advantage, profit
vor teil haft	advantageous, profitable
Vorder teil nm	front, front part
zer teil en	separate, disperse
Zer teil ung	division, separation
zu teil av	fall to one's share
zu teil en	allot to, allocate; apportion; distribute, delegate, supply
Zu teil ung	allotment, allocation, apportionment, distribution; supply
Unter ab teil ung	subdivision, branch, subunit
zu er teil en	award, allot, assign
un ge teil t	undivided
ab ur teil en	decide a case; condemn s.o.; criticize severely
be ur teil en	judge s.t.; review a book, criticize a work of art
Be ur teil ung	judgement, review; estimation
ver ur teil en	condemn, sentence, convict
Ver ur teil ung	condemnation, sentence
Vor ur teil nn	prejudice
vor ur teil s los	unprejudiced
Vor ur teil s los ig keit	freedom from prejudice; openmindedness
be vor teil en	take advantage of; overreach
über 'vor teil en	take advantage of, deceive
Ueber vor teil ung	taking advantage of, deception
un vor teil haft	unprofitable, disadvantageous; unbecoming clothes
Vor aus ab teil ung	advance force, reconnaissance force
be teil ig en	give s.o. a share, make s.o. a partner
sich be teil ig en	take part in, participate in
Be teil ig ter	person concerned, participant
Be teil ig ung	attendance, participation; share, interest, partnership
un be teil ig t	indifferent to
be nach teil ig en	wrong s.o., handicap s.o.
Be nach teil ig ung	disadvantage, handicap, discrimination; injury, damage

---

teuer	a	dear, costly, expensive; valuable; precious, cherished, beloved

	Teuer ung	dearness, high prices; dearth, scarcity, famine
be	teuer n	protest; swear; assert, assure of
Be	teuer ung	protestation; assertion, solemn declaration
über	'teuer n	overcharge
ver	teuer n	raise the price of

	tief a	deep; profound; low; bass voice, low-pitched tone
	Tief nn	low pressure area, low
	Tief e	depth; deepness; profoundness, profundity; deep, abyss
un	tief a	shallow
Un	tief e	shallow, shoal
ver	tief en	deepen; hollow out; heighten an emotion
sich ver	tief en	deepen; hollow out
Ver	tief ung	deepening; hollow, cavity; recess; absorption
zu	tief st av	deeply, intensely; badly

	Tier nn	animal; creature; beast
	Tier chen	insect, bug
	tier isch	animal; bestial, brutish
Ge	tier nn	animals
Un	tier nn	monster
Ur	tier chen nn	protozoan

	Tisch nm	table; board
	Tisch ler	joiner; cabinetmaker
	Tisch ler ei	joinery; joiner's workshop
auf	tisch en	dish up, serve up
Nach	tisch nm	desert, sweets
Neben	tisch nm	next table

	Titel nm	title; heading; title to, title-deed; securities
be	titel n	entitle, name; call, style s.t.
Unter	titel nm	subheading; subtitle, caption

	Ton nm	tone, sound; musical note; pitch, accent, stress; clay
	tön en	sound, ring, resound; orate, hold forth
	ton isch	tonic
	ton los	soundless; unstressed; toneless
	Tön ung	tinge, shading, tint; tone
ab	tön en	shade, tone down
be	ton en	stress, accent; emphasize; declare emphatically
be	ton t	stressed; emphatic, insistent
Be	ton ung	accentuation
er	tön en	resound, ring out
Miss	ton nm	discordant tone, dissonance
Ober	tön e np	musical overtones
über	'tön en	drown out
Unter	ton nm	undertone; overtone
ver	ton en	set to music, compose
Ver	ton ung	composition, music

voll tön end		full-toned, sonorous, rich
un be ton t		unaccented, unstressed

trag bar		portable, wearable; bearable; acceptable, reasonable
Trag e		handbarrow
träg e	a	lazy, indolent, idle, slothful, sluggish, inert
trag en		carry, take, convey, transport; lift, support, bear
sich trag en		dress; wear well; have one's mind occupied with
Träg er		carrier, bearer, porter; wearer; champion; girder
Träg erin		carrier, bearer, porter; holder, wearer; champion
Träg heit		laziness, indolence, sluggishness, inertia, inactivity
Ab trag	nm	payment, installment
ab trag en		carry off, take away; demolish, wear out
ab träg lich		injurious, harmful, detrimental
An trag	nm	offer, proposition, proposal; application, request; appeal
an trag en		propose
Auf trag	nm	order, command; charge; appointment; assignment, direction
auf trag en		serve up, lay on; commission; boast; wear out
Aus trag	nm	end, decision, settlement; issue
aus trag en		carry out, deliver; report, divulge; transfer, determine
Be trag	nm	amount, value, sum, total
Be trag en	nn	behaviour, conduct
be trag en		amount, come to, run up to, total; take
sich be trag en		behave o.s.
Bei trag	nm	contribution, share; subscription, fee, dues
bei trag en		contribute to; promote, help
Ein trag	nm	entry; registration; prejudice
ein trag en		carry in; register; enter; list, record
ein träg lich		profitable, lucrative
Ein träg lich keit		profitableness, productiveness
Ein trag ung		entry; registration
Er trag	nm	produce, proceeds, profit, income, earnings; yield, crops
er trag bar		supportable, bearable, tolerable
er trag en		bear, endure, stand, tolerate; suffer
er träg lich		supportable, bearable, tolerable, sufferable
fort trag en		carry away, carry off
ge trag en	a	solemn, measured, slow; worn, second hand
her trag en	s	bring here, carry hither
hin trag en		carry there
mit trag en		carry with others; share
Nach trag	nm	supplement, addition; addendum, postscript
nach trag en		carry after, add to; bear a grudge against
nach träg er isch		vindictive, resentful
nach träg lich		supplementary, additional; further, later
Ueber trag	nm	carrying over, sum carried forward; transfer; balance
über trag bar		transferable; alienable; assignable, negotiable; translatable

Ueber trag bar keit	transferability, negotiability
über 'trag en	transport, carry over, bring forward; transfer, delegate; transmit
über trag en	figurative, metaphorical
Ueber trag ung	transfer, carrying over; assignment, delegation; transmission
un trag bar	intolerable, unbearable, past endurance; unwearable
Ver trag nm	agreement, contract, treaty, bargain, arrangement
ver trag en	endure, bear, stand, tolerate, suffer
sich ver trag en	agree, harmonize, get along, be compatible; be consistent
ver träg lich	sociable, peaceable, friendly, amicable, good-natured
ver trag lich	stipulated, contractual, agreed upon
Ver träg lich keit	good nature, peaceable disposition, sociability, compatibility
Vor trag nm	essay, address, speech, performance; lecture, report, talk
vor trag en	carry forward; recite, declaim; lecture on; propose
weit trag end	long-range, far-reaching, important, portentous
zu trag en	carry to, report, tell, repeat
sich zu trag en	happen, come to pass, take place
Zu träg er	tell-tale, informer, gossip
Zu träg erei	gossip, telling tales
zu träg lich	advantageous; useful, wholesome
Zu träg lich keit	usefulness, wholesomeness
zusammen trag en	carry together, compile; glean
Zwischen träg er	talebearer, telltale, scandal monger
be an trag en	propose; apply for, file a petition, make a motion
Gegen an trag nm	counter-motion, counter-proposal
be auf trag en	charge with, authorize, commission, empower
Be auf trag te	commissioner, nominee, deputy, mandatory
un er träg lich	intolerable, unbearable, insufferable
ab ge trag en a	worn out, threadbare, shabby
hin über trag en	carry over, carry across
un über trag bar	not transferable, inalienable, unassignable, non-negotiable
her um trag en	carry around; divulge
un ver träg lich	unsociable, quarrelsome
Un ver träg lich keit	unsociableness, incompatibiltiy
da von trag en	carry off, obtain, catch
un zu träg lich	disadvantageous, unhealthy; unwholesome, unsuitable
Un zu träg lich keit	inconvenience, disadvantage, failure; discord
Brief träg er	mailman, postman

trau en	marry, join in marriage
sich trau en	dare, venture, risk
Trau er nf	sorrow, affliction, grief; mourning
trau er n	mourn for
trau er voll	mournful, sad

trau lich	intimate; cozy, snug
Trau lich keit	intimacy; coziness
be trau en	entrust with s.t., confide s.t., commit s.t. to one's care
Fern trau ung	marriage by proxy
sich ge trau en	dare, venture; risk
miss trau en	distrust s.o., have suspicions about s.o.
Miss trau en nn	distrust
miss trau isch	distrustful; suspicious, wary; doubtful, diffident
ver trau en	trust
Ver trau en nn	trust, confidence
ver trau en s voll	trustful, trusting
ver trau lich	confidential; intimate, familiar
Ver trau lich keit	confidence, intimacy, familiarity
ver trau t	intimate, familiar
Ver trau t heit	familiarity
Zu trau en nn	confidence
zu trau en	think s.o. capable of s.t.
zu trau lich	confiding, trusting; unafraid, friendly, tame
Zu trau lich keit	confidingness; tameness
an ver trau en	confide, entrust

trau r ig	sad; grieved, sorrowful; mournful, melancholy; sorry
Trau r ig keit	sadness; grief, sorrow; melancholy, wretchedness
Trau ung	marriage ceremony; wedding
be trauer n	mourn for s.o.; mourn the loss of
ver trauer n	spend time in mourning

Traum nm	dream; reverie, daydream; vision
träum en	dream of, daydream, be in a reverie
Träum er	dreamer; visionary
Träum erei	dreaming; reverie, day-dream, musing
träum er isch	dreamy; musing, bemused
traum haft	dreamlike
er träum en	dream of, imagine, envision
ver träum en	dream away
ver träum t	dreamy, sleepy

treff en	hit, strike
sich treff en	meet; gather, assemble
Treff er	hit, good shot
treff lich	excellent; exquisite, choice
Treff lich keit	excellence, choiceness
an treff en	meet with, find; come across, chance upon
auf treff en	strike, hit, impinge
Be treff nm c	business reference; subject
be treff en	befall, come upon, visit; affect, touch; concern; refer to
Be treff ende	person referred to, person in question
be treff s p c	with regard to, with respect to; concerning
ein treff en	arrive

Hinter	treff en	nn	rear guard, reserve
über	'treff en		excel, outdo, outstrip s.o.; surpass, exceed, beat s.t.
Voll	treff er		direct hit
vor	treff lich		excellent, splendid, superior, superb
Vor	treff lich keit		excellence, superiority
zu	treff en		be right, be true, be correct, come true
zusammen	treff en		meet; coincide, concur
Zusammen	treff en	nn	meeting, encounter; coincidence, concurrence
an be	treff en		as regards this matter; as far as I am concerned
un über	treff lich		unsurpassable, matchless, peerless
Un über	treff lich keit		unsurpassability, matchlessness
un zu	treff end		incorrect; unfounded

	treib en		drive, work, operate; propel, float, drift; shoot forth
Treib	en	nn	driving; doings, activities; goings-on; bustle, activity
Treib	er		driver; beater, oppressor; propeller; picker
ab	treib en		drive away, repulse; drift away; abort
Ab	treib ung		abortion
an	treib en		push on, urge on
An	treib er		slave driver; pacemaker
auf	treib en		drive up; obtain, raise money; swell up
aus	treib en		drive out, expel
Aus	treib ung		expulsion, exorcism
be	treib en		pursue studies; run a business; urge on, hasten s.o.
Be	treib ung		exercise, carrying on; management
bei	treib en		collect debts; exact taxes; requisition
'durch	treib en		drive s.t. through; strain, sift s.t.; carry s.t. through
ein	treib en		drive in cattle; recover debts; collect taxes
fort	treib en		drive away; drift, drift away
hinter	treib en		hinder, prevent; thwart
Hinter	treib ung		hindrance, prevention
über	'treib en		exaggerate, overdo
Ueber	treib ung		exaggeration
'um	treib en		drive s.o. around; worry
unter	'treib en		understate
Unter	treib ung		understatement
ver	treib en		expel from, banish
Ver	treib ung		expulsion, banishment
vor	treib en		drive
weg	treib en		drive away; drift away
zu	treib en		drive towards, drive on
zurück	treib en		drive back, repel, repulse
zusammen	treib en		drive together, bring together
hin auf	treib en		crowd up to s.t.; drive up prices
hin aus	treib en		drive out; crowd out
um 'her	treib en		knock around, drift
sich her um	treib en		hang around, roam about

aus ein			
ander	treib en		disperse, scatter

	treid:	siehe trag	
Ge	treid e	nn	grain, cereals; corn; crop; windrow

	trenn bar		separable; detachable
	Trenn bar keit		separability
	trenn en		separate; sever, divide; detach, isolate; separate spouses
sich	trenn en		separate from; part, separate
	Trenn ung		separation, severance; disconnection; segregation; division
ab	trenn bar		separable, detachable
ab	trenn en		separate, detach; unstitch a seam, rip off
sich ab	trenn en		separate, detach, remove o.s.
Ab	trenn ung		separation, severance; unstitching
auf	trenn en		rip up, rip open; undo, unpick a seam
los	trenn en		sever, separate; unsew, unstitch
un	trenn bar		inseparable
Un	trenn bar keit		inseparability
zer	trenn en		rip up a garment
un zer	trenn lich		inseparable

	tret en		tread, step, walk, stride; treadle, pedal; work, kick
ab	tret en		tread down, wear out; transfer; yield; withdraw, resign
Ab	tret er		transferrer; door mat
Ab	tret ung		cession, surrender; transfer; resignation, abdication
an	tret en		enter upon an office; set out on a journey
auf	tret en		kick open; step on; proceed; behave, act; appear, perform
aus	tret en		step out, go out; resign from, leave, withdraw; emerge; wear out
be	tret en		tread on, tread upon; enter
be	tret en	a	beaten; frequented; embarrassed
bei	tret en		enter into; agree to, assent to, accede to; join
'durch	tret en		tread through, wear holes in
ein	tret en		enter, come in, step into; join; happen, occur, arise
hin	tret en		step forth
nieder	tret en		trample down
über	'tret en		break, violate, trespass on, offend against
'über	tret en		step over; overflow; cross, go over to, change over to
Ueber	tret er		transgressor, trespasser, offender
Ueber	tret ung		transgression, violation, infringement, encroachment
'unter	tret en		seek shelter
ver	tret bar		justifiable, defendable, fungible
ver	tret en		represent, replace; deputize for; answer for; attend to

Ver	tret	er	representative, deputy; substitute; advocate; agent, salesman
Ver	tret	ung	representation; replacement; substitution; agency
vor	tret	en	step forth, come forward; project, protrude
weg	tret	en	step aside; break ranks, fall out of ranks
zer	tret	en	trample down, tread under foot, crush
zurück	tret	en	step back, stand back, draw back; recede, retreat; resign, retire
zusammen	tret	en	come together, meet, unite; trample down
her an	tret	en	step near, step up to, approach s.o.
her aus	tret	en	step out; come forward with
un be	tret	en	a	untrodden; unbeaten
her ein	tret	en	step in, enter
wieder 'ein	tret	en	re-enter
aus ge	tret	en	a	trodden-down; beaten path
ent gegen	tret	en	step up to, advance towards; stand up to, oppose
gegen über	tret	en	step in front of, face
her vor	tret	en	come forward, step forth; emerge, come out; bulge the eyes
hin zu	tret	en	come up to, approach; join a company; be added to, accede
da zwischen	tret	en	interpose, intervene

---

	treu	a	faithful, true; loyal; devoted, staunch; trusty; faithful
	Treu	e	faithfulness; loyalty; faith
	treu	lich	faithfully; truly
	treu	los	faithless, disloyal, perfidious, treacherous
	Treu	los ig keit	faithlessness; infidelity; perfidy, treachery
be	treu	en	care for, attend to, look after, nurse; assist
Be	treu	er	attendant, caretaker; relief worker
Be	treu	ung	care
ge	treu	a	faithful, true, loyal, trusty, staunch
Ge	treu	er	faithful followers
ge	treu	lich	faithful, true, loyal, trusty, staunch
un	treu	a	unfaithful, untrue, disloyal
Un	treu	e	unfaithfullness, disloyalty; infidelity
ver un	treu	en	embezzle
Ver un	treu	ung	embezzlement, misappropriation

---

	trieb:	siehe treib	
	Trieb	nm	sprout, young shoot; driving force, impulse, instinct, urge
	trieb	haft	instinctive, animal-like; carnal
Ab	trieb	nm	clearing of timber; downward pressure; distillation
An	trieb	nm	drive, propulsion; impulse, impetus, urge; incentive
Auf	trieb	nm	bouyance; lift; impetus, stimulus; drive; upward trend
Be	trieb	nm	undertaking, firm, company, enterprise; rush, traffic
be	trieb	lich	relating to an enterprise; operational, operating, internal

be	trieb	sam	active, busy, bustling, industrious, diligent; fussy
Be	trieb	sam keit	activity, bustle, industry, diligence; fussiness
durch	trieb	en a	cunning, crafty, wily, sly; mischievous
Durch	trieb	en heit	cunning, craftiness, wiliness, slyness
Ge	trieb	e nn	gearing, gear transmission, gear mechanism; drive
über	trieb	en a	overdone; exaggerated, excessive, extreme; overdrawn
Ueber	trieb	en heit	exaggeration; extravagance, extravagancy
Um	trieb	nm	machinations, intrigues, subversive activities; bypass
Ur	trieb	nm	basic instinct
Ver	trieb	nm	sale, market; distribution
Vor	trieb	nm	road heading; drifting; rate of advance; propulsive thrust

	trift:	siehe treib	
Ab	trift	nf n	leeway, drift; right of pasture

	trink	bar	drinkable, potable
	trink	en	drink, carouse, imbibe, drink in
	Trink	er	drinker; drunkard, alcoholic
an	trink	en	begin to drink from; get drunk, get tipsy
aus	trink	en	drink up; empty, drain, finish one's glass
sich be	trink	en	get drunk
Er	trink	en nn	drowning
er	trink	en	be drowned, drown
mit	trink	en	drink with others
ver	trink	en	drink away money, spend time drinking
zu	trink	en	drink to, raise one's glass to

	tritt:	siehe tret	
	Tritt	nm	tread, step, pace, footprint, footstep, footfall; kick
Ab	tritt	nm	departure, exit; lavatory, toilet
An	tritt	nm	beginning, start, setting out; taking possession of
Auf	tritt	nm	incident; quarrel, argument; appearance, scene; step
Aus	tritt	nm	stepping out; leaving; resignation, withdrawl; exit; emergence
Bei	tritt	nm	accession, taking part; joining
Ein	tritt	nm	entry, entrance; beginning; setting in, joining; admission
Rück	tritt	nm	resignation, retirement; retreat, rescinding; withdrawal
Ueber	tritt	nm	going over; change, conversion; joining
Vor	tritt	nm	precedence
Zu	tritt	nm	admission to, entrance, admittance
Zusammen	tritt	nm	meeting, association, congress
Wieder ein	tritt	nm	re-entry

	trock	en a	dry; arid
	Trock	en heit	dryness; aridity; drought
	trock	n en	dry up, wipe dry; desiccate; dehydrate, drain; air

ab	trock n en	dry up, wipe dry
auf	trock n en	dry up; mop up
aus	trock n en	dry up, dessicate; parch; drain; season wood; wipe dry
ein	trock n en	dry in, dry up; shrivel up
ver	trock n en	dry up

	troff: siehe treff	
be	troff en a	affected by, concerned; stricken with; embarrassed
Be	troff en heit	embarrassment, perplexity, bewilderment
un über	troff en a	unsurpassed, unmatched, unequalled, unexcelled

	Trost nm	comfort, consolation, solace
	tröst en	console, comfort, solace; soothe; cheer up
	Tröst er	comforter, consoler
	Tröst erin	comforter, consoler
	tröst lich	comforting, consoling; cheering
	trost los	disconsolate; desolate; cheerless; bleak, dreary
	Trost los ig keit	desolation, despair, bleakness, dreariness; wretchedness
	Tröst ung	consolation, comfort; soothing words
ge	trost a	confident, hopeful; without hesitation; safely; always
un	tröst lich	inconsolable, disconsolate
ver	tröst en	feed with hopes; console; put off

	trüb e a	cloudy, muddy, thick; dull; dim; dismal, gloomy
	Trub el	turbulence, bustle, fuss; milling crowd
	trüb en	cloud; dim, dull; tarnish, darken; spoil, dull
sich	trüb en	become strained
	Trüb heit	muddiness, turbidity; dullness; cloudiness; gloom, dreariness
	Trüb sal nf	affliction; misery; distress; grief, sorrow
	Trüb ung	making muddy, rendering turbid; dimming, clouding
be	trüb en	grieve, afflict, sadden
be	trüb lich	distressing, sad, deplorable
Be	trüb nis	grief, sorrow, affliction, sadness
sich ein	trüb en	become cloudy, become overcast
Ein	trüb ung	cloudiness, overcast sky
un ge	trüb t	unclouded, clear; untroubled, serene

	trunk: siehe trink	
	Trunk nm	drink, potion; drinking, drunkenness
	trunk en a	drunken, drunk, inebriated, intoxicated
	Trunk en heit	drunkenness, inebriation, intoxication
be	trunk en a	drunken, drunk, intoxicated
Be	trunk ene	drunken person, drunk, inebriate
Be	trunk en heit	drunkenness, intoxication
Um	trunk nm	drink
voll	trunk en a	completely drunk, intoxicated, inebriated
Voll	trunk en heit	total intoxication, total inebriation

an ge trunk en a		slightly drunk, intoxicated, tipsy; opened bottle

trunn: siehe trenn	
ab trünn ig	unfaithful, disloyal, renegade; apostate, faithless

tu n		do, perform, make
Tu n nn		doings, activities, proceedings; action, conduct
tu n lich av		practicable, feasible, expedient
tu n lich st av		if possible, whenever practicable
ab tu n		put off, lay aside; abolish; finish off; settle an affair
An tu n		put on clothes; do s.o. honor; inflict; insult, injure
auf tu n		open
sich auf tu n		expand; yawn; get started
be tu lich		obliging, considerate; officious
dar tu n		prove, show, demonstrate, make evident, substantiate
Ge tu e nn		idle doings, fuss
hin tu n s		put, place
mit tu n		join in doing; help
nach tu n		copy s.o., imitate s.o.
'um tu n s		put on
sich 'um tu n s		apply for; look around for
un tu n lich		impracticable, unfeasable
ver tu n		spend, squander, waste
sich ver tu n		make a mistake
weg tu n		put aside; remove
zu tu lich		attentive, not timid, friendly, confiding
Zu tu lich keit		attentiveness; complaisance
Zu tu n		assistance, help
zu tu n		shut, close; add
zu tu n lich		attentive, not timid, friendly, confiding
Zu tu n lich keit		attentiveness; complaisance
zurück tu n		put back into its place
zusammen tu n sich		put together
zusammen tu n		associate; unite, join, combine
hin ein tu n		put in, put into; add to
sich her vor tu n s		distinguish o.s.
zu vor tu n		outdo, surpass s.o. in s.t.
da zu tu n		add

tucht: siehe tu	
tücht ig	able, fit; capable, efficient; clever, proficient, excellent; good
Tücht ig keit	ability, fitness; efficiency; cleverness; **proficiency**; excellency
un tücht ig	unfit, incapable; inefficient; incompetent; unseaworthy
un tücht ig	inept, unqualified; incapable, unable, incompetent
er tücht ig en	make fit, train; strengthen, harden
Er tücht ig ung	training, strengthening, hardening

	tug:	siehe tu
	Tug end	nf	virtue, quality, good quality
	tug end haft	virtuous, honest; chaste
	Tug end haft ig keit	virtue, virtuousness; honesty, integrity, chastity
	tug end sam	virtuous, chaste
un	tug end	vice, bad habit; failing, fault

	tunk:	siehe tauch
	Tunk e	sauce; gravy
	tunk en	dip s.t., steep s.t.
ein	tunk en	dip s.t. in, sop s.t. in, dunk s.t. in

	Tür	nf	door
Hinter	tür	nf	back door
Neben	tür	nf	side door
Vorder	tür	nf	front door

	üb en	exercise, practice; drill, train; cultivate the arts
	üb lich	usual, customary; conventional; common, ordinary; normal, standard
	Üb ung	exercise; study; practice; use, custom
aus	üb en	exercise; practice; conduct, perform, carry on an activity
Aus	üb ung	exercise; practice; performance, execution; perpetration
ein	üb en	practice s.t.; train, coach, drill s.o.
ge	üb t	practiced, skilled, versed, experienced; trained
Ge	üb t heit	skill, practice, experience
ver	üb en	commit, perpetrate, play pranks
Vor	üb ung	preliminary practice, preparatory exercise
un ge	üb t	untrained, unpracticed; inexperienced

	über	av	above, over, more than; all over
	über fäll ig	overdue
	über mäss ig	excessive; immoderate; undue
	üb r ig	left over, remaining; residual; odd; superfluous
	üb r ig ens	av	by the way, incidentally
dar	über	av	over that, over it, above it; on top of it; across it; meanwhile
gegen	über	p	opposite, facing, across from; towards; compared with
her	über	av	over here, across, this side
hin	über	av	over, over there; to the other side
vor	über	av	along, by, past; gone by, over; finished, done with
er	üb r ig en	save money; spare time
sich er	üb r ig en	be unnecessary, be useless, be superfluous

	um	p	about
	um	av	about; about, near, towards, at; by
dar	um	av	around that, around it, about that
her	um	av	about, around
wieder	um	av	again, anew; on the other hand; in turn

| hin wieder um | c | on the other hand, in return |
| hin wieder um | av | again, once more |

	unter	p	under, below; beneath, underneath; among; during
dar	unter	av	under that, under it; underneath, below; among them, including
her	unter	av	down there, down here; down with it
hin	unter	av	down there, downwards
mit	unter	av	now and then, sometimes, occasionally
zu	unter st	av	right at the bottom
da hin	unter	av	down there

	Vater	nm	father; sire
	väter lich		fatherly, paternal
	väter lich er seit s		on one's father's side
	vater los		fatherless
	Vater schaft		paternity, fatherhood
Ur	vater	nm	first father, ancestor
Vor	väter	np	forefathers, ancestors
Gross	vater	nm	grandfather

	Volk	nn	people; nation; race; populace, the common people, mob, rabble
	Völk chen		crowd
	Völk er schaft		people; tribe
	völk isch		national, racial
	Volk s tum	nn	nationality, nationhood; national characteristics
	volk s tüm lich		national, popular
	Volk s tüm lich keit		popularity
Ur	volk	nn	primitive people; aborigines
be	völk er n		people, populate, settle; frequent, throng, swarm in
Be	völk er ung		population; inhabitants, people; populace
ent	völk er n		depopulate, unpeople
Ent	völk er ung		depopulation
über	'völk er n		overpopulate
Ueber	völk er ung		overpopulation

	vor	av	before, in front of, forward, forwards
be	vor	c	before
da	vor	av	before it, in front of it
her	vor	av	forth, forward; out
zu	vor	av	before, previously; first, beforehand

	wach:	siehe weck	
	wach	a	awake
	Wach e		watch, guard; police-station; sentry, sentinel
	wach en		be awake; watch over, guard; keep an eye on
	wach sam		watchful, vigilant; alert
	Wach sam keit		watchfulness, vigilance
	Wäch t er		watcher, guardian, keeper; watchman; automatic controller

auf wach en	awaken, wake up
be wach en	watch over, guard; shadow; mark, cover
Be wach ung	guard; custody
durch 'wach en	stay awake all night, keep watch all night
er wach en	awaken, wake up; start up
über 'wach en	watch over; superintend; control; inspect; monitor
Ueber wach ung	supervision, control, inspection; surveillance, monitoring
un be wach t	unwatched, unguarded

wachs en		grow; increase; extend, expand; develop
Wachs tum	nn	growth; increase, development; expansion
an wachs en		take root; grow on; grow, increase, augment, rise; accumulate
An wachs ung		accretion, increment
auf wachs en		grow up
aus wachs en		sprout; grow up, reach one's full growth; heal up; outgrow
sich aus wachs en		grow into, develop into
be wachs en		grown over with, covered with; stocked with
'durch wachs en		grow through
durch wachs en	a	streaky, marbled
ein wachs en		grow in
ent wachs en		outgrow, grow out of
er wachs en	a	grown-up, adult
er wachs en		arise, develop, spring from; accrue from, accrue to
Er wachs ene		full-grown; of age
Ge wächs	nn	plant, vegetable; herb; produce, growth
ge wachs en	a	natural, undisturbed
nach wachs en		grow again; grow up
ver wachs en		grow together; close up, heal up; become overgrown
ver wachs en	a	deformed, crooked; hunchbacked; dense, thick
Ver wachs ung		deformity
Zu wachs	nm	increase, increment, accretion
zu wachs en		become overgrown
zusammen wachs en		grow together
her an wachs en		grow up
her aus wachs en		sprout out, grow out
hin aus wachs en		outgrow
hin ein wachs en		grow into one's part
aus ge wachs en	a	full-grown; full-fledged

Wachs	nn	wax
wachs en		wax s.t.
wächs ern	a	wax; waxen, waxy
ein wachs en		wax s.t., wax a floor
ver wachs en		rub with the wrong type of wax

Waff e	weapon; arm; branch of the armed forces
waff en fäh ig	capable of bearing arms

waff en los	weaponless, unarmed
waff n en	arm
be waff n en	arm; equip with arms, provide weapons
Be waff n ung	arming; arms, weapons
ent waff n en	disarm
Ent waff n ung	disarming, disarmament
un be waff n et	unarmed, defenseless

wäg bar		weighable; ponderable
Wag nis	nn	venture, risk, hazard
ab wäg en		weigh out; level; weigh, consider carefully
aus wäg en		weigh s.t. out
sich 'durch wag en	s	venture through
er wäg en		weight, consider, deliberate; examine; take into account
Er wäg ung		consideration, reflection
ge wag t		daring; risky, precarious; risque
sich hin wag en	s	venture to, venture near a place
un wäg bar		imponderable
Un wäg bar keit		imponderability
sich vor wag en		venture forward
sich her an wag en		venture near, dare to approach
sich her aus wag en		venture out
sich hin aus wag en	s	venture out
sich hin ein wag en		want to go in
sich her vor wag en		venture forth

Wahl	nf	choice; alternative; selection; option
wähl bar		eligible
Wähl bar keit		eligibility
wähl en		choose; select, pick out; take one's choice; elect
Wähl er		elector, voter; selector
wähl er isch		particular; choosy, dainty, fastidious
Wähl er schaft		constituency; voting population
wahl frei		optional, elective
wahl los		indiscriminate
Aus wahl	nf	choice, selection
aus wähl en		choose, select, pick out, single out
'durch wähl en	t	dial through
er wähl en		choose, select, pick; elect, vote for
Fern wahl	nf t	telephone direct distance dialing
Nach wahl	nf	special election
Ur wahl	nf	preliminary election
Vor wahl	nf	preliminary election
Wieder wahl	nf	re-election
'wieder wähl en		re-elect
aus er wähl en		choose, select

wahr	a	true; real, genuine; proper; sincere, frank, open
wahr haft		true, veritable; truthful, veracious
wahr haft ig		true, veritable; truthful, veracious
Wahr haft ig keit		truthfulness, veracity

	Wahr heit	truth
	wahr lich av	truly, in truth; verily
sich be	währ en	prove good; prove a success; stand the test
	Be währ ung	verification; release on probation; crucial test
für	wahr av	indeed, truly
ge	währ en	become aware of; perceive, observe; discover, discern
un	wahr a	untrue, false
un	wahr haft ig	untruthful, insincere
Un	wahr heit	untruth, falsehood
sich be	wahr heit en	prove to be true
ver	wahr los en	neglect
Ver	wahr los ung	neglect; demoralization
be	wahr heit en	verify

	wahr en	watch over; guard, defend; preserve, look after, protect
	währ en	last, continue
	währ end c	while, whilst; whereas, while
	Wahr ung	maintenance; safe-guarding, protection of interests
	Währ ung	currency; gold standard
be	wahr en	keep, preserve
Be	wahr er	keeper, custodian
Be	wahr ung	keeping; preservation
fort	währ en	last, continue, persist
fort	währ end av	continual, continuous; constant, perpetual
ge	wahr en	become aware of, perceive, observe, notice; discover, catch sight of
Ge	wahr sam nm	custody, care; safekeeping; control, detention
Ge	währ nf	guarantee, warrant, security, surety
ge	währ en	grant, allow, accord; concede; give, yield; offer
Ge	währ ung	granting, allowing
ver	wahr en	keep, guard
Ver	wahr ung	keeping, guard; charge, custody; safekeeping
auf be	wahr en	keep; preserve
Auf be	wahr ung	keeping, preservation, storage

	Wald nm	wood, forest; woodland, wooded area
	Wäld chen	little wood, grove
	wald ig	woody, wooded
	wald reich	rich in forests, well-wooded
	Wald ung	wooded area, woodland, forest
be	wald et	wooded, woody
ent	wald en	clear of forest, deforest
Hinter	wäld ler	backwoodsman
Ur	wald nm	primeval forest, jungle

	wand: siehe wend	
	Wand nf	wall; partition; screen, panel
	Wand ung	side, inner wall; wall of a blood vessel
Vor	wand nf	pretext, pretence; plea, excuse, subterfuge

Zwischen	wand	nf	partition, wall, bulkhead

Auf	wand	nm		expenditure, expense, costs; waste; luxury, pomp
Aussen	wand	nf		exterior wall
Be	wand	t nis		condition, state; circumstances
Ein	wand	nm		objection
Ge	wand	nn	p	garment, gown, dress, attire, vestment
	ge	wand	t	agile, quick, clever, skillful; ingenious; easy, experienced
Ge	wand	t heit		agility, quickness, dexterity, cleverness, skill; fluency
Rück	wand	nf		back wall, rear wall
	ver	wand	t a	related to, akin to, kindred; congenial; cognate
Ver	wand	te		relation, relative, kinsman
Ver	wand	t schaft		relationship, relations; congeniality, affinity
	ver	wand	t schaft lich	allied, congenial, kindred
an	ge	wand	t	practical, applied science
un	ge	wand	t	unskillful, awkward, clumsy
an	ver	wand	t a	related to
un	ver	wand	t	fixed, unmoved, steadfast

	wandel:	siehe wend	
	Wandel	nm	change
	wandel	bar	changeable; variable
	Wandel	bar keit	changeableness, inconstancy
	wandel	n	walk; wander, travel
sich	wandel	n	change, alter, vary
	wand	l ung s fäh ig	versatile, adaptable, changeable, capable of change
	Wand	l ung	change, transformation; rehabilitation, conversion
ab	wandel	en	vary, modify; decline a noun, conjugate a verb
Ab	wandel	ung	modification; noun declension, verb conjugation
an	wandel	n	befall, seize; come over s.o., come upon s.o.
um	wandel	bar	transformable, convertible
um	'wandel	n	walk around s.t.
'um	wandel	n	change, transform, convert; turn s.t. into s.t.
um	'wandel	n p	walk around s.t.
un	wandel	bar	immutable, unchangeable, unshakable
Un	wandel	bar keit	immutability
ver	wandel	n	change; turn, convert; transform
An	wand	l ung	fit, slight attack; sudden impulse
Um	wand	l ung	transformation, transmutation, conversion; promotion; assembly
Ver	wand	l ung	conversion, change, transformation, metamorphosis; reduction

	wander:	siehe wend	
	Wander	er	wanderer, traveler; hiker
	wander	n	wander, travel; ramble, hike; migrate; shift; creep
	Wander	ung	walking-tour, hike
	Wand	r erin	wanderer, traveler; hiker
ab	wander	n	wander away; drift away; migrate

Ab wander ung	migration; exodus
Aus wander er	emigrant
aus wander n	emigrate, migrate; get out of range
Aus wander ung	emigration, immigration
be wander t	experienced, skilled in; well-acquainted with, proficient in
durch 'wander n	wander through, pass through
Ein wander er	immigrant
ein wander n	immigrate
Ein wander ung	immigration
Rück wander er	returning emigrant
unter 'wander n	infiltrate
Unter wander ung	infiltration
zu wander n	immigrate
un be wander t	inexperienced, not versed in, unskilled in
her um wander n	wander around

warm a	warm, hot
Wärm e	warmth; heat; temperature
wärm en	warm, make warm, make hot; heat
Ab wärm e	waste heat
an wärm en	warm up, take the chill off; preheat
auf wärm en	warm up; bring up again, rake up, rehash
durch 'wärm en	warm through
sich 'durch wärm en	warm o.s. through, get warm
er wärm en	warm, heat
sich er wärm en	grow warm; warm up
Er wärm ung	warming
vor wärm en	warm up, preheat

warn en	warn of, caution against
Warn er	warner, admonisher
Warn ung	warning; admonition; caution
ent warn en	sound the all-clear signal
Ent warn ung	all-clear signal
ver warn en	warn off, admonish; caution
Ver warn ung	warning, admonition; caution
Vor warn ung	early warning

Wart e	watch-tower; look-out; switchboard gallery; level
wart en	wait; stay
Wärt er	attendant; guard; prison warden, keeper
Wärt erin	female attendant; nurse
Wart ung	attendance, tending; nursing; maintenance, servicing
ab wart en	wait for, await
ab wart end	observant, temporizing
An wärt er	aspirant; candidate; applicant
An wart schaft	candidacy, qualification, expectancy; reversion
auf wart en	wait on, attend on
Auf wart ung	attendance, service; visit
er wart en	expect; look forward to; wait for, await; anticipate

Er	wart	ung	expectation; hope; expectancy
ge	wärt	ig	expecting; expectant of
zu	wart	en s	wait; wait and see
un er	wart	et	unexpected; unforeseen, as a surprise

ab	wärt	s av	down, downward
auf	wärt	s av	upward, up; uphill
aus	wärt	ig	out-of-town; non resident; foreign, external
aus	wärt	s av	outward; away from home; out of doors, out of town; abroad
ein	wärt	s av	inward
Gegen	wart	nf	presence, present
gegen	wärt	ig av	present
her	wärt	s av	on the way here, this way
hinter	wärt	s av	backward
nieder	wärt	s av	downward, down
rück	wärt	ig	rear, at the back
rück	wärt	s av	back, backwards
unter	wärt	s av	downwards
vor	wärt	s av	forward, onward
wider	wärt	ig	unpleasant, disagreeable; repulsive; disgusting, loathsome
Wider	wärt	ig keit	unpleasantness, repulsiveness, nastiness, nuisance
ge	wärt	ig en	expect, await; be prepared for, reckon with
ver gegen	wärt	ig en	bring s.t. to mind; visualize s.t., realize s.t.
Ver gegen	wärt	ig ung	realization, visualization

	wasch bar	washable; fast color
	Wäsch e	wash; washing; laundry; linen; underwear; lingerie
	wasch en	wash; launder; shampoo; scour
	Wäsch er	washer; laundryman
	Wäsch erei	laundry; scouring mill for wool
	Wäsch erin	washerwoman, laundress
	Wasch ung	washing; ablution
ab	wasch en	wash off; wash down body, bathe; sponge off; wash away
auf	wasch en	wash up
aus	wasch en	wash out, cleanse; rinse, bathe; erode
Ge	wäsch nn s	balderdash, nonsense
Unter	wäsch e	underwear, underclothing
ver	wasch en	use up in washing; washed out, faded; pale; vapid
un ge	wasch en a	unwashed

	Wasser nn	water
	wasser arm	ill supplied with water; arid
	wässer ig	watery; diluted, weak
	wasser n	land on water, touch down on water
	wässer n	water; irrigate; soak, steep; wash; hydrate
	wasser reich	abounding in water; of high humidity
	Wasser ung	landing on water, splashdown
	Wässer ung	watering, irrigation; soaking, steeping; washing
	wäss r ig	watery; diluted, weak

Ab wasser	nn	waste water, sewage
be wässer n		water; irrigate
Be wässer ung		watering, irrigation
ent wässer n		drain
Ent wässer ung		drainage, draining
Ge wässer	nn	waters
Ober wasser	nn	upper water
ver wässer n		water, dilute; water s.t. down

Wechsel	nm	change; reverse; exchange; succession, fluctuation; bill
wechsel haft		changeable, alterable
wechsel n		change; vary; exchange
wechsel voll		changeable; eventful
Wechs l er		money-changer; exchange banker
ab wechsel n		alternate; vary
aus wechsel n		exchange, interchange; replace; change
Aus wechsel ung		exchange, interchange; replacement; changing
ein wechsel n		change; exchange; cash s.t.
Rück wechsel	nm	re-draft, re-exchange
'um wechsel n		change money
ver wechsel n		change by mistake; exchange; confound; confuse with
un ver wechsel bar		unmistakable
Ab wechs l ung		change, alternation, variation; variety, diversity; diversion
Ver wechs l ung		mistake; confusion; mix-up
ab wechsel nd		alternate, alternating; varying; periodic

---

weck en	awake, waken, call; rouse
Weck er	awakener; alarm clock; bell; ringer
auf weck en	rouse from sleep, awaken s.o.; rouse, animate, enliven
ein weck en	preserve, pickle; pot; can
er weck en	awaken; rouse, stir up; raise; arouse, excite
Er weck ung	resuscitation, revival
ge weck t	alert, wide-awake, lively; bright
auf er weck en	raise from the dead; restore to life, resuscitate
Auf er weck ung	raising; resuscitation
auf ge weck t	intelligent, bright, alert, quick-witted

---

weg	av	away, off; gone; lost
Weg	nm	way; path; road; route; manner, method; course; direction; errand
Ab weg	nm	detour; wrong way
ab weg ig		devious, misleading; wrong, out of place; irrelevant
Aus weg	nm	exit, way out
aus weg los		hopeless
Aus weg los ig keit		hopelessness
be weg en		move, stir; set in motion; carry, convey; fluctuate, vary

sich be weg en			move, stir
be weg lich			movable, moving, mobile; flexible; portable
Be weg lich keit			mobility, movableness; flexibility
Be weg t heit			agitation, turbulence; emotion
Be weg ung			movement, motion
be weg ung s los			motionless, immobile
Be weg ung s los ig keit			immobility
Hin weg	nm		the way there
hin weg	av		away, off
Neben weg	nm		byroad
Rück weg	nm		return way; return route
Um weg	nm		roundabout way, detour
un weg sam			impassable, pathless
Un weg sam keit			impassability
unter weg s	av		on the way, en route; in transit
ver weg en	a		daring, bold, audacious; rakish
Ver weg en heit			boldness, audacity, dare-devilry, temerity
vor weg	av		beforehand; from the beginning, to begin with
zu weg e	av		manage s.t., succeed in doing s.t.; materialize, come off
fort be weg en			move on, move away; propel, drive
Fort be weg ung			locomotion; progression
Gegen be weg ung			countermovement
un be weg lich			immovable; motionless; fixed, rigid, stationary
Un be weg lich keit			immovableness, immobility
un ent weg t	av		unswerving, unflinching, stalwart
kein es weg s	av		by no means; not at all, in no way

weh	a		sore, painful, aching
Weh	nn		pain; grief, woe
Weh e			drift
Weh en	np		labor-pains, travail
an weh en			blow upon, breath against
Fern weh	nn		wanderlust
Nach weh en	np		afterpains
'um weh en			blow down
um 'weh en			blow around, waft around, fan
ver weh en			blow away; scatter; cover with snow
Ver weh ung			sand drift, snow drift
zu weh en			blow toward; block up with sand

weich	a		soft; tender; supple, pliable; tender-hearted
Weich e			flank, side; groin; switch
weich en			give way, yield; fall back, retreat; ease off, recede
Weich heit			softness; tenderness; smoothness; suppleness; flabbiness
weich lich			soft, tender; sloppy; weak, effeminate; indolent
Weich ling			weakling, sissy, softie
ab weich en			deviate, diverge
auf weich en			soften, mollify; soak, moisten; temper
'durch weich en			soften; soak, drench
ein weich en			soak, steep, macerate

er weich en		soften; mollify; move, touch
er weich end		softening; emollient
Er weich ung		softening; mollification
ver weich lich en		render effeminate, coddle
Ver weich lich ung		effeminacy, softness
sich er weich en		relent, yield, give in

ab weich en		deviate, diverge
ab weich end		divergent, varying
Ab weich ung		deviation; difference, discrepancy
aus weich en		turn aside, make way; avoid; dodge
ent weich en		escape, run away, abscond
zurück weich en		fall back; give ground
un aus weich lich		inevitable, unavoidable

weil	c	because, since
weil and	av	formerly, erstwhile, onetime; deceased
Weil e		a while, a time; leisure
weil en		stay; linger, tarry
Weil er		hamlet
ver weil en		stay, linger
zu weil en	av	at times, sometimes; occasionally, now and then
un ver weil t		without delay, immediately

wein en		weep for, shed tears over, cry
wein er lich		tearful, lachrymose; whining, crying
sich aus wein en		cry one's fill, have a good cry
be wein en		weep for, deplore, lament, mourn
Be wein ung		mourn over the loss of, bewail the death of
nach wein en		mourn over the loss of, bewail the death of
ver wein t		tear-stained; red with tears

Wein	nm	wine; vine
Nach wein	nm	inferior wine from the last pressing

Weis e		manner, way, mode, fashion, style
weis e	a	wise; sage, prudent
weis en		point out, show
Weis er		pointer; signpost
weis heit s voll		wisdom
weis lich		wisely, prudently
Weis ung		direction; instruction, order
ab weis en		refuse, reject, turn down; dismiss, beat back, repulse
Ab weis ung		refusal, rejection; dismissal, repulse; rebuff
an weis en		teach, instruct; direct, order; assign, allot
auf weis en		show, present; exhibit, produce
Aus weis	nm	statement, certificate, identification papers, permit
aus weis en		expel, eject; banish, exile; deport, evict; present, prove
sich aus weis en		establish one's identity, show one's papers, show o.s.

Aus weis ung	expulsion; deportation; eviction; proof of identity
Be weis nm	proof, argument, evidence, exhibit, demonstration
be weis bar	provable, demonstrable
Be weis bar keit	demonstrability
be weis en	prove, show, evidence; establish; demonstrate; substantiate
ein weis en	direct, guide; install; assign to; vector a plane
Ein weis ung	guidance; installation; assignment; vectoring; briefing
Er weis nm	render, do; prove
er weis en	prove, show; render
sich er weis en	show o.s., become apparent, become clear
er weis lich	provable, demonstrable
Hin weis nm	reference; hint, allusion; instruction; pointer; indication
hin weis en	point out s.t., draw attention to s.t., indicate s.t.; hint at s.t.
Miss weis ung	aberration, variation
Nach weis nm	proof, evidence, indication, reference; information; list; direction
nach weis bar	provable, demonstrable; traceable, detectable; evident
nach weis en	point out, refer to, prove, establish; identify; detect
nach weis lich	demonstrable, evident, authentic
Nach weis ung	evidence; voucher; record, certificate
über 'weis en	assign, transfer; refer to; devolve upon; remit
Ueber weis ung	remittance; transmission, transfer; assignment
unter 'weis en	teach, instruct
Unter weis ung	instructions, information, indoctrination
Ver weis nm	reprimand, reproof, censure; reference
ver weis en	banish, exile
ver weis en	refer to a page; remit money; reprove, reprimand
Ver weis ung	banishment, expulsion; reference
Ver weis ung	reference
vor weis en	show, produce, exhibit
zu weis en	allot to, appropriate, assign to; introduce; recommend to
Zu weis ung	assignment, appropriation, allotment
zurück weis en	send away, send back; decline, refuse, turn down; repulse
Zurück weis ung	refusal, rejection; rebuff, repulse; dismissal, repudiation
un ab weis bar	not to be refused; imperative, peremptory; inevitable
un ab weis lich	not to be refused; imperative, peremptory; inevitable
Gegen be weis nm	proof to the contrary
un be weis bar	unprovable, undemonstrable

weit a	distant; wide; broad, spacious; vast, immense; loose

Weit e		wideness, width; diameter
weit en		widen; enlarge; expand; stretch; widen, broaden
weit er	a	wider; more distant; farther, further; additional, further, moreover
Weit er e	nn	what follows, the rest, everything else
Weit ung		widening
aus weit en		widen; expand, stretch, spread; extend
Aus weit ung		widening; expansion; extension
un weit	p	not far from, close to
er weit er n		widen, enlarge, expand, extend; dilate
sich er weit er n		widen, enlarge, expand, extend; dilate
Er weit er ung		widening, expansion, enlargement
so weit		so far as, as far as

Welt	nf	world
welt lich		worldly, mundane; secular, temporal, profane
Aussen welt	nf	outer world
Innen welt	nf	world within us, inner life
Mit welt	nm	the present generation
Nach welt	nf	posterity, future generations
Ober welt	nf	upper world
über welt lich		ultramundane
Um welt	nf	environment, the world around us
Unter welt	nf	underworld, hades
Ur welt	nf	primeval world
ur welt lich		primeval, antediluvian
Vor welt	nf	former ages; prehistoric world
vor welt lich		prehistoric; antediluvian
ver welt lich en		secularize
Ver welt lich ung		secularization

Wend e		turning point; turn; front vault; dismount
Wend el	nf	coil, helix
wend en		turn around, turn over; reverse, change direction
wend ig		nimble, agile, maneuverable; flexible; versatile, resourceful
Wend ig keit		nimbleness, agility, maneuverability, flexibility, versatility
Wend ung		turn, turning, facing, change
ab wend bar		preventable, avertible
ab wend en		turn away, parry, prevent; alienate
ab wend ig		alienate; withdraw
an wend bar		applicable, available for, practicable
An wend bar keit		applicability, practicableness
an wend en		employ, apply, make use of
An wend ung		application, use
auf wend en		spend, waste
Auf wend ung		expense, expenditure
aus wend ig	av	by memory, by heart; exterior, outside, outward
be wend en		leave it at s.t., acquiesce in
ein wend en		object to, demure, plead
Ein wend ung		objection; exception; protest; defense, plea

ent wend en		steal, pilfer, embezzle, misappropriate
Ent wend ung		pilfering, purloining, embezzlement, misappropriation
in wend ig		interior, inward, inside, internal
über wend lich		whipped
'um wend en		turn over
ver wend bar		available, usable, applicable, practical
Ver wend bar keit		availability, utilization, utility, usefulness
ver wend en		apply to, employ in, use, utilize; spend, expend, invest
Ver wend ung		application, use, utilization, investment; intercession
weg wend en		turn away, avert
zu wend en		turn towards; procure for s.o.; let s.o. have, give; devote to
Zu wend ung		gift, donation; allowance; gratification; bestowal
un ab wend bar		inevitable, fatal
not wend ig		necessary
Not wend ig keit		necessity

---

	werf en		throw, fling, hurl, cast, toss; drop; project, emit
sich werf en			buckle, distort
Werf er			pitcher; mortar, launcher
Werf t	nm	shipyard, dockyard
ab werf en			throw off, cast off; yield a profit; shed, discard
an werf en			throw first; set in motion, start, crank up; throw into gear
auf werf en			cast up; fling open a door; dig; raise a question
aus werf en			throw out, fling out; eject, reject; vomit, disgorge
Aus werf er			ejector, extractor
be werf en			throw upon, throw at; pelt; rough-cast, plaster
ein werf en			throw in; break; mail a letter; object; interject
ent werf en			design, plan, sketch, outline; draw up, devise; project
fort werf en			throw away
hin werf en			throw down, fling down; write down
nach werf en			throw s.t. after s.o.
nieder werf en			throw down; crush, supress; overwhelm
'über werf en			throw over; slip on; huddle on
sich über 'werf en			fall out with, quarrel
'um werf en	s	overturn, upset; throw over; put on; overthrow, knock down
unter 'werf en			subdue, subject, subjugate
Unter werf ung			subduing, subjection; surrender, acquiescence
ver werf en			reject, refuse, repudiate, abandon; dislocate
sich ver werf en			warp; be dislocated
ver werf lich			blameable, objectionable, reprehensible
Ver werf lich keit			blameableness, reprehensibleness, badness
Ver werf ung			rejection; warping, fault; dislocation
vor werf en			throw forward, throw before; reproach, upbraid with, blame for
weg werf en			throw away, cast away

zu werf en	throw to; fill up; slam the door
zurück werf en	throw back, repulse; reflect; reverberate, echo; bend back
zusammen werf en	throw together; confound; mix up, jumble up; lump together
hin aus werf en	throw out, cast out, expel; fire s.o.; throw away
hin über werf en	throw across
her um werf en	throw around; turn sharply
her unter werf en	throw down; dump
hin unter werf en	throw down
'durch ein ander werf en	mix up, muddle up

wert a	worth; worthy; dear; esteemed, valued
Wert nm	value; worth; equivalent; price; asset; standard; valence; use
wert en	value; appraise; judge; classify; rate; score; evaluate; admit
Wert ig keit	valence
wert los	worthless, valueless; useless; futile
Wert ung	valuation; appraisal, estimate; rating; judging; scoring
wert voll	valuable, precious
ab wert en	devaluate, devalorize
Ab wert ung	devaluation
auf wert en	revalorize
Auf wert ung	revalorization, revaluation
aus wert en	evaluate; analyze, interpret; estimate; make full use of
Aus wert ung	evaluation; analysis; interpretation; utilization
be wert en	value; price; assess, estimate, appraise; rate, grade
Be wert ung	valuation, estimation, assessment
Bei wert nm	coefficient
ent wert en	depreciate, devaluate; withdraw money from circulation
Ent wert ung	depreciation, devaluation; withdrawal; defacement, cancellation
Gegen wert nm	equivalent
'um wert en	revalue, convert
Um wert ung	revaluation, conversion of currency
ver wert bar	realizable; usable; convertible, negotiable
ver wert en	utilize, make use of; evaluate; realize; commercialize, exploit
Ver wert ung	utilization; realization; commercialization; exploitation
voll wert ig	full, of full value; up to standard
'über be wert en	overvalue

Wes en nn	being, creature; entity; essence, substance; nature; bearing
wes en haft	substantial, real; characteristic
wes en los	unsubstantial; unreal, shadowy

wes ent lich	essential, substantial; material, vital; fundamental
ab wes end	absent, away; not in; missing; absent-minded, lost in thought
Ab wes ende	absentee
Ab wes en heit	absence, absenteeism
An wes en nn	property, real estate, premises
an wes end	present
An wes en heit	presence; attendance
Un wes en nn	nuisance; excesses
un wes ent lich	unessential, immaterial, unimportant, negligable
ver wes en	putrefy, decay, decompose
Ver wes er nm	administrator; vice-regent
ver wes lich	corruptible, putrefiable
Ver wes ung	decay, putrefaction, decomposition
un ver wes lich	incorruptible
Un ver wes lich keit	incorruptibility

Wetter nn	weather; storm, bad weather; thunderstorm
wetter n	be stormy; storm, thunder; swear at s.o.
Un wetter nn	stormy weather; thunderstorm

wicht: siehe wieg	
Wicht nm	creature, elf, goblin, gnome; fellow; little person
Wicht e	specific gravity, weight per unit volume
wicht ig	important, momentous; essential; vital; weighty
Wicht ig keit	importance, import, moment; seriousness
Ge wicht nn	weight; load
Ge wicht nn h	weight; load
ge wicht ig	weighty, heavy, ponderous; important, momentous; influential
un wicht ig	unimportant, insignificant
Un wicht ig keit	insignificance
Gegen ge wicht nn	counterweight, counterpoise, counterbalance
Ueber ge wicht nn	overweight; preponderance, superiority
Unter ge wicht nn	underweight

Wickel nm	roller, roll, packing
wickel n	wind, roll, coil; reel, spool; wrap up; swathe
ab wickel n	unwind, reel off, uncoil, adjust, liquidate debt; effect
auf wickel n	roll up, turn up; wind, spool; unwind, unfold, unwrap
aus wickel n	unwrap, unfold, unswathe a baby
ein wickel n	wrap up; envelop, swaddle a child; trick s.o.
ent wickel n	develop, evolve, work out, cultivate, form
sich ent wickel n	develop, evolve, form, grow; deploy
um 'wickel n	wind around, lap around; tape; cover; wrap up
ver wickel n	entangle; embroil, engage in; complicate a matter
zusammen wickel n	wrap up; roll up
un ent wickel t	undeveloped
her um wickel n s	wind around, wrap around, twist around
aus ein ander wickel n	disentangle

Ab wick l er	liquidator
Ab wick l ung	unwinding; transaction, settlement; execution, carrying out
Ent wick l er	developer
Ent wick l ung	development
Ver wick l ung	entanglement, implication; complication; confusion, tangle
Weiter ent wick l ung	development

wider p	against, contrary to, in opposition to, versus, in the face of
wider lich	repugnant, repulsive; distasteful, disgusting
Wider lich keit	repulsiveness; loathsomeness
wider wärt ig	unpleasant, disagreeable; repulsive; disgusting, nasty; odious
Wider wärt ig keit	unpleasantness, repulsiveness; nastiness; nuisance
wid r ig	adverse, untoward, contrary
Wid r ig keit	contrariety, unpleasantness; repulsiveness, loathsomeness; adversity
an wider n	disgust, nauseate, sicken
er wider n	return, reciprocate; reply, answer, rejoin; retort
Er wider ung	return, reciprocation; retaliation
zu wider p	contrary to, opposed to, against; repugnant, distasteful, hateful
un er wider t	unanswered; unreturned, unrequited

Wieg e	cradle
wieg en	weigh; have a weight of
sich wieg en	rock; sway, seesaw, teeter
ab wieg en	weigh out
auf wieg en	offset, compensate for, make up for
aus wieg en	weigh out; balance out
ein wieg en	rock child to sleep; lull s.o. to sleep
ge wieg t s	experienced, seasoned; smart, shrewd, clever, astute
nach wieg en	weigh over again, check
über 'wieg en	outweigh
'über wieg en	outweigh
vor wieg en	preponderate, predominate

wiegel: siehe wieg	
Auf wiegel ei	incitement, instigation, agitation; sedition
auf wiegel n	stir up, incite, instigate, agitate
Auf wiegel ung	incitement, instigation, agitation; sedition

wies: siehe weis	
er wies en a	proven, shown; rendered
un be wies en a	not proven, not demonstrated
an ge wies en a	dependent on; on one's own

Will e nm	will; volition; intention; determination
will en los	lacking will-power, irresolute; spineless

Will en los ig keit	lack of will-power; indecision
will en t lich	deliberately
will ig	willing, ready; docile
will ig en	consent to s.t., agree to s.t.; approve of s.t.
Will ig keit	willingness; zeal
ge will t	willing, prepared, ready, inclined; determined
Un will e nm	indignation, displeasure, anger; unwillingness
un will ig	indignant, displeased; annoyed, angry; unwilling, reluctant
Wider will e nm	aversion, dislike, loathing; reluctance
wider will ig	unwilling, reluctant; grudging
be will ig en	grant, allow, accord; license; appropriate; allocate
Be will ig ung	grant, allowance; vote; allocation, allotment; license
ein will ig en	consent, agree, acquiesce in, approve of
Ein will ig ung	consent, approval

Wind nm	wind; flatulence
wind ig	windy, windswept; giddy, frivolous person; precarious, shaky
Ab wind nm	down-current
Auf wind nm	up-wind, up-current, anabatic wind
Gegen wind nm	head wind

Wind e	winch, windlass, hoist; reel
Wind el nf	diaper, baby's napkin
wind en	wind, twist, twirl; coil; reel
wind en	squirm, writhe; wind, meander; wriggle
Wind ung	winding, turn, convolution; bend, coil; thread of screw
ab wind en	reel off, unwind
auf wind en	wind up; lift, jack up, hoist, raise, weigh anchor
'durch wind en	wind through
sich 'durch wind en	wind through, worm one's way through
Ge wind e nn	winding; garland, festoon; wreath; skein; coil
um 'wind en	wind around, entwine
sich her aus wind en	extricate o.s. wriggle out of s.t.
aus wind en	wring out
über 'wind en	overpower, overcome; conquer
Ueber wind er	conqueror
Ueber wind ung	conquest; overcoming, surmounting
ver wind en	overcome, get over

Winkel nm	angle; corner, nook; recess; chevron; square; phase angle
winkel ig	angular; full of corners, crooked lane; angled
Gegen winkel nm	corresponding angle
Innen winkel nm	interior angle
Neben winkel nm t	adjacent angle

Winter nm	winter
winter lich	wintry

Nach winter nm	late winter, second winter
über 'winter n	pass the winter; hibernate
Ueber winter ung	hibernation

---

wirk en	work wonders, cause, effect; knit, weave; knead dough
Wirk er	knitter, weaver
Wirk erei	knitting, weaving
wirk lich	real, actual; true, genuine, substantial
Wirk lich keit	reality, actuality; truth; real life
wirk sam	effective, efficacious, efficient; operative
Wirk sam keit	efficacy; effectiveness; efficiency; impressiveness
Wirk ung	effect; action; consequence; result; reaction
wirk ung s los	inefficacious, ineffectual, inefficient
Wirk ung s los ig keit	inefficacy, inefficiency
wirk ung s voll	impressive, effective, efficient, effectual, forcible
wirk ung s weise	mode of action; working; mechanism
aus wirk en	work out; knead dough; effect, bring about
sich aus wirk en	take effect, operate, make itself felt
Aus wirk ung	effect; result, outcome; consequence, impact, aftermath
be wirk en	effect; cause
durch 'wirk en	interweave
ein wirk en	act on s.o., have an effect on s.o., influence s.o.
Ein wirk ung	action, operation, effect; influence
er wirk en	obtain, procure; effect, bring about
Fern wirk ung t	distant effect; radiation effect; telepathy
Gegen wirk ung	countereffect, reaction
mit wirk en	cooperate, contribute to, assist in, take part in
Mit wirk ende nf	performer, actor, player
Mit wirk ung	cooperation, contribution, assistance, concurrence
nach wirk en	act afterwards; produce an after-effect, be felt afterwards
Nach wirk ung	after-effect, consequences
Neben wirk ung	secondary effect
rück wirk end	reacting; retroacting; having retroactive effect
Rück wirk ung	retroaction; retrospectiveness
un wirk lich	unreal
un wirk sam	ineffective, inoperative, inefficient; inactive
Un wirk sam keit	inefficiency, inoperativeness
ver wirk en	forfeit; incur, be liable to a penalty
zurück wirk en	react; have a retroactive effect
zusammen wirk en	cooperate, collaborate, work together; combine
ent gegen wirk en	counter a view, work against a plan; counteract s.t.
ver wirk lich en	realize, translate into reality
Ver wirk lich ung	realization
sich ver wirk lich en	be realized, materialize; come true

Wirt nm	host; landlord; innkeeper, saloonkeeper
wirt lich	hospitable; habitable
Wirt schaft	housekeeping; economy; trade and industry, economics

wirt schaft en	keep house, run the household; economize
Wirt schaft erin	manageress; housekeeper
Wirt schaft ler	economist, economic expert
wirt schaft lich	economic; financial; commercial; thrifty; efficient, profitable
Wirt schaft lich keit	economy; good management; efficiency; profitability
be wirt en	entertain, treat to
Be wirt ung	entertainment, reception
un wirt lich	inhospitable, desolate
ab wirt schaft en	get ruined, ruin o.s. by mismanagement
be wirt schaft en	cultivate, till a field, manage, administer; ration
Be wirt schaft ung	cultivation; management; administration; control, rationing
Miss wirt schaft nf	maladministration, mismanagement
un wirt schaft lich	uneconomical, unthrifty; inefficient
ver wirt schaft en	squander away
ab ge wirt schaft et	ruined by mismanagement; exhausted, run down
her um wirt schaft en s	rummage around
Land wirt nm	farmer; agriculturalist
Land wirt schaft	agriculture, farming; farm
land wirt schaft lich	agricultural; rural, agrarian

Wisch nm	wisp of straw; scrap of paper
wisch en	wipe, mop
sich wisch en	wipe one's mouth; mop one's brow
Wisch er	windshield wiper; slush brush; stump for drawing
ab wisch en	wipe off, dust off; mop, sponge
auf wisch en	wipe up, mop up, clean up
aus wisch en	wipe out; wipe off, obliterate, efface; sponge out
'durch wisch en	invincible, impregnable, insurmountable; insuperable
ent wisch en	slip away, escape; give s.o. the slip, elude s.o.
er wisch en s	catch, get hold of
ver wisch en	wipe out, blot out; efface; blur, obscure; smear
sich ver wisch en	become effaced, get blurred; vanish, become indistinct
weg wisch en	wipe off; sponge off; blot out

wiss: siehe weis	
wiss en	know about, know of
Wiss en nn	knowledge; learning; scholarship, erudition; information
Wiss en schaft	science; knowledge; intelligence
Wiss en schaft ler	man of learning, scholar; scientist, scientific man
wiss en schaft lich	scientific
wiss en t lich	knowing, conscious; willful, deliberate
ge wiss a	sure, certain, positive, fixed
Ge wiss en nn	conscience
ge wiss en haft	reliable, accurate, exact; scrupulous, thorough; careful
Ge wiss en haft ig keit	conscientiousness; reliability, accuracy, exactness

ge wiss en los	without conscience, unscrupulous; irresponsible, reckless
Ge wiss en los ig keit	unscrupulousness; irresponsibility, recklessness
Ge wiss heit	certainty, conviction; assurance, certitude
ge wiss lich av	certainly, surely, definitely
mit wiss en	joint knowledge; cognizance, privity
Mit wiss er	person in on a secret; confidant; accessory, privy
Mit wiss er schaft	cognizance, knowledge
un wiss end	ignorant, uninformed; untaught, unlearned; innocent
Un wiss en heit	ignorance; innocence, guilelessness
un wiss en schaft lich	unscientific
Un wiss en schaft lich keit	lack of scientific accuracy
un wiss en t lich	unwitting, unknowing, unconscious
Vor wiss en nn s	foreknowledge, prescience
vor aus wiss en	foresee, anticipate, foreknow
un ge wiss a	uncertain, unsure; indefinite; doubtful, dubious, questionable
Un ge wiss heit	uncertainty, unsureness; doubt, dubiousness; vagueness
sich ver ge wiss er n	make sure of, ascertain
Natur wiss en schaft	natural science

wog: siehe wieg	
Ge wog en heit	favor, affection
um 'wog en	wash around

wohn en	live with; dwell, reside, lodge
wohn haft	resident, living
wohn lich	comfortable, livable; cozy, snug
Wohn ung	dwelling, habitation; lodgings, apartment, accomodation
An wohn er	neighbor
be wohn bar	habitable
Be wohn bar keit	habitable condition
be wohn en	inhabit, live in; reside in, occupy
Be wohn er	inhabitant, resident; citizen; occupant, inmate; tenant
bei wohn en	assist at, attend; witness
Bei wohn ung	presence, attendance; sexual intercourse
Ein wohn er	inhabitant, resident
inne wohn en	be inherent in; be proper to, be characteristic of
um wohn end s	neighboring
Um wohn er s	inhabitant of the neighboring district, neighbor
un wohn lich	uncomfortable, cheerless
Mit be wohn er	co-inhabitant; fellow lodger
un be wohn bar	uninhabitable
un be wohn t	uninhabited; unoccupied, vacant; deserted
Ur be wohn er	original inhabitant, native
Ur ein wohn er	original inhabitant, native

ent wöhn en	disaccustom

Ent wöhn ung		weaning
ge wöhn en		accustom, habituate, get used to; inure to; familiarize
sich ge wöhn en		get accustomed to; become familiar with
Ge wohn heit		habit, wont; custom, practice
ge wöhn lich		common, general; ordinary, commonplace; usual, customary
ge wohn t		habitual, usual, wonted; traditional, customary
Ge wöhn ung		accustoming, habituation; inurement, acclimatization
ver wöhn en		spoil, coddle, pamper
ver wöhn t		pampered, spoilt; fastidious
Ver wöhn ung		spoiling; pampering
ab ge wöhn en		give up, leave off
an ge wöhn en		accustom
An ge wohn heit		habit, custom
ausser ge wöhn lich		extraordinary
sich ein ge wöhn en		accustom o.s. to, acclimatize; get used to
Ein ge wöhn ung		acclimatization; familiarization
un ge wöhn lich	a	unusual, uncommon; abnormal, odd, novel
un ge wohn t		unaccustomed

Wolk e		cloud; flaw
wolk en los		cloudless, clear
wolk ig		cloudy, clouded; overcast
sich be wölk en		cloud over, become cloudy; darken, overshadow
Be wölk ung		clouding; cloudiness, clouds
sich ent wölk en		clear, brighten
Ge wölk	nn	clouds
sich um 'wölk en		cloud over, darken

woll en		will; wish, desire; want; demand, claim; intend, be about to
hin woll en	s	want to go
zurück woll en		wish to return, want to go back
her aus woll en	s	want to get out
hin aus woll en	s	wish to get out
hin ein woll en	s	want to go in
un ge woll t		unintentional

Woll e		wool
woll en	a	woolen; worsted
woll ig		wooly
Ge wöll e	nn	undigested pellets from birds of prey

Wort	nn	word; term, expression; saying, word; word of honor
Wort e	np	words
wört lich		verbal, literal; word-for-word
wort reich		abundant in words; verbose, wordy
Wort reich tum	nm	abundancy of words; verbosity
Bei wort	nn	epithet; adjective

Für	wort	nn	pronoun
Nach	wort	nn	afterword in a book
Vor	wort	nn	foreknowledge, prescience
be für	wort	en	plead for; advocate, recommend; support, endorse
Be für	wort	ung	recommendation, endorsement, support

	wucher:	siehe wachs 1	
	Wucher	nm	usury, profiteering
	Wucher	ei	usury
	Wucher	er	usurer, profiteer
	wucher	isch	usurious, profiteering
	wucher	n	grow rampant, proliferate; spread rankly; practise usury; profiteer
	Wucher	ung	rank growth, proliferation; excrescence, tumor; vegetation
über	'wucher	n	overgrow, overrun

	wuchs:	siehe wachs 1	
	Wuchs	nm	growth; build, physique; stature, development
An	wuchs	nm	growth, growing of young trees; marine growth on a ship
Auf	wuchs	nm	upgrowth, young growth; vertical accretion
Aus	wuchs	nm	outgrowth; abuse; excresence, protuberance; products; aberrations
Be	wuchs	nm	vegetation, plants; marine growth, barnacles
Miss	wuchs	nm	misgrowth, monstrous growth, monstrosity
Nach	wuchs	nm	younger generation; offspring, progeny; trainees, recruits
ur	wüchs	ig	earthy; natural, native, original, elemental; rough, sturdy
Ur	wüchs	ig keit	earthiness; naturalness, originality; roughness, ruggedness

	wund	a	sore; galled, chafed; wounded
	Wund	e	wound, injury, lesion, abrasion, cut, sore
ver	wund	bar	vulnerable
ver	wund	en	wound
Ver	wund	ung	wounding, injury
un um	wund	en a	frank, plain, flat, blunt
un ver	wund	bar	invulnerable
Un ver	wund	bar keit	invulnerability

	Wunder	nn	miracle; wonder, marvel; prodigy
	wunder	bar	wonderful, marvelous; miraculous, astounding, fabulous
	wunder bar er weise av		miraculously; strange to say, mysteriously
	wunder	lich	quaint, odd, strange; whimsical; peculiar; eccentric
	Wunder	lich keit	strangeness, oddity; whimsicality; eccentricity
	wunder	n	surprise, astonish
sich	wunder	n	wonder at, be surprised at, be astonished at
	wunder	sam p	wondrous, wonderful
	wunder	voll	wonderful, marvelous, admirable

Be	wunder	er	admirer
Be	wunder	erin	admirer
be	wunder	n	admire, marvel at
Be	wunder	ung	admiration
ver	wunder	lich	astonishing, remarkable; wondrous, odd, strange
ver	wunder	n	astonish, amaze
Ver	wunder	ung	astonishment, surprise, amazement

Wunsch	nm	wish, desire; request; ambition
wünsch en		wish, desire; want; request
wünsch en s wert		desirable
wunsch ge mäss		as requested, as desired, according to one's wishes
wunsch los		worthy of, deserving, dignified
er wünsch t		desired, wished-for; desirable
ver wunsch en	a	enchanted; haunted
ver wünsch en		curse; enchant, bewitch
Ver wünsch ung		curse, imprecation
zurück wünsch en		wish back
un er wünsch t		undesirable, unwelcome

Würd e	dignity; position of honor, title, office
würd e los	undignified
würd e voll	dignified; solemn, grave
würd ig	worthy of; deserving of; dignified
würd ig en	appreciate, value; mention honorably; assess; praise
Würd ig ung	appreciation, assessment; valuation
un würd ig	unworthy; disgraceful; degrading
Un würd ig keit	unworthiness
ent würd ig en	degrade, disgrace, debase
Ent würd ig ung	degradation, debasement, disgrace
her ab würd ig en	degrade, abase; lower s.o. to the level of s.t.
Her ab würd ig ung	degradation, abasement

wurf:	siehe werf	
Wurf	nm	throw, cast, pitch; release
Würf el		cube, die, dice
würf el ig		cubical; chequered
würf el n		play dice, throw dice
Ab wurf	nm	throwing down, dropping; throw-off
An wurf	nm	throw-off, first throw; plastering, roughcast
Auf wurf	nm	mound, embankment
Aus wurf	nm	throwing out, ejection; eruption; spitting; refuse; outcast
Be wurf	nm	plastering, rough plaster, rough cast
Ein wurf	nm	slit, slot; letter box; charging, feeding; objection
Ent wurf	nm	design, plan, project; scheme, draft, blueprint
Ueber wurf	nm	wrapper, shawl; hasp
unter würf ig		submissive, obsequious
Unter würf ig keit		submission, submissiveness, obsequiousness
Vor wurf	nm	reproach, blame, reproof

vor	wurf s voll	reproachful
Zer	würf nis	discord, difference, disunion, disagreement, dissension, quarrel
ge	würf el t	checked, checkered, check-pattern; diced
zusammen	würf el n	jumble up, mix up in confusion

	Würz e	spice, condiment; seasoning, flavor; fragrance
	würz en	spice, season, flavor; give zest to, ginger up
	würz ig	spicy, well-seasoned, aromatic; piquant
Ge	würz nn	spice

	Wurzel nf	root; stem; bulb; carrot
	wurzel los	rootless
	wurzel n	take root, send out roots
an	wurzel n	strike root, take root
ein	wurzel n	take root, strike root
ent	wurzel n	uproot, unroot, deracinate
Ent	wurzel ung	uprooting
ver	wurzel t	deeply rooted in; firmly rooted
ein ge	wurzel t	deep-rooted; engrained, inveterate

	wuss: siehe wiss	
be	wuss t	conscious, known; deliberate; be conscious of s.t.
Be	wuss t heit	consciousness, awareness
be	wuss t los	unconscious, insensible, senseless
Be	wuss t los ig keit	unconsciousness, insensibility, senselessness
un be	wuss t	unconscious; unaware; instinctive, involuntary, subconscious
unter be	wuss t a	subconscious, marginal

	Zahl nf	number, figure; numeral, cipher, digit
	zahl bar	payable
	zähl bar	countable, computable
	zahl en	pay, settle, pay off; meet
	zähl en	count, number, keep score
	Zahl er	payer
	Zähl er	counter, teller; numerator; meter
	zahl los	numberless, innumerable, countless
	Zahl ung	payment, settlement, clearance, disbursement
	Zähl ung	counting, count, numeration, census, metering, registering
ab	zähl en	count out
ab	zahl en	pay s.t. off; pay s.t. in installments
Ab	zahl ung	partial payment, installment
An	zahl nf	number, quantity
an	zähl en	make a first payment; pay on account
an	zahl en	pay on account; pay a first installment on s.t.
An	zahl ung	partial payment, installment; deposit, downpayment
auf	zähl en	enumerate s.t., count up s.t., name s.t.
Auf	zähl ung	addition; enumeration, specification
aus	zahl en	pay out; pay s.t. off

aus zähl en		finish counting s.t.; count s.o. out in boxing
Aus zähl ung		count s.t. over
Aus zahl ung		payment; transfer of money by telegram
be zahl en		pay; discharge, settle a bill; pay for
Be zahl er		payer
Be zahl ung		payment; full settlement; fee, remuneration; pay, salary
'durch zähl en		count over
ein zahl en		pay s.t. in
Ein zahl er		depositor
Ein zahl ung		payment, bank deposit
er zähl en		tell, relate, narrate; tell stories
Er zähl er		narrator; writer, story teller
Er zähl ung		narrative; tale, story
her zähl en		enumerate s.t., count up s.t., name s.t.
hin zähl en		count down
mit zähl en		include in the account; be included in the account
nach zähl en		count s.t. over again
nach zahl en		pay late; pay in addition
Nach zahl ung		additional payment
rück zahl bar		repayable, redeemable, refundable
Rück zahl ung		repayment, reimbursement, refund; redemption
Ueber zahl nf		numerical superiority, majority
'über zähl en		count s.t. over
über zähl ig		surplus, supernumerary
Un zahl nf		endless number, legion
un zähl bar		countless, innumerable
un zähl ig		countless, innumerable
sich ver zähl en		miscount, make a mistake in counting
voll zähl ig		complete, integral; full strength; in full force
Voll zähl ig keit		completeness
vor zähl en		enumerate
weiter zahl en		pay further
zu zähl en		allot to, add to; count out to s.o.
zu zahl en		pay extra
Zu zahl ung		extra pay
zurück zahl en		pay s.t. back
zusammen zähl en		add up, count up
vor aus zahl en		pay in advance
Vor aus zahl ung		prepayment, anticipated payment
ab be zahl en		pay off debt; pay in installments
aus be zahl en s		pay s.t. to s.o.
nach be zahl en		pay afterwards, pay the remainder
Nach be zahl ung		subsequent payment
un be zahl bar		priceless; invaluable
un be zahl t		unpaid; outstanding accounts
nach er zähl en		repeat; retell
Nach er zähl ung		repetition; adaptation; reproduction
weiter er zähl en		pass a story on, not keep a story to o.s.
'wieder er zähl en		repeat, paraphrase, retell
un ge zähl t		unnumbered, innumerable, untold, numberless, countless

un voll zähl ig	incomplete
hin zu zähl en	add to
vor aus be zahl en	pay in advance, prepay
Vor aus be zahl ung	advance payment, prepayment

Zahn nm	tooth; fang; tusk; gear, cog
zahn en	cut one's teeth, be teething
zähn en	indent, notch; denticulate
zahn los	toothless
Zähn ung	serration; toothing
aus zahn en	tooth, indent
ver zahn en	tooth, gear a wheel; indent, dovetail; interlock
Ver zahn ung	tooth system, toothing
ge zähn t	toothed, cogged; notched; dentated; perforated

Zaun nm	fence
ab zäun en	fence off
ein zäun en	fence in
Ein zäun ung	enclosure; fence
um 'zäun en	fence in, enclose
Um zäun ung	enclosure, fence

Zeich en nn	sign, token; symbol; mark; indication, symptom; omen; warning
zeich n en	draw, delineate; design; draft, sketch, outline; sign; underwrite
Zeich n er	draughtsman, draftsman
Zeich n ung	drawing; sketch; design; illustration, figure, diagram; signature
Ab zeich en nn	mark of distinction; badge
an zeich en	sign, indication, mark; symptom; omen, warning
Gegen zeich en nn	countersign, check
Ver zeich nis	list, catalog; register; inventory, roll; index
vor zeich en	omen; prognostic; signature; accidental sign; preliminary symptom
ab zeich n en	copy, draw, sketch; mark off, check off an item
an zeich n en	mark, note; index
auf zeich n en	draw, sketch; note down; register, record
Auf zeich n ung	drawing; note; entry; record
aus zeich n en	mark out; label, ticket, price goods
sich aus zeich n en	distinguish o.s., excel
Aus zeich n ung	marking
be zeich n en	mark; label; designate, name; point out, show; characterize
be zeich n end	characteristic, typical; indicative of
Be zeich n ung	expression, manifestation
'durch zeich n en	trace
ein zeich n en	draw in, mark in; enter; slot; insert
Ein zeich n ung	mark, entry; subscription
ge zeich n et	drawn; signed
gegen zeich n en	countersign; endorse
Gegen zeich n ung	countersignature

nach zeich n en	draw from a model, copy; trace
Nach zeich n ung	copy, tracing
über 'zeich n en	oversubscribe
unter 'zeich n en	sign
Unter zeich n er	signer; subscriber
Unter zeich n ete	undersigned
Unter zeich n ung	signature, signing
ver zeich n en	note down; record, register; list, quote; misrepresent
vor zeich n en	draw s.t. for s.o., show s.o. how to draw s.t.
Vor zeich n ung	drawing copy, pattern, design
aus ge zeich n et	distinguished, decorated; excellent, outstanding, fine
mit unter zeich n en	add one's signature to; countersign
kenn zeich n en	characterize; mark

zeig en	show; present; point at, indicate; stand at; demonstrate
sich zeig en	show o.s.; appear, make an appearance; show up, turn up
Zeig er	hand
An zeig e	announcement, notification, notice
an zeig en	notify, announce; advise; point to; advertise; denounce
auf zeig en	show, present, set forth; make evident; point out; disclose
be zeig en	show, express, exhibit, manifest
Be zeig ung	expression, manifestation
her zeig en	show, let see
hin zeig en	point there, point at s.o.
vor zeig en	produce, show; exhibit
Vor zeig ung	producing, showing; exhibition
Vor an zeig e	advance notice, preliminary announcement

Zeit nf	time; times, days; hours; tense; epoch, era, age; period
zeit ge mäss	seasonable, opportune, timely; modern, up-to-date; current
zeit ig	early; mature
zeit ig en	mature, ripen; produce, call forth
zeit lich	temporal; time; chronological
Zeit lich keit	temporal state, temporality
zeit los	timeless
Zeit ung	newspaper, journal; gazette; tidings
bei zeit en	early; in good time, on time
Ge zeit en np	tide
Un zeit nf	at the wrong time, inopportunely; prematurely
Ur zeit nf	primitive times, dawn of history
Vor zeit nf	antiquity, times of old, days of yore
vor zeit en av p	in former times, formerly; once upon a time
vor zeit ig	premature
zu zeit en av	at times

Zwischen	zeit	nf		interval, interim, intervening period
Frei	zeit	nf		spare time, leisure time
gleich	zeit	ig		at the same time
Jahr es	zeit	nf		season, time of the year
Lehr	zeit	nf		apprenticeship, year of apprenticeship
Mahl	zeit	nf		meal, repast
Schul	zeit	nf		school days, time spent in school

	zeug:	siehe zieh		
	Zeug	nn		stuff, material, cloth, fabric; tools, things; trash, junk
	Zeug e	nm		witness
	zeug en			engender, beget, procreate, generate, produce, create
	zeug en			testify as witness
	Zeug in			female witness
	Zeug nis			testimony, evidence; deposition; certificate; school grade, mark
	Zeug ung			procreation, generation
be	zeug en			testify, bear witness to, certify
Be	zeug ung			testimony, attestation
er	zeug en			beget; manufacture; generate, grow, raise, form; breed
Er	zeug er			begetter; father, parent; producer, manufacturer, generator
Er	zeug nis			production, product, growth; fabric; merchandise, goods
Er	zeug ung			production, generation, manufacture, making; procreation
über	'zeug en			convince of, persuade, induce
Ueber	zeug ung			conviction, certainty, assurance, belief, persuasion
Unter	zeug	nn	s	underwear
Ur	zeug ung			abiogenesis
Neben er	zeug nis			byproduct
Flug	zeug	nn		airplane
Werk	zeug	nn		tool

	zicht:	siehe zeih		
Ver	zicht	nm		renouncement, sacrifice; waiver, disclaimer, release; abandonment
ver	zicht en			do without s.o., go without s.t.; renounce, resign; disclaim

	zieh en			pull, draw, tug, haul; make out; cultivate, breed
sich	zieh en			extend, stretch, run, warp, distort
	Zieh ung			drawing of lots; drawing of securities
ab	zieh en			draw off; remove; strip; distill; sharpen; print; subtract
an	zieh en			draw, pull on, put on; pull; tighten; attract
an	zieh end			attractive; interesting
An	zieh ung			attraction
auf	zieh en			draw up, open; pull up, raise; wind up a watch; bring up

aus zieh bar	telescopic, extensible; removable
aus zieh en	draw out, pull out, extract; undress; depart
be zieh bar	habitable, ready for occupancy; obtainable
be zieh en	cover with; occupy, move into; get, obtain; take in
sich be zieh en	become cloudy; refer to, relate to, appeal to
Be zieh er	subscriber, customer; importer; drawer
Be zieh ung	reference, connection, relation, regard, respect
durch 'zieh en	draw through, pass through, run through; thread
ein zieh bar	recoverable, collectible; retractable
ein zieh en	draw in, pull in; seize, draft; enter; soak in; retract
Ein zieh ung	drawing in; collection, cashing, withdrawing; calling up; seizure
ent zieh en	take away; abstract; deprive s.o., dispossess s.o.; extract
sich ent zieh en	shirk, evade, elude, withdraw from
Ent zieh ung	withdrawal, deprivation; abstraction; extraction; denial
er zieh en	bring up, raise, rear; educate
Er zieh er	educator, tutor, pedagogue, teacher
Er zieh erin	governess, lady teacher
er zieh er isch	educational, pedagogic
Er zieh ung	education; breeding, upbringing, rearing; manners
fort zieh en	draw away, drag away; emigrate, migrate; move on, leave
her zieh en	near, go here; come to live in a place
hin zieh en	draw to, attract; move to
hinter 'zieh en	defraud, evade; embezzle
Hinter zieh ung	defraudation, evasion
los zieh en s	set out, pull away; march
mit zieh en	drag along; march along with
nach zieh en	draw after, drag along; trace; tighten; follow
Rück zieh er s	retractor muscle; overhead kick; backdown
'über zieh en	draw over, cover with; put on, pull over
über 'zieh en	cover with, put over, coat; overdraw; stall; overlay
Ueber zieh er	overcoat, greatcoat, topcoat
'um zieh en	pull down; change clothes; cover, wrap, draw around
sich um 'zieh en	change one's clothes
'unter zieh en	put on underneath; pull under, draw under
unter 'zieh en	subject to
ver zieh en	move to, remove to; distort; draw; screw up one's face
sich ver zieh en	warp; hang badly; drag; disappear, vanish; dissolve; disperse
voll 'zieh en	execute, fulfill, carry out; accomplish; consummate, solemnize
Voll zieh er	executor
Voll zieh ung	execution, accomplishment
vor zieh en	draw forth; prefer
weg zieh en	pull away, pull aside; remove; march away
zu zieh en	draw together, tighten; pull together, shut; consult; invite

zurück zieh en	draw back, take back, withdraw; call in; move back, return
sich zurück zieh en	retire, withdraw, back out, retreat
zusammen zieh en	draw together, contract; assemble; concentrate, condense; oppress
sich zusammen zieh en	gather, shrink up, collect, contract; draw nearer
Zusammen zieh ung	contraction, constriction, shrinking; concentration
her ab zieh en	draw, pull down
her an zieh en	draw near, pull up; attract, interest in; educate
her auf zieh en	draw up, pull up; approach, draw near
hin auf zieh en	pull up, go up
her aus zieh en	draw out, take out, pull out, extract; move out
hin aus zieh en	drag out, draw out; put off, prolong
ein be zieh en	include, cover; incorporate in
her bei zieh en	draw in, drag in
vor bei zieh en	draw past, pass by
her ein zieh en	draw in
hin ein zieh en	pull in, draw into; involve in, implicate; incorporate
an er zieh en	breed s.t. into s.o.
um 'her zieh en	run around, roam around
hin über zieh en	draw over, pass over; move to the other side
her um zieh en	draw about; wander around
her unter zieh en	draw, pull down
her vor zieh en	draw forth
hin zu zieh en	add, include, draw into; consult, call in
aus ein ander zieh en	draw asunder; lengthen; deploy

Ziel	nn	aim; end, target, object; objective; destination; purpose
ziel en		take aim, level, sight
ziel los		aimless, purposeless
ab ziel en		aim at s.t.; be meant to do s.t.
er ziel en		obtain, attain, get; achieve; score; make a profit
hin ziel en		draw, pull; draw out, drag out, protract

ziem lich	av	pretty, fairly, rather, tolerable; about
ge ziem en		be becoming, befit s.o.
sich ge ziem en		be becoming, befit s.o.
ge ziem end		becoming, seemly, fitting, decent, due, proper
un ziem end		unseemly, unbecoming; indecent

Zimmer	nn	room; apartment
zimmer n		timber; carpenter; make, construct; frame
Hinter zimmer	nn	backroom
Neben zimmer	nn	adjoining room
Vor zimmer	nn	antechamber
Vorder zimmer	nn	front room
Wohn zimmer	nn	living room, parlor

zog:	siehe zieh	
zög er n		hesitate, waver; linger, tarry, delay
Zög ling		pupil
Be zog ener		drawee, payer
ge zog en a t		drawn weapon, rifled weapon
un er zog en a		uneducated; ill-bred
ein ge zog en a		retired, solitary; called up, drafted, inducted
Ein ge zog en heit		retirement
un ge zog en a		rude, uncivil, ill-bred; naughty
Un ge zog en heit		rudeness; naughtiness
Zurück ge zog en heit		retirement, seclusion, privacy, solitude
Erz her zog nm		archduke
Erz her zog in		archduchess
erz her zog lich		archducal
Erz her zog tum		archduchy
ver zög er n		delay, retard; slow down, protract
Ver zög er ung		delay, retardation, lag; deceleration, braking

zu av		too
da zu av		to that, thereto; for that purpose; in addition, besides
her zu av		near, close; nearer, closer
hin zu av		to the spot, near; there
all zu av		altogether too, all too
nah e zu av		almost, nearly
wo zu		for what, what for

zug:	siehe zieh	
Zug nm		draw, pull, jerk; stress, suction; procession; train; draft
Züg el		rein, bridle, curb, restrain
züg el los		unbridled, unrestrained, inordinate; licentious, dissolute
Züg el los ig keit		dissoluteness, licentiousness, looseness
züg el n		rein, pull up, bridle, curb, check
zug ig		drafty
züg ig		speedy, free, easy, uninterrupted; efficient
Züg ig keit		easy flow of traffic
Ab zug nm		departure, retreat; discount; copy, proof; trigger; print
ab züg lich		deducting the charges
An zug nm		approach, entering; suit, dress, apparel
an züg lich		invective, offensive, satirical; personal
An züg lich keit		invective
Auf zug nm		elevator, hoist; procession, parade; train; attire; appearance
Aus zug nm		drawer; tray; departure, emigration; removal; extract; abstract
Be zug nm		covering, cover, pillow case; subscription; purchase; fees; salary
be züg lich		relative, respecting
Durch zug nm		passage; draft; circulation; girder

Ein	zug	nm	entry, entrance, move, moving in; collection; indentation
Fern	zug	nm	long-distance train
Gegen	zug	nm	countermove; corresponding train
Rück	zug	nm	withdrawal, retreat, return
Ueber	zug	nm	coating, film, covering, cover; case; slip; crust; lining
Um	zug	nm	procession; remove, removal; demonstration
Ver	zug	nm	delay, default
Voll	zug	nm	execution, accomplishment
Vor	zug	nm	preference, advantage, priority; merit, excellence, privilege
vor	züg	lich	excellent, superior, exquisite, especially, particularly
Vor	züg	lich keit	excellence, superiority, choiceness
Weg	zug	nm	removal, departure
Zu	zug	nm	immigration, influx; increase; arrival; reinforcements
zu	züg	lich p	plus, adding, including
rück be	züg	lich g	reflexive
un ver	züg	lich	immediate, prompt, forthwith, right away, right now
be vor	zug	en	prefer, favor, give preference
Be vor	zug	ung	preference, favoritism

	zugel:	siehe zieh	
un ge	zügel	t	unbridled, unrestrained, unruled; dissipated; without restraint
Nach	züg	l er	straggler, camp follower

	zwang:	siehe zwing	
	Zwang	nm	compulsion; obligation, constraint; pressure, force, command
	zwäng	en	squeeze s.t. into s.t., cram s.t. into s.t.
	zwang	haft	forced, enforced, forcible; compulsive, obsessive
	zwang	los	casual, informal, free and easy; unceremonious, unconstrained
	Zwang	los ig keit	casualness, informality; unconstraint, freedom
	zwang	s mäss ig	forced, enforced, forcible, compulsive, obsessive
	zwang	s weise	compulsory, obligatory, forced, enforced
'durch	zwäng	en	force s.t. through, ram s.t. through
ein	zwäng	en	squeeze s.t. in, wedge s.t. in; constrain, straitjacket s.t.
hin durch	zwäng	en	squeeze s.t. through
hin ein	zwäng	en	squeeze s.o. into s.t., force s.t. into s.t.

	zwei	nu	two
	Zwei	er	pair of oars, pairs; two deciliters of wine; two-pfennig coin
	zwei	er lei	of two kinds, of two different sorts
	zwei	fach	double, twofold, dual; two-ply; binary
	Zwei	heit	duality; dualism

	zwei mal av	twice
	zwei mal ig	done twice, repeated twice
	Zwei sam keit	twosomeness
	zwei wert ig	bivalent, divalent; two-valued
ent	zwei av	in two; broken, in pieces; torn; exhausted, worn out
ent	zwei en	disunite, divide, separate
sich ent	zwei en	fall out, break, split; quarrel
Ent	zwei ung	disunion, division, separation; quarrel, strife; split, rupture

	zweifel: siehe zwei	
	Zweifel nm	doubt; uncertainty; misgiving; suspicion
	zweifel haft	doubtful, dubious; questionable; precarious
	zweifel los	undoubted, doubtless
	zweifel n	doubt
	Zweif l er	doubter, skeptic
an	zweifel n	doubt, call into question, dispute
be	zweifel n	doubt, call in question, refuse to believe
un	zweifel haft	undoubted, indubitable
ver	zweifel n	despair, be in despair, abandon hope
Ver	zweif l ung	despair

	Zweig nm		branch, bough
Ab	zweig nm		branch
ab	zweig en		branch off
Ab	zweig ung		branching-off; bifurcation
Ge	zweig nn	p	branches, boughs
sich ver	zweig en		branch out, ramify
Ver	zweig ung		ramification, branching

	Zwing e	ferrule; clamp
	zwing en	compel, constrain, force, make; oblige; conquer, overcome
	Zwing er	tower, dungeon; kennel; bear-pit; cage
auf	zwing en	force s.t. upon s.o., push s.t. down s.o.'s throat
be	zwing en	defeat, beat; master, overcome, restrain; conquer
Be	zwing er	conqueror, subduer
Be	zwing ung	mastering; conquest
er	zwing en	force; enforce; compel obedience
un be	zwing bar	invincible; impregnable

	zwung: siehe zwing		
er	zwung en	a	forced, unnatural, artificial, strained, simulated
ge	zwung en	a	find o.s. compelled to do s.t.; forced, constrained; unnatural
Ge	zwung en heit		constraint, stiffness, unnaturalness
un ge	zwung en	a	free and easy, casual, unceremonious, natural, unaffected
Un ge	zwung en heit		ease, casualness; naturalness, unaffectedness